Morrison's China

Morrison's China

*The Collected Journalism and 'Reminiscences'
of George Morrison*

Introduced and Edited by

Simon Holberton

THE
HERMES
PRESS

Published by The Hermes Press
info@thehermespress.com.au

First published 2025

Copyright © Simon Holberton, 2025

The moral right of the author has been asserted.

All rights reserved. Without limiting the rights under copyright restricted above, no part of this publication may be reproduced, stored in or introduced into a retrieval system, or transmitted, in any form or by any means (electronic, mechanical, photocopying, recording or otherwise), without the prior written permission of the copyright owner and publisher of this book.

The published articles of George Ernest Morrison are in the public domain in all jurisdictions.

The 'Reminiscences' manuscript and photographs are courtesy of the Mitchell Library, Sydney and reproduced with permission.

 A catalogue record for this book is available from the National Library of Australia

ISBN: 978 1 7642884 0 8 (pbk)
ISBN: 978 1 7642884 1 5 (hbk)
ISBN: 978 1 7642884 2 2 (ebk)

Cover image: Morrison with Sun Tien-fu, his senior servant, c. 1905
Back cover images: Morrison dressed as a scholar, China c. 1893 (top) and leaning against a log in New York, 1887 (bottom)
Inside cover: the bookplate Morrison pasted into every book in his library

Designed and typeset by Helen Christie, Blue Wren Books
Printed and bound by Ingram Spark

For my children Alexandra and Nicolas

THE STRUGGLE OF MAN AGAINST POWER
IS THE STRUGGLE OF
MEMORY AGAINST FORGETTING.

Milan Kundera

Contents

Preface ix

A Correspondent in China

Introduction 1

1. Morrison Ventures Forth 53
   'The Trans-Manchurian Railway' 57
   7 March 1898

2. A Coup in Peking 79
   'The Situation in China After the Coup D'état' 85
   16 November 1898

3. Kill the Foreigners 93
   'The Siege of the Peking Legations' [Part 1] 101
   13 October 1900
   'The Siege of the Peking Legations' [Part 2] 139
   15 October 1900

4. An Imperial Procession 189
   'The Chinese Court's First Railway Journey' 193
   13 March 1901

5. Japan Defeats Russia 203
   'Port Arthur From Within: "Discreditable Surrender"' 207
   25 January 1905

6. The Funeral of the Empress ... 213
'China: The Funeral of the Empress Dowager' ... 215
27 November 1909

7. Morrison's Last Hurrah ... 221
'Across China and Turkestan' [in 12 parts] ... 225
5 March to 26 September 1910

8. The End of Imperial China ... 311
'The New Chinese Army: Its Qualities and Defects' ... 317
21 October 1911

9. Morrison's life in China after journalism ... 327

An Australian Odyssey

10. A Pleasant Excursion ... 353
'Across the Australian Continent on Foot' ... 357
by George Ernest Morrison, 1883

Memoirs

11. Morrison's Life ... 375
'Reminiscences' ... 377
dictated by G. E. Morrison to his wife, c. 1915

Bibliography ... 501
Index ... 505

Preface

Since his death in 1920 George Morrison has been the subject of a number of books. There have been at least three biographies, of which Cyril Pearl's 1967 *Morrison of Peking*[1] remains the most comprehensive and in many ways, despite its frustrations and lack of references, the most comprehensive. Morrison's correspondence has been edited in two excellent scholarly volumes by Lo Hui-Min for Cambridge University Press[2] and my debt to him is spread like confetti throughout the footnotes. Three volumes of Morrison's photographs of Old China were published in China in 2005 with a Chinese and English commentary, and, lastly, Linda Jaivin, a China scholar who also writes diverting erotic fiction, has made Morrison's affair in 1904 with May Ruth Perkins, an American socialite, the central element in her novel, *A Most Immoral Woman*.[3]

How remarkable it is, therefore, that among all the volumes devoted to Morrison not one has reproduced any of the work that made him famous, namely, his journalism. This book aims to fill this gap by representing a selection of his journalism from *The Times* during his period in Peking for the newspaper from 1897 until 1912. Additionally,

---

1 Angus and Robertson, 1967. The other two biographies are Frank Clune's *Chinese Morrison*, Sydney: Angus and Robertson, 1940 and Peter Thompson and Robert Macklin's book, *The Man Who Died Twice*, Sydney: Allen & Unwin, 2014.
2 *The Correspondence of G. E. Morrison 1895–1912* (Vol. 1), Cambridge: Cambridge University Press, 1976; *1912–1920* (Vol. 2) Cambridge University Press, 1978.
Shen Jiawei, *Old China through G. E. Morrison's Eyes*, 3 vols. Fujian Educational Trust, 2005.
3 London: *Fourth Estate, 2009*.

for the first time we publish an edited version of his 'Reminiscences', his projected but incomplete memoirs, together with an annotated text of his 1883 article for *The Age* newspaper of Melbourne, 'Across the Australian Continent on Foot', which gives an account of his solo 2,043 mile (3,288km) trek from Normanton on the Gulf of Carpentaria to Melbourne.

In deciding upon which of Morrison's dispatches from China to reproduce I have sought to present a selection that highlights some of the main issues with which the Chinese Empire had to grapple, specifically, the encroachment of Russia on its periphery, the high and low politics of the Imperial court, and the convulsive Boxer rebellion of 1900 which became a lightening rod for anti-foreigner sentiment that reached to the top of the Chinese government. In addition there are some pieces that shed a different light on China, namely Morrison's amusing tale of the Chinese court's first railway journey, and his monumental account of his last big trek, this time across Chinese Turkestan. Two of the articles here—the account of the Boxer rebellion, and Across Chinese Turkestan—are each nearly 30,000 words each in length. They were sent as 'letters' (what we would today call 'feature' articles) and helped to make and reinforce his reputation as the most knowledgeable writer on China at the time. I believe they make rewarding reading more than 100 years after their first publication.

Most of the words in this book are, therefore, those of Morrison himself. My contribution, aside from the footnotes, consists of one long essay at the beginning of this book and another, recounting Morrison's life after journalism, at the end of the section containing his China journalism. I also introduce each of the selected pieces and place them in time and space. In my contributions here I have sought to stay close to my subject and have, therefore, lent heavily on Morrison's archive, his memoir, his diaries, his letters and, importantly, his photographs. As the footnotes show, in addition to Dr Lo, I have also benefited from the work of Sarah Paine on China, Russia and Japan; Cyril Pearl, Morrison's biographer; and, among others, John King Fairbank and Jonathan Spence, two scholars who have written standard histories of modern China.

For the present volume, aside from the exigencies of locating his stories in back issues of *The Times*, reproducing Morrison's journalism presents a number of difficulties, chief among them being the transliteration of Chinese names and places into English. During Morrison's time the Wade-Giles method of transliteration was a new innovation. Before 1892, when Herbert Giles published his *English-Chinese Dictionary* (based on a system first developed by Thomas Wade), transliteration of Chinese into English had been ad hoc, though based mostly on the Nanking dialect; the use of the Wade-Giles system changed that phonic foundation to the Peking dialect, something the Chinese Communist Party retained when, in the 1950s, it devised the *Hanyu Pinyin* system, with its own unique orthography, and made the Peking dialect the language of instruction in Chinese schools and, by extension, worldwide. In reproducing Morrison's text, I have decided to retain his transliterations, which loosely follow Wade-Giles, and to leave it to the footnotes to give the current Pinyin version of the names of places or persons referred to. The Chinese capital city is referred to throughout as Peking, the English term for the Chinese capital since the 18th century, and the old English names for Canton and Shanghai are also retained.

The other two works by Morrison in this volume were composed at opposite ends of his writing career. He was 21 years old when he wrote the first of these which is an account of a 2,043 mile (3,288km) trek he took on foot in the summer of 1883 from Normanton, on the Gulf of Carpentaria, to Melbourne, the capital city of the then Crown colony of Victoria, a route that retraced, in large part, the one taken by the ill-fated Burke and Wills expedition of 1860–61. The second, much longer work, he called 'Reminiscences', and it is a memoir he dictated to his wife, Jennie, in Peking. The date of composition is unknown except that it post-dates August 1912, the month of his marriage to Jennie Robin Wark. The title page says it was prepared by his wife. In 1912, Morrison was 50 years old and had eight years left to live, the last one and half years of those eight was spent in Europe, first Paris for the Peace Conference, then England, in a fruitless quest to find relief for the disease that killed him. The 'Reminiscences'—the last substantial piece of prose he composed for public consumption—does not read like the words of a dying man. The composition is likely, therefore, to have taken place in Peking around 1915.

The Mitchell Library, part of the State Library of New South Wales, is the custodian of the manuscript of 'Reminiscences' which consists of 128 typewritten pages, double spaced. This manuscript contains Morrison's handwritten corrections. In the Library it is designated "ML MSS 312/32" and it is this text which is reproduced here.

I have endeavoured to be comprehensive in my annotation of all the texts in this volume. In all of his writing Morrison made few allowances for his readers' knowledge of contemporary Chinese affairs and he rarely contextualised the individuals he mentioned in his journalism, expecting his reader to know the persons concerned. He was similarly unhelpful in the other works in this volume. Such assumptions about his readers' knowledge of persons and places is untenable today, and may well have been so when he wrote, and I have accordingly offered short descriptions of them in the footnotes where possible.

I have made use of Morrison's extensive photographic archive that was bequeathed to the Mitchell Library by his widow Jennie. The archive is particularly rich in postcards of contemporary China and in Morrison's own excursions in photography, such as recording the funeral procession of the Empress Dowager in November 1909, and his travels in western China in 1910 for a series of articles, here brought together, focussing on Chinese Turkestan. Given the continuing issues surrounding Chinese rule of the so-called New Territories (Xinjiang) Morrison's observations on his travels are still relevant.

I want to record my thanks to the Mitchell Library, Sydney, for allowing me to publish the 'Reminiscences' and for giving their consent to use and quote from his correspondence and diaries and to use the photographs. I want also to thank Nicholas Tolhurst and my wife, Kerryn, for reading and correcting earlier drafts of the manuscript. Additionally I want to thank Pauline Hopkins who line-edited the manuscript; she spotted many infelicities and inconsistencies and improved the text. Helen Christie has designed a handsome volume. All errors are, of course, my own.

PREFACE

A NOTE ON THE TEXTS

I have endeavoured to produce here a facsimile of the works published in this volume. In doing this I have preserved what was the accepted style of the time. Today we write Mr without a full point after the 'r'; in Morrison's time it took a full point. Words such as 'favour' and 'honour' were written without the 'u' in a way that today accords with American rather than today's standard English spelling. These are minor issues when set against the transliteration of Chinese names and places, discussed above. In the text I have reproduced them as Morrison wrote them. On their first mention I have used the footnotes to render the names and places as readers would encounter them today, so that Li Hung-chang, the great 19th century Chinese statesman, is Li Hongzhang in the footnotes, and Tientsin is rendered Tianjin, according to the Pinyin method of transliteration. For the conversion of currencies to today's value I have used the Bank of England's online Inflation Calculator.

A Correspondent
in China

> CHINA IS THE THEATRE OF THE WORLD'S
> CHIEF PERFORMANCE FOR THE NEXT FEW YEARS;
> AND WE MAY WATCH THE UNFOLDING OF THE
> DRAMA WITH ADDED INTEREST FROM THE FACT
> THAT THE MAN WHO IS TO TELL US MOST
> ABOUT IT IS AN AUSTRALIAN.
>
> A. B. 'Banjo' Paterson
> *Evening News*, Sydney, 21 January 1903

Introduction

George Ernest Morrison was one of the most extraordinary individuals Australia has produced. He trained as a medical doctor, first at the University of Melbourne then later at Edinburgh where he completed his degree. He practiced his profession in Spain, Morocco and in Australia at Ballarat, in his home colony Victoria, where he was head of surgery at the district hospital.

It is not, however, for his contributions to medical science that George Morrison is remembered. His reputation is one of an enterprising explorer, a writer, who was, from 1897 until 1912, one of the world's most influential journalists. During that time he was the Peking Correspondent for *The Times* of London, the leading newspaper of the world's most powerful state and empire. What he wrote was closely followed and acted upon in the principal capitals of the world. He was exceptionally well-informed and he wrote with authority, so much so that Britain's foreign secretary had to admit that he was often better informed, and certainly more timely, than his own Foreign Office officials. If Australia were a country that had heroes, Morrison undoubtedly would be one of them.

Morrison's time in China occurred at one of those 'hinge' moments in history when the existing order was shifting and about to give way to the new. He did not conceptualise it in this way, of course; such moments are apprehended only with the benefit of time and distance from events. But, from that distance, we can see that, for China, this time marked a turning point in its long history—not one of triumph, but rather one of defeat and (from the point of view of China's current rulers) humiliation,[1] and possibly renewal.

George Morrison was born on 4 February 1862 in Geelong, an emerging colonial town situated 70 kilometres west of Melbourne. His father, George, was educated at the University of Aberdeen and was recruited from Scotland by the Presbyterian Church in Victoria to found a school for boys in Geelong, much as his brother had done in Melbourne with the creation of Scotch College. George Snr's school, Geelong College, exists to this day as one of the city's leading fee-paying (and now) co-educational schools.

Morrison's education was typical of its day: classical languages (Latin and ancient Greek); mathematics; science; and lots of sport. It equipped him well for his future careers and gave him a facility for languages. In addition to Latin he had French, Spanish and some Chinese, but most of all the skills to write a clear and vigorous English sentence.

Of the place of his birth, Geelong, Morrison later wrote, it was: "One of the healthiest and most delightful towns in Victoria with a climate like that of the Mediterranean."[2] His adolescent diaries are filled with records of school sports, family holidays at Queenscliff, and endless tallies of rabbits and assorted wildlife that he shot on his solitary explorations of the Bellarine Peninsula. The Geelong in which he grew up was a place that was, however, contracting. The lure of gold propelled growth in towns in central Victoria to Geelong's north where big discoveries had been made. As Susan Priestly observed:

> In the two decades after 1861, the golden capitals, Ballarat and Bendigo, doubled in size to outstrip Geelong, the original second city to Melbourne. The population of Geelong and its suburbs declined from 23,000 to 19,000 and the town displayed an 'utter want of liveliness' despite its wide streets and excellent

---

[1] A thoughtful discussion of Chinese narratives around the so-called 'century of humiliation' is provided by Alison A. Kaufman (2011). 'The "Century of Humiliation" and China's National Narratives'. US-CEASR Commission. Washington, US Government. <https://www.uscc.gov/sites/default/files/3.10.11Kaufman.pdf>.
[2] See Chapter 11: 'Reminiscences', p. 378, this volume.

INTRODUCTION

botanic gardens, private schools, and public institutions, its many buildings of 'good taste', its wool stores and woollen mills. Large ships continued to be based from its wharves by a stony reef, and even the rail traffic tended to bypass Geelong in favour of Melbourne.[3]

The dullness of his daily environment served only to fuel his sense of adventure and his ambition to travel. In his late teens, his hero was Henry Moreland Stanley, the correspondent for the *New York Herald Tribune* who, in 1871, gained worldwide renown for leading an African expedition in search of Dr David Livingstone, a British missionary feared dead, whom he found in Tanzania, uttering the memorable line: "Dr Livingstone, I presume." In 1879–80, Morrison conceived of a book about Australian explorers and he went as far as to sketch potted biographies of Oxley, Hume and Hovell, Sturt, Mitchell, and Barker, to name just some. He planned to dedicate the book to Stanley ("the greatest traveller of this or any other age") and added to the title page, "I may here remark in parenthesis that it is my fixed determination to do something great 'Some day.'"[4]

Morrison's early journalism, of which one example is published later in this volume, was written very much with Stanley hovering over him. It is of the 'exploration' genre and was produced mostly in the long summer holidays after he finished his schooling at Geelong College and then during the summer holidays for the first two years of his medical studies at the University of Melbourne.

When he finished secondary school in Geelong, he walked 1,050 kilometres from Queenscliff, on the coast south-east of Geelong, to Adelaide along the coastal and inland routes. After his first year of

---

3 Susan Priestly, *Making Their Mark*, McMahons Point: Fairfax, Syme & Weldon Associates, 1984, p. 72.
4 George Ernest Morrison, 30 November–28 December 1880, MLMSS 312/2/Item 07, Mitchell Library. On the first page of the diary is the following inscription: "George Ernest Morrison / Scotch College / Melbourne / 4.5.80 which I read as 4 May 1880. Thereafter follows the Dedication and Preface and then biographical sketches of the principal Australian explorers. Morrison discontinued this project and used the remaining pages of the diary to begin his daily account of his travels down the Murray River, beginning on 30 November 1880.

medical studies, his next exploration was a trip down the Murray River. He used a Nautilus canoe, a canoe capable of deploying sails, on a 2,200 kilometre stretch of the river from Albury to a coaching stage called Cockatoo Wells[5] on the Coorong in South Australia and then returned to Geelong by steamer. Another holiday saw him taking passage on the *Lavinia*, a brigantine, off the coast of north Queensland where he sought material for an exposé of the trade in what was then referred to as '*kanakas*', Pacific Islanders who were 'recruited' as indentured labour in the Queensland sugarcane fields. This series of articles brought him notoriety,[6] with questions about the treatment of Islanders being asked not only in Brisbane of the colonial administration but also of the Colonial Secretary on the floor of the House of Commons in London. The pursuit of this story took him to Far North Queensland and, at its conclusion, he was to do something he had always wanted—to walk from the Gulf of Carpentaria to Melbourne. Indeed, he was to take the route that largely followed the ill-fated Burke and Wills expedition of 1860–61 which, having reached the Gulf, foundered on the return journey with the loss of its leaders and four of the five others.

The same fate did not befall Morrison. Just before Christmas, 1882, he set off from Normanton, recalling in his 'Reminiscences':

> I travelled alone and unarmed, like any ordinary sundowner. Except on rare occasions I slept in the open. I was never molested, and I reached Melbourne, within the time appointed, having covered the 2043 miles (3288 km) in 123 days, including all stoppages.[7]

Morrison's account of his journey across Australia brought him into contact with David Syme, the legendary publisher/editor of Melbourne's *The Age* newspaper. Syme was impressed with the young

---

5 It was at Cockatoo Wells where he met an hotelier who had travelled widely in Spain and who planted in Morrison a strong desire to visit the country. Cockatoo Wells is around 30 km from the town of Naracoorte.

6 By February 1900, when he was famous, the Queensland premier Philip Callanan would host a lunch for Morrison *en route* to Peking from visiting relatives and friends in Melbourne.

7 'Reminiscences,' p. 387.

Morrison's account of his walk across Australia and, with the possible annexation of New Guinea in the air,[8] Syme commissioned Morrison to lead an exploration of New Guinea, hitherto the province of its tribal inhabitants, a small number of missionaries, ornithologists and traders. Morrison accepted this commission with alacrity, all the more made keen by the element of competition introduced by news that *The Argus*, *The Age's* more conservative and influential rival in the Melbourne market, was also funding an expedition to New Guinea.

Morrison's expedition, however, was a disaster from beginning to end. Travel in New Guinea was extremely difficult, at least for Europeans, once one ventured beyond Port Moresby, due to the density of the jungle and the lack of defined routes through it. In September 1882, Morrison was nearly killed when he was attacked by tribesmen. Two spears struck him, one spear point lodging in his face, the other in his abdomen.

"One of them penetrated my stomach just under the chest," he wrote in his account of the attack for his series for *The Age*, "the other entered the hollow of my right eye and stuck in the bone at the bottom of the bridge of my nose."[9]

In a pre-modern medical age, it is remarkable that Morrison did not die either from his injuries or the infections that could have been expected to follow. He survived his ordeal and disowned the series of articles that appeared under his name, claiming he barely wrote a word of them.[10] He does not dwell on the New Guinea visit in his 'Reminiscences' preferring instead to describe the precariousness of his health.

---

8 At the Intercolonial Conference of 1883 the colonies were agreed that New Guinea should be annexed by Britain but couldn't agree on the timing. In 1890, Henry Parkes lamented that failure. "... if Australia could have spoken with one voice in the year 1883 New Guinea would have belonged to Australia." Cited in C. M. H. Clark, *Select Documents in Australian History 1851–1900*, Sydney: Angus and Robertson, 1953, p. 475.
9 George Ernest Morrison, 'Exploration of New Guinea,' *The Age*, 9 February 1884, p. 13.
10 "I'm only partly responsible for the series of articles on my journey subsequently published. The narrative I wrote was called 'My Failure in New Guinea'. But the exigencies of the newspaper required the adoption of a less modest title. I had no copy to speak of." 'Reminiscences,' p. 387.

Portrait of George Morrison.
Mitchell Library, Sydney

It seemed to me as though I had been lamed for life. The point was in my throat for 169 days, and was then extracted without chloroform, through my right nostril, by the leading surgeon of my time in Australia, Mr, afterwards Sir Thomas, Fitzgerald.[11] The other point remained in my body 260 days.[12] In the meantime, I had gone home to Edinburgh to continue my medical studies when it was cut out from the extra peritoneal tissue above the external iliac artery by Professor John Chiene,[13] the professor of surgery in the University of Edinburgh. I was a patient in the students' ward of the Edinburgh Infirmary, and my case attracted some attention.[14]

Morrison's memoirs elide the reasons for his departure from the University of Melbourne but he had, in fact, failed his exam in *Materia Medica*, the name then used for what we now call pharmacology. He had misdiagnosed an ailment and recommended the wrong medicine to relieve it. He appealed the poor mark, and may well have rued his decision to put himself forward for honours. Even the entreaties of his parents were not enough to persuade the examiner (whom Morrison describes elsewhere as "a man of intemperate speech")[15] to change his assessment. Off to Edinburgh University he was sent.

Two years later, Morrison successfully graduated from the university. Restlessly and purposelessly he travelled, first to America then Jamaica. It was while in Jamaica that he decided to go to Spain. His interest in Spain had been kindled by the bar owner he met in Cockatoo Wells at

---

11 Sir Thomas Naghten FitzGerald, 1838–1908, Irish, arrived in Melbourne in July 1858. He was a brilliant surgeon, noted for his diagnostic skill, who rose to the top of medical practice in colonial Australia.

12 A marginal note in the manuscript says: "? longer—does not tally with the dates." Indeed not; from the date of the injury (3 October) until Prof. Chiene's successful operation (1 July), 271 days had elapsed.

13 John Chiene, 1843–1923, professor of surgery at Edinburgh University; president of the Royal College of Surgeons. The Chiene Medal is to this day presented to the top surgery graduate of Edinburgh University. Morrison was to study under him. When he came to publish *An Australian in China* in 1895, he dedicated it to John Chiene MD "who gave me back the power of locomotion."

14 'Reminiscences,' pp. 388–389.

15 George Morrison, *An Australian in China,* London: Horace Cox, 1895, p. 32.

the end of his trip down the Murray River. That interest had developed into an itch that needed to be scratched. He secured passage on a ship to New York where he unsuccessfully tried to get employment as a doctor. Then, through the kindness of a stranger, he returned to Edinburgh to pursue his Spanish dreams.

Fortuitously, in the Scottish capital he made contact with the Senior Medical Officer of the Rio Tinto mining company, the forerunner of today's mining conglomerate. Morrison was taken on as a company doctor at its eponymous mine in Andalusia.

After less than a year, he left and went to Morocco where he found temporary employment attending to the medical needs of the Sharif of Fez. A plan to further his medical studies in Paris at the Pitié-Salpêtrière Hospital with the celebrated Dr Jean-Martin Charcot, one of Europe's leading neurologists and a teacher of Sigmund Freud, came to nothing. He was attracted more to the *la vie parisienne* than to medicine. He resolved to return to Melbourne where he applied for, and was accepted, to head the district hospital at Ballarat. He was 29 years old. He takes up the manner of his appointment in the 'Reminiscences':

> I reached Australia on the 3rd of December 1890 and four months later, on the 21st of April 1891 I was appointed resident surgeon of the Ballarat district hospital, an appointment I held for two years. This was in some ways the most coveted hospital appointment in Australia, for the city is interesting, the climate glorious and the pay was generous. In giving me the appointment the committee paid attention to other factors than mere vulgar medical knowledge. On paying my visits before the appointment was made, I called first on the most aggressive member of the committee, Mr. George Smith, a market gardener who had been in his time a handy man with his fists. When I spoke to him of my desire to be appointed, he said:–
>
> "Wasn't you the young man walked across Australia."
>
> I said I was.
>
> He said:– "We all admired that plucky feat. I don't think we will go far wrong if we appoint you."[16]

---

16 'Reminiscences,' pp. 403–404.

INTRODUCTION

His time in Ballarat started well and ended badly. If the letters pages of *The Star*, Ballarat's local newspaper, are any guide, he was widely appreciated by his patients. Not a week went by without one or more writing to *The Star* to praise him for his treatment of them or a family member. Almost from the time he got to Ballarat, however, there were pressures to reduce costs and therefore the services available at the hospital. Before his appointment, the hospital had run into financial difficulties and the response was to demand ward closures and reduce nursing staff, both measures which Morrison vigorously opposed. *The Star*, in keeping what was then accepted practice, published anonymous letters (signed 'Subscriber', or 'Miner') that attacked Morison personally for being too young (the 'boy doctor') or being overpaid. The issue that caused his resignation, however, was the pressure the board brought to renegotiate the terms of his employment. The board wanted to cut his salary, then a substantial £450 a year, which he agreed to, but the sticking point was their demand to reduce his notice period to one month. In February 1893, he jumped before he was pushed. He resigned and left Ballarat with a purse of gold sovereigns as a parting gift from colleagues.

Morrison was 31 years old and he decided to go north to Asia, initially toying with the idea of practising medicine in the Philippines on account of his fluency in Spanish, but a visit to Manila resulted in no success. Medicine's loss was journalism's gain. He shuttled between Hong Kong, Shanghai, Tianjin, Peking and, when down and out in Japan, he conceived of a journey from Shanghai to Rangoon, capital of Burma.

> I was really hard up in Japan, in Kobe, when I sold my telescope for $12. I truthfully wrote to a friend in Australia telling him that I had come round from Yokohama on my first shirts studs, that I was at present living on my telescope, and that I hope to return to Shanghai on my surgical instrument case. And that happened. In Kobe I had conceived the idea of crossing China to Burma, and on my return to Shanghai, I telegraphed home for money, and with the assistance then sent me I set out on my journey, an account of which I have published in *An Australian in China*.[17]

---

17 'Reminiscences,' p. 405.

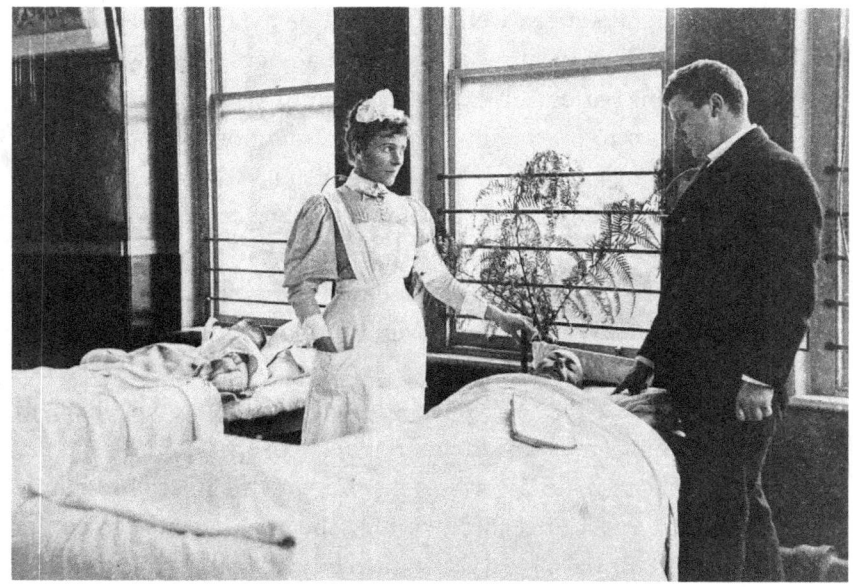

Dr Morrison, Ballarat District Hospital, c. 1892.
Mitchell Library, Sydney

Morrison, dressed as a scholar, with his porters, c. 1893.
Mitchell Library, Sydney

INTRODUCTION

This was Morrison's first encounter with China, a country that would occupy his talents for the rest of his life, and be the source of his fame and legacy. In An Australian in China, Morrison writes with a bluff nonchalance how "easily and pleasantly" a distance of 3,000 miles (4,830 kms) can be covered. The journey consisted "simply" of a voyage of 1,500 miles up the Yangtze River to Chungking,[18] followed by "a quiet, though extensive, excursion" of another 1,500 miles on foot, "taken by one who spoke no Chinese, who had no interpreter or companion, who was unarmed, but who trusted implicitly in the good faith of the Chinese."[19]

It was on this visit that Morrison began his relationship with China. The Australia in which he had grown up harboured a "strong racial antipathy to the Chinese" and he carried that prejudice with him to China. However, his experience of travelling in China caused him to change his mind "to one of lively sympathy and gratitude ... I shall always look back with pleasure to this journey, during which I experienced, while traversing provinces as wide as European kingdoms, uniform kindness and hospitality, and the most charming courtesy."[20]

Morrison is a perceptive observer of China. His book is enlivened by myriad details of daily life and he was not afraid to write ironically about what he observed, which indeed became a hallmark of his journalism. Trade, industry and the influence of foreigners were all high on his list of things to write about. He was assiduous in meeting foreign consuls and members of the Imperial Customs Service for intelligence about local affairs. He was kindly towards the missionaries stationed there, although entirely sceptical of their ability to convert the Chinese to Christianity, due in part to the inherent distrust the Chinese had for foreigners, but

---

18 Known today as Chongqing.
19 *An Australian in China*, p. 1. All quotations in this paragraph are from this book. Travelling 'unarmed' is something Morrison always liked to note. He did the same in the account of his 1883 trek across Australia, his adventure in New Guinea, and he would do so again in his account for *The Times* of his trip across Chinese Turkestan in 1910.
20 ibid., p. 2. It is noteworthy that he concluded his last major series for *The Times*—an account of his travels in western China and Turkestan—with complimentary remarks about the "unfailing friendliness and ... constant courtesy" of the Chinese he encountered. *The Times*, 26 September 1910, p. 5.

also to the way in which the missionary community, broadly defined, went about the business of persuading the Chinese of the Christian godhead.

> The Chinese recognise a supreme God, or are believed to recognise a supreme God—"High Heaven's ruler" (*Shangtien hou*), who is "probably intended," said Williams, "for the true God." The Mohammedans, when they entered China, could not recognise this god as identical with the only one God, to whom they accordingly gave the Chinese name of "true Lord" (*Chên Chu*). The Jesuits, when they entered China, could not recognise either of these gods as identical with the God of the Hebrews, whom they accordingly represented in Chinese first by the characters for "Supreme Ruler" (*Shang ti*), and then subsequently by the characters for "Lord of Heaven" (*Tien Chu*). The Protestants naturally could not be identified with the Catholics, and invented another Chinese name, or other Chinese names, for the true God; while the Americans, superior to all other considerations, discovered a different name still for the true God for whom they assigned the Chinese characters for the "the true Spirit" (*Chên Shên*), thereby suggesting by implication ... that the other spirits were false ... Obviously the Chinese are a little puzzled to know which of the contending gods is most worthy of their allegiance.[21]

His new regard and sympathy for the Chinese did not blind him to the realities of daily life in China, and the all-pervasive scourge of opium use.[22] He witnessed the widespread cultivation of the 'poppy' on the upper reaches of the Yangtze River and throughout Sichuan, through which he walked and rode, well away from 'foreign' influence. He

---

21 ibid., pp. 112–113. The various Christian sects not only used different names for God, in an attempt at ecclesiastical product differentiation, they also actively sort to undermine their 'competitor' sects by claims of heresy and the like, thereby raising further questions in Chinese minds as to the doctrines of the faith.

22 For a thorough overview of opium, its use, trade and prohibition, in China since the beginning of the 17th century, see 'Opium' in Jonathan D. Spence, *Chinese Roundabout: Essays in History and Culture,* New York: Norton, 1992, pp. 228–256.

questioned bien pensant criticism in London that laid all the blame for China's opium problem at the feet of British and foreign traders. He quotes Li Hung-chang,[23] the Viceroy of Chilli, admitting that the poppy was "surreptitiously grown" in some parts of China against Imperial edicts. "Surreptitiously grown in some parts of China!" exclaimed Morrison. "Why from the time I left Hupeh[24] till I reached the boundary of Burma, a distance of 1,700 miles, I never remember to have been out of sight of the poppy. Li Hung-chang continues: "I earnestly hope that [the London Society for the Prevention of the Opium Trade], and all right minded men in your country, will support the efforts China is now making to escape from the thraldom of opium." And yet you are told

---

23 Li Hongzhang, 1823–1901, whom we will meet frequently, was an official who tried to modernise China. He was for a time *de facto* in charge of China's foreign relations and he administered a large area of China centred on Tianjin. A brilliant scholar-official, Li was a statesman, diplomat, politician and military leader. In his day, he was compared to Bismarck, the dominant continental European politician of the final quarter of the 19th century. However, unlike Bismarck, who built a nation, it was Li's lot to preside over the breakup of the Chinese Empire. He was unable to prevent the collapse of the Qing dynasty's 'tribute' system, which kept Vietnam, Korea, Okinawa, among others, quiescent and in the Chinese orbit. He forged an alliance with the Russian Empire that took vast tracks of Chinese territory.

From 1870–1895, Li was Viceroy at Tianjin and from that position was China's principal interlocutor with foreigners, especially in times of crisis. On his watch Korea's bonds to China were severed and he settled the Franco-Chinese war in 1885 by ceding Vietnam to France. He represented China after its defeat in the Sino-Japanese War of 1894–95, signing the Treaty of Shimonoseki which ceded Taiwan and Okinawa to Japan as well as the Liaoning peninsula, which Japan was later forced to retrocede to Russia.

In business, he started the China Merchants Steamship Company in 1872 (a company later resurrected by Deng Xiaoping after China's re-embrace of modernisation in the 1980s), coal mines in Kaiping, producing 250,000 tonnes a year, and he favoured railways which brought him into opposition with the Empress Dowager. He told Ito Hirobumi, the Japanese statesman, in 1895 that, "Affairs in my country have been so confined by tradition that I could not accomplish what I desired … I am ashamed of having excessive wishes and lacking the power to fulfil them." For a fuller account of Li's life and career see 'Li Hung-chang', by William J. Hall in A.W. Hummel, *Eminent Chinese of the Ch'ing Period*. US Government Printing Office, Washington DC, 1943, vol. 1, pp. 464–471. Li's life cries out for a modern biographer.

24 Known as Hubei today.

Li Hung-chang with members of his family (detail) c. 1900.
Mitchell Library, Sydney

that the largest growers of the poppy in China are the family of Li Hung-chang."[25]

I will have more to say below about Morrison's qualities as a journalist, but suffice to say, his book about his travels in China turned out to be a winning addition to his application for a position on *The Times*. It showed him to be resourceful, fearless, independent, sceptical and, above all, a good writer. These were not, however, qualities that recommended him to *The Argus* in Melbourne, probably the country's leading broadsheet newspaper at the time.

In 1894, on Morrison's return to Australia (having narrowly escaped death, again) and preparing to write his book, his friend, Theodore Fink, a Melbourne lawyer with good media connections, approached Edward Cunningham, editor of *The Argus*, who said: "It is impossible, he can't write up to our standards."[26] Not for the first time did Australia

---

25 Morrison, *An Australian in China*, op. cit., pp. 41–42. Among his many sins, poppy cultivation is not one commonly levelled at Li.
26 Pearl, op. cit., p. 72.

lose a talented journalist to Fleet Street, though this may be the earliest recorded example.

Morrison cast about for a job in Australia. He could have returned to Ballarat as a doctor on a salary of £1,000, a considerable sum and more than twice what he previously earned, but at Fink's urging he decided to go to London and took a lesser-paid job as a ship's surgeon for £30. He arrived there in February 1895 and set about selling his manuscript. It was bought for £75 (more than £7,300 today) by Horace Cox, publisher of *The Field*, a popular magazine for the huntin', shootin' and fishin' set. While Morrison waited for the book's publication, he spent his time in the British Museum library writing his dissertation for his medical doctorate. The *Hereditary Transmission of Various Malformations and Abnormalities* was accepted by Edinburgh University on 1 August 1895. He was now Dr Morrison, a title he would use for the rest of his life.

He set about trying to become a newspaperman. He first tried directly approaching editors. There was trouble in Venezuela, he spoke Spanish; perhaps there might be an opening? These approaches were to no avail. He was advised to try *The Times*; he hesitated, not knowing quite how to approach such a venerable institution. He knew no one. It is one of the ironies of Morrison's move into journalism, a profession which he regarded as one dedicated to the pursuit of truth, that it was an error in his book about China that drew him to the attention of Sir William Gowers,[27] an eminent authority on nervous diseases, and a man who proved to be his entrée into British journalism. Morrison, who deployed his medical knowledge to write with authority about the health of the Chinese, had written: "No people are more cruel in their punishments than the Chinese, and obviously the reason is that the sensory nervous system of a Chinaman is either blunted or of arrested development."[28] Sir William had read this with interest and invited Morrison to a meeting at his house. There he introduced him to

---

27 Sir William Richard Gowers, 1845–1915, was a pioneering British neurologist and hailed as one of the greatest clinical neurologist of all time. He practised at the National Hospital for the Paralysed and Epileptics (now the National Hospital for Neurology and Neurosurgery). Morrison remained in touch with Gowers for many years.
28 Morrison, *An Australian in China*, op. cit., pp. 97–98.

Sir Henry Howorth,[29] an historian of the Mongol peoples. During their discussion, Morrison confided in them his desire to join a newspaper. Gowers decided to see what he could do. As can happen, Gowers knew George Buckle,[30] editor of *The Times* (they were both members of the Athenaeum, a gentleman's club) and encouraged Buckle to consider Morrison for a position. The timing was propitious, as *The Times* wanted to appoint a correspondent at Peking. Events moved quickly. By the end of October, Morrison had been to meetings with the paper's managing editor and to dinner parties with the foreign staff and editor. He was clearly a 'fit'. He was offered the job as *The Time's* Peking correspondent and the next month he left England for Saigon, having negotiated a pre-posting tour of France's involvement in Indochina.

The Times in Morrison's Day

The Times' reputation was built not only on its longevity—it was first published in 1785—but on the quality of its reporting. It gave exhaustive coverage to the proceedings of the House of Commons and the Lords, the latter a much more important chamber in the 19th century than today as many of Britain's prime ministers were peers and thus answered questions in the Lords. *The Times* afforded similar coverage of the courts, building a reputation as source of authoritative record on Britain's evolving common and statute law. It was, however, the newspaper's foreign coverage that further set it apart from its domestic competition. This began in the early 19th century with its accounts of the Battle of Trafalgar (1805) and the Battle of Waterloo (1815), which

---

29 Sir Henry Hoyle Howorth, 1842–1923, Conservative politician, barrister, historian. He wrote a three-volume history of the Mongols and a separate biography of Genghis Khan and his ancestors, together with a three-volume history of the English church up to the eighth century.

30 George Earle Buckle, 1854–1935, a fellow of All Soul's Oxford, was appointed editor of *The Times* at the age of 30 and remained editor for 28 years, until 1912. His career was marred by the publication of forged letters attributed to Charles Parnell, an Irish nationalist. In retirement Buckle completed the biography of Disraeli left incomplete by the death of William Monneypenny, adding four more volumes, and edited and published three volumes of Queen Victoria's letters.

it most unusually published on its front page, a space typically reserved for short, classified advertisements.

It was, however, William Howard Russell's coverage of the Crimean War in 1854 that transformed foreign reporting in general, and underlined the power of the press in particular.[31] The war was a disaster for the men who fought and died in it, and Russell's vivid and sympathetic coverage of fighting men and his forensic account of the incompetence and mismanagement by the commanding general, Lord Raglan, and the War Office, led to the collapse of Lord Aberdeen's government and his ousting as Prime Minister. Russell's reputation was burnished further by Alfred Tennyson's use of his reports for his celebrated and much recited poem, *The Charge of the Light Brigade*. By the time Morrison joined *The Times* it stood at the top of the news production system in Britain in terms of influence if not profitability. It had become a newspaper of record and, in addition to home news, that 'record' now encompassed Britain's imperial role in world affairs. Everything that happened in the world was of interest to the editors of *The Times*, more so if it affected Britain's interests, especially her commercial interests.

When Morrison went to meet C. F. Moberly Bell,[32] manager of *The Times*, on Thursday 24 October 1895, *The Times* bore very little resemblance to the newspaper that is published today. For a start it was a broadsheet newspaper twice the size of the tabloid format that the paper introduced in 2004. The other difference one would immediately notice was that the front page did not consist of the day's most important news, but to many small, classified advertisements. Moreover, except for advertisements on page one and often on page two as well, little

---

31 John Simpson, *We Choose to Speak of War and Strife: The World of the Foreign Correspondent*, London: Bloomsbury, 2016, pp. 41–47. Provides and excellent anecdotal account of the evolution of foreign reporting in the English-speaking world.

32 Charles Frederick Moberly Bell, 1847–1911, was Managing Director of *The Times* from 1890 until his death in 1911. He was a journalist and authority on Egypt about which he published three books before being brought to London to improve *The Times*' business operations. Under his management *The Times* expanded its foreign coverage, launched its still published Literary and Educational supplements, and entered into business with the *Encyclopaedia Britannica*. He was a great supporter and friend of Morrison's. He helped engineer the sale of *The Times* to Alfred Harmsworth, later Lord Northcliffe, in 1908.

of the news content appeared in a fixed place in the run of pages that followed. The page carrying the 'Contents', which guided readers to where the news in the newspaper resided and carried *The Times*' leading article, could appear on page five, seven, or nine. The contents page did, however, have predictable features: the top of the furthest left-hand column listed the important contents of the newspaper; then followed a brief summary of each article; then, after two horizontal ruled lines, came its Leading Articles, in which *The Times* 'thundered' about the issues, large and small, of the day.

The day George Morrison went to meet Moberly Bell, *The Times* opined on a ship-building dispute that had reached an important point of negotiation by management and unions in Carlisle; the indebtedness of London's local government; and a rather long apology for it having published incorrect information the previous day about the contretemps between Britain and the United States over Venezuela. "The story which reached us from New York yesterday was so inherently improbable that it hardly, perhaps, merits serious contradiction"[33]—which rather begs the question as to why it was published in the first place. If Morrison had been a careful reader of *The Times*, he might have lit upon a report of a speech by George Curzon, Under-Secretary for Foreign Affairs[34] to the Conservative Association at Kingston-on-Thames in south-west London. Page eight of the newspaper happened that day to be filled mostly with Ecclesiastical Intelligence—reports of meetings of the bishops of the Church of England. However, at the bottom of the page, on the left, was Curzon giving his defence of colonialism and its challenges, starting with the role of the Foreign Office for which he was largely responsible, and whose actions he defended on the floor of the House of Commons. It is worth quoting in full, as there is little in it with which Morrison, a loyal imperialist, would have disagreed. It also concludes with the 'special' interest Britain had with commerce in the

33 *The Times*, 24 October 1895, p. 7.
34 George Nathaniel Curzon, 1859–1925, 1st Marquess Curzon of Kedleston, Conservative grandee, Viceroy of India. His quip about journalists intelligently anticipating facts was applied to Morrison. Curzon was the government's spokesman for foreign affairs in the House of Commons, given that Lord Salisbury Prime Minister and Secretary of State for the Foreign Office was a member of the House of Lords.

INTRODUCTION

Far East, one of the key reasons *The Times* wanted a correspondent in China:

> The Foreign Office was not merely an institution whose duty it was to safeguard British possessions and colonies, to maintain friendly relations with foreign Powers, and to preserve the balance of power, but it had also the task of providing for the necessary and legitimate expansion of British commerce and the good of the race. In the terrific pressure of competition it was essential that new openings be found and new markets procured. There were some who saw in this necessary expansion a lust for territorial aggrandizement. To such the British Empire was an ogre which was anxious to pounce upon unprotected persons and unappropriated territories; but they recognized that expansion was a physical and commercial necessity. It was for them to show that what they won in the era of conquest they could hold in the era of competition. In the Far East, where there was reason to fear that our position was affected, the commercial position of England was engaging special attention.[35]

Absent from the edition of the newspaper the day he met Moberly Bell was a form of reportage the editors internally called a 'letter'. This should not be confused with Letters to the Editor that originated from readers. Unlike today, where Letters to the Editor occupy a dedicated section on the newspaper and its website, in the 1890s, readers' letters were distributed throughout the newspaper without any apparent relevance to the news articles around them. The 'letters' the Foreign Department received from its correspondents abroad were, however, entirely different. They received prominent display and were generally very long. They were, in form and substance, both subjective, often being written in the first person and, by turns, analytical and descriptive, opinionated and factual, and, like readers' letters, they were posted to the newspaper by mail. Here, the contest between cost of delivery and the demands of timeliness was decisively won by the former. The only

---

35 Report: Mr. G. Curzon and Kingston-on-Thames, *The Times*, 24 October 1895, p. 8. This account is written in reported speech, it is not a verbatim transcript of what Curzon said.

*One of Morrison's telegrams, 24 June 1901,
about punishments for Boxer rebels, including Prince Tuan.*
Mitchell Library, Sydney

alternative to the postal service was the telegram. Telegrams were paid for by the word, and *Times*' correspondents' letters could number into the thousands, and therefore they would have been prohibitively expensive to send in telegraphic form. In the case of Morrison's letters, it would have cost many hundreds, perhaps thousands, of pounds to send them as a telegram.[36] The post entailed quite a long delay between receipt by the Foreign Department and publication, a delay they seemed unconcerned about.

---

36 Reliable data on the costs of telegrams at this time is difficult to obtain. Morrison wrote to his mother on 12 July 1898 noting, *en passant*, that "I sent a telegram to *The Times* costing about £100 [£11,200 today]—I spend thousands of dollars telegraphing for them." ML MSS 312/42 letter book. In 1915 it cost $US 0.57 cents a word, which, in today's money equates to $18 a word. See *Communication Difficult with Australia*, Commerce Reports, US Department of Commerce, Washington D.C., no. 178, 31 July 1915.

INTRODUCTION

Morrison Leaves for the Far East

Morrison's desire to tour Indochina before he went to Peking had greatly amused his employer, but *The Times* wanted him and so they acceded to his wishes and he visited Indochina and the then Kingdom of Siam (now Thailand) before taking up his post at Peking. To facilitate this, he was appointed Special Correspondent with a brief to look into the situation in Indochina. Demonstrating great forbearance, *The Times* allowed him to spend the next year familiarising himself with affairs in Indochina, especially the machinations of the French, who were keen to expand their considerable influence in the region. He also looked into Siam's reform movement and was hugely impressed with it. The imperialist in him even praised it as a way to avoid colonial conquest. The explorer in him was satisfied with an expedition through the border regions of northern Thailand and Burma that resulted in him visiting Yunnan in southern China.

There was method in his madness, as his main interest was Anglo-French rivalry in Indochina. China had been the dominant cultural influence for centuries before the French annexed Cochin-China in a war from 1858–1862. Cochin-China encompassed much of the Mekong River delta area of present-day Vietnam and Saigon (now Ho Chi Min City) was its principal city. North of it was Annam, the largest swathe of territory, in which the royal capital Hué was located. Still further north was Tonkin, where Hanoi was situated.

Before western colonialism, Vietnam and Cambodia were tributary states of the Chinese Empire; their envoys made regular visits to Peking at which they presented their tribute to the Emperor and performed the kowtow at an Imperial audience. Vietnam even used Chinese as the official language of record. France saw Indochina as central to the creation of the French Empire in the Far East and, in furtherance of those interests, fought a war with China in 1884–85 for control of Annam. This war was resolved after a series of Chinese naval and coastal defeats and was settled by the Treaty of Tientsin that ceded Tonkin and Annam to France, which were both incorporated into French Indochina in 1887. France had succeeded in slicing off a large portion of the Chinese Empire to the south.[37]

Morrison was hugely impressed by Siam and its modernising ruler King Chulalongkor, although it was the king's half-brother Prince Damrong Rajanubhab, noted for his reform of the Thai education system, with whom he mostly dealt. Siam afforded Morrison an opportunity for exploration and for his travels, he engaged a resourceful local, Ah Heng,[38] who would become his interpreter and assistant during his whole time in China. The two travelled widely on horseback throughout northern Thailand and into Yunnan in southern China. This journey is recounted in his 'Reminiscences'.

On the eve of his arrival in Peking, Morrison had a comprehensive series of reports about affairs in Indochina behind him. But he was receiving mixed messages from senior editorial executives in London. On the one hand, *The Times*' manager C.F. Moberly Bell told him that "your letters have been excellent and we are perfectly satisfied with what you have done,"[39] and, on the other, was the mixed reaction to his Indochina series by *The Times*' leading foreign affairs columnist (and soon to be head of the Foreign Department) Valentine Chirol,[40] a man with whom Morrison was to have a respectful, friendly, if stormy and sometimes acrimonious relationship. *The Times* had indulged Morrison's

---

37 By 1907, France had extended control over Cambodia to Laos as well.
38 In his 'Reminiscences', Morrison describes Ah Heng as a "Chinese Siamese half-caste – a man of exceptional courage, resource and linguistic ability who spoke good English, Siamese, Lu Shan, and Swatow Chinese." Lu Shan (or Leshan) is a Chinese dialect spoken in Sichuan while Swatow (Shantou) dialect is called Chaoshan and is widely spoken among Thai and Cambodian persons of Chinese descent. See page 415, this volume.
39 Lo, op. cit., 1976, p. 40. Letter to Morrison, 12 November, 1896.
40 Sir Ignatius Valentine Chirol, 1852–1929, was a distinguished journalist, author, historian and diplomat who was head of the Foreign Department (Foreign Editor) of *The Times* from 1892 until 1912. He coined the term 'Middle East' for a series of articles he wrote for the paper and published as a book in 1903. An arch imperialist he was described by Sir Neill Malcolm, "as the friend of viceroys, the intimate of ambassadors, one might almost say the counsellor of ministers … one of the noblest characters that ever adorned British journalism." Chirol was knighted for his service to journalism and rejoined the Foreign Office in 1912. He was active in the Balkans for the Foreign Office and was part of the British delegation to the Versailles Treaty talks in 1919. He wrote authoritatively on foreign policy.

interest in Indochina and published his reports prominently. In April 1897, with Morrison now in Peking, Chirol sought to reset Morrison's journalistic mission and wrote to him in the following terms:

> For our purpose, the incidents and adventures of travel must always be merely subsidiary to the general information and enlightenment we require for the *furtherance of British interests and of Imperial policy*. [Emphasis added] In one word, what you seem to me to lack in some measure is a sense of perspective. You must try and focus your lens to our eyes, remembering always that we are a very long way off and only want to look through the big end of the telescope. Picturesque details should be the garniture, not the foundation of your work.[41]

The Situation in China

When Morrison arrived in Peking in the spring of 1897, the Chinese Empire was teetering on collapse. It had recently faced an humiliating defeat by Japan in the Sino-Japanese War of 1894–95[42]—a defeat that was doubly humiliating because not only had Japan's army and navy outclassed their Chinese opponents, but this was the first time an Asian power had inflicted defeat on China in 250 years, indeed since the barbarian Manchu's swept aside the Ming and adopted the name Qing[43] as their rule name. For the Empire's Manchu rulers and their Chinese officials, defeat by Japan amounted to a grievous loss of 'face'[44]—that most important of external approbations, the gain of which adds lustre to reputation, the loss of which renders the recipient reduced and

---

41 Lo, op. cit., p. 38, n. 1.
42 See S. C. M. Paine's *The Sino-Japanese War of 1894–1895: Perceptions, Power and Primacy*, Cambridge: Cambridge University Press, 2003.
43 Ch'ing according to the Wade-Giles system.
44 See Hsien Chin Hu, 'The Chinese Concepts of "Face"', *American Anthropologist*, Jan-Mar 1944, vol. 46, no. 1, part 1, pp. 45–64. Also, Valentine Chirol defined face thus: "In and above all things the central Government has to 'save its face'—i.e., to maintain those immutable forms and appearances which, in the private as well as the public life of the Chinese, have nothing to do with realities, but entirely overshadow them." 'The Far Eastern Question', *The Times*, 26 September 1895, p. 6.

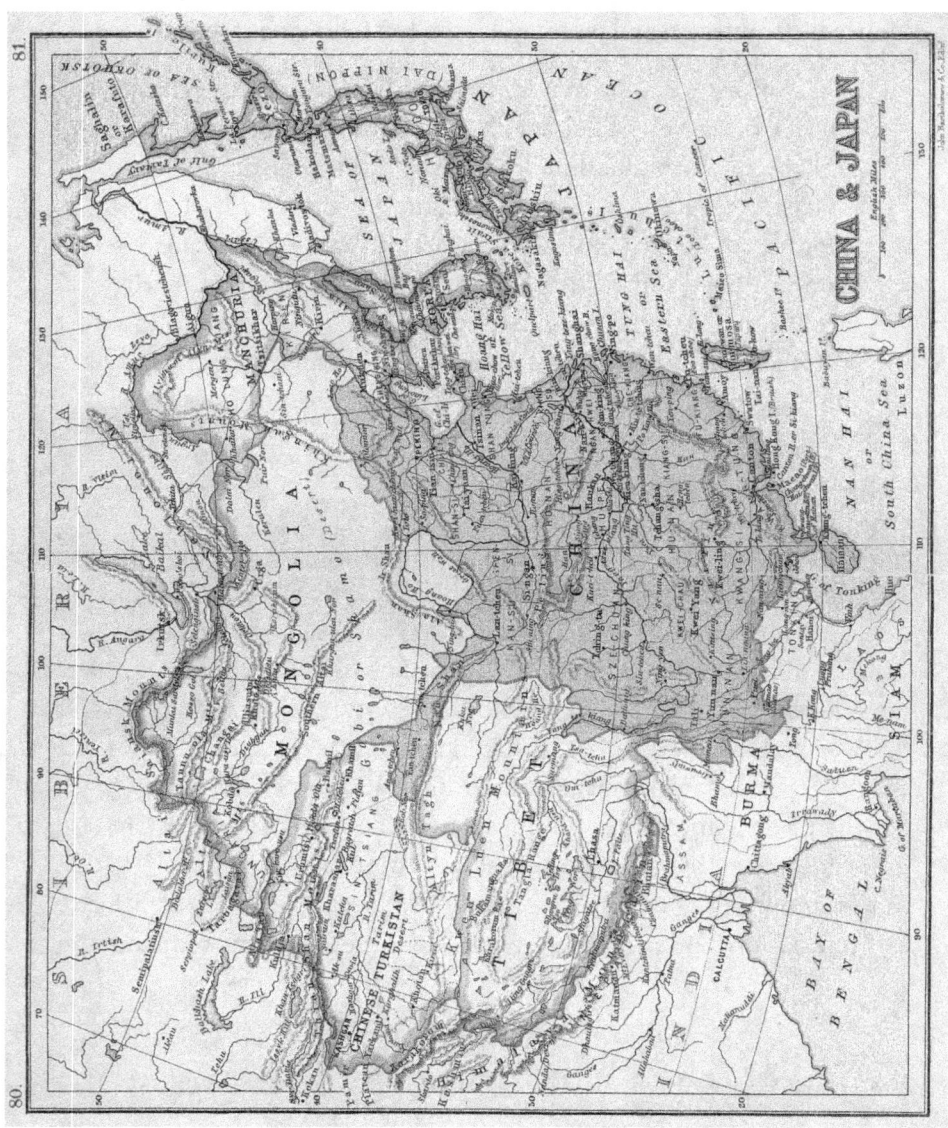

The Chinese Empire. 'Core' China is the darker shaded area in the middle with Chinese Turkestan and Tibet north west and the Mongolias to the north, Manchuria to the north east. From: J G Bartholomew, A Literary & Historical Atlas of Asia, *Lindon: J M Dent (nd) c. 1910.*

INTRODUCTION

sometimes contemptible in the eyes of his peers. The defeat by Japan was, however, the least of the problems the Empire faced. More than the Qing's failure to address the threat posed by more powerful Western and westernised countries was the cumulative effect of a century of internal rebellion that had undermined the legitimacy of Manchu rule, who appeared perilously close to losing their so-called 'Mandate of Heaven'.

To understand the China that Morrison encountered it would be helpful to banish from one's mind the notion one may have of China today. At the end of the 19th century the Chinese Empire—for it was an Empire rather than a single nation state—was fracturing. The Empire's rulers, the Manchu Qing aristocracy, were struggling to maintain order over their vast inheritance.

Compounding their problems was the reality that in very few places were China's borders fixed and defined, other than where it met the ocean. Its land borders were fuzzy, porous and ill-defined. The 18 provinces that largely defined Han Chinese settlement extended from Hebei in the north to Guangdong in the south and from Zhejiang in the east to Yunnan in the west. China was surrounded by a number of tributary states over which it exerted degrees of control and suzerainty. These were:

- Annam (Vietnam); Khmer (Cambodia) and the Burmese States to the south;
- To the west, Tibet and its eastern projection, Amdo Tibet (today Qinghai province);
- To the north-west were the recently conquered Muslim New Territories (Sinkiang, or Xinjiang);
- To the north, the Mongolias, Inner and Outer;
- To the north-east, Manchuria (the ancestral lands of the ruling Qing dynasty); and
- On the north-eastern border, the tributary state, Korea.

The Empire's vassals extended further east to the Ryukyu Islands (now part of Japan) where its king, based on Okinawa, paid tribute to the Qing. Looser control was exercised over Taiwan, inhabited by an aboriginal people, foreigners and some Chinese. Over the previous 1,000 years even the Japanese had occasionally sent tribute to the Emperor.

Such, therefore, was the scale of the Chinese, or 'Celestial' (as it called itself) Empire at the beginning of the 19th century. By the time Morrison resigned from *The Times* in 1912 to become Political Adviser to Yuan Shih-kai,[45] President of the Republic of China, the Empire had been much reduced.

The 18th century had been the golden era for the Manchus, a nomadic Asiatic people from Manchuria who had overthrown the Ming in 1645 and who adopted 'Qing' as their reign name, and ruled China through the established Chinese bureaucracy. Their governance had been remarkably stable, with just three emperors—K'ang Hsi, Yong Cheng, and Chien Lung[46]—reigning from 1661 until 1796. Over this 135-year span, most of the accretions to Chinese territory and the creation of an "inner Asian Empire"[47] were accomplished, amounting to a near doubling of the territory under Chinese control. Yet, in the last few years of Chien Lung's long life (he died in 1799 having abdicated in favour of his heir Jiaqing in 1796) signs of disquiet in the Empire had already appeared. Rebellion stalked the land.

In particular was the White Lotus Rebellion, in the decade between 1794 and 1804, which engulfed Sichuan, Hubei and Shaanxi provinces, and proved a harbinger of anti-Manchu rebellion that would come to characterise the last century of the dynasty's rule. The White Lotus rebels were nativist and anti-Manchu. They were actuated by a

---

45 Yuan Shikai, 1859–1916, played an important role in early 20th century Chinese politics. He was a senior official in the Qing administration and a driving force behind the adoption of western military methods for the creation of a modern Chinese army. He held senior administrative positions—governor of Shandong and viceroy of Zhili—before falling out of favour with the Qing court towards the end of Tsu Hsi life (1908). During this time he thoroughly modernised the military, his Beiyang Army being its strongest unit, and was an able civilian administrator who introduced the first local elections in China as well as education reform, among others. As the Chinese empire crumbled and Qing rule collapsed he emerged as the most qualified man to assume political control of the Republic of China, assuming the role of President in 1912. As President he lived like an Emperor and soon decided he wanted to be one. His attempt failed and he died soon after.

46 The three emperors' names are now transliterated as Kangxi, Yongzheng, and Qianlong.

47 This is the phrase used by F. W. Mote in his *Imperial China 900–1800*, Cambridge Massachusetts: Harvard University Press, 1999, p. 945 for map of China c. 1800.

combination of religion (a Buddhist folk religion that focussed on the Eternal Mother as the object of veneration) and a desire to revive the (Chinese) Ming dynasty, although they were unable to agree on who the leader should be. The Jiaqing emperor finally quashed them by using a combination of Manchu forces and Chinese militia but, as J. K. Fairbank observed: "To discerning scholars versed in the lore of the dynastic cycle, the fortunes of the Qing dynasty seemed to be turning downward."[48]

Indeed they were. Jiaqing's difficulties were far from over. In 1813, the Eight Trigrams Uprising occurred and, like the White Lotus rebellion, it too had a touch of millenarianism to it, as well as a Buddhist gloss and the pointed aim of the removal of the Manchu. Unlike the White Lotus uprising, which was located in the west and north west of China, the Eight Trigrams rebels were located in provinces much closer to Peking—Shandong, Hebei and Chihli.[49]

The leader of the Eight Trigrams, Lin Qing,[50] (1770–1814) was born in a village outside Peking to a father who was a minor official in the Peking government. Lin was educated but poor. He started work as an apprentice in a herbal medicine shop. After his father's death, he managed to succeed him in his official role, a role that gave him access to government funds for the repair of the Grand Canal. He embezzled some of those monies and opened a tea shop, the profits of which he gambled away. After that, he enjoyed years of restless travel and itinerant work. He travelled both to Manchuria, where he worked in construction, then south to the Yangzi River delta and the city of Suzhou, where he had a relative. There he worked in a number of positions, including as a junior official in the magistrate's office. It was on his return north that Lin joined a religious sect drawing its beliefs from millenarian Buddhism; believing that daily observance of prayerful ritual would insulate adherents from the dangers of fire and flood. Lin was an able proselyte and was rewarded with a beating from the local magistracy

---

48 John King Fairbank, *The Great Chinese Revolution: 1800–1985*, London: Chatto & Windus, 1987, p. 65.
49 Also known as Zhili.
50 This account follows Jonathan D. Spence, *The Search for Modern China*, New York: W. W. Norton, 1990, pp. 166–168.

for being too vocal. Generally, however he was ignored. His skills in herbal medicine and knowledge of officialdom enabled Lin to inspire and motivate local villagers. He raised money from them in exchange for promises (no more than IOUs) of future land allocation.

Lin's rising status enabled him to join forces with other Buddhist leaders. He started to promote himself as the future Buddha of Maitreya, who had been sent by the Eternal Mother to prepare him and his followers for the new great cycle of history. This sounded like a forecast of dynastic change. "We wait only for the northern region to be returned to a Han [Chinese] emperor / Then all-that-is will again be under a single line."[51]

Lin plotted the assassination of Jiaqing and, such was his support network, he was able to suborn some senior eunuchs in the Forbidden City to assist him. The attack on the Forbidden City in September 1813 failed and resulted in some 100 deaths and casualties. Overall, however, an estimated 20,000 members of the Eight Trigrams society were put to the sword in the ensuing months. Jiaqing was curious about Lin's motives and wanted to find out more about his proposed rebellion. Lin was brought before the Emperor, but refused to elaborate on his reasons for rebellion. He was executed by 'slicing'— a form of execution more colloquially known as 'death by a thousand cuts'. As Jonathan Spence observed, groups such as Lin's constituted a "latent potential for rebellion," his "casual accumulation of followers and money, the generalised grievances, and the broad religious claims were typical of many other such groups formed in north China over subsequent decades."[52]

The Eight Trigrams uprising was contained. As the 19th century wore on, domestic rebellion would grow and grow to an extent that nearly toppled the Qing. Of these uprisings, three stand out as worthy of note: the Taiping Rebellion (1853–1864); the Nian Rebellion (1851–1868); and the Muslim rebellions in far western China (1855–1873, 1880s). It is to those we now briefly turn.

---

51 ibid., p. 168.
52 ibid.

INTRODUCTION

At their height the rebellious Taipings (the Heavenly Kingdom of Great Peace—*Taiping Tianguo*) ruled over 30 million persons from their capital at Nanking (Nanjing). The rebellion was led by Hung Hsiu-ch'uan,[53] a failed scholar from the Hakka minority in Guangdong, who declared himself to be the Heavenly King of the Taiping and the younger brother of Jesus Christ. His understanding of Christianity was informed by his reading of Protestant tracts that introduced the Bible to Chinese readers, particularly by the American southern Baptist Issacher Jacox Roberts, "who gave him examples of how to pray, preach, sing hymns, catechise, confess one's sins, baptise and otherwise practice fundamental Protestantism."[54]

By the late 1840s when Hung's followers numbered more than 20,000, he raised an army in the south. In 1851 it moved decisively northwards capturing Hankuo and Wuchang.[55] In early 1853, the army descended on the Yangtze and took Nanking, which was made the Taipings' Heavenly Capital. Hung's converts were imbued with the belief that God had instructed them to destroy the Manchu (Qing) dynasty and replace it with a new order of brotherhood and sisterhood. Unlike the passivity of Taoism, or the quietism of Buddhism, Taiping Christianity drew on the 'church militant' tradition of Protestant activism. It "was a unique East-West amalgam of ideas and practices geared to militant action, the like of which was not seen again until China borrowed and Sinified Marxism-Leninism, a century later."[56]

What is surprising about the Taiping rebellion is not its failure, but its longevity. The rebellion tied down the Qing dynasty for more than a decade in one the bloodiest civil wars the world has seen; one that claimed, possibly, as many as 25 million lives. It was brought to an end by the ruthless generalship of Tseng Guo-fan,[57] commander of the crack Xiang army. They were aided by a decision by the western powers to

---

53 Hong Xiuquan, 1814–1864.
54 Fairbank, op. cit., p. 74.
55 Today part of the mega city of Wuhan
56 Fairbank, op. cit., pp. 75–76.
57 Zeng Guofeng, 1811–1872, was a scholar-official and military leader who played an important role in the defeat of the Taipings and who reformed the Xiang Army. He was part of the modernising 'Self-Strengthening Movement' which sought to marry Confucian values with western military technology.

support the Qing with a foreign mercenary army, the 'Ever-Victorious Army', headed first by an American, Frederick Townsend Ward and, after his death, by the British artillery officer, Charles 'Chinese' Gordon.

In the meantime in the Second Opium War, the British, French and the Russians were able to extract further concessions. In 1860, an enfeebled Manchu court in Peking was tied down with domestic rebellion and unable to resist western demands for further opening of the Chinese Empire, not only to foreign trade, but to the accepted (Western) method of intercourse between nations. This included having resident ambassadors stationed at Peking, dealing with a recognisable 'foreign ministry' that, in turn represented the policies of the government of China.

The Qing were fortunate in one respect—the other large domestic rebellion, the Nian Rebellion, made no attempt to join forces with the Taiping. Had they done so it is entirely likely that the Chinese Empire would have met a much earlier end.

The Nian, unlike the Taiping, the Eight Trigrams and the White Lotus rebels, were not a millenarian sect founded in religion. Neither were the Nian initially led by a unified leadership motivated by a coherent aim. The rebellion took 50 years to coalesce and was given an important boost by the floods in the early 1850s. In China the rivers periodically flooded and one of the duties of the government was to make sure the levies held. The budget for these works was large and the temptation to embezzle it larger still for the government officials who were meant to disburse it. The floods acted as a recruiting sergeant for the Nian. At the same time its organisation improved. In 1852, the leaders of 18 separate Nian groups agreed that Chang Lo-hsing,[58] a landowner from northern Anhui province, should be their leader. In 1856 he was elected Lord of the Alliance and given the title Great Han Prince with the Heavenly Mandate—a title that underlined his ethnicity (Chinese) and his legitimacy (the Mandate of Heaven) in contradistinction to the Manchu (foreign) occupant of the Dragon Throne.

---

58 Zhang Luoxing, 1810–1863.

INTRODUCTION

The Nian commanded an army of some 30,000 to 50,000 troops. This was not a very large force by Chinese standards, but the Nian became adept at what we would now call guerrilla warfare. They were mobile and well-armed and able to cut the lines of communication of the Manchu, who were then occupied with suppressing the Taiping Rebellion. They were also proficient in entrenching themselves in well-defended redoubts, often moated and defended with canon.[59] They were less proficient in winning the hearts and minds of local people, in spite of injunctions from their leaders to treat the common folk well. They were noted for their looting and rape, so much so that villagers fled their dwellings on news that the Nian were headed their way.

The Manchu also began to send higher-calibre officers leading better-trained troops to fight the Nian. Chief among them was a Mongol general who was chamberlain of the Imperial guard in Peking. General Senggelinqin had distinguished himself in battles against the Taiping, especially one that saw the Taiping defeated less than 30 miles from Tianjin. He stopped the British at Dagu in 1859, but was unable to prevent them from entering Peking in 1860 (for which he was punished). Later that year he was ordered to suppress the Nian and travelled south with a force of Mongol and Manchu cavalry. He cornered the Nian leader Chang, in north-western Anhui, and killed him. He was unforgiving in battle and struck terror in the Nian and local populations. An officer in the Qing army at the time wrote: "Who would have expected that the atrocities of the Imperial Army would be so much worse than the rebels themselves."[60]

Despite the death of Chang, the Nian had depth in leadership. The Nian harried the Manchus, leading the army on endless fruitless chases. In 1865 they led Senggelinqin and his army on a chase through Jiangsu, Henan and Shandong provinces, finally tricking the Manchus into a deadly ambush. Senggelinqin was killed, as were most of his troops, their 5,000 horses were booty for the Nian.

Tseng Guo-fan was called back into service; his victory over the Taiping uprising giving expectations of a quick result. He had disbanded

---

59 Spence, op. cit., p. 185.
60 ibid., p. 186.

the Xiang army, however and was not able to deploy a fighting force of equivalent deadliness. Meanwhile his protege, Li Hung-chang, had been made Governor General of Liangjiang (the provinces of Jiangsu, Jiangxi) and he resupplied Tseng with troops.

Li came from Anhui and the troops recruited had problems transferring their full loyalty to Tseng. Once this became understood in Peking the court ordered them to swap jobs: Tseng became Governor General and Li took command of the army (called the Huai Army after the river that flows through Anhui). It was an inspired switch. Li, a brilliant official who had topped his year in the competitive examinations, proved an able commander. It took time, but by 1868 his army had cornered the remnants of the Nian in Shandong and they were put to the sword.

Li was ennobled and showered with honours. He was to become one of the most powerful officials in the last quarter of the 19th century, a man who directed the Empire's foreign relations and did much to promote the modernisation of the Chinese economy and administration. During that time he was dubbed the Bismarck of China. Unlike Bismarck who expanded Germany's borders and built up Germany to become continental Europe's most powerful state, Li oversaw the contraction of the Chinese Empire, mostly due to Russia's audacious land grabs, China's defeat by the Japanese in 1894–95 Sino-Japanese War, and the Empire's continued weakness in the face of European pressure to open its economy. Morrison would meet Li after his arrival in Peking in 1897 and bristled at Li's attempt to bribe him. He would, however, keep a close association with him through William Pethick,[61] Li's American secretary, who was a valuable source of inside information.

---

61 William N. Pethick, c. 1840–1902, an American diplomat and secretary to Li Hongzhang, the high Qing official. Pethick went to China after the Civil War with a letter of recommendation from Abraham Lincoln. He served twice as US Consul in Tianjin (1873–75 and 1885–93) and was a fluent in Chinese. Pethick distinguished himself during the 1900 Boxer Uprising, leading a group of 10 US soldiers to save Chinese Christians. He is described in a report by Captain J. T. Myers of the US Marine Corps as "a veteran of our civil war, whose knowledge of China and the Chinese language and whose personal bravery while under fire rendered his services of the greatest value to the besieged." *Peking: Report of Captain John T. Myers,*

INTRODUCTION

The other great rebellion against Qing rule—and this time it was an uprising against Chinese colonialism—was the Muslim uprising in China's west that lasted from the 1850s to the 1880s. It was the Chien Lung[62] emperor who coined the term Sinkiang (Xinjiang, or New Territories) for the lands in the far west that his army conquered in the 1750s. These lands were settled by Muslim Uighur people and many others including Kirghiz and Mongol who traversed its vast inhospitable terrain. The subjugation of Xinjiang was not far short of genocide, with an estimated 80 per cent of the population of Kashgaria (northern Sinkiang) dying from war, or war-induced disease.[63] In the 19th century these and adjacent lands were called Chinese Turkestan.

In 1910, Morrison set forth on his last big expedition when he travelled more than 3,000 miles across China to finish his journey in Tashkent on the eastern edge of the vast Russian Empire in Central Asia. He produced a 12-part series for *The Times*, which is collected together and reproduced here for the first time since it was originally published.

The Muslim rebellion was led, for most of the time, by Yaqub Beg[64] who was born in the Khanate of Kokand, now Uzbekistan. He was finally defeated by Tso Tsung-tang[65] after a 10-year war of attrition notable for Tso's scorched earth approach to regaining territory. It also drew the attention of the Ottomans (who conferred upon Beg the title Emir of Kashgaria) and the Russians and British who, to China's great displeasure, separately signed agreements with him. The response of the Qing to the Muslim rebellion and steep population decline was to take direct administrative control of Sinkiang and allow Han migration.

---

26 September 1900, Naval History and Heritage Command. He was one of Morrison's key informants about politics and business.

62   Qianlong.

63   S. C. M. Paine, *Imperial Rivals: China, Russia and Their Disputed Frontier,* London and New York: Routledge, 2015, p. 113, pp. 126–127.

64   Beg was a Tajik born in Piskent, present day Uzbekistan in 1820; he died in 1877.

65   Zuo Zongtang, 1812–1885. Qing official experienced in military and civilian affairs. In 1863 he was appointed Governor-General of Zhejiang and Fujian provinces. He is remembered for his generalship in suppressing Muslim uprisings in Shaanxi and Gansu (1867–77) and for the bloody reconquest of Xinjiang (1875–78) from Muslim 'rebels' and Russian encroachment. For a fuller biography see Tu Lien chê, 'Tso T'sung Tang', *Eminent Chinese of the Ch'ing.* vol. 2, pp. 762–767.

"En Chine Le gâteau des Rois et ... des Empereurs," H. Meyer. 1898.
Public domain

This act of settler colonialism, so different from the way the Qing administered other tributary states on its periphery, such as Tibet,[66] sowed the seeds of Han/Muslim conflict, which is still with us today.

Rebellion against the Manchus underlined the ruling Qing dynasty's weakening grip on power. The Qing response to rebellion was brutal. During the period 1850–1873 China's population contracted by some 60 million persons, from an estimated 410 million at mid-century to 350 million by the early 1870s.[67] Rebellion occupied much of the attention of the Peking government. It weakened the dynasty's bargaining power with the other great threat it faced—foreign demands for the Empire to open itself to the world of international trade and commerce.

---

66 Of course Mao Zedong was to change this policy after his bloody invasion of Tibet in the 1950s and promote the Sinicisation of Tibet.
67 Fairbank, op. cit., p. 81.

INTRODUCTION

When Morrison arrived in Peking it was just over 100 years since Lord Macartney's ill-fated mission to the court of the Chien Lung emperor which had sought to open trade and diplomatic ties between Britain and the Chinese Empire. China, however, recognised no other country as its equal and Chien Lung insisted on treating Macartney as a representative of a barbarian people who had come to pay him tribute. Macartney was required to kowtow which he refused to do. Chien Lung left Macartney with a letter to carry. "The Celestial Empire," Chien Lung wrote to George III in 1793, "does not value rare and precious things ... we have never valued ingenious articles nor do we have the slightest need for your country's manufacturers."[68]

And there matters rested until the 1830s when the trade in opium became too big for the Chinese authorities to ignore. Opium consumption in China, which began in the 17th century, grew strongly in the 18th century, on the back of domestic Chinese poppy cultivation and production of refined opium.[69] It was an elite recreational drug and was initially consumed by mixing opium with tobacco, also locally produced. Indian opium was, however, more powerful than China's domestic product and it commanded a premium price and was much sought after by users. But it had become too popular and the deleterious effects of long-term use were of concern to the government (riddled as it was itself with users).

A stockpile of opium was burned at Canton in 1839 and the response by the British and US navies (the first time the two had fought on the same side)[70] is known as the First Opium War. The settlement of that war—the Treaty of Nanking, 1842—partially succeeded where Macartney had failed. China opened five places, the so-called Treaty Ports, to foreign trade. It accepted foreign diplomatic representation at those ports, although no diplomatic presence in Peking and it also agreed to the extraterritorial application of foreign laws to foreigners in those ports. Lastly, it ceded Hong Kong, a 'barren rock' at the mouth of the Pearl River delta, in perpetuity to the British. Such was the basis

---

68 Alain Peyrefitte, *The Collision of Two Civilisation: The British Expedition to China in 1792–4*, Trans. Jon Rothschild, London: Harvill, 1993, p. 291.
69 Spence, 'Opium', op. cit., pp. 228–256.
70 Robert Tombs, *The English and their History*, New York: Knopf, 2016, p. 560.

upon which the Chinese Empire moved squinting and hesitant into the harsh light of international relations, just as European powers jostled to extend their power across the globe.

The proximate cause for the Second Anglo-Chinese War at the end of the 1850s was the seizure of a British trading ship, the *Arrow*, in October 1856 on the orders of Ye Mingchen, the provincial governor resident at Canton. He stopped it because he was in the process of suppressing a local rebellion and may have thought it was a Chinese vessel. This incident may well illustrate the law of unintended consequence in that the *lorcha*[71] in question was Chinese-owned and crewed, but flying the Red Ensign on account of being registered in Hong Kong. This 'insult' to the British provided a thin justification for bombarding Canton and hunting down Commissioner Yeh (as the British referred to Ye Mingchen). The war, which was joined by France and received support from the US and Russia (more of whom later) ended in 1859 with the entry of British and French troops into Peking and the looting and burning of the Imperial Summer Palace.

This was the first time a hostile foreign force had entered the Chinese capital since the Manchus overthrew the Ming in the mid 17th century. The second war resulted in a clutch of new treaties being negotiated and signed. One of them, the *Convention of Peking*, resulted in the creation of a nascent Chinese foreign ministry, called the Tsungli Yamên[72] and the establishment of a diplomatic quarter in Peking for the housing of foreign ambassadors and their staff. A further indignity for the Chinese was having to cede vast areas of the Empire to the west and north for incorporation into the Russian Empire.

Russia's defeat in 1856 in the Crimean War by a coalition consisting of Ottoman, British and French forces severely wounded Russian pride and effectively ended Russia's westward expansion. The Tsar and his advisors turned their attention to central Asia and the Far East and

---

71 A hybrid vessel with a European hull and Chinese sails.
72 The Tsungli-Yamên (Office for the Management of the Business of All Foreign Countries), was the government body in charge of foreign affairs in late Imperial China. It was established in 1861 after the Convention of Peking. It was abolished by the Qing government in 1901 in the wake of the Boxer uprising and replaced with a Foreign Office (Waibu) of ministerial rank.

The Sino-Japanese War was substantially fought in Korea. This three panel woodblock print represents the Battle of Pyongyang, 15September 1894. The Chinese soldier left carries the banner General Nie Shicheng, whose army the Japanese defeated. Lieutenant-General Nozu Michisura (1840–1908), commander of the Japanese army in Korea, and, right, the dashing Lieutenant-Colonel Fukushima Yasumasa (1852–1919), later made general and raised to the peerage. Print is dated September 1897.

there they found they shared an ill-defined border with the Chinese Empire. From about 1850 to 1914 the Russian Empire would absorb or bring under its control more than 3.3 million square kilometres of Chinese territory,[73] and area equalling the size of modern India. The seized territories included vast areas in the far west of China bordering Xinjiang, outer Mongolia, and large tracts of Manchuria to the north and east. By comparison, the area of Hong Kong occupied by the British (the premiere commercial imperialists in China) would be easily lost in the rounding up of Russia's land grab as Hong Kong amounted to not much more than 1,100 square kilometres, or 0.03 per cent of Russia's total acquisitions.

While few of the western European powers or the United States raised much concern about the activities of the Russians, Russia's great rival in north China, Japan, was acutely aware of its plans. Japan saw Russian involvement in north China and especially Korea as directly affecting Japanese interests. And this was the putative cause for Japan's war with China.

Japan's military prowess took the European powers by surprise, and its military successes met with lavish praise in the Western press. Japan had embarked on modernisation barely 25 years before the war and it arrived on the international scene having shown itself to be a master of western military technology and practice. Japan shamed China, which resorted to racist descriptions of the Japanese as "dwarves" and "pirate dwarves" in all official Chinese communiqués on the conflict. For its part, Tokyo forced on Peking an humiliating peace settlement—the Treaty of Shimonoseki, 1895. This treaty ceded to Japan Formosa (Taiwan) Okinawa, and large tracts of land on the northern shore of the Bohai Sea and the Liaoning peninsula, including the important ports of Port Arthur and Dalian. It also required China to recognise the independence of Korea, thereby severing another tributary state

---

[73] Paine, *Imperial Rivals*, op. cit., p. 3. and pp. 28–29. "By the Treaty of Aigun [Russia] acquired sovereignty over 185,000 square miles of territory along the northern bank on the Amur River; by the Treaty of Peking it took 130,000 square miles along the northern Manchuria coastline between the Ussuri River (Wu-su-li chiang) and the sea; and by the 1864 Treaty of Tabagatai it gained an additional 350,000 square miles of territory in north east Sinkiang [Xinjiang]."

from the Celestial Empire's control.⁷⁴ In retrospect, this Sino-Japanese War fired the starter's gun for the Battle for the Concessions—that unedifying spectacle of European imperialists competing for economic concessions in China. No sooner had the ink dried on the *Treaty of Shimonoseki* than the Triple Intervention occurred, when Russia, France and Germany leaned on Japan to relinquish control of its concessions on the Liaoning Peninsula to Russia. The Japanese would not forget.

For the Russians, the capture of the Liaoning Peninsula was profoundly consequential. Russia's port at Vladivostok was unnavigable for four months of the year due to sea ice. With Port Arthur, Russia had an all-weather port that gave them access to the Pacific. This had important implications for the Trans-Siberian railway as well, which could now terminate at Port Arthur, if a rail line traversing southern Manchuria could be built.

Arrival in Peking

When Morrison arrived in Peking on 15 March 1897, he was 35 years of age and decidedly uneasy. Looking back at that time some 15 or so years later he was to write: "That first summer in Peking, I recall with shuddering."⁷⁵ Although he had long dreamt of a career in journalism this was the first time he had been employed as a full-time journalist. Of his first months in the Chinese capital he says: "Everything was in darkness. The work was unfamiliar. Ignorance of the springs of Chinese action was universal and I was the most ignorant of all."

In his correspondence with friends and colleagues during that first year, Morrison vented his frustration with getting to grips with China. In April he wrote to Moberly Bell that he was trying to inform himself about what was happening in Peking "but it is extremely difficult to sift the truth."⁷⁶ He went on to recount a meeting he had with Li Hung-

---

74 The French in their war with China 1884–85 severed Annam (the northern part of Vietnam) from the Empire's control. By 1885, after the Third Burmese War, the British controlled all Burma and began to administer it as a province of British India. Burma had been a tributary state of the Chinese Empire before the 1820s.
75 'Reminiscences,' p. 433.
76 Lo, op. cit., p. 45. Morrison to Moberly Bell, 8 April, 1896

chang, who was Viceroy of Chili from 1870–95 and the statesman at the centre of China's economic development and foreign relations.

> [He] had the impudence to ask me if a money payment would induce me to write to *The Times* advocating a doubling of the import duties without compensation. The crafty old man is failing, he now looks his face age of 76, and it can not be long before he must be laid aside from physical infirmity.[77]

In May he wrote to J.O.P. Bland, *The Times*' correspondent in Shanghai, that "there was something deadly in this atmosphere." He went on to say,

> it is almost impossible to ascertain the truth and the constant strain of one's judgement is wearing down and heartbreaking. Living in Peking one would get to distrust one's own brother.[78]

He set about to meet people, especially well-placed foreigners in China's Imperial Maritime Customs Service. The customs service was one of those curious colonial institutions that was dominated by a cadre of gifted foreign linguists led by Sir Robert Hart,[79] an Ulsterman who had lived in China since 1863. The customs service provided the Chinese government with its only secure form of revenue, a source, moreover, that was not subject to theft and skimming by Manchu and Chinese officials in the way so many other sources of finance raised by the Chinese government were. Sir Robert initially held himself aloof from

---

77 ibid., pp. 45–46. Li lived another five years and died in 1901.
78 Lo, op. cit., p. 81.
79 Sir Robert Hart, Bt, 1835–1911, British official serving the Qing dynasty as Inspector-General of China's Maritime Customs Service from 1863–1908 which Hart staffed with a cadre of brilliant foreign linguists, mostly British but also Americans and Western Europeans. Himself a formidable linguist, with equally formidable powers of organisation, he transformed Chinese Customs into the single most important source of revenue for the Chinese Government and expanded its operations to include managing lighthouses, China's first postal service, and source of diplomatic advice. To the extent that the Chinese trusted any foreigner they trusted Hart—his Chinese nickname was "our Hart". He was given Chinese honours of the highest rank including the Red Button, a Peacock's Feather and the Order of the Double Dragon, among others. He was created a baronet in 1893. He married Hester Breedon in 1866 and had three children with her; they separated in 1882 when Hart went to live with his Chinese mistress, Ayou, with whom he also had three children.

INTRODUCTION

Sir Robert Hart, the Inspector General of the Chinese Imperial Maritime with a Chinese government's newspaper.
Mitchell Library, Sydney

Morrison, but not so one of his senior deputies, Alfred Hippisley,[80] who, based at Tianjin, supplied Morrison with a steady stream of authoritative information. And his meeting with Li Hung-chang had not been entirely fruitless either. There he met William Pethick,[81] a former US consul in Tianjin who was employed as Li's American secretary. Pethick would become a useful source for Morrison on internal Chinese politics.

Morrison arrived in China in what we can now see as the lull before the storm. China's defeat in the war with Japan of 1894–95 had refocussed foreign minds on the spoils to be had through exploitation of an enfeebled and disintegrating Chinese Empire. Internally, elite opinion was increasingly becoming anti-foreign with the policy of accommodation to foreigners, exemplified in the career of Li Hung-chang, discredited and out of favour. Li's most recent service to the Empire had been the negotiation of the Treaty of Shimonoseki, but

---

80 Englishman Alfred E. Hippisley, 1848–1939, joined the Imperial Chinese Maritime Customs Service in 1867 and was tipped to succeed Hart but illness forced his retirement in 1910. He was central in the United States' embrace of the 'Open Door Policy' toward foreign trade and investment in China, persuasively arguing the case to Secretary of State John Hay who promoted it as US policy.

81 See note 63 for Pethick's details.

from a Chinese perspective it was hardly a triumph, and, as we will see later, was an event that galvanised a further (failed) push towards modernisation by the Kwang Hsu[82] emperor. The Treaty ceded to Japan large areas of Chinese territory somewhat reduced by the 'Triple Intervention' of Russia, France and Germany, which forced Japan to relinquish control of the Liaoning Peninsula. The principal beneficiary of that arm-twisting was Russia, which secured not only a terminus for the Trans Siberian Railway, but a warm water port at Port Arthur. No one had surveyed Russia's Far East empire and ambitions before. Morrison's decision to make Russia's railway in Manchuria the subject of his first big exploration of China speaks to his strategic sense, but it must also have been a relief to him to leave Peking in June 1897 and do what he liked best—be a wanderer.

Morrison as a Journalist

> Twelve years ago, I was sent to Peking, having had no previous journalistic work. The instructions given to me were simply that I was to tell the truth without fear or favour and during the time that I have been in the Far East, I hope that I have carried out these instructions and that I have endeavoured to allow no personal prejudice or predilection to interfere with my work or to colour any cable I have been able to send to the great journal I am serving. I feel indignant when I read in the papers that I am for-this or anti-that country. I am an Englishman and all I think about and all that I desire to serve are the interests of my own country.[83]

It is interesting to note that Morrison sees no contradiction, or at least, tension, in his avowed pursuit of "truth without fear or favour," and his desire "to serve ... the interests of my own country." This was entirely consistent with the note Valentine Chirol wrote to him when he arrived

---

82 Guangxu, 1871–1908.
83 Pearl, op. cit., p. 196. Morrison was addressing the Yokohama Foreign Board of Trade annual dinner in 1908.

in Peking about providing 'intelligence' for *The Times* that furthers British Imperial policy.

The country referred to is Great Britain, not the emerging Australian nation, the place of his birth, and, which, by the time he spoke in Yokohama, was barely seven years old. We should not be surprised that he describes himself as an Englishman; he was viewed by his employer as a Colonial Englishman. Proud as he was of his Australian origins (he always travelled with a volume of his friend A. B. 'Banjo' Paterson's verse[84]), most of his life he was a British subject from the Colony of Victoria. He was a product of Empire and a staunch believer in the civilising power of the British and their imperial mission. His views about imperialism rarely obtruded in his journalism about China, a civilisation and people he admired. Indeed, he seems to be equally disgusted by the behaviour of many of the European Powers in China as he is with ineffectiveness of the Chinese government to deal with them. His views about colonialism, however, were on full display in the account of French administration in Indochina that he produced for *The Times* before he moved to Peking. From today's standpoint, the views are noxious in their naked racialism, yet they reflect the way in which 'race' was a lens through which many viewed the newly globalised world.[85]

> If there is one fact more clearly demonstrated than any other, it is that the colonisation done by the French in Cambodia has not gained for the French, any more than it has in Annam and Tonking [Vietnam], the goodwill of the subject races. How can it be otherwise? The French colonist treats the native capriciously

---

84 They got to know each other and first met in Peking 1901. On 21 January 1903, Paterson wrote to Morrison, "I am editing the above organ of misinformation [*The Evening News*]. If you can look in and see me I would be glad." (ML MSS 312/45) Morrison did see Paterson and it resulted in Paterson writing a favourable profile of him.

85 When, in 1921, C. E. W. Bean began to publish his multivolume history of Australia's involvement in the World War 1, he framed the conflict, in part, in terms of a battle of race. "The Australian came of a race whose tradition was one of independence and enterprise, and within that race itself, from a stock more adventurous and for the most part physically more strong than the general run of men." Bean, *The Story of ANZAC*, Sydney: Angus & Robertson, 1937, 6th ed., pp. 4–5.

with alternate kindness and harshness, with insolent hauteur or with impudent familiarity. A Britisher is characterised by a certain racial absence of admiration for colour, especially for the colour of a hybrid. His gall rises when he sees, as I have so often done in Cochin-China and Cambodia, a French functionary seated at the same table and cracking jokes with half-caste Annamites and bastard Malays. Capriciousness or familiarity in dealing with races who are capricious by nature and so admire firmness, and who regard familiarity as a confession of inferiority, is a fatal error.[86]

Morrison's news coverage of China was firmly focussed on the activities of European and American business interests in China. London was the leading capital market of the world and it financed Chinese loans and industrial investment in China. The City of London, was therefore keenly interested in his telegrams detailing the latest twists and turns in what Lord Salisbury had called "the battle of the concessions". In what today would be called his 'feature' articles, and then were called 'letters', he provided a richer diet of story and observation, though one still couched in terms of the interests of foreigners in the progress of China.

Morrison came to the task of journalism with an unusual set of life experiences, experiences that prepared him well for discerning truth from falsehood and the character of the persons with whom he came into contact. It is worth considering this experience that was to cohere in a man who became one of the, if not, the most influential journalist of his time.

Morrison's imagination was captured, at an early age by the romance of exploration. He would tell friends and associates in London: "I have been a wanderer since my 18th year."[87] In his late teens and early 20s he sought to emulate his hero Henry Stanley, the great American explorer/journalist of High Imperialism. In his summer holidays, which in

---

86 Morrison, 'From Cochin-China to Cambodia,' Our Special Correspondent, *The Times*, 7 April 1896, p. 10. One may note here that Morrison never wrote about the Chinese in these terms.

87 'G. E. Morrison', *The Times*, 17 July 1900, p. 4. This is from Valentine Chirol's 'obituary' of Morrison that was prematurely published by *The Times* at the height of the Boxer uprising. See 'Kill the Foreigners,' later in this volume.

Australia straddle the New Year, he explored Australia. First, he trekked along the southern coastline of Australia from Queenscliff at the mouth of Port Philip Bay in Victoria to Adelaide, the capital of South Australia. The next summer, he canoed down the Murray River. His most daring piece of Australian exploration, however, was his 2000 mile trek across Australia—north to south—from the Gulf of Carpentaria to Melbourne, again solo, unarmed and completed in just over 200 days. This not only underlined but must also have reinforced a resourcefulness and resilience in Morrison, and given him the ability to make quick, accurate judgements of strangers met along the way. Accounts of these adventures, and others, were published in the local Melbourne press. Much of this juvenilia journalism is just that – juvenilia; however, it is worth reproducing his account of his walk across Australia if only for the sheer audacity of the trek and uniqueness of the achievement. It has not been reproduced since it was first published in *The Age* on 19 May 1883, and is printed later in this volume with explanatory notes. Morrison never lost his desire for travel. His curiosity for strange lands would stay with him until his last great journey through Chinese Turkestan, an account of which he wrote for *The Times* in 1910 and which is reproduced here.

His medical experience—the 'objective' way in which his medical training conditioned him to look at people—also sharpened his powers of observation and judgement. In 'Reminiscences' he recounts a number of instances, one from Spain, another from his trip back to Australia as a ships' doctor, where he dealt with malingerers. While in Ballarat as the head surgeon for the district hospital, he regularly gave evidence before the courts and was cross-examined about the causes of death. It is not unreasonable to assume that this honed his skills in the gathering and presentation of evidence, a not unrelated activity to serious journalism. To the cauldron of influences that shaped him must also be added that he had faced death many times, often displaying great physical courage. The first time was in New Guinea where he sustained wounds from two spears; the second, on his journey back from China to Australia after his 1894 walk across that vast country. From Burma he went to India and contracted a debilitating, and nearly fatal, remitting fever; and lastly, during the siege of Peking in 1900 when he was seriously wounded in the leg. Throughout that siege, he ministered to the injured and dying, as well as taking part in rescue operations that took him outside the flimsy protective area of the Legations.

Murray Sayle,[88] a great Australian journalist who spent the last 30 years of his life in Japan, would say to young journalists he encountered: "There are two ways of getting to know a country. You can learn its language or read its history." Like most of us, Morrison did both but with the accent decidedly on the latter, very much as Sayle was later to do. Morrison amassed a vast library of some 24,000 volumes by the time he sold it to a Japanese aristocrat in 1917.[89] His collection included some of the earliest versions in Latin of Marco Polo's travels in China; he gathered a near complete collection of the writings of Catholic priests in Japan and China about the countries in which they resided; he amassed the largest collection of missionary texts and pamphlets as relates to Christian proselytising in China, as well as many thousands of 19th century accounts of Asian and Far East exploration in English, French and German among others. Morrison read prodigiously. He was an able linguist. He had been schooled in ancient Greek and Latin – the latter language in good enough shape for him to assist an uncle in writing a Latin primer for school students—and he had good Spanish and French. He claimed not to know Chinese, a comment that perhaps reflected his high standards, as there is ample evidence that he knew enough Chinese to negotiate daily life. However, to read and write Chinese is a mighty task, especially for one in his 30s who had never previously encountered it. He always travelled with Ah Heng, his assistant, and he engaged the services, among others, of Sir Edmund Backhouse,[90] a brilliant linguist

---

[88] Murray Sayle, 1926–2010, was a foreign correspondent and investigative reporter, especially for London's *Sunday Times*. He made his home in Japan in 1975 for 30 years. He made this comment to the author in 1985.

[89] Baron Hisaya Iwasaki, 1865–1955, scion of the Mitsubishi conglomerate, provided the £35,000 (£2 million today) for the purchase of Morrison's books. The collection today forms the heart of the Toyo Bunko (Oriental Library) in Tokyo and contains many rare treasures.

[90] Fabulist, forger, fraud, Backhouse was an extraordinary figure whose life has been examined by Hugh Trevor Roper in *A Hidden Life: The Enigma of Sir Edmund Backhouse*, London: MacMillan. 1976. Backhouse's written Chinese was so good that he could himself forge the diary of Jung Lu, a Manchu aristocrat, and have it taken, initially, for an original document.

who lived in Peking, to translate the Chinese government documents and the vernacular press for him when needed.

Morrison did not take long to become one of the leading journalists of his day. He spent the first year or so of his time at *The Times* traversing Indochina, and then from the beginning of 1897, he was in Peking. On his Indochina assignment he produced a series of detailed 'letters' (long, discursive feature articles) for the paper that looked closely at French Indochina and at Siam (modern day Thailand). As *The Times* ruefully noted in his premature obituary, these letters were "graphic and instructive," however, they "attracted more attention, perhaps, in Paris than in London."[91] Difficult as his entry into Peking news gathering had been, by mid-1898 Alfred Hippisley, the number two official at China's Imperial Maritime Customs, could write, "you have now established a world-wide reputation. The accuracy of your information has been borne testimony to in all parts and by all sorts of persons, and your experience and knowledge of China are now by themselves of great value."[92]

Morrison had shown himself to be an exceptional news hound, a provider of what Valentine Chirol, *The Times*' foreign editor, would call "intelligence." These were short reports, 'telegrams' no more, and five or six paragraphs long (sometimes shorter), about the state of multi-million pound loan negotiations between the Chinese government and foreign lenders, details of the funding of the latest railway or mining "concession," and diplomatic news about secret treaties between China and third countries, particularly Russia. Britain had no interest in ruling China, as it had ended up doing in India, but it had a strategic interest in making sure no other country ruled it, or obtained economic benefits injurious to Britain. Indeed, British interest in China was primarily economic. As the world's largest economy and biggest creditor nation British capital was intimately involved in the economic modernisation of China. Morrison's frequent telegrams alerted the City and Westminster that there was someone in Peking keeping on top of developments.

---

91 'G. E. Morrison', op. cit., p. 4.
92 Lo, op. cit., p. 88. Hippisley himself is worthy of greater study. An Englishman, he persuaded US Secretary of State John Hay to embrace, and enunciate, the Open Door policy towards China trade.

Morrison and some important members of the Tsungli Yamên (forerunner to the Foreign Ministry), 8 August 1899.
Mitchell Library, Sydney

Morrison with his household staff, c. 1905.
Mitchell Library, Sydney

INTRODUCTION

These telegrams were an important part, perhaps the major part, of his reputation for providing timely and accurate news about foreign involvement in China. They were also a source of embarrassment to the British Government who found that senior ministers were often unable to respond to questions in the House of Commons about affairs in China. Reporting by British diplomats in China lagged the timeliness of Morrison. This led to the celebrated remarks by George Curzon, Under Secretary of State of Foreign Affairs and later Viceroy of India, on the floor of the Commons when pressed as to why the Foreign Office was failing to provide timely news of events.

> It is the business of Her Majesty's representatives abroad to report to us facts of which they have official cognisance, and to obtain confirmation of them before they telegraph. I hesitate to say what the functions of the modern journalist may be; but I imagine they do not exclude the intelligent anticipation of facts before they occur ... the journalist whose main daily duty is speed is likely sometimes to get the advantage over the diplomatist whose main object is accuracy.[93]

When in Bangkok, Morrison had got to know Maurice de Bunsen,[94] the British consul at Bangkok. As with so many people he met in life he maintained a correspondence with Bunsen. The latter wrote to him in November 1897 that he had dined with Moberly Bell of *The Times* "and I was glad to note that you were well appreciated in that quarter." But it was the compliment he paid Morrison apropos his journalism

---

93 ibid., p. 79, note 2. Curzon to the Commons on 9 March 1898. He was harried by MPs to respond to Morrison's stories later that March 1898. He was called to respond to a report about the Russian plan to lease Port Arthur and Dalian. Curzon could not confirm the report, which later turned out to be accurate.

94 Sir Maurice William Ernest de Bunsen, Bt, 1852–1932, a British diplomat of German extraction (his grandfather was the Prussian ambassador to London) was Consul General in Bangkok 1894–1897. He went on to be Ambassador in Lisbon, Spain and Austria. He was influential in British policy towards the Ottoman Empire and South America.

that is worth quoting. "You have the gift of seeing and understanding," de Bunsen wrote.[95]

A sense of his celebrity—and of being "an exceptional man"—is conveyed by a profile of Morrison written by Australia's great 'bush' poet Banjo Paterson, then editor of *The Evening News* in Sydney, in 1903.

> Dr Morrison lives for the most part at Peking, where he is in touch with the best informed Chinese circles. But he moves constantly about, travelling in men-of-war, on tramp steamers, on mule litters, on pony back, or on his feet, as occasion demands. He is a powerful, wiry man, of solid and imposing presence and those who know him best in China say that he has mastered the secret of all Chinese diplomacy – bluff … For the rest, a keen knowledge of men, a gift of diplomacy, and a dogged Scotch persistency pull him through his difficulties.
>
> It needs an exceptional man to hold his own in such troubled waters; every day there is some new rumour, some new threat, some new difficulty. What are the Russians doing, what the Germans, what the Americans? He has to report, and report faithfully, every move in the game in which the stakes are millions, and the counters are the lives of men.[96]

The 'intelligent anticipation of facts' was on full display in January 1912, months before Morrison left *The Times* for his new role as political advisor to Yuan Shi-k'ai, the first president of the Republic of China. Two thousand years of imperial government of China was on the brink of collapse, about to give way to republican government. Morrison had the scoop on everyone.

Three decks of headlines gave the essentials:

---

95 de Bunsen to Morrison, 7 November 1897, Mitchell Library MSS 312/42 letters 1895–1897.

96 'Dr Morrison: A Notable Australian', *The Evening News*, 21 January 1903. From *Collected Prose of A. B. 'Banjo' Paterson*, eBook No.: 0607731h.html, Project Gutenberg Australia, Walter Morse (ed).

INTRODUCTION

LAST DAYS OF THE MANCHU DYNASTY.
A REPUBLIC BY IMPERIAL DECREE.
YUAN SHIH-KAI AND THE PRESIDENCY.
(From Our Own Correspondent)
Peking, Jan. 16. 1912.

The steps towards abdication are quickening. I have excellent authority for believing that within three or four days a momentous Edict will be issued, and that it will go further than was expected, not only announcing the abdication of the Throne, but decreeing the establishment of a Republican Government in China, the people to elect the President. In this way, it is believed, the Republic will be regarded by the nation as a Constitutional Republic legitimately succeeding the Monarchy by the Imperial will.

It is confidently believed, in spite of suggestions to the contrary, that the Republican leaders at Nanking will recognize the paramount claims of Yuan Shih-kai to the Presidency, knowing that he alone among Chinese statesmen has great administrative experience and commands a powerful following among both Manchus and Chinese, the devotion of the best troops of the Empire, and confidence and respect abroad.

Morrison's 146-word telegram was out in its timing—the Imperial edict was not published until 12 February that year—but correct in every other respect. The Manchu Qing dynasty abolished itself by Imperial edict and in the same document ordained the creation of the Republic of China.

Yuan Shikai, though ultimately a disappointment, became the President of the Republic of China after Sun Yat Sen, who had been 'provisional' president, stepped aside. He essentially accepted the rationale given by Morrison in favour of Yuan: his administrative experience, his following among local elites, and the support he had among the army.

～

Pagoda behind the Summer Palace, Peking, c. 1905.
Mitchell Library, Sydney

Chapter 1

MORRISON VENTURES FORTH

"Your letter on the Manchurian railway was most interesting and arrived just in the nick of time."[97] So wrote Valentine Chirol, *The Times'* Foreign Department head, on 31 March 1898. Morrison's assessment of the railway, reprinted here, was datelined 20 December 1897 but was not published until 7 March 1898—such were the exigencies of a journalism that relied on the postal services for the communication of dispatches and also on, what is to us today, a curious journalistic convention of *The Times* to print 'letters' from its correspondents. These were timeless 'think pieces' designed to get under the skin of the place from which they were written and were at once personal and analytical.

Morrison set off on his trip to Manchuria "early in the rains"[98] (last week of July 1898) and did not return to Peking until towards the end of November. His journey covered many hundreds of miles, by boat, horse, foot and *tarantass*, which was a covered unsprung four-wheeled cart widely used in Russia. In the company of Ah Heng, his manservant and assistant, he met everyone in Russian officialdom that was possible, name checking some of Russia's leading empire builders; he was an acute observer, from the role of prison labour in the Russian construction of

---

97 Lo, op. cit., pp. 75–76.
98 ibid., p. 51.

the railway to the importance of illegal gold in the economy. He had a keen eye for the engineering challenges facing the Russians. Interesting too is the way he seeks to make the unfamiliar familiar with comparisons to other British 'possessions': rolling country is compared to the plains of Manitoba, an important town is likened to Johannesburg, yet another is the Botany Bay of the area.

By the time Morrison got to Peking, Imperial Russia loomed as one of the determinant powers of China's future. News of a wide ranging 'secret' treaty[99] between St Petersburg and Peking had emerged in December 1896 only adding and giving substance to concerns about Russia's steady expansion eastwards, as the treaty seemed to suggest that China, in the wake of its recent defeat by Japan, had thrown its lot in with Russia. It now appeared as if China were prepared to allow Russia a wide latitude of operations in the north east of its country.

Morrison's decision to make the proposed Manchurian railway the subject for his first large article of *The Times* was, therefore, an astute decision. Russia was one of the most aggressively expansionist imperialists and it had been expanding its borders for a very long time. It has been estimated that in the four centuries up to the end of the 19th century, Imperial Russia had grown by an average of 10 square miles per day.[100] Since its defeat in the Crimean War, Russia had been hungry for territory in the Far East. By the Treaty of Aigun,[101] (1858) and confirmed by the Treaty of Peking (1860), which the Chinese subsequently regarded as "unequal," Russia increased its penetration of China's northern lands significantly by the acquisition of vast tracts of land that extended its frontier to the northern and western shores of the Amur and Ussuri rivers.

In pursuit of eastward development, it was busy building a railway across its vast country and sought a terminus at a better port than it already possessed at Vladivostok, itself a former Manchu possession.

---

99 *The Times* published the text of this treaty in its edition of 8 December 1896, p. 8, under the headline: 'Text of the Russo-Chinese Treaty'. It was followed by another more discursive story under the headline 'The Secret Treaty Between Russia and China', on 5 January 1897, p. 7.
100 Stephen Kotkin, *Stalin: Paradoxes of Power 1878–1928*, New York: Penguin, 2014, p. 11.
101 Aihui today.

Imperial Russia now wanted to build a railway through Manchurian lands south of the Amur and to take the line as far as Port Arthur[102] on the Liaoning peninsula, thereby securing an all-weather port for trade and the projection of Russian power into the Pacific.[103] The recently signed treaty allowed this development.

This ambitious plan was the unintended consequence of the First Sino-Japanese War of 1894–95. The treaty that ended this war, the Treaty of Shimonoseki, 1895, ceded to Japan the Liaoning peninsula (including Port Arthur), in addition to Formosa (Taiwan), the former tributary state of Okinawa, and allowed Japan free rein in the former tributary state of Korea over which China relinquished its suzerainty in favour of Korean 'independence'. For Japan these treaty gains in Manchuria and Korea presented a solution to two pressing problems—a lack of industrial resources allied to over-population, and a buffer between the Japanese home islands and Imperial Russia. It also vaulted Japan into a leading position on the Chinese mainland, especially in the north of China. These were, however, gains that Russia could not countenance and together with Germany and France (though not Britain) it successfully brought pressure to bear on Tokyo to retrocede to Russia its interests on the Liaoning peninsula, the so-called Triple Intervention. With this, the touch paper had been lit for what became known as the Battle of Concessions, an unedifying competition between Japan and the European powers to enlarge their spheres of influence in the decaying Chinese Empire.

In this competition, Imperial Russia was ably represented in Peking by Count Cassini[104] who succeeded in deepening Russia's relationship

---

102 Lushun today.
103 Railway construction propelled Russia's eastward expansion. Between 1895 and 1905, Russia nearly doubled the length of its rail network, from 16,155 miles to more than 40,500 miles. The cost of eastward expansion was much cheaper per mile than westward construction. In 1910, a British analyst estimated that European rail construction cost on average £10,504 a mile (£1 million in today's money), whereas construction of the "Asiatic" network cost on average £5092 (£520,000) a mile. See John Thomas Bealby, *Railways* in main Russia article, *Encyclopaedia Britannica*, Cambridge: Cambridge University Press, 11th ed., 1910, vol. 23, p. 891.
104 Arturo Paul Nicholas Cassini, Marquis de Capuzzuchi de Bologna, Count de Cassini, 1836–1919, was a diplomat with the Russian government for 55 years, who in 1891 was

with the Chinese. Secretly the two countries devised a plan for closer relations which included, among other things, the extension of the railway through Manchuria to the Pacific, to be financed by the Russo-Chinese Bank (solely funded by the Russians). The architect of this policy on the Chinese side, and the recipient of a 3 million ruble bribe,[105] was Li Hung-chang, an official for whom the word 'eminent' might have been coined. He had had a storied career in the military and government affairs and was, at the time of the Japanese war, one of the most senior officials in the Chinese government. Yet as Morrison ruefully observed about Li in his 'Reminiscences', Li was unable "to recognise modern conditions and his policy of playing of one power against the other invariably involved his country in costly difficulties with both powers."[106] The Japanese treaty was to mark the beginning of the end of Li's political career and policy of balancing foreigners' interests, although he was to provide one last service to the Empire at the conclusion of hostilities between China and the foreign powers after the Boxer Uprising of 1900 when he signed for China the Boxer Peace Protocol with the Allied Powers.

However, all that lay in the future. Morrison's first big article had been a huge success. On 31 March 1898, in the letter previously referred to, Chirol, after offering some advice as to how Morrison could have made a three-part series of his Manchurian journey, concluded: "For myself I may say that the way in which you have distinguished yourself has been a great personal satisfaction to me."[107] Morrison had been with *The Times* in Peking for just one year.

---

appointed to the post of envoy extraordinary and minister plenipotentiary to the Chinese Imperial Court at Peking. He refused to present his credentials to anyone but the Emperor, a demand with which the Chinese finally complied.

105 Paine, op. cit., pp. 185–186. The bribe roughly equates to £54 million today.
106 'Reminiscences,' p. 449.
107 Lo, op. cit., p. 76.

'The Trans-Manchurian Railway'

(From Our Own Correspondent)
Peking, 20 December 1897[108]

During the past few months I have had an opportunity of travelling across Manchuria, along the course of the projected Trans-Manchurian Railway.

From Vladivostok[109] I went up the Amur and Shilka rivers to Stretensk,[110] the limit of practical navigation, and then returned to Vladivostok across country. Generally speaking, I guided my journey by land so that I might meet the Russian engineers proceeding to their stations. The final route of the railway has not yet been determined. Three times already its direction has been altered, and the guiding principle in each change of direction has been to bring the railway further to the south so as to loop on to Russian territory an ever-increasing area of Manchuria.

Briefly stated, the chief features of the new railway are as follows:- The railway is termed the Chinese Eastern Railway, a title ingeniously devised to "save face" of the Chinese. Shares can only be held by Russians and by Chinese, the result of which arrangement being, of course, that every share is held by Russians, not one single share is held by Chinese. The railway is to connect the Trans-Baikal section of the Siberian Railway with Vladivostok. It is to be built by Russian engineers, protected by Russian soldiers, with Russian capital, and with Russian material, and it will pass through territory which, though now

---

108 Published Monday 7 March 1898, p. 9.
109 Vladivostok was Manchu (Chinese) territory until the Russians took it from the Qing in the 1860 Treaty of Peking.
110 Located on the right bank of the Shilka river, founded in 1689.

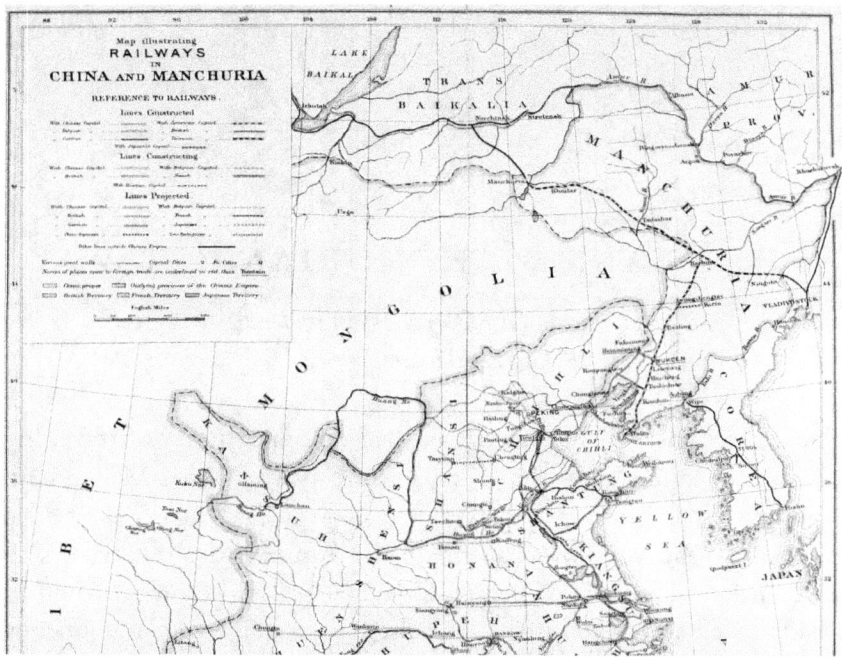

Detail of map showing Manchurain railways from Railway Enterprise in China: An Account of its Origin and Development, *p. 38, by Percy Kent, published by Arnold, London, 1907.*
No known copyright

Chinese, may soon have ceased to be an integral portion of the Middle Kingdom. The railway is to be completed and in full running order before August 28, 1903, and 80 years later it is to become the property of the Chinese Government,[111] provided, of course, that the Chinese Government is still in existence. Finally, the railway is financed by a private commercial enterprise, supported by the Russian Government, known as the Russo-Chinese Bank, which, as its name denotes, is partly Russian and partly Chinese. The Russians hold all the shares and retain

---

111 This appears to be a rare error by Morrison. According to the text of the Treaty as published in *The Times* on 8 December 1896, p. 8, under the headline 'Text of Russo-Chinese Treaty' (a Reuters dispatch lifting the Treaty's text from the *North China Daily News*), the Treaty provides for the railway's retrocession to China after 30, not 80, years. At that time, 1933, the Japanese had invaded Manchuria making transfer moot. Stalin took until 1953 to relinquish Soviet ownership of the railway.

1 | 'THE TRANS-MANCHURIAN RAILWAY'

the exclusive control, management, and profits; the Chinese provide the clients and compradores, some of the under clerks, and all the servants. It is a conjunction of interests typical of Russo-Chinese combinations generally.

In the course of my journey I went first from Vladivostok to Khabarovka[112] on the Amur. This is the seat of the Governor-General, who has under his supreme control all that vast territory of Siberia from Lake Baikal eastward to the sea. Only lately this city has been joined to Vladivostok by rail. The line is 487 miles in length, and 10 years, from September, 1887, to September, 1897, were required for its completion. The Trans-Manchurian Railway, three times as long, through a country three times as difficult, is to be completed within six years.

It is interesting to note that much of the work on this railway was done by convicts, drafted from the penal settlements of Saghalien.[113] At one time as many as 1,200 men were employed on the section approaching Khabarovka. Fear was, generally expressed that the introduction of so large a body of criminals would bring with it a formidable increase in crime. But the experiment was a complete success, and during three years there was not a crime other than the trifling offence of drunkenness discovered among them. I saw a detachment of convicts at their work. I examined their papers and tasted their food, and I can but add my testimony to evidence which is already overwhelming of the humanity with which the prisoners are treated. The convicts slept in well-found barracks; they were well clad and well nourished. They had no reason to complain of their lot. Their papers proved that in nearly every case generous remissions had been granted in the terms of their penal servitude. Imperial clemency has had during the last few years many occasions for exercise. The ascension of the Tsar to the Throne, the Imperial marriage, the coronation, have each been associated in the prisons of far Siberia with the lightening of punishment. In many cases the original sentence had been reduced to one-half. Men condemned to hard labour for ten years in 1890 were already entitled to their ticket-of-leave. On the railway the Government farms out the convict labour.

---

112 Here Morrison uses the name the present day Khabarovsk had until 1893. The town dates for 1858 when Russia gained Chinese territory through the Treaty of Aigun.
113 Sakhalin today.

A junk on what is thought to be the Amur River, Manchuria.
Mitchell Library, Sydney

A Russian paddle steamer on the Sungari (Songhua) River, c. 1900.
Mitchell Library, Sydney

One month's work counts as one month and a-half. By this means the acquisition of the ticket-of-leave is still further hastened.

There is abundant steam communication on the Amur and Shilka. Both rivers are lighted and buoyed, and are free from ice from May to October. When the railway is completed to Stretensk a constant stream of traffic will pass from this route to and from the East and Europe. To one travelling up the river the prospects everywhere are of uninterrupted progress. All along the northern bank at distances of from 20 to 30 miles the Cossack stanitzas,[114] founded by Muravieff[115] prior to 1858, have grown into thriving villages. Agriculture is increasing, immigration is encouraged.

The great plains between the Bureya and the Zeya,[116] which have everywhere been thrown open to selection, are as fertile as the plains of Manitoba. Conditions of life are trying and infant mortality is high, but the race that survives is a splendid race physically, hardy, enduring, and independent.

Chief of the towns on the Amur is Blagovestchensk,[117] the Johannesburg of Siberia, a city of 40,000 inhabitants, whose wealth is in gold. It contains the finest merchant palaces in all Eastern Asia. It is situated at the junction of the Zeya, that navigable affluent down whose waters in 1644 Poyarkoff[118] first reached the Amur. Blagovestchensk is the market of the Zeya goldfields; joined by rail as it eventually will be

---

114 The word means Cossack village.
115 Count Nikolay Nikolayevich Muravyov-Amursky, 1809–188, was a Russian statesman and one of the driving forces behind Russia's eastward expansion to the Pacific via Siberia and Manchuria. As Governor-General of Eastern Siberia, he pressured China for access to lands north of the Amur river. He was responsible for concluding the Treaty of Aigun with the Qing government in 1858, which ceded to Russia 185,000 square miles on the northern bank of the Amur river. In 1860, he claimed what was to be called Vladivostok for the Russian Empire.
116 The Zeya-Bureya Plain remains one of the most fertile regions in the Russian Far East. The Bureya river is 623 km long and flows into the Amur at Pashkovo in Russia. The Zeya is about 1,240 km and is a major left bank (Russian) tributary of the Amur joining it near Blagoveshchensk.
117 Blagoveshchensk today has a population of around 250,000 and is situated at the confluence of the Amur and Zeya rivers.
118 Vassili Danilovich Poyarkov, c. 1597–c. 1670, was the first Russian explore of the Amur region.

with the heart of Manchuria, it is destined to become a very important city. At present it is dependent upon Manchuria for its grain, its hay, its cattle and food-stuffs, and its cheap labour. Its new governor is General Gripski, its new *commissaire de frontière* is the famous geodesist and explorer Colonel Bronislas de Grombtchefsky,[119] whose name is so intimately associated with the rectification of Russian frontiers in Central Asia. He had just returned on his steam launch from inspecting the main water routes of Manchuria. His appointment in the present crisis of affairs is ominous for China.

The most profitable trade of Blagovestchensk is the illicit dealing in unminted gold,[120] which is smuggled across the river to the Chinese towns of Aigun[121] and Helampo.[122] The trade has assumed very large proportions, and I am satisfied that much of the gold believed to come from the ruins of Manchuria is really the product of Siberian goldfields. The mines on the Zeya are very rich.[123] I know one which lately celebrated the output of its sixteenth ton of gold. Whilst gold is worth 42 times its weight in silver in Shanghai, it can be purchased in Blagovestchensk for 32 times its weight in silver. Its cheapness, especially in winter when the diggers come in from the workings, attracts many buyers from Japan and from foreign firms in the north of China. Free trade in gold is not, permitted; all gold must be sent to the nearest assay office and there sold to the Government at a price arbitrarily determined

---

119 Bronislav Ludwigovich Grombchevsky, 1855–1926, was a Polish officer in the Imperial Russian Army and an explorer/spy, famed for his participation in the so-called Great Game. Grombchevsky traveled extensively in the Far East and Central Asia during the period 1888–92. He is regarded as the Russian counterpart to the British military-explore Sir Francis Younghusband. The two rivals famously met in 1889 when they were exploring the Raskam Valley in Xinjiang for their respective governments. Grombchevsky rose to the rank of Lieutenant-General but was cast down in the aftermath of the 1917 Bolshevik revolution. Exiled to Siberia he was assisted in escape by the Japanese. He ended up in Poland where he died in poverty.
120 A coin or currency that has not yet been stamped or marked by an official minting authority.
121 Called Aihui Town today. Aigun gave its name to the Treaty of Aigun,
122 Helampo is today known as Heihe and is situated on the Amur opposite Blagoveshchensk, which were connected by a two-land bridge in 2019.
123 Founded in 1879 as Zeysky Sklad and enjoyed rapid growth and was until the early 1930s was one of Russia's primary gold producers.

by the Government. But the methods are so cumbrous, the nearest assay office at Irkutsk is at such a prodigious distance, the delays are so great, and the price determined by the Government so much below the market value, that a premium is put upon illicit dealing. A small proportion of the gold is sent to Irkutsk, the bulk of the remainder finds its way into Manchuria. Nearly all supplies paid for by Russian dealers on the Manchurian side of the river are paid for in gold and not in silver.

The head of navigation on the Shilka is Stretensk,[124] a town of Jews. It will be the terminus of the Trans-Siberian Railway, and will displace Kiakhta[125] as the centre of the overland tea trade between China and Siberia. The cumbrous transport by camel will be abolished and, an important change in commercial trade routes effected. This assumption is based upon the fact that by the Stretensk route after the railway to Irkutsk has been finished the freight on tea will be reduced one-half. For example:– the freight charges on tea carried from Hankow to Tientsin, and thence by the overland route through Kalgan and Kiakhta to Irkutsk are, assuming that five camels carry one ton, £20 10s. the ton. The same tea sent from Hankow by steamer to Nikolaievsk,[126] by river steamer to Stretensk, and then by train to Irkutsk will pay, assuming that on the railway freight is one penny per ton a mile, £8 a ton.

One hundred miles beyond Stretensk the branch railway that is to cross Manchuria is expected to leave the main line at the village of Metrophanof. Nothing, however, is yet known for certain. During the rainy season just past the whole country was under water. Floods of unprecedented magnitude, 14 feet higher than the highest flood ever before recorded, simply obliterated the entire railway work already completed between Chita and Nertchinsk.[127] Two years' work will be

---

124 Now spelt Sretensk, it was founded in 1689 and is situated on the right bank of the Shilka River.
125 Kyakhta today is an historic border town on the Kiakhta River that was founded in 1727 following the Treaty of Kiakhta, the second treaty governing trade between Russia and the Qing which lasted until 1860. This treaty also allowed the Russians to establish an Orthodox church in Peking which became an important centre for Russian scholarship about China.
126 Nikolayevsk today.
127 Nerchinsk lent its name to the first treaty between the Manchus and the Russians, the 1689 Treaty of Nerchinsk which resolved border and trade issues. Border markers

A tarantass, similar to the one Morrison used in Manchuria.
Mitchell Library, Sydney

required for repairing the damage done. A new basis will have to be taken for calculating the, levels and the whole course of the railway from the main line to Mongolia may require reconsideration. The railway will enter Manchuria at Staro Suruhaitui.[128] To this point I drove in a tarantass[129] from Stretensk crossing eastwards to Nerchinski Savod, near the Argun,[130] and then coasting down the Russian frontier to the crossing place. Nerchinski Savod is the chief town of an Imperial estate, a truly Imperial estate, whose extent is measured by the thousand square miles. It is governed by a distinguished general, who holds his appointment direct from the Throne. It has 3,500 inhabitants, it has schools, colleges, and hospitals, and the general standard of comfort is a high one. Gold and silver are found in the neighbourhood. The convict settlement is 12 miles from the town. It contains only 400 convicts, the numbers in accordance with a tendency apparent throughout Siberia having

  were in Manchu, Russian and Latin (as was the text of the treaty).
128 An historical settlement on the north (left) bank of the Argun River, Starto-Suruhaitui was founded in the late 17th century as a Cossack wintering post to enable the Russians to consolidate their territorial gains along the Argun frontier. It became a significant customs point on the Chinese/Russian border.
129 A four-wheeled horse-drawn Russian carriage without suspension.
130 The Argun merges with the Shilka River to form the Amur River.

1 | 'THE TRANS-MANCHURIAN RAILWAY'

General view of a boarder guard post, Manchuria, c. 1900.
Mitchell Library, Sydney

recently been reduced. Prison labour in Siberia is being supplanted by the labour of free men. The free population is increasing more rapidly than are the means of existence, and the time is, I believe, approaching, when Siberia will cease to be the penitentiary of Russia.

All the way down the Russian frontier of the Argun every 20 or 30 versts[131] there are small Cossack villages peopled from the Trans-Baikal. Immigration is encouraged and the population, despite the rigours of the climate, is constantly on the increase. A splendid race of men are the Russian settlers, every man is a soldier, every man is armed, every man is capable of great endurance, hardy and disciplined, every man is a good horseman, and has a horse to ride as hardy as himself. Down the Mongolian side you have nothing but the wind-swept hills, no natives, no habitations, while the harvests grown near the river bank are gathered by Russians as if on their own soil. On both sides of the river the pastures are splendid and horse and cattle thrive, but the country is as treeless as the plains of Australia. There is not one single tree from near Nerchinski Savod southwards for 200 miles, and, more remarkable still, there are no Chinamen. Absorption of some of the Mongol races may be seen in Eastern Siberia, but the exclusion of Chinese west of

---

131 A Russian measure of length, about 1.1 kilometres.

the Trans-Baikal frontier is singularly complete. All down the frontier my Chinese servant was as great an object of curiosity as he would have been in an English village.

Staro-Suruhaitui on the Argun, the frontier stanitza, through which the railway is to be admitted into Manchuria, is a small village of 100 log cabins, with a ferry crossing over the river. A Mongol commissaire de frontière resides here and visés the Russian and Manchu passports of travellers. One hundred miles to the south-east is the Chinese frontier town of Hailar.[132] It is reached by a lonely road over the steppes unsheltered from the wind, the only fuel being dried cow-dung, the only dwellings Mongol yurts made of stretched sheepskin. But Hailar itself is a busy town much frequented by Russians who come here to purchase cattle, sheep, and horses, flour from Tsitsihar,[133] brick tea from Tientsin, and samshu,[134] that fiery spirit, which is Chinese vodka. Payment is made in gold and paper roubles, or in silver, but mainly in gold illicitly purchased from Siberian gold diggers. Hailar is the headquarters of the engineers of the first of the seven sections of the Trans-Manchurian Railway. It is a mud town of 2,000 inhabitants composed exclusively of emigrants from Shansi. It is a town of men and has no women. It has no inns. Russians come here unmolested and unarmed. Hardy fellows, they bivouac in the open air, and shelter in the temples when it rains. From Hailar the railway as originally projected was to be carried to the river Nonni[135] at Tsitsihar, a distance of 350 miles. But this route has been abandoned and a more southerly route will be followed to the Sungari[136] at Petuna.[137] By both routes the nature of the country passed

---

132 Hailar was founded in 1734 and today has a population of more than 350,000. It is a major transportation hub. It is on the western line of the Trans-Siberian express route.
133 Known today as Qiqihar, it was founded in 1691 as a garrison town to defend the northern frontiers against Russians. It was the capital of the region in Qing and Republican times. Soviet Russia, led by Zhukov, defeated the Japanese here in 1939 in a battle that tempered Japan's willingness to fight the Soviets during WW2.
134 A thrice distilled rice spirit.
135 Nenjiang (or New River), a 1370 km river that flows through Heilongjiang and at times marks the border between China and Inner Mongolia.
136 Sungari is the Manchu name for what the Chinese today call the Songhua River, the largest tributary of the Amur River, or Heilung River.
137 Petuna (Boduna) is part of Songyuan city today in Jilin province. It is the Manchu name for an early settlement. It was founded in the mid-17th century by the Qing as a

1 | 'THE TRANS-MANCHURIAN RAILWAY'

General view of the city of Girina (Jilin) on the Sungari (Songhua) River, c. 1900.
Mitchell Library, Sydney

over is the same. A plateau of considerable elevation to the base of the Khingan mountains, a steep ascent to the pass, and an abrupt descent, and then down through a marshy country bubbling with water through swamps and marshes to the valley of the Nonni[138] and Sungari. On the Mongolian plateau there is no vestige of a village. Every 20 miles there is a Mongol tent, every 40 miles a well-kept station house, while at an occasional lonely house, for warmth half sunk into the ground, a few exiles from within the Great Wall make a scanty livelihood building high-wheeled Mongol carts for the meagre traffic. It is a lonely, desolate country. The few inhabitants are poverty-stricken. Everywhere you pay for little favours with a slice sawn from a slab of brick tea.

The plateau is some 2,200ft. above the sea level, and rises gradually to the base of the Khingan mountains, 2,750ft. One Mongol tent at Erekte[139] marks the commencement of the ascent over the mountain range. The road winds up among the pines and reaches the summit at

shipbuilding centre for the navy operating on the Sungari (Songhua) and Amur river systems. A military governor was stationed there since 1676.
138 The Nonni is the Manchu name for the Nen River, the largest tributary of the Sungari which meets it at Da'an.
139 Erekte is a district in the Govi-Altai Provinve of south western Mongolia.

the pass, 3,650ft., amid beautiful scenery, at the temple to the "Goddess of Mercy." An instructive contrast is witnessed in this temple. Side by side with the tawdry trappings of Chinese devotion and the disjointed goddess made of painted mud are Russian tarantasses and the arms of Russian soldiers. For these are the headquarters of the two engineers detached from the Intelligence Department of the War Office, to study the Khingan mountains. And this will be the headquarters of a Polish engineer, to whom has been intrusted the second section of the railway. His chief difficulty will be to find a practicable pass for the railway over the mountains. So far as the preliminary surveys have yet determined, the only possible route necessitates the cutting of a tunnel several thousand feet in length, but there is still hope, of course, that this may be avoided. The descent from the temple is very steep, the road falling 1,000ft. in four miles, in a pass so narrow and rugged that there seems but little space for development.

Once across the mountain range you have left the basin of the Argun[140] and are in the vast area drained by the Nonni. Following down the course of the Yalo river[141] you wind through inhabited steppes to the vast swampy plain, which the inundation of the Nonni annually buries deeply under water. Half-way down I met one party of Russian engineers, and by and by two more, moving through the solitudes with carts and tents, with servants, and flocks of sheep. The engineers were picked men, big bearded men, whom the Chinese being apt to estimate years by the length of the beard, would reverence for their age. There were assistant engineers, doctors, and Chinese interpreters, and escorts of Cossack soldiers. The armed escort was needed for work more than for protection, but it is different in Manchuria proper. For 200 years Manchuria has been the dumping ground of Chinese criminals. The valley of the Nonni presents formidable difficulties to the engineer. For months in the year it is almost impassable. Five deep channels,

---

140 The Argun River rises in Inner Mongolia and flows west for 1,620 km. It joins the Shilka at Pokrovka to form the Amur (Heilong Jiang) River. The Treaty of Nerchinsk (1689) defined it as the border between the Celestial Empire (the Qing) and Russia And reaffirmed by the Treaty of Aigub (1858). Site of Sino-Soviet conflict in 1969; order settled in 2008.
141 Yalu River.

one of them 300 yards in width, drain the basin, while the intervening country is subject to annual inundations. It is estimated that between the dry ground on the west, abreast of Tsitsihar and the city itself, eight miles of bridge-work will have to be constructed. The enormous expense involved in such an undertaking is obvious.

Tsitsihar lies to the east of the river. It is a town of 30,000 inhabitants, the capital of the province of Heh Lung Kiang,[142] and seat of residence of the Chiang-Chun or military governor. The town is much frequented by Russians who come here from Blagovestchensk and Khabarovka[143] to purchase live stock and food stuffs. Russian soldiers escort the engineers and guard the railway stores. Russian words are current. Russian roubles are accepted by the native bankers. The most important Chinaman in the service of Russia, Chih-Fon-Tai of Khabarovka, has one of his chief branches here. Russian railway offices are being built outside the city, the construction anticipating the subsequent connexion by railway of Blagovestchensk with Tsitsihar and Petuna. One Russian merchant in Blagovestchensk has also an agency here. The Russians march through the town with an air of possession which powerfully impresses the Chinese. They treat the people uniformly well and a *plébiscite* as to the desirability of Russian occupation would open the eyes of the Chinese mandarins. The Nonni is navigable to Tsitsihar. The Chiang-Chun has a steam launch, which, during the summer runs with despatches to Petuna and Kirin, while steamers belonging to Chih-Fon-Tai have already opened trade with Khabarovka. Hitherto foreign goods in Tsitsihar have been almost without exception imported by land from Niuchwang.[144] Chinese soldiers are much in evidence in Tsitsihar. They are Manchu bannermen armed with an extraordinary variety of rifles, from the old Tower muskets bought by the Chinese in the belief that they were the weapons with which England won the battle of Waterloo,[145] to the most

---

142 Heilungjiang (literally meaning Black Dragon River) is the province today and the name by which the Chinese also call the Amur River.
143 Now Khbarovsk.
144 Today know as Yingkou. Niuchwang was one of the Treaty Ports created by the Treaty of Tianjin (1858) and is situated on the north-east coast of the Liaodong Gulf in Liaoning province.
145 As Morrison tells us in his 'Reminiscences' these rifles were sold to the Chinese by Louis Spitzel, a man of mysterious origins, who, for a while, was a jeweller in

modern repeating rifles. Varieties of most of the weapons discarded in Europe during the present century are found in Manchuria. The most common pattern is the Mauser carbine of 1871. The Chinese have learned nothing from the Japanese war. I saw in Manchuria no rifle that was not rusty. It is "fool pidgin,"[146] the Chinese think, to waste on a rifle the oil that may be needed in the opium lamp.

Tsitsihar is described as the Botany Bay of China. Its inhabitants as well as other inhabitants of the province of which it is the capital, have been to some degree recruited from the Chinese criminal classes.[147] The country has an evil reputation even in China. There is nothing, however, in the demeanour of the people to indicate the nature of their origin. Criminals are difficult to distinguish in China, and all that can be justly said of this portion of Manchuria is that a certain proportion of its inhabitants are Chinese officials and servants who have been found out, or, to speak more correctly, who when found out have not had means sufficient to move the scales of justice in their favour, and so were deported. Judged by the European standard, there is hardly an official in China—who is not a criminal. Peculation, embezzlement, malversation of public moneys, bribery, and extortion are the recognized methods by which mandarins grow rich in the "Middle Kingdom." Probably never in the history of any other country was there a more gigantic service of fraud and embezzlement than in the manipulation of public moneys during the recent war with Japan. Yet one of the public men, whose hands were most deeply stained with corruption, is not in Manchuria at all but is one of the honoured representatives of his country abroad.

From Tsitsihar to Petuna I kept down the east side of the Nonni, though the railway going southward to Kirin must follow the west side. I crossed the deep swamps that mark the junction of the Nonni and Sungari and entered Petuna. The distance is 180 miles, and the entire country has been under the plough. The "league-long furrow " is never ending. A few years ago this country was a waste, but the stream of immigration has been unceasing. Where there were a few mud huts

---

Melbourne, before travelling to China to make his fortune. See p. 440, this volume.
146 That is, a "fool's business."
147 Not so disreputable today, Qiqihar is the second largest city in Heilongjiang province, has a population of about 4.5m, and is a hub of heavy manufacturing.

clustered round the post-station there are now thriving villages, with countless busy inns catering for a traffic that is always becoming greater. The soil is rich alluvial. The elevation of the plain above the sea level is only 600ft. The river that drains it travels 1,500 miles before reaching the sea, and as the country is treeless and subject to sudden and heavy rains no cause tending to inundation is lacking. The river even in ordinary seasons is very wide; in places it expands into lakes so broad that the other bank is often below the horizon. At the junction of the Nonni and the Sungari the width is measured by miles.

At a day's march from the junction is the important town of Petuna, a city of 60,000 inhabitants, whose numbers are being added to with enormous rapidity. From here southwards to Kirin[148] the country is among the most fertile and most thickly peopled in the Empire. It is the granary of Manchuria. Its harvests already supply the mills of Siberia; its wheat will yet compete in the grain markets of the world. Petuna, from its position on the navigable Sungari, will be an important depôt of the railway, and Russians are stationed here in considerable force. In the railway camp on the other side of the river the engineer Prince Hilkof[149] has his quarters surrounded by a complete staff and a sufficient escort of Russian soldiers. Last season three steamers reached Petuna from Habaroosk[150] on the Amur, the round passage occupying 12 days, four days down stream and eight days up stream. A bonus of 3,000 roubles was paid for each voyage. At the same time Tsitsihar on the north and Kirin on the south were both proved to be within three days by steamer from Petuna. An important traffic here awaits development; the river is open from May to October. Next season the flotilla of 10 steamers and 40 barges built in England to the order of the Russo-Chinese Bank for the transport of railway material will begin its systematic navigation.

It is curious to observe how easily the Chinese in Manchuria have become reconciled to the navigation by steam of its inland waters. Obstruction is the only force in China upon whose operation one can

---

148 An old romanisation for Jilin, which, along with Heilongjiang and Liaoning, is one of the three north-east provinces of modern China.
149 Prince Mikhail Ivanovich Khilkov, 1834–1909, councillor of state, minister for communication and transportation at the time of Morrison's visit.
150 Now known as Khabarovsk.

always rely, but nowhere does obstruction yield more readily to the exhibition of force. By the treaty of Aigun of 1858 confirmed by the treaty of St. Petersburg of 1881, the, Sungari was opened to Russian commerce, but until a few years ago Russian merchants attempting to ascend the river were turned back by the Chinese, an indignity to which the Russians submitted, so feared and respected was the "latent" power of China.

Kirin with its 200,000 people is the second greatest city in Manchuria. It is beautifully situated on a bend of the Sungari. Its wealth is enormous, and the standard of comfort of its inhabitants a very high one. No advantage of position or environment is wanting to justify the Russians in selecting this as the chief centre of the Trans-Manchurian Railway. There is, first, its position in relation to Port Arthur,[151] to which point, as to the eventual terminus of the railway, Russian engineers are now making preliminary surveys; there is, secondly, the richness of the surrounding territory, where foodstuffs could be procured sufficient to provision the whole army of Siberia; and, finally, there is its vulnerability, for the Russian frontier posts Poltafka[152] and Novolievsk are both within 14 marches of the city.

Wood is abundant in Kirin, floated down in huge rafts from the mountain sources of the Sungari, in the Chang Pai Shan. There is timber sufficient to supply sleepers to half the railways of Asia. Coal is also abundant, but of inferior quality. Household black coal is delivered at the door for 8s. per ton. Twenty miles north of the city, however, an excellent brown coal is found, which is stated to be equal to the brown coal used on the Hungarian railways. It is worked only in shallow pits with the crudest of methods under foreign supervision and by the aid of modern machinery the output is capable of infinite expansion. For two years past this field has been carefully studied by a Russian mining expert.

The Russification of the city is proceeding. Samovars are seen in every inn. Russian engineers, escorted by Cossacks, drive in tarantasses

---

151 A much contested naval area at the beginning of the 20th century. Today the port is called Lushun and is further along the Liaoning Peninsular from Dalian, another great port supporting the Chinese economy.
152 Poltavka is a small rural town on the Sino-Russian border.

1 | 'THE TRANS-MANCHURIAN RAILWAY'

through the crowded streets. The Russians have little more to gain in Manchuria. They have the right to mine, the right to build houses and import all kinds of machinery for railway and mining use. They have the right to unrestricted navigation of inland waters, and they have the right to protect themselves by force, independent of Chinese. And with it all the Chinese are content and they are prepared to welcome any further change which would remove them from the exactions of their own officials. The dread of the Chinese during war is not of the enemy so much as of the undisciplined rabble called Chinese braves, who enlist solely to pillage the people whom they are sent to protect. The Russian Colonel Grombtchefsky was in Kirin in August in a river steamer belonging to the Government at Blagovestchensk. Through some oversight no official went out to meet him. He thereupon anchored his steamer abreast of the Governor's yamên and blew the steam whistle until the whole city knew of his arrival. The respect that was shown him was abject. Russians to the number of two or three, hundred live in Chinese barracks beyond the west gate of the city. The flag that waves above them is typical of the Russian alliance in regard to Manchuria. It is the Chinese Imperial flag with the Russian colours set in the upper righthand corner. The Chinese in Kirin regard the Russian occupation as unavoidable, and are therefore arranging to take advantage of it by introducing wares acceptable to Russians and by learning Russian. No branch of the Russo-Chinese Bank has yet been established here, the important Russian exchange business being satisfactorily handled by the Rang Sheng Ch'ing, a Chinese bank whose correspondents are in every important town in North China. Kirin has an arsenal consisting of a number of large buildings crowded with a medley of machinery, mostly German rejects. The arsenal is mainly a repairing shop, though it is capable of manufacturing 10,000 Hotchkiss and 9,000 Mauser cartridges per day. Since the war with Japan, Yingalls are the only weapons made here; they are long weapons with a barrel like a gas-pipe, and their advantage in Chinese estimation is that the detonation on discharge will itself terrify any heart that is not a Chinaman's. To much better service has the arsenal been put in the minting of dollars, which by edict are current throughout the province. They have the arbitrary exchange value of 2.200 cash, they are rough in workmanship and made of debased silver, but they are an immense advance upon the native currency.

A part from its position as one of the chief markets of British goods sent inland from Niuchwang, Kirin possesses a local interest to Englishmen as the spot where in December, 1895, a peculiarly gross insult was offered to our nation by Chinese officials. The case is worth recalling, as it proves once more, though further proof is hardly needed, what absolute bad faith the Chinese ever show in their dealings with civilized Powers. In Kirin, in December, 1895, Ao Ling, the prefect, summoned before him the native evangelist of the Irish Presbyterian Mission and without trial caused him to be cruelly beaten. His offence was that he had acted as intermediary in the purchase of a site for the new mission hospital. He was thrashed in the presence of two English missionaries who had accompanied him to the Yamên, and who between the blows were foully reviled by the prefect. A guard of soldiers specially sent by the military Governor kept order during the flogging. It was some time before the insult could be made known, for by order of the authorities messages from the foreigners were refused at the telegraph office. Once it was reported a demand was made that the prefect should be dismissed. In April, 1896, the prefect was recalled to Peking, nominally for degradation, but actually to receive unofficial approbation of his act. In September assurance was given that the prefect would never again hold office, yet two months later he was impudently restored to his former post in Kirin. Remonstrance on our part again caused his removal, but the removal was in the nature of a reward, for the Chinese Government at once appointed him Prefect of Kuang Cheng Tzu, a post in the same province still more lucrative than that of Kirin. This, post he still holds.

At Kirin the railway will cross the Sungari and go east to Omoso[153] 120 miles, and then north-east to Ninguta 100 miles further. Two mountain ranges of no great altitude, densely wooded with elm and pine, lie athwart the course. They will have to be crossed then the valley of the Hurka will be entered and followed down past Lake Bilten to

---

153 Omoso's precise location is not certain. Morrison describes it as a village of 2,000 but it does not appear to exist today.

Ninguta. Large inns provide for a considerable traffic. Every 20 miles along the route there is a guardhouse, with 30 or 40 soldiers of the usual type of the "look see" Chinese brave. The first pass (2,000 feet) is the Lao Yeh Ling—"His Excellency" pass—so called because the summit is crowned by a temple to his Excellency the God of War. The second pass is 2,800 feet above the level of the sea (1,700 feet above the plateau), and is the highest on the road. It is the Chang Kwang Tsai Ling. The intervening country is hilly, but the gradients are easy.

As far as Omoso the tide of immigration has spread, and it is moving onward irresistibly. Fertility is the chief characteristic of the country, and the only check to immigration are the fears, more or less imaginary, of brigands. The road is currently believed to be infested with brigands, who are described as "Red Beards," and are mainly the creatures of fear. Their distinction "Hung Hus"—"Red Beards"—seems to indicate that they were originally imagined as coming from the Russian side of Manchuria. No doubt there are brigands, and no doubt there has been since the war an increase in lawlessness. After the war troops were disbanded and camps broken. Soldiers brought from the other end of the empire were given a few strings of cash and turned adrift to find their way home as best they could. Necessity drove many to become banditti. But the reports are much exaggerated. Insurance offices in Kirin and other large cities in the north insure wagoners against the risk of loss by brigandage. Brigandage must therefore exist, and its extent would not be minimized by the insurance offices. The authorities themselves, however, cannot consider the road unsafe. My passport would indicate that I was a traveller of some importance, though I had only one servant with me. Yet to the most dangerous portion of the road I was escorted by two Chinese foot soldiers, armed with rusty muzzle-loaders. I passed a few heads in cages, and at one place I met a brigand being carried in a cart to execution in Kirin. He had been caught red-handed. Between his legs as he sat was the head of his companion, placed there to remind the poor living wretch of the cheerful fate that was in store for him.

Omoso, the half-way town where the road turns off to Hun-chun, is a village of 2,000 inhabitants, with a garrison of 160 soldiers. In Manchuria you gauge the importance of a town by the size and number of its pawnshops, which are in reality the only safe store-houses of the natives. Omoso has no pawnshop, and is therefore of no importance.

But the harvest gathered in the fields round about it is magnificent. Between Omoso and Ninguta the most remarkable feature is the Stone Lake, a wide bed of lava which sounds hollow and vibrates to the passage of the cart. Ninguta occupies a beautiful site on the river Hurka.[154] It is a town of 10,000 inhabitants and the headquarters of Russian engineers who have for months past been searching unsuccessfully for a railway route to Lalin. It is a busy town with a telegraph office. Everything foreign imported here comes through Vladivostok and Poltafka, its chief article of import being salt, which is admitted across the frontier duty free. This is a fact worth attention. Salt is a Government monopoly in China, and recognizing this we agreed, in our convention relating to the Burmese frontier, to prohibit the importation of salt into Yunnan from Burma. This clause may therefore be revised when the time comes for tariff revision. The chief exports from Ninguta eastward are bean-oil, flour and maize, and live stock for the soldiers in Siberia.

From Ninguta to Poltafka on the Russian frontier a practicable route for the railway has been discovered. This is indeed the only section of the railway of which even preliminary surveys have been completed. Its length is 193 miles, and the chief difficulty to be contemplated is the cutting of a tunnel 1,400ft. in length. The route zig-zags across the mountains, the steepest passes being those across the watershed between the Eurka and the Mô-Ling-ho and that between the Mô-Ling-ho and the Suifun. The Mô-Ling-ho is the river that becomes the Muren and enters the Ussuri at Iman; the Suifun is the river that separates the Chinese frontier town of San-cha-kou and the Russian Poltafka. In the descent from the mountains to the valley of the Suifun the path winds down a defile in whose lower reaches lie the straggling huts of the mining village of Warugo. All the country-side is pitted with shallow gold workings. Then the plain opens out and the bare hills seen beyond are in Russian territory. Down the broad valley flows the Suifun in several channels, watering alluvial fields, every acre of which is cultivated.

---

154 Morrison uses the Manchu name for Ning' An, which is today located within Mudanjiang City. It was an important frontier town for the Qing and founded in the 1650s and was the seat of the Military Governor of the region.

Between the second and third channels is San-cha-kou,[155] a town held by 400 braves, and beyond the third is Poltafka. It was pleasant to the traveller to see again the broad roads, the clean log cabins and post-station, the homely church, the stalwart men and officers in uniform of the Russian village. A squadron of cavalry of trans-Baikal Cossacks, among whom are many Mongol Buriats[156], guards the frontier. Their effective strength may at any time be increased tenfold from the garrison at Nikolski. It is a day's drive in a tarantass to Nikolski on the Ussuri Railway; a few hours later and the train leisurely arrives at Vladivostok. At this point I finished my journey and then hastened back to Peking. The conclusions I drew from my journey were patent.

As to the railway, is is evident that little progress has been made, and that another season will be needed before the final route can be determined. The difficulties encountered are greater than were expected. All the engineers I met seemed to think the demand reasonable that the line should be finished within six years. Railway construction in Manchuria possesses one great advantage. The means of communication are splendid; transport can be effected by land in winter, the rivers are open in summer. Work can be began simultaneously at several points on the projected line—at Metrophanof on the Trans-Siberian Railway, reached by steamer from Stretensk, at Petuna and Kirin, both connected by steamer at Singuta, reached by boat on the Hurka, and at Nikolski on the railway already constructed. There can be no lack of cheap labour, despite the fact that the railway for some hundreds of miles will pass through country inhabited only by Mongol nomads. When the line is finished the saving in distance, comparing the new line with the old, will be found to be much less than was originally expected. By the old route, round the bend of the Amur from Stretensk through Khabarovka to Vladivostok, the distance was estimated at 1,592 miles; of this, 487 miles, the section between Vladivostok and Khabarovka, have been constructed, and 1,100 miles more are required to complete the connexion. By the short cut which the new railway is to follow from Metrophanof through Hailar, Petuna, Kirin, Ninguta, and Poltafka, to

---

155 Sanchakou is now located within Dongning City, Heilongjiang. It has a sizeable Korean population.
156 A Mongol ethnic group from southern Siberia more commonly known as Buryats.

Vladivostok, the distance is estimated at 1,410 miles, of which 68 miles have been constructed and 1,372 miles more are required to complete the connexion. Thus the new line will be 152 miles shorter than the old line.

What now in relation to China and Russia is to be the future of Manchuria? What must happen? On the one side you have Siberia, a country very extensive but comparatively poor, where every peasant is a soldier, belonging to a powerful military aggressive people, and on the other you have Manchuria, a rich country undefended and peopled by a race devoid of patriotism who would regard with indifference any change of masters so long as they themselves were not molested, and who moreover have by treaty already granted permission to their masterful neighbours to patrol their country with an unlimited number of armed men. The great mass of the people of Manchuria are Chinese immigrants who regard their adopted country as lying beyond the pale of China proper. Under no circumstances is it possible to conceive a national rising of the people. Large bodies of Russian troops can, from several points of Siberia, be simultaneously moved into the country. Should such an advance take place the soldiers can obtain from the Chinese all the coolies, all the supplies, all the carts and transport needed, and the Chinese, so far from resisting the invasion, will rejoice at the opportunity of earning money so easily. Siberia is already largely fed by Manchuria, which has indeed become almost a necessary adjunct to the Russian province.

It seems to me then that so long as China and Russia are permitted to go their own way untrammelled by international complications, the absorption of Manchuria by Russia—always, of course, as the reward of friendship to China—is inevitable. But there is another factor in the situation. And though nearly every Russian I met on my journey spoke with unconcealed derision of her pretensions, the importance of Japan in relation to the future of Manchuria cannot be disregarded.

Chapter 2

A Coup in Peking

On 22 September 1898, Imperial China's last and best chance of reforming itself was snuffed out when Dowager Empress Tsu Hsi[157] staged a palace coup against her nephew the Emperor Kuang Hsu.[158] This brought to an end 100 days of whirlwind reforms that Kuang Hsu had initiated in the hope of rapidly modernising China. It also brought back in to power Tsu Hsi, a Manchu aristocrat who had been China's *de facto* ruler from the 1860s until her 'retirement' in 1889.

Morrison wrote the assessment of the coup published here three weeks after it was staged. By then Tsu Hsi had moved with deliberation to ensure that Kuang Hsu was confined to house arrest within the Forbidden City, that his advisers were executed, and most importantly, that officials loyal to her were back with their hands on the levers of power. Virtually to a man (with the exception of herself, all were men) they were also Manchus.

During the 100 days (from June to September 1898), Kuang Hsu issued no fewer than 38 major decrees covering all aspects of the Qing government, from its administration, education (controversially changing the method of competitive examination for admission to the

---

157 Cixi, 1834–1908, Dowager Empress. Other names for her include Xiaoqin, Yehonala, and in this text, Tsu Hsi.
158 Guangxu, 1871–1908, died on 14 November, a day before the Empress Dowager Tsu Hsi herself died. He was 37; after an examination of his remains in 2008 his cause of death was determined to be a massive dose of arsenic.

scholar class), law, economy, technology, military, and police systems. In this endeavour, the Emperor was guided principally by a young scholar from the south (Canton) Kang Yu-wei.[159] Kang, like many of the younger generation of scholars, was horrified by China's loss to Japan in the Sino-Japanese war of 1894–95 and excoriating in his criticism of the Treaty of Shimonoseki brokered by Li Hung-chang which had resulted in a huge loss of territory and an even larger loss of 'face'. Such was Kuang Hsu's interest that Kang's first meeting with him lasted five hours. Kang also presented him with two extended essays:[160] the first on the fate of Poland, which was dismembered by Prussia, Austria and Russia at the end of the 18th century; and, the second on the reforms in Japan, known as the Meiji Restoration, which lead to that country's rapid modernisation, current military might and ability to face down foreigners. The message was clear: modernise or perish. Kuang Hsu listened.

It is hard not to feel sympathy for Kuang Hsu. He had been reared in the Forbidden City all his life, under the watchful eye of Tsu Hsi. In 1887, he became Emperor and for the next two years ruled under his aunt's guidance. She retired from active involvement in government affairs in 1889. In the early 1890s, Kuang Hsu "gave evidence of becoming a strong-willed and contentious ruler"[161] and in 1898 he promoted a group of court advisors who wanted him to lead a programme of profound reforms comparable to those embarked upon by the Emperor Meiji of Japan an 1868.

While the good intention of the 100 Day reforms is hard to fault, the announcement and prosecution of the reforms made little-to-no allowance for the impact their implementation would have on established power and pecuniary relationships in the Chinese government. Kuang Hsu's reforms produced few winners among the interest groups most affected: the entrenched power structure of Manchu aristocrats and

---

159 Kang Youwei, 1858–1927. F. W. Mote provides a sympathetic and scholarly appraisal Kang's thought in his *China and the Vocation of History in the Twentieth Century: A Personal Memoir*, New Jersey: East Asian Library Journal in Association with Princeton University Press, 2010, pp. 68–79.
160 Spence, op. cit., p. 230.
161 Mote, op. cit., p. 68.

their Chinese enablers. The reform of education, in particular, was seen as an attack on the Empire's scholar mandarinate and, more importantly, those aspiring to work for it.

By September 1898, Kuang Hsu was a pathetic and isolated figure, a man who realised what was needed but was unable do anything. On 7 October, *The Times* man in Hong Kong had an interview with Kang You-wei. In this interview Kang allowed copies to be made of letters the Emperor had written to him in his final days in power. One, dated 16 September, read:

> We know that the Empire is in very troublous times. Unless we adopt Western methods it is impossible to save it. Unless we remove the obstructive Conservative Ministers, superseding them by young intelligent men with knowledge of Western affairs, it is impossible to effect reforms, but the Dowager will not agree. I have repeatedly advised her Majesty, but she becomes enraged. I am afraid I shall not be able to protect my Throne. You are hereby commanded to consult your colleagues and see what assistance you can give to save me. I am very anxious and distressed. I am anxiously awaiting your assistance.[162]

Morrison, in a letter soon after the coup to J. O. P. Bland, his colleague in Shanghai, vented his frustration at the failed reform programme, not because he saw no need for it, but rather with the ham-fisted way in which was implemented. He asks Bland, somewhat rhetorically:

> Do you believe that that reform probably the most important of all altering the methods of examination could have been introduced in China in the crude form in which it was promulgated without inflicting infinite hardship upon hundred and thousands of poor devils who were then deprived of the fruits of the work without any compensation? The repeal of this reform more than anything else strengthened the hands of the party of the Empress.[163]

---

162 'Kang Yu-Wei and the Emperor' (From our Correspondent) Hong-Kong, Oct. 6, *The Times*, 7 October 1898, p. 3.
163 Lo, op. cit., vol. 1, p. 97.

Morrison's account of the *coup* is gimlet-eyed and possibly for this reason Bland thought it was pro-Empress Dowager and anti-reform. Morrison responded: "I am here simply to chronicle the facts or rather to chronicle what the balance of evidence shows to me are facts." He added that he would continue to accept statements made to him "by independent men whose judgement I have previously tested and not found wanting."[164] Later in the letter he wrote, "I am as much in favour of reform as any man and that when I think of the Chinese masses I have in my mind's eye the teeming millions of the interior rather than the foreign-improved thousands on the coast."[165]

Tsu Hsi[166] was a remarkable woman by any standard. She exercised power in a country that had only once before tolerated a woman in control, the Empress Wu (AD 624–705) during the Tang dynasty. She was the daughter of a middle-ranking official who was cashiered for desertion during the Taiping Rebellion. She was Manchu, of the Yehe Nara clan. At the age of 17 she was selected to enter the Palace as a junior concubine of Emperor Wen-sung (1831–1861). Her status was raised to that concubine of the second class when she produced a male child and her seniority further improved for that child was the only male heir of the Emperor. She learned about affairs of state from Wen-sung who let her order his official papers. Wen-sung died in August 1861 at Jehol,[167] a Manchu palace city 225 km north east of Peking. He ensured Tsu Hsi would have a role in state affairs when he gave her one of the two seals of state that needed to be affixed to any Imperial decree during the regency of his infant son and heir. The other seal was held by the Empress Tzu-an, 1837–1881. Eight men were entrusted with the regency whose first decision was to confer upon the two women the title of Empress Dowager. Between August and November 1861 there was much jockeying for position at the top of government. This was

---

164 ibid.
165 ibid., p. 98.
166 For this account of Tsu Hsi I have relied up the works of Fairbank, Spence, and the biography of Tsu Hsi by Fang Chao-ying in Arthur W. Hummel (ed.), *Eminent Chinese of the Ch'ing Period*, vol. 1, pp. 295–300.
167 Today known as Chengde. In the early 18th century Emperor Kangxi made Jehol his summer residence and began construction of the 'Summer Resort', a palace situated in magnificent gardens.

2 | A COUP IN PEKING

resolved by a military *coup* in support of the two Empresses Dowager, the beheading of one of the regents and the banishment of the other seven. Thus was inaugurated 'Listening from behind Screens to Reports on Governmental Affairs,' as rule by the two Dowagers was termed. Tsu Hsi was fortunate in that Tzu-an was neither "able nor ambitious," characteristics that she possessed in abundance.

It took until 1881, when Tzu-an died and Tsu Hsi became the sole regent of by now another child emperor, that she fully consolidated her power. She ruled until Emperor Kuang Hsu married Tsu Hsi's niece in 1889. She retired to the Summer Palace, much of it ravaged by Anglo-French forces in 1860, and oversaw its rebuilding—diverting much of the budget for the Empire's navy to the opulent reconstruction of her residence, including ships carved from large pieces of marble. As Teng and Fairbank observe:

> With a dominant will and an understanding of human nature, she controlled high personages through forceful leadership, flattery, money, the delegation of authority, and unabashed power, as might be necessary, and generally succeeded in lining them up to support her. She could play the role of a helpless widow with a young child, and make it hard for men in the society of China to refuse her requests. Alternatively she could be ruthlessly insistent on her wishes and threatened the use of her authority to do away with any opponent ...
>
> Another less publicised aspect of the Empress Dowager's conduct was addiction to taking gifts or bribes from her officials. This had been done by every Manchu emperor before her and by almost all officials throughout the dynasty, but she carried it to an extreme ... much to the demoralisation of the government service.[168]

She used her considerable political talents primarily to preserve the Manchu prerogative. Up to this point, she was opposed to modernisation as it implied the adoption of alien Western ways. Pro-modernisation

---

168 S. Y. Teng, and J. K. Fairbank, *China's Response to the West: A Documentary Survey 1839–1923*, Cambridge Mass: Harvard, 1979, p. 89.

officials, such as Li Hung-chang, had to struggle with her to win approval for the construction of railways, which she hated, and modern steam driven ships, especially for the navy. She was implacably anti-foreign and, as we shall see, gave encouragement to the Boxer rebellion which, at its heart, wanted to kill all foreigners in China and Chinese Christians. Following her return to Peking after the Boxer rebellion she acceded to many of the reforms she had prevented her nephew from implementing. That proved too late to save Manchu rule. Tsu Hsi was known as the Old Buddha by local Chinese who to this day preserve the ability to poke fun at their rulers though the use of nicknames. Some, like the present Chinese leadership are humourless[169] and suppress these names, but Tsu Hsi was not concerned about her nickname and may well have even enjoyed it.

As Morrison explains Kang escaped from Peking with the aid of the British, though he does not mention the name of the mail steamer that Kang boarded. It was the HMS *Ballaarat*, preserving the old spelling of Ballarat, the central Victorian town where Morrison had practiced medicine in the early 1890s.

---

[169] China has banned images of Winnie-the-Pooh on the internet for reasons of *lèse majesté*. Someone had suggested Winnie resembled Xi Jingping, general secretary of the Chinese Communist Party. When Chris Patten, the last British governor of Hong Kong arrived there in 1992, the locals immediately mocked his portly demeanour by calling him *fei pang*, "Fat Patten." He wisely laughed it off.

'The Situation in China After the Coup d'état'

(From Our Own Correspondent)
Peking, 11 October 1898[170]

The restoration of the Regency is complete. The Empress-Dowager is in power; the poor, weak little Emperor is more than ever a mere figurehead. He is said to be virtually a prisoner within the Palace. His death has already been announced a dozen times and once officially by the Taotai[171] in Shanghai to the British Consul General. But there was a motive in that official announcement inasmuch as the Taotai wished to justify his conduct in offering a reward for Kang Yu-wei. "The Emperor was dead," he said, "poisoned by Kang Yu-wei." But the Emperor is at this moment alive, although it cannot be denied that his life is in jeopardy. There are still two parties within the Palace—the party of the Emperor, with its leaning towards reform, however wild and impracticable, and the party of the Empress-Dowager, the incarnation or all that is anti-foreign, conservative, retrograde, and reactionary. While the Emperor lives his living is a source of unrest to the Empress-Dowager, who fears the bribed dagger of a eunuch or the poisoned cup handed by some one in the service of the Emperor. On the other hand, the Empress-Dowager knows that the Emperor is a poor, weak, yielding creature, who will henceforth issue her behests as though they were his own. Can she, even if he were dead, obtain a greater measure of power during the tutelage of his successor? That is the factor which must determine

---

170 Published on Saturday 26 November 1898, page 6.
171 Taotai was the title given to the Chinese provincial officer responsible for the civil and military affairs of a district, abolished shortly after the establishment of the Republic in 1911.

Tsu Hsi (Cixi), 1835–1908, Dowager Empress of China.
Wikimedia Commons

whether the Emperor is to live or to die. His health is always bad. He has hypospadias[172] and suffers much; he is probably consumptive, and the life he leads, especially during the winter, is the worst possible for one of his habit. In some measure the people have been prepared for his death by the issue a few days ago of an Imperial edict notifying that the ill-health of the Emperor was increasing and summoning to the Court the most distinguished Chinese physicians from the provinces. his successor has already, it is said, been chosen by the Empress-Dowager, and is understood to be a grandson of Prince Tun, a boy of ten. The Empress-Dowager would thus be able to act once more as Regent during the minority of a third Emperor.

The successor whom she is reported to have chosen is in the legitimate line of succession, and, what is most essential, belongs to a later generation than that of the Emperor. For purposes of ancestral worship, the keystone of the Chinese religious system, it is necessary that the Emperor should pertain to a later generation than that of the person whose manes[173] he has to adore. Tuna Chi, the last Emperor, and Kwang Hsü, the present Emperor, were first cousins, and it is not in accordance with tradition or the elaborate ceremonial prescribed by the Board of Rites or with the teachings of ancestral worship that Kwang Hsü should be qualified to perform the ancestral sacrifices. It was in

---

172 A congenital malformation of the penis where the opening is not at its point but on its underside.
173 The souls of dead ancestors.

2 | 'THE SITUATION IN CHINA AFTER THE COUP D'ÉTAT'

protest of this violation of the right of succession that the censor Wu-ko-tu[174] committed suicide in the presence of the Emperor during one of the Imperial visits to the ancestral tombs. There were other irregularities in this succession. When the last Emperor died his widow, Ahluta,[175] was pregnant. Had the child been a son, even though born posthumously, he would have become the Emperor and the mother would have become the Empress-Regent and virtual ruler. But the child was never born. Ahluta sickened and died—"committed suicide from grief," it was said; the Regency passed a second time into the hands of the two Empresses-Dowager and of Prince Kung, who selected forthwith as Emperor the poor, weak boy whose chief qualification in their eyes was his known inability to beget children. The Emperor's death will not therefore affect the situation in Peking, a successor being already provided in the person of a young Prince who is the legitimate heir, and whose youth at the same time secures to the old Empress the undisturbed enjoyment of supreme power.

The Empress-Dowager presides at all meetings of the Cabinet, sometimes seated beside the Emperor, sometimes by herself. She receives all memorials, drafts all edicts, and acts in every way as the controlling force of the Central Government. Simultaneously with her return to power there has been some consolidation of the power of the Manchus. No question of the loyalty of the Manchus to their own dynasty can possibly be entertained. A Manchu Jung, he succeeds to the power formerly wielded by Prince Kung, a Manchu is now Viceroy of Chi-li, another is Viceroy of Szu-chuan, a third is Viceroy of Yun-nan and Kwei-chau, while a Chinese Bannerman is Viceroy of Che-kiang and Fo-kien. There are also more provincial treasurers Manchus than formerly, and a small proportion more of provincial Judges. But, on the other hand, all the provincial Governors in China, with two exceptions,

---

174 Wu Ko-tu, 1812–1879, an official known for his strict Confucian principles, objected to Tsu Hsi's selection of her nephew as the Guangxu emperor, and, in a blunt memorial to her demanded that she clarify the imperial succession. He committed suicide by poison at the tomb of the Tongzhi Emperor.

175 Ahluta, 1854–1875, was a high born Manchu princess with connection to the Asian Gioro imperial lineage. She was rumoured to be pregnant when the Tongzhi emperor died in 1875. Events surrounding her death are murky. She might have committed suicide or have been starved to death on Tsi Hsi's orders.

The Summer Palace, Forbidden City, where Emperor Kwang Hsu was sequestered for the rest of his life after the coup.
Mitchell Library, Sydney

2 | 'THE SITUATION IN CHINA AFTER THE COUP D'ÉTAT'

are Chinese, including those of Shan-tung, Ho-nan, and Shan-si provinces, where there are no viceroys and where the chief power is vested in the hands of the Governor. There is a dearth of men among the Manchus capable of filling high office, even according to Chinese standards. An interesting feature in the situation is that Li Hung Chang has not yet returned to office, although he has still the title of Senior Grand Secretary.

Have the Russians been concerned in this *coup d'état*? Of this I can find no evidence. Though they act in Peking in open sympathy with the movement, they have no doubt encouraged it, and its success so far has been to their advantage. That it is to the advantage of the Russians that the present rotten and effete dynasty remain on the throne cannot be disputed. They naturally hail with satisfaction the downfall of Chang Yin-huan,[176] who was put under surveillance on the day of the coup d'État and subsequently handed over to the Board of Punishments. A Cantonese also—the most powerful Cantonese in China—he was charged with having harboured Kang Yu-wei. His execution was, it was reported, decreed for early on the morning of September 26. Late the previous night the British Minister and the Japanese *Chargé d'Affaires* intervened, pleading with Li Hung Chang to use his influence and prevent such a crime. Whether due to this intervention or not the death-sentence was not passed, but a punishment almost equally severe was substituted. A few days later Chang Yin-huan, one of the most enlightened men in China, who was special envoy to the Queen's Jubilee, was sentenced to be rigorously banished to Chinese Turkestan. He was acquitted of all complicity with the crimes of Kang Yu-wei, but he was apparently convicted of being "crafty and treacherous." He will probably survive the journey. His downfall is a serious reverse to British influence in Peking, and indeed to all progress along western lines. Though venal and corruptible, like all Chinamen, he had rendered great services to his country in the introduction of enlightenment and knowledge in dealing

---

176 Chang Yin-huan, 1837–1900, was a diplomat. He was concurrently Vice-Minister of Finance and a Minister of the Tsungli Yamên, as well as joint superintendent of railways and mines. He represented China at Queen Victoria's Diamond Jubilee in 1897 and was the first Chinese to be knighted by the British Government. During the Boxer rebellion, while in exile, Tsu Hsi's advisers ordered his execution.

with foreign affairs. As an advocate of progress he has been eliminated. And other prominent men, such as Chen Pao-chen,[177] the Governor of Hunan, have also been removed. Their crime was progress: the article of faith of the party in power is retrogression.

Undoubtedly, however, the Japanese have supported Kang Yu-wei and his schemes. The last night Kang Yu-wei passed in Peking was in the Japanese Legation with the Marquis Ito.[178] He and all his followers have been on terms of close intimacy with most of the Japanese in Peking, both official and unofficial. One of the tenets of Kang's faith was an alliance with Japan, the adoption of Japanese reforms—Japan to be the model—Chinese soldiers to be trained in Japan, Chinese ships to be commanded by Japanese officers. One of the first books he caused to be translated was the "History of the Reformation in Japan." The proposed visit of the Emperor to Tien-tsin was to be the prelude of a longer journey to the Mikado in Japan. That all the reforms of Kang have now been cancelled is a reverse to the Japanese, who ardently desire to see a new China. It is a reverse also to many English missionaries, who extended to Kang Yu-wei the benefit of their counsel and the advantage of their sympathy. No support whatever, either direct or indirect, had been given to Kang Yu-wei and his party by any British official. And the fact that the mail steamer upon which he took passage from Shanghai and Hong Kong was convoyed by a British cruiser, the Bonaventure, has given a totally erroneous impression to the Central Government that the British Government was in sympathy with the reformer, and through him with the revolutionary movement now operating in several parts of the Empire.

---

177 Chen Bao-zhen, 1831–1900, as provincial governor of Hunan launched ambitious reforms in the fields of education, military modernisation, industrialisation, and press freedom. He was a key allay of Kang Youwei. Chen officially died of an illness.
178 Itō Hirobumi, 1846–1919, four-time prime minster of Japan who oversaw that country's modernisation after Japan's self-imposed isolation ended, under foreign pressure, in the 1860s. Itō negotiated with Treaty of Shimonoseki with Li Hung-Chang after Japan defeated China in the Sino-Japanese War. Reformers in China were conflicted over Japan; they looked to Japan's experience with modernisation as a possible template for China; yet, culturally they looked down on the Japanese and were appalled by Japanese encroachments on Chinese territories in emulation of European powers.

2 | 'THE SITUATION IN CHINA AFTER THE COUP D'ÉTAT'

Chang Chih-Tung, Governor General of Hebei and Hubei, with unknown British officer, 14 May 1903.
Mitchell Library, Sydney

The outlook is not reassuring. Much depends upon the loyalty of the Yang-tsze provinces, and in this connexion the proposed visit of Marquis Ito to Chang Chih-tung[179], the viceroy of Hunan and Hupeh, causes some uneasiness among the official classes here. The Marquis Ito they regard as an arch-revolutionist.

---

179 Zhang Zhidong, 1837–1909, a powerful conservative Official. A brilliant scholar, Chang was fierce in condemnation of Russian and French encroachments on the Chinese Empire's territory. He was a moderniser who started a mint in Canton, and a press there dedicated to the publication of Confucian classics; when Viceroy at Wuhan he promoted the development of railways and built China's first steel works, using coal and iron ore from central China. He coined the slogan: "Chinese learning from the fundamental (Confucian) principles; Western learning for practical application." It proved not to be a winning combination. Morrison regarded him as on of the more effective Chinese ministers.

The Marquis has left Peking. His mission here is regarded as a failure. He despairs of reform in China. In Peking he found no statesman, no man willing to take responsibility, no man standing conspicuously above his fellows. He thinks that no reform in the Court is possible so long as the Court remains in Peking; the removal of the capital is a necessity. And no reform of the finances of the Empire is possible until the problem is dealt with of abolishing the expenditure of the £3,000,000 per annum (£340 million in today's money) now absorbed by the vast hordes of Manchu retainers dependent upon the Court.

Chapter 3

KILL THE FOREIGNERS

In early October 1898, Morrison received a note from Sir Claude MacDonald, Britain's resident Minister at Peking. "Have you heard anything of the above?" he inquired. Enclosed with Sir Claude's note was a letter that had been sent to him on 6 October by Edward G. Hillier,[180] the agent of the Hongkong and Shanghai Banking Corporation in Peking. Hillier wrote:

> My Compradore [Wu Tiao-ching[181]] tells me that the common talk of the streets last night was a certain remark said to have fallen from one of the members of the Council,[182] that advantage should be taken of the present opportunity, when there is only a handful of foreigners here to exterminate the lot and burn the Legations: my man, walking behind a group of the Yamên-underling-type last night, heard this quite seriously discussed.

---

180 Hillier, 1857–1924, had been stationed in Peking since 1891. He represented British financial interests in China and was involved with virtually all important foreign loan negations with the Chinese government.
181 Wu Tiao-ching, 1850–1928, apprenticed to foreign trading firms in Shanghai he became fluent in English. Advised Hong Kong Bank, also became a first Chinese manager of the Imperial Bank of China, working alongside western employees. Adviser to Yuan Shikai on fiscal policy.
182 The Council of State, established in 1729, was responsible for the government of the Empire. Though of no fixed number it usually consisted of two Manchus, two Chinese, with the presidency held by one of the royal Princes, implying a Manchu majority.

Of course we have heard this sort of thing before, but, in view of current events [i.e. the recent *coup*], you might think it well to bring it to bring the matter to the notice of the [Tsungli] Yamên. I can not ascertain which member of the Gd [Grand] Council is credited with the suggestion, but I should think it rests between Yung-lu and Kang-yi; from what one can judge nothing would be to silly for the former.

Coming as this letter did during the fallout of the previous month's *coup* Morrison filed the letter away. Besides, as Hillier pointed out "we have heard this sort of thing before". Morrison's reply, if he wrote one, has not come down to us. Yet Hillier's letter was prescient in that it contained some key elements that would be present in the Boxer Uprising that occurred 20 months later: the desire, verging on a plan, of the Chinese government to "exterminate the foreigners" underlined by the involvement of officials at the highest level of the government, among whom Jung-lu[183] (as his name is more usually rendered) and Kang-yi[184] were two. Jung-lu, a favourite of the Dowager Empress, survived his suspected complicity in the rebellion; Kang-yi was not so fortunate, he was executed for his active encouragement of the Boxers. Soon members of the royal family would lend their support to the Boxers.

The origins of the Boxers are obscure but were founded in a group practicing martial arts, hence the term 'boxer' to describe their elaborate arm movements in conflict. Overlaying the martial arts aspect of the group was a set of magical beliefs that adherents believed would render them invulnerable to Western weapons. Sadly when hostilities were fully underway the Boxers met the reality of bullets and many thousands died. "Where is the magic now," rhetorically asked two senior Mandarins who jointly petitioned the government to withdraw support for the

---

183 Jung-lu, 1836–1903, was a Manchu of the Gualgiya clan. His career was made in the military, holding crucial posts in Xi'an and Peking, finally, after the Sino-Japanese War being elevated to the Tsungli Yamen and the Grand Council. See his biography by Fang Chao-ying in Hummel, vol. 1, pp. 405–409.

184 Kang-i, 1837–1900, a hardline conservative Manchu who rose through the bureaucracy to become a trusted adviser to Tsu Hsi. Opposed to the 1898 Reform movement, supported the Boxer rebellion, and Qing military confrontation with foreign powers.

Boxers.[185] They saw the Boxers as little less than brigands, and compared them to the White Lotus rebels and the Eight Trigrams movement of earlier times. Their advice fell on deaf ears. The government supported the Boxers whom they described as "patriots" whose slogans included "Support the Qing, destroy the foreign". One of the galvanising events that helped propel the Boxers was the German occupation of Kiao-Chau[186] in Shantung province—the place of Confucius' birth—and the arrogation to itself of rights to develop railways and mines. This was the opening land grab in the Battle for Concessions occasioned by the aftermath of the Sino-Japanese War; the pre-text for German action, though, was the murder of two German catholic priests in late 1898. The most thorough investigation of the origins of the Boxers, in English at least, is by Joseph Esherick[187] who had access in the 1980s to Chinese sources. He found that the Boxers were a broad-based agrarian movement in the west of Shandong and their beliefs reflected popular culture of the time, one that emphasised martial arts, a sectarian attitude to religion, and beliefs in spirit possession that resulted in invulnerability. He found no connection to the White Lotus rebels.

The foreign community in Peking, which might have numbered as many as 500[188] persons in 1900, was slow to react to the rise of the Boxers, although Sir Claude MacDonald minister at the British legation had been sending telegrams to London about the Boxers since the beginning of the year.[189] When, after an extended visit to Australia and

---

185 In June 1900, Hsu Ching-ch'eng and Yuan Ch'ang memorialised (petitioned) the throne to withdraw its support for the 'bandit' Boxers. They wrote three times during June and July and after the third memorial they were executed. See Teng and Fairbank, pp. 190–193 for the texts of their three memorials.
186 Qingdao today.
187 Joseph W. Esherick, *The Origins of the Boxer Uprising*, Berkeley and Los Angeles: University of California Press, 1987.
188 This is the estimate of Peter Fleming in his *Siege of Peking*, Rupert Hart-Davis, London, 1960.
189 In July 1900, with the siege not yet over, the British government laid before parliament all the correspondence it had entered into with the Chinese government, and the cables it had received from its embassy in Peking. Numbering some 277 items, it is an exercise in 'open government' that successors might do well to emulate. Correspondence respecting the Insurrectionary Movement in China, July 1900, London HMSO.

Japan, Morrison got back to Peking on 4 April he went to see Sir Claude that afternoon. He recorded in his diary "Boxers ceasing agitation"—his first mention of them, and rather off the mark. For the next 10 days he busied himself with cataloguing his growing library, meeting foreign businessmen and diplomats, but then, on 15 April, Akira Sugiyama, of the Japanese Legation came to visit him.

"The Boxer movement he says is increasing. It is extending further to the north. It was in Shantung; it is now in Chili. Should nothing be done? I think there should be."[190]

Sugiyama would have the unfortunate distinction of being the first foreigner to be killed by the Boxers in Peking when they attacked the Legations, but that would not happen until 11 June. From the 15 April onward, Morrison's Dairy has almost daily records of either rising concern among the foreign community about the Boxers, although some, such as the one of the 16 April, recorded an alternative explanation of events. "According to Jonathan Lees ... the danger is scarcity of rain which is attributed to the disturbance of the *Feng Shui* by foreigners. If rain comes Boxers will soon disappear."[191]

Feng Shui (wind and water) is a form of geomancy for the regulation of the good and evil influences in nature as they affect human affairs. It is designed to maximise the good and limit the evil by the skilful orientation of objects (such as houses and tombs, and within both the position of windows and doors) in space. The Chinese put, and continue to put, great store in *feng shui*. Similarly it was common for the Chinese to view natural phenomena (such as drought, flood or earthquake) as natural prefigurations of forthcoming disturbances in human affairs, or as the result of malign influences, such as the presence of foreigners or Christians. It was not, therefore, unreasonable for foreigners to link the north China drought in early 1900 with increased anti-foreign activity. Even Morrison, a gimlet-eyed observer of Chinese affairs, resorted to this form of reasoning and as late as 18 May could record in his *Diary* "I said to Sir Claude "the first shower and the movement expires.

---

190 Morrison's diaries are kept at the Mitchell Library in Sydney. His diary for 1900, herein referred to as *Diary*, has been transcribed and I quote from this transcription.

191 Nearly a month later, Morrison still clung to the view that an end to the North China drought would bring an end to the "disturbances." See *Diary*, 5 May 1900.

3 | KILL THE FOREIGNERS

Yesterday some rain fell. Just my luck. I wire in the morning the alarming Boxer movement and in the afternoon rain falls."

Such optimism persisted but was short lived and soon the diaries are recording details of Boxer reprisals against foreigners, especially Christians, and more especially still, Catholics.

The position of the Catholic church in China had lately become controversial. Led in Peking by a brilliant Lazarist priest by the name of Pierre-Marie-Alphonse Favier-Duperron,[192] the Church had managed to reframe its status so that its bishops were placed on an equal footing with Manchu/Chinese viceroys and the governors; the Vicars-General ranked with the treasurers, provincial judges and Taotai; and, priests with prefects. This dual power structure was bound to cause problems. Who could definitively decide upon what? How could a foreigner overrule a Chinese official? As Henri Cordier, the doyen of French oriental scholars, noted with Gallic understatement: "This decree was signed at the suggestion of Bishop Favier of Peking, but its wisdom has been much disputed."[193] The powers Favier won for the Catholic church would turn out to be illusory although not before their news had stoked further Chinese animosity towards Christians and disgust at their government's weakness. It is difficult to be precise as to how much fuel this added to the fire but common sense suggests it ranks among the contributory causes to what followed.[194] Whatever the case it was something that preyed on Morrison's mind and in 1908 he successfully lobbied Liang Tun-yen,[195] president of the Waiwupu (Foreign Ministry and successor to the Tsungli Yamen), to rescind the privileges Favier had won for the Catholic Church.

---

192 Known as Monsignor and later Bishop Favier, 1837–1905. His account of the Chinese capital (*Péking histoire et description*. Pekin: Imprimerie des Lazaristes au Pe-Tang, 1897, 2 volumes) is highly regarded. Bishop since 1899, Favier led the defence of the Cathedral and the preservation of many hundreds of Chinese Christian refugees who had there sought sanctuary.
193 Cordier wrote the essay on the Catholic church in China for the *Catholic Encyclopaedia*, 1908, vol. 3.
194 See Pearl, op. cit., p. 197.
195 Liang Dunyan, 1857–1924, industrialist and diplomat. Liang was a pragmatic diplomat, he worked to return the railways to Chinese ownership. He supported Yuan Shikai but broke with him over the letters imperial pretensions.

Meanwhile, Morrison continued to record instances of anti-foreign activity, especially against Christians (Chinese converts and western missionaries). Then on 16 May he relates what his 'boy', possibly Ah Heng whom he used for demotic intelligence gathering, had found out about the unrest, as well as other informants for the missionary community that Morrison met that day.

> "According to my boy 8,000,000 men are to descend from heaven and exterminate the foreigners.[196] Then rain will come. Foreigners were poisoning the wells. Says Mrs. [Emma] Smith, the Manchu Government is to make a determined effort to drive us all out … E Ho-Chuan means Righteousness, Peace in Harmony – Fists. The movement may become serious especially if a leader can be found. People easily excited but there is no leader. Many stories of pillaging … [Rev. Frederick] Turner says there were some boxers practising. One lad of 16 bared his chest to [Auguste] Chamot saying, "The foreign bullet may strike me here, tapping his chest, but will not hurt me."[197]

Throughout the rest of May Morrison daily recorded examples of Boxer attacks on Christians. He was also attentive to the behaviour of the Boxers who "never pass a temple without prostration," and who believe when they go into a trance "they awake impervious to the foreigners' bullets. Armed with swords and spears, no guns. All knives and swords have doubled in value. Shops working day and night to supply demand."[198]

The news kept getting worse. On May 23, Morrison went to see his bookbinder, who was located near Peitang, the Catholic Cathedral

---

196 Morrison used this figure in his magnum opus about the Boxers.
197 Morrison, *Diary for 1900*, entry for 16 May. His transliteration of the Boxer name is wrong, it is usually transcribed as 'I-ho-chuan'. His translation is essentially accurate, but is usually rendered 'Righteous and Harmonious Fists'. Mrs Smith is probably Emma Jane Smith, wife of Rev. Arthur H Smith, missionary and author of *China in Convulsion*, F. H. Revell Co., New York, 1901, 2 vols; Turner is probably Rev. Frederick Storrs Turner, 1834–1916, a British clergyman and campaigner against the opium trade; Chamot is Auguste Chamot, a Swiss hotelier who ran the Hôtel de Pékin in the Legation quarter.
198 *Diary*, entry for 19 May.

in Peking. He saw "several hundred" refugees crowding the cathedral grounds. Either side of the west door are tents with eight or 10 unarmed solders each inside them. The Boxers, he noted, "grow with their success and the Europeans will not be safe. On the banners of the boxers are the two characters – Abolish the Westerners."[199] Two days later placards posted describe "An admirable way of destroying foreign buildings."

Then, a few days later, Morrison went to Tientsin to take the temperature. Gloom prevailed. He lunched with Edward Drew,[200] an American who worked for the Imperial Maritime Customs, and his family. At the lunch he met Emma Smith again. "She is firmly convinced that a general massacre of all the foreigners in Peking is contemplated. She believes it, having received secret information. Yet there is no evidence to show that the warning is more important than it has ever been before. Constantly we have been warned."[201]

In the days that followed it became clear that the Boxers and their helpers in government were setting out to isolate Peking. The rail yards at Fengtai were destroyed, along with a carriage especially built for the Empress Dowager. More importantly, that destruction meant that rail communication with Tianjin was severed as was the telegraph.

Morrison recounted some of the stories above and many more. *The Times* published his account of the siege over two days, beginning on Saturday 13 October 1900 and concluding on Monday 15 October. His story is datelined 14 August, the day the siege was lifted, an exercise in dramatic license to be sure. In all, his account amounts to some 28,000 words and is a vivid description of the origins (as known to foreigners them) of the Boxers, insight into palace intrigue, and set piece accounts of key moments during the 55 days the siege lasted. In a postscript he is generous in remembering the bravery of others but silent about his own. Morrison's skills as a doctor and surgeon were invaluable during the siege and his personal bravery noteworthy. He was also wounded in the leg which slowed him down, somewhat. His friend A. E. Hippesley quoted the following in his obituary of Morrison in 1920:

---

199 ibid., entry for 28 May.
200 1843–1924.
201 ibid., entry for 26 May.

Although not a military man, Dr. M had proved himself one of the most important members of the garrison being always in motion and cognisant of what was going on everywhere, being by far the best-informed person within the Legation quadrangle. To this must be added a cool judgement, total disregard for danger, and a personal sense of responsibility to help every one to do his best.[202]

Communication with the outside world was virtually impossible during the siege. Most of the China-based reporting of the event originated in Shanghai and was based on rumour. These rumours were transmitted and resulted in *The Times* publishing a number of erroneous obituaries,[203] in particular one of Sir Claude MacDonald, British Minister at Peking, Sir Robert Hart, and Morrison himself. He joked later that the praise heaped upon him enabled helped him secure a pay rise.

The Boxer uprising ended in humiliation for the Qing government. In September 1901 a 'Protocol' was signed by Li Hung-chang, executing his last official duty for the Empire, and the representatives of 11 foreign powers. It was punitive.[204] Ten high officials were executed, examinations were suspended in 45 cities, the Legation quarter in Peking was enlarged, fortified and garrisoned, and 45 Qing forts were destroyed. An indemnity of more than $300 million was to be paid over 40 years. Its conclusion did, however, result in change in attitude by Tsu Hsi to reform. Many of the reforms the Emperor had tried to introduce in 1898 were dusted off and effected during the last seven years of the Old Buddha's life.

---

202 A. E. Hippisley, 'Dr George Ernest Morrison', *The Geographical Journal*, vol. 56, no. 2, August 1920. Hippisley was quoting the Rev. A. H. Smith's *China in Convulsion*, New York: F. H. Revell Co., vol. 1, p. 345.
203 The three obituaries mentioned occupied the entirety of page 4 of *The Times* for Tuesday 17 July 1900.
204 Fairbank, op. cit., pp. 138–139.

'The Siege of the Peking Legations'

(From Our Own Correspondent)
Peking, 14 August 1900[205]

One of the ancient sages of China foretold that "China shall be destroyed by a woman." The prophecy is approaching fulfilment. When the Empress-Dowager, in September, 1898, seized once more the reins of power, who could have foreseen that she was to lead her country with such swiftness to destruction? The anti-foreign, anti-Christian movement which has now culminated in the occupation of Peking by the allied Powers and the destruction once for all of China's power as a nation was from the outset encouraged and fostered by the Empress-Dowager and by the ignorant reactionaries whom she selected as her advisers.

The Origin of the Boxers

The foundation of the "Boxers" can be traced to one man, Yu Hsien,[206] who, when Prefect of Tsao-chau, in the south-west corner of Shan-tung, organized a band of men as local militia or tribunes. For them he revived the ancient appellation of "I-Ho-Ch'iian," the Patriotic Harmony Fists. Armed with long swords, they were known popularly as the Ta-tao-huei, or Big Knife Society.

---

205 Published Saturday 13 October 1900, pp. 5–6.
206 Yu Hsien (Yu Xian), 1842–1901, a Manchu who was an high official of the Qing government, outspokenly anti-foreign and anti-Christian. He rose to prominence first in Shandong and then, during the Boxer uprising, as Governor of Shansi where he was held responsible for a massacre of Christians and subsequently executed.

Company of Boxers in Tianjin, c. 1900.
Library of Congress Prints and Photographs Division Washington, DC

After the occupation of Kiao-chau Bay[207] the society grew in force, the professed objects of its members being to oppose the exactions of native Catholics and to resist further German aggression. They became anti-Christian and anti-foreign. They became a religious sect, and underwent a fantastic kind of spiritual training of weird incantations and grotesque gymnastics, which they professed to believe rendered them impervious to the sword and to the bullet of the white man. Three deities they specially selected as their own-namely, Kwanti, the God of War and patron deity of the present dynasty, Wang Cheng-tze, an incarnation of Laotze, and the Joyful Buddha of the Falstaffian Belly. They made Taoist and Buddhist temples their headquarters. Everywhere they declared that they would drive the foreigner and his devilish religion from China.

To encourage this society its founder, Yu Hsien, was in March, 1899, appointed by the Throne Governor of Shan-tung. In four years he

---

207 By Germany in 1898–99—its 'prize' in the Battle for Concessions that had swept China.

had risen from the comparatively humble post of Prefect to that of the highest official in the province.

The "Boxers" had grown in power till they had become a menace to the maintenance of law and order, and were terrorizing large districts of the province. In the district where they had originated they came into collision with the authorities; they were attacked by the military commander of the district, and 91 were killed and many imprisoned. This was on October 25 of last year (1899). But the attempt to suppress the society of which he was the founder did not meet with the approval of the Governor. The military officer was deprived of his command. The district magistrate was degraded, and "Boxers" who had been made prisoners were liberated.

Upon Yuan Shih-kai's appointment as Governor after the murder of the English missionary, Mr. Brooks, he received instructions to suppress the "Boxers," but not to employ force in doing so; he was warned that among their members were patriotic and good men and that to punish them indiscriminately would not be in accordance with the wishes of high heaven.

The Empress-Dowager and the Boxers

From Shan-tung the "Boxers" spread into the adjoining province of Chi-li,[208] the metropolitan province. It was from the first noticeable that all the teachers of the "Boxer" cult were Shan-tung men. "Boxers" could only have spread into the region of the capital by the sanction, if not by the encouragement, of the Court. They inoculated the Empress-Dowager with a belief in their doctrine and in their supernatural power, of resisting the foreigner. Never has ignorance been so disastrous.

Edicts published in the *Peking Gazette*[209] recognized the association officially. Secret societies have always been forbidden by the Government as hotbeds of sedition, but this society, being anti-

---

208 Chi-li no longer exists as an administrative district in north China. It was composed of parts of the modern provinces of Hebei, Henan, Shandong, including the provincial-level municipalities of Peking and Tianjin.
209 The *Peking Gazette* was the publication that recorded the decisions, laws and edicts of the Chinese government.

Christian and anti-foreign, was pampered as patriotic in its aims and loyal in its constitution. Besides, its appearance in the metropolitan province opportunely coincided with a state of unrest that had become alarming. There was famine in the land, no rain had fallen. The winter wheat had failed, the spring wheat could not be sown, and 95 per cent of the land was untilled. The price of grain had risen and there was widespread misery and discontent. The feeling arose that these misfortunes were attributable to the enmity of high heaven, offended by the usurpation of the Empress-Dowager and the deposition from all real power of the Son of Heaven, the rightful Emperor. At this juncture the society entered the province. Its propaganda spread like wildfire. "It is the foreigners who are eating the country. It is the foreign religion which has called down upon China the wrath of heaven. It is the cursed foreign railways and telegraphs which have diverted the good influences from on high." Resentment against the Empress-Dowager was turned into wrath against the foreigner and fury against his religion.

Thus the wily woman diverted from herself the popular clamour. She encouraged the growth of "Boxer" trainbands, seeing in them possible means of protection for her dynasty, and she fanned the wrath against the Christians by cunningly devised edicts comparing "Boxers" with Christians to the disadvantage of the latter. Grave insinuations against the Christians grew into open attacks culminating in a decree ordaining their extermination. The Imperial Court became thus the patrons of a movement which was to sweep the country clear of the foreigner and "let the seas separate us." Prince Tuan,[210] the father of the Heir Apparent, became the chief of the "Boxers," while other prominent men known to be in their counsels were Duke Lan, his younger brother, Hsu Tung, the tutor of the Crown Prince, Xang Yi, the "Great Extortioner," and Chao

---

210 Prince Tuan (also known as Duke Lan), 1856–1923, was a Manchu prince of the late Qing dynasty, a leader of the Boxers and patron of them at the highest level of the Chinese government. He supported the Empress Dowager in her opposition to reform initiated by the Guangxu emperor, was virulently anti-foreign and arranged for Cixi to meet the leader of the Boxers, Cao Futian. After the uprising was put down, he lived until 1917 in exile in Urumchi in far western China. Morrison met him there in 1910, see p. 262. Tuan returned to Peking in 1917; he was regarded as something of a hero for his anti-foreign stance.

3 | 'THE SIEGE OF THE PEKING LEGATIONS'

Shu-chiao,[211] the president of the Railway and Mining Bureau, a board founded to prevent railways and mines from being opened, and Li Ping Heng,[212] the degraded Governor of Shan-tung, who had been cashiered, in obedience to the demands of Germany, never to hold office again, yet had been subsequently appointed to a high post in the, Yang-tsze Valley, the British sphere.

When, after an absence of eight months, I returned to the capital last April, I found "Boxers" everywhere in evidence and the most serious alarm among the missionaries as to the course events were taking. Boys were being drilled by teachers from Shan-tung and were, being armed with knives and swords. Knives had already risen to double their usual value and cutlers were reaping a harvest. Anti-foreign literature was being sold in the streets. Christian servants were being warned that they were "doomed men." Yet those who were not missionaries regarded the movement with contempt. No rain had fallen, and it was believed that much of the excitement would disappear after the first shower.

In May the drought continued and the excitement grew. It was reported that 8,000,000 men were to descend from heaven and exterminate the foreigners. Then rain would come. Christians had offended the gods by worshipping the devils' religion and Heaven's wrath had been incurred, no rain had been sent, and thousands were starving. To inflame the ignorant still more against the foreigner it was reported that foreigners were poisoning the wells. Then the crusade began in the southern part of the province against the native Christians. They, the Urmoatze or "secondary devils," were to be first attacked, and when they had been exterminated the white men were to be ended. Heartrending stories came from the province of murders of native Christians, of the pillaging and burning of Christian property. On the 15th the Catholic Fathers and Monsigneur Favier reported that the persecution was the most serious which had been witnessed in China since the outbreak in Szu-chuan, and that it was spreading with alarming

---

211 Chao Shu-Chiao, 1848–1901, topped his year in competitive examinations and rose to be Minister of Justice, Mayor of Peking, Yamen Minister and Grand Councillor (1899–1900). His seniority meant that he was condemned to commit suicide (clumsily and badly done) for his part in the Boxer uprising rather than face execution.
212 Li Ping Heng, 1830–1900, Chinese Imperial official, Provincial Governor.

Peitang Cathedral, Peking.
Mitchell Library, Sydney

3 | 'THE SIEGE OF THE PEKING LEGATIONS'

rapidity. Refugees began pouring into Peking and the Catholics began arming. Wherever strong enough they intrenched themselves in Catholic villages and offered armed resistance to persecution. Christian families living unprotected in the country abandoned everything and fled for protection to the Catholic centre near Paoting-fu[213] or to the parent churches in Peking. The Pei-tang,[214] the great Catholic Cathedral at Peking, rapidly filled with refugees.

The Bishop urged that foreign guards should be at once brought to Peking. To bring guards to Peking he argued was more effective than to bombard a port. In 1898, at the time of the coup d'État, the effect of bringing guards was an immediate restoration of tranquillity. The present movement was a popular one, and was regarded favourably by the Government. Bring troops to Peking and the Government would at once suppress the movement in order to save the face of China, whose humiliation in having foreign guards to preserve order in the capital would be witnessed by the entire world. The "Boxers" were not so much anti-Christian as anti-foreign. Their strength was growing daily, and soon the Europeans would not be safe. It was urgently necessary to bring guards.

On May 19 two ominous incidents occurred. One of the medical teachers at the University, received word excusing him from attending the medical school for 25 days. His work took him across the South City, where anti-foreign placards were numerous. The enforced leave given him was prompted by fears for his personal safety. A Chinese boy was detected dropping something into a well. Seized and interrogated, he declared that he had been hired by the foreigners to poison wells. On the same afternoon, the 19th, two missionaries who had bravely ventured a far as Chochou and Liang Hsiang in the heart of the "Boxer" district between Peking and Pao-ting-fu returned to the city. It was an alarming tale they had to tell. The country was alive with "Boxers."

---

213 Now known as Baoding it is situated about 150km south of Peking in Hebei province.
214 Pei-tang (Beitang) is an historic church in Peking, originally erected on land donated by the Kangxi Emperor in 1703. The present building dates from 1864 and in 1887 was moved to its current location following an Imperial request. An important site of Catholicism in China, Beitang was shuttered in 1827 for some years, and again during the Boxer uprising.

Two well-known teachers of the London Missionary Society had been seized by the mob, carried before the "Boxer" priests, and put through the mockery of a trial. Having recited the formula and burned incense, the priests pretended to become entranced and receive guidance from Heaven. "Do with the 'secondary devils' as you will; no harm can come to you" was the verdict given to satisfy the mob. Refusing to abjure their faith, the teachers were backed in pieces and thrown into the river. The magistrate could give the missionaries no protection, and he besought them not to linger in his district. Already he had lost face and influence, for, in an attempt to suppress the "Boxers" at Matou, he had gone there with some cavalry and infantry, but his own soldiers sympathized with the "Boxers"' and betrayed him into their hands. He had been seized by the "Boxers" and held to ransom.

Diplomatic Action in Peking

The movement was gathering in volume, and excitement was increasing in Peking. On the 20th a meeting of the Diplomatic Body was held, when it was decided to address a joint note to the Yamên calling upon the Government to take immediate steps for the suppression of the "Boxers," as otherwise the Ministers would be compelled to adopt measures for their own protection. Unanimity is not the predominant characteristic of the Diplomatic Body in Peking, and it is possible that the Tsung-Li-Yamên recognized this, and did not attach much weight to the communication. On a previous occasion, in connexion with the disturbances, a joint note in the form of an ultimatum sent by the American, British, German, and Japanese Ministers, fizzled out like a damp squib. Italy and her ultimatum had greatly weakened the power of threats upon the Chinese. Besides, the action of the Russian Minister, who, while supporting the conjoint action of the Diplomatic Body, was accustomed at such a crisis as this to send despatches direct to the Empress-Dowager through Prince Ching,[215] was not calculated to force China into the belief that all the foreign Powers were acting in accord.

---

215 Prince Ching, I-k'uang, 1836–1916, descended from the emperor Kao-tsung, his family fell from prominence but was raised up again by his efforts. He was famously corrupt, preferring to negotiate the size of emolument himself rather than through the usual

3 | 'THE SIEGE OF THE PEKING LEGATIONS'

To all protests by the Ministers the Yamên replied by ridiculing the fears of the foreigners and giving assurances. It was boys they said, who were going through the "Boxer" drill—ignorant boys who thus found a pastime. An edict entirely unsatisfactory was issued on the 23rd, exhorting the unruly to disperse quietly to their homes. It was most cunningly worded so as not to offend the "Boxers," who were secretly lauded as loyal and patriotic, and yet was so contrived as to delude the foreign Ministers into not bringing their guards to Peking. Then overwhelming evidence was produced to prove that the movement had the official cognisance and approval of the Government, for "Boxers" began drilling on the official drill grounds—in the Yamên of the Mongolian Superintendency, in the grounds of the great barracks near Li Hung Chang's temple, in the palaces of Prince Tuan, the father of the Heir Apparent, and of Duke Lan, his brother, and finally in the Imperial palace itself, the eunuchs trained outside by the Shan-tung leaders being their teachers. Evidence, afterwards duly confirmed, pointed to Prince Tuan's palace as the headquarters of the sect. All the retrograde Ministers who have assisted China down the path to Avernus,[216] Hsu

---

way, an intermediary. He inherited family estates in 1850 and in 1884 he was made Prince of the Second Degree to which was attached his historic family's designation Ch'ing. That year he was made chief member of the Office of Foreign Affairs, the Tsungli Yamên. In 1885 he was appointed on of the controllers of the Board of Admiralty. In 1894 the Empress Dowager raised his to the Prince of First order. He fled Peking with the court in 1900, returning in 1901 to participate with Li Hung-chang in the peace settlement. In 1903 he became chief Grand Councillor, the most powerful official in the empire. From May-November 1911 he was Prime Minister. He resigned and was made Privy Councillor. P'u-i abdicated in December 1911 and Ch'ing resigned and moved to Tientsin where he subsequently died.

216 Morrison is here demonstrating the benefits of his classical education. Avernus is a lake near Naples which fills the crater of an extinct volcano. It was described by Virgil in Book 6 of his *Aeneid* as the entrance to the underworld.

Tung,[217] Kong Yi,[218] Li Ping Heng[219] and Chao Shu-chiao were in direct communication with the "Boxer" leaders.

Placards were posted throughout the city headed "An admirable way of destroying foreign buildings." Refugees crowded into the Pei-tang. Services for those outside were suspended at all four Cathedrals, and women were excused from coming to church. They had been threatened and terrorized in the street. Among the refugees were many burned and wounded, who had escaped massacre in the country.

On May 21 some hopes were given that an attempt was to be made by the Government to check the movement. A message received from the Tien-tsin Consuls on that day announced that a Colonel Yang and 70 soldiers proceeding to Pao-ting-fa to attack the "Boxers" had been caught in an ambuscade and had all perished. For a little time we thought that the soldiery were being employed against the murderers of Christians. Investigation, however, proved that the story, which had been communicated to the foreign Consuls by the interpreter to the Viceroy had no foundation in fact. Colonel Yang had been murdered while, with a party of 70 men in the country, but there had been no conflict with the "Boxers." None of his men had been attacked and he himself seems to have fallen a victim to an act of private revenge. Far from suppressing the "Boxers," the soldiers, especially the anti-foreign rabble of General Tung-fuh-siang,[220] openly fraternized with

---

217 Xu Tong, 1819–1900, was a conservative official opposed to reform. He was Tsu Hsi's Grand Secretary.
218 Here Morrison probably means Gang Yi, 1837–1900, who was a prominent conservative official along with Xu and Li who opposed reform. He was a Manchu and a keen supporter of the Boxers.
219 Li Pengheng, 1830–1900, prominent conservative o opposed to reform and supporter of the Boxers. A trusted adviser to Tsu Hsi, Hw as appointed Imperial Commissioner for Military Affairs and commanded Chinese forces opposing the Eight-Nation Alliance during the sieges of Tianjin and Peking.
220 Dong Fuxiang, 1839–1908, Chinese general from the western province of Gansu who commanded an effective force of Muslim Hui soldiers. He participated in the Dugan Revolt (1862–1877) on the side of Yaqub Beg but defected to the Qing forces in exchange for official position. In 1890 he was stationed at Aksu, Kashgaria in the far west of China but was brought east by the Sino-Japanese War of 1894. He returned to the west in 1895 to put down another Dungan revolt. In 1898 he and his force of 10,000 were in Peking for preparation for war against foreigners. He supported the Boxers in

3 | 'THE SIEGE OF THE PEKING LEGATIONS'

the "Boxers," being addressed by them in affectionate terms as "blood brothers."

Foreigners who had friends among the Chinese received private warning to leave Peking; their lives were in danger; a massacre of the Europeans was impending. Gardeners and washermen employed by foreigners left their work and went into hiding. Teachers and servants in the employment of foreigners who were not Catholic ran away into the country. It was becoming unsafe for the Chinese to work for the foreigner.

On the 28th of May a messenger came into Peking to announce that the Lu-han railway between Lu-ku-chiao and Pao-ting-fa had been destroyed, and that the lives of the French engineers at Chang-hsin-tien, five miles beyond Lu-ku-chiao were imperilled. The station had been burnt and the engineers were besieged in their houses. Later word came that Feng-t'ai, the first station on the Peking-Tien-tsin line, had been attacked by "Boxers" and the station burned. The engine sheds were in flames and the whole country-side was in alarm. At once it was regarded as noteworthy that General Tung-fuh-siang had, been received in audience by the Empress-Dowager. Word that the station was to be burnt on that day had been sent some days before to all the surrounding villages.' In expectation of the burning, "Boxers," or sympathizers, had left in the morning for Feng-t'ai, announcing that they were going to witness the conflagration. The smoke could be seen from Peking and from all the temples in the western hills. No sooner had the flames started than the rain so long and ardently desired burst over the country. High heaven had signified approval of the work. So propitious a sign gave great encouragement to the "Boxers." After the Tien-tsin massacre of 1870, a similar phenomenon occurred, susceptible of the same interpretation. Fortunately, an engine had been kept in waiting at Feng-t'ai, and by this the engineers and other *employés*, nearly all of whom were British, escaped to Tien-tsin before the attack.

1900 and his troops were responsible for hacking to death Akai Sugiyama, the Japanese diplomat, among others. He lost all official positions after the rebellion was put down. He returned to Gansu with a personal force of 5,000, and died there.

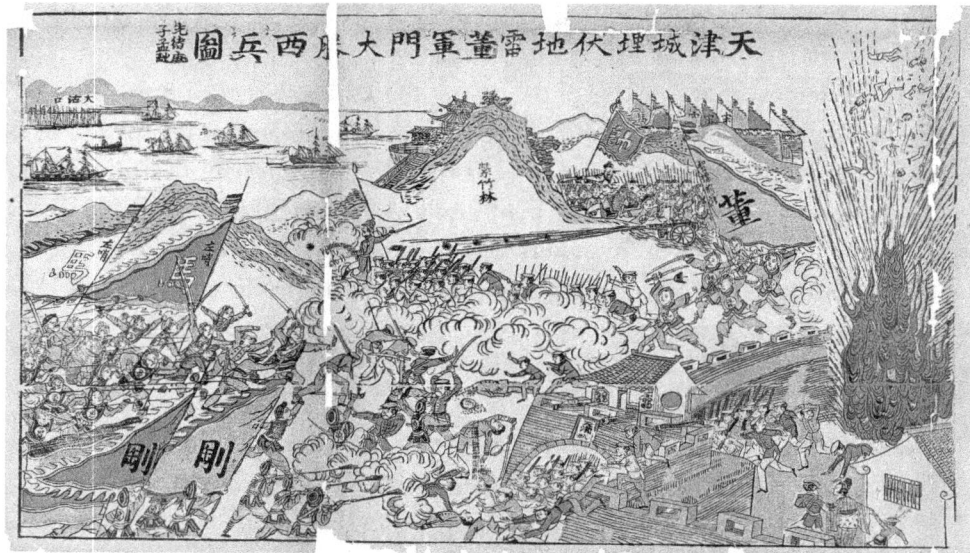

How the Chinese saw it. The defence of Tianjin from foreign invasion, 1900.

But great and inevitable anxiety was felt for the safety of the French engineers at Chang-hsin-tien, 15 miles from Peking, for the country was swarming with "Boxers," with whom the soldiers were fraternizing. Their rescue on the 29th was due to the courage of M. Auguste Chamot,[221] a Swiss gentleman long resident in Peking, who, accompanied by his wife, a lady of remarkable physical courage, by a young Australian named Dupree, and four French gentlemen, rode out through a country seething with excitement, and the same evening brought safely back to Peking every member of the party, 13 men, nine women, and seven children. An hour after the party escaped their houses were set fire to and looted by the very soldiers who had been sent to protect them. This prompt and daring rescue was one of the best incidents of the siege; often has the Legion of Honour been conferred for services less meritorious.

---

221 *The Times* used Monsieur, here abbreviated as M for French honorifics and Herr in respect of German males.

3 | 'THE SIEGE OF THE PEKING LEGATIONS'

Arrival of the Legation Guards

Peking was becoming more excited day by day. Foreigners riding near the Yung-ting-mên were assailed with stones by Imperial soldiers "sent to protect foreigners." Foreign guards were sent for. The Chinese made a last effort to assure the foreign Ministers that they were not needed, that the excitement was abating, and that soon all would be quiet. They attempted to throw difficulties in the way of the troops coming, but finally agreed that they should come. Sir Claude MacDonald[222] for his part notified the Yamen in peremptory terms that the time for patience had passed, that the foreign guards were coming, and that if any attempts were made to obstruct them they would come in tenfold greater numbers. The train service, though dislocated, continued, and in the evening of the 31st of May, too late to allow a demonstration in the streets, the Marine guards, British, Japanese, American, French, Italian, Russian, arrived. They numbered in all some 340 men. Though the hour was late and the gates had to be kept open, they marched past respectful and gaping crowds of thousands of Chinese, past grovelling officials, and battalions of soldiers—an unthinkable humiliation for the capital of what Lord Salisbury[223] once ventured to characterize as a nation of 400,000,000 of brave people.

---

222 Colonel Sir Claude Maxwell MacDonald, 1852–1915, British soldier and diplomat, who held important diplomatic positions in China and Japan. Until the mid-1880s MacDonald was on army service in Africa where he ended up Commissioner and Consul-General in Brass in the West African Oil Rivers Protectorate (present day Nigeria). He left the army in 1896 and, having caught the eye of Lord Salisbury, was that year appointed HM Minister in China with representation in Korea as well. He negotiated the 99-year lease on the New Territories adjacent to Hong Kong which expired in 1997 and resulted in the reversion to Chinese sovereignty of Hong Kong in its entirety. He distinguished himself as leader of the foreign community on Peking during the Boxer uprising of 1900. That year he swapped jobs with Sir Ernest Satow in Tokyo, becoming ambassador there when the status of the legation was raised to that of an embassy.

223 Robert Arthur Talbot Gascoyne-Cecil, 3rd Marquess of Salisbury, 1830–1903. Lord Salisbury was three time British prime minister, foreign secretary known for his policy of "splendid isolation" from entanglements abroad, especially in Europe. His last period as PM was 1895–1902. A man of formidable intellect but of melancholy disposition, a Victorian titan indeed. He was descended from William Cecil, Lord Burghley, principal advisor to Elizabeth I and James VI.

Guards were mounted at the Legations, and the streets, except for the crowds that thronged the Legation quarters to see the foreign soldiers, resumed their usual appearance. As usual in these conjoint international expeditions, there had been serious blunders. In the first place, the British force numbered, when leaving Tien-tsin, 100 men, not one too many; but Russia was sending only 75 men. Accordingly the British Consul detrained 25 of his men in order that the number of British might correspond with the number of Russians. Our power of defence in the large Legation was seriously affected by the loss of this detachment. Our authorities seemed to consider that the troops were being called to Peking for a demonstration only; accordingly they sent with them an antiquated five-barrel Nordenfeldt of 1887 pattern which consistently jammed every fourth round.

Still worse was it with the Russians. They left their 12-pounder on the platform at Tien-tsin but brought the 80 rounds of ammunition, and these, when the communications were subsequently out, they sank in the bottom of the well to save them from falling into the hands of the enemy.

Two days later the Austrian and German guards came to Peking, and two days after that train communication with Peking was interrupted. The immediate effect of the presence of foreign guards was an abatement of excitement in the city itself, but in the country the harrying and murder of native Christians continued. Then the "Boxers" grew bolder and attacked the Europeans. On June 2 reports reached Peking that a party of foreign engineers employed on the Lu-han railway south of Pao-ting-fu had been attacked when escaping by the Tachinig river to Tien-tsin, and that of the party of 30 eight men and one woman were missing, of whom there were grave reasons to fear that five were dead. Then a day later word reached us of the brutal murder at Yunag-ching near the Peking-Tien-tsin railway, of Mr. Robinson and Mr. Norman, two missionaries of the Society for the Propagation of the Gospel.[224] Mr. Robinson had been first killed, but Mr. Norman had succeeded in fleeing for refuge to the Yamen of the magistrate, and by him was given

---

[224] The Society was established by the Church of England during the reign of William III in 1701 to promote Christianity in north America. It began work in China in 1863.

3 | 'THE SIEGE OF THE PEKING LEGATIONS'

up to the fury of the mob and done to death. The destruction of the railways continued, and reports of the burning of new stations come in daily.

On the 4th Sir Claude MacDonald had a meeting with the Tsung-li-Yamên. It was a very serious meeting, for it concerned the murder of the two British missionaries. Four members were present. In the midst of the Minister's protest one member was found fast asleep. "There you have China," said the Minister. "What can you do with such a people?" And in the meantime, while the crisis was impending, the Empress-Dowager was giving a series of theatrical entertainments in the Summer Palace.

Attitude of the Chinese Government

Some action was, however, taken by the Chinese Government, but its effect was to encourage the movement which it was pretending to check. Pressed by the foreign ministers to issue a decree quelling the outbreak, the Government published an edict on June 6 which screened the "Boxers," compared them with Christians to the disparagement of Christians, and attributed the recent outbreak to lawless persons "Who had falsely joined the "Boxers" for their own evil, just as bad characters, it alleged, became Christians to defeat the ends of justice. Profound indignation was caused by the decree, Not a single "Boxer" or "lawless person" had been arrested, though they numbered tens of thousands, but to cast ridicule on the foreigners another edict insolently announced that one man, creating a disturbance by street brawling, had been arrested and would be punished. Here are a few extracts from the decree. No reference whatever was made in it to any act of murder, nor to the systematic massacre of native Christians by the "Boxers." It said:–

> *The Christians have now been propagating their religion in China for many years, and the missionaries have no other object than that of exhorting people to virtuous conduct. Heretofore the Christians have not utilized the Church as a means of causing trouble, so that the people and the Christians have lived together in amity, each following his own doctrine. Now, however, the churches and Christians have become very numerous throughout the Empire, so that discontented*

and reckless characters have found their way into their ranks without the missionaries' being able in every case to discriminate between the good and the bad. Such bad characters have become Christians merely as an excuse to insult and oppress the rest of the population, and to tyrannize over the districts in which they dwelt, although, of course, the missionaries have in no way signified their approval of such proceedings.

As to the 'Patriotic Harmony Society of "Boxers,"' they have recently been practising military drill for the preservation of their bodies and the protection of their homes, and in no way making a disturbance or trouble. Now we have repeatedly issued edicts instructing the officials to repress firmly all disturbances without regard to people being members of the society or not, the only question being whether they are bad characters, and they are to be dealt with most rigorously if they create disturbances. Converts and 'Boxers' alike are one and all the little children of the Throne, and we regard them with an equal love which in no way discriminates between, the 'Boxer' and the Christian.

Then the decree announced that Chao Shu-chiao, one of the most rabid anti-foreign Mandarins in China, had been appointed to report upon the condition of things in the "Boxer" districts. This appointment was a further exemplification of the bad faith of the Government, for he was appointed solely because he was known to be one of the chief supporters of the "Boxer" brotherhood.

Missionaries in Peking began collecting together into the larger mission compounds for common protection. Many ladies went for safety into the British Legation. Railway communication was now severed and the telegraph communication threatened. Our isolation was being completed.

In the country disaffection spread to the districts to the east of Peking, and the position of the American missionaries at Tung-chau became one of great danger. It was decided to abandon their great missionary establishments, and with the native Christians that could follow them to come into Peking. They asked for an escort, but Mr.

Conger[225] felt himself compelled to decline one, on the ground that he did not venture to send the small body of men that he could spare from the Legation through so dangerous a district. Protection must be looked for from the Chinese Government. What soldiers could not be sent to do one fearless American missionary succeeded in doing. Late in the evening of June 7 the Rev. W. S. Ament, of the Board Mission, left Peking in a cart, and with 20 other carts journeyed 14 miles to Tung-chau through a country palpitating with excitement. It was an act of courage and devotion that seemed to us who knew the country a deed of heroism. His arrival was most opportune. He brought safely back with him to Peking the whole missionary body then in Tung-chau five men, including the author of "Chinese Characteristics," 11 ladies, and seven children, together with their Christian servants.

Before leaving the missionaries formally handed over their buildings, schools, colleges, and chapels to the protection of the Chinese Government. Their trust was at once betrayed. Scarcely had they reached Peking before the mission property was in flames, burnt by the very soldiers sent by Government to have them in safe keeping. Every foreign building in Tung-chau was razed to the ground, and there is every reason to fear that every Christian in the neighbourhood who had failed to escape to Peking was butchered. On arrival in Peking the missionaries, dismayed by the wreck of their years of work in China, held a conference and decided to send the following cable over the head of the Minister direct to the President at Washington:–

President McKinley, Washington,
June 8th, 1900.

'Boxers' destroy chapels, massacre hundreds Christians. Threaten exterminate all foreigners. Tung-chau abandoned. Tsunhua Pao-ting-fu extreme danger. Chinese troops useless. Peking Tien-tsin daily threatened. Railways destroyed. Telegraphs cut. Chinese Government paralyzed. Imperial edicts

---

225 Edward Hurd Conger, 1843–1907, was the United States' Minster in Peking, having previously been a US congressman from 1885–1890, and US Minister to Brazil. He left Peking in 1905 to be US ambassador to Mexico, but resigned that year due to ill-health and returned to his home in California.

double-faced, favour 'Boxers.' Universal peril unless situation promptly relieved. Thirty Americans convened regard outlook practically hopeless.

It would be interesting to know if this telegram ever reached Washington.

On the 7th Lao Fa and Lang Fang, two more stations on the railway, were burnt. Then word came that the foreign-drilled soldiers of General Nieh[226] sent from Lutai to guard the railway had fired upon the "Boxers" and killed "some hundreds," and the news gave us encouragement. Immediately after, however, the Legations learnt that General Nieh had subsequently to the fight wired to Yung Lu[227] asking if he should continue to fire upon the "Boxers," and had received the reply, "Disperse them by pacific means; don't fire." And the indication of policy thus given was confirmed immediately after by the ominous intelligence that General Nieh's troops had been recalled to Tien-tsin and Lutal as punishment for having fired upon the "loyal and patriotic brotherhood." Clearly the sympathies of the Government were with the "Boxers."

---

226 General Nie Shicheng, 1830–1900, fought the French (1885) and the Japanese (1895). He initially suppressed the Boxers but then withdrew, retuning to battle with foreign forces when they landed in Tianjin in July 1900. Killed in battle.

227 Better known as Jung-Lu, 1836–1903, he was a mercurial Manchu and close ally of Dowager Empress Tzu-hsi (Cixi), a member of the Plain White Banner. Official in the Ching government starting in the Board of Works. During the British and French invasion of Peking in 1860 he was in charge of the police in the suburbs of Peking. He was soon noticed by the Empress Dowager. He 'retired' in 1879, under a cloud, but retained his rank as commander of the Peking Gendarmerie. He was recalled in 1887, made a chamberlain of the Imperial Bodyguard, followed by Tartar General of the Manchu garrison at Xi'an in 1891 until 1895. He returned to Peking in 1895 to head the police and serve in the Tsungli Yamen. At the end of the Sino-Japanese War in 1895 he became president of the Board of War and in 1896 Associate Grand Secretary. He led the reorganisation of the army and was responsible for Yuan Shikai's appointment to Chili. He was opposed to reform and was anti-foreign; in 1895 'memorialised' the Emperor advising against the establishment of railroads, mines, telegraph lines, paper currency, factories, a modern army and navy, Westernized schools, and even the post office. The only foreign thing he did not condemn was firearms which could be used to oppose foreign aggression. He kept his head down during the Boxer uprising and in spite of his tacit support he managed to profit from it. He was appointed Grand Secretary in succession to Li Hung-chang. Jung-lu died soon afterwards. A man with a finger in every pie.

3 | 'THE SIEGE OF THE PEKING LEGATIONS'

The construction of the railway from Tien-tsin to Peking had been strenuously opposed by the Chinese on the ground that it would permit the passage of foreign troops to the capital; its destruction could hardly be regarded by them as a calamity, but rather as strengthening the position in the capital.

More troops were sent for to reinforce the Legation guards in Peking, but they were sent for too late. Already many miles of the railway had been torn up, and it was hopeless to expect an early restoration of communication. The movement was spreading northwards, the railway works at Tongshan were threatened, the missionaries in Kalgan were menaced, and the Russian Greek church at Tung Ting An, 35 miles north of Peking, one of the oldest churches in the north of China, was burnt to the ground.

On June 9 one of the secretaries of the Tsung-li-Yamên, a Manchu who has been abroad and speaks French with fluency, called as an intermediary upon Sir Claude MacDonald. He is a frequent visitor at the British Legation and has no anti-foreign prejudices. An incident occurred in connexion with his visit that gave cause for thought, Sir Claude bluntly said to him that he had been informed that a massacre of the foreigners in Peking had been determined on by the present anti-foreign Government. A Chinese would have laughed away the suggestion, but the secretary changed colour and, assuming a look of serious gravity, said nothing. Sir Claude was so convinced, from the man's manner, that treachery was contemplated that he reported the incident to his colleagues. Then peremptory messages were sent ordering up the reinforcements. They were to leave Tien-tsin next day, come as far as possible by rail, and then march overland. At an audience with the Tsung-li-Yamên later in the day the American Minister was struck with the arrogant, almost insolent, bearing of the Ministers. What matter, they said to him and to the other foreign representatives, if the railway was destroyed. "What did your Excellency do before the railway was constructed; how did you get along then?"

The Empress-Dowager and the Emperor, who had been for some time past at the Summer Palace returned to Peking, entering the city at the same hour by different gates. Large escorts of cavalry and infantry accompanies them; Manchu bannermen in large numbers were posted on the walls. It was noticeable that the bodyguard of the Empress was provided by the renegade Mohammedan rabble of Tung-fuh-siang, who had long been a menace to foreigners in the province. The return of the Court was expected to have a tranquillizing effect upon the populace. But this was not the case, Students were attacked when riding in the country; our racecourse, grand stand, and stables were burnt by "Boxers" armed with knives; Europeans could not venture along the streets outside the foreign quarter without being insulted. People were saying everywhere, "The foreigners are to be ended." Streets were being patrolled by cavalry, but there was every fear that the patrols were in league with the "Boxers," who were marching through the streets bearing banners inscribed "Fa Ching Mieh Yang." "Protect Pure (the Dynasty), exterminate the foreigner."

Hatamen, Peking.
Mitchell Library, Sydney

Foreign Preparations for Defence

The London Mission and the Society for the Propagation of the Gospel handed over their buildings to the Chinese authorities, holding them responsible for their safe keeping, and all missionaries and their families went to the British Legation.

The American Board Mission likewise delivered over their valuable property to the Government and fell back upon the great Methodist

Episcopalian Mission near the Hatamen Gate, beyond the foreign quarter. Tung-chau missionaries and their families and several hundred Christian converts were already gathered there. Steps were at once taken to fortify the compound. Under the direction of Mr. F. D. Gamewell[228] deep trenches were dug, earthworks thrown up, and barbed-wire entanglements laid down. Watch was kept and sentries posted, provisions laid in, and all preparations made to withstand a siege. Twenty marines and a captain from the American Legation were sent as a guard, and some spare rifles were obtained from the British Legation. Converts were armed with pikes and knives, and a determined effort was to be made in case of attack. The mission was, however, absolutely at the mercy of any force holding the high city wall and Hatamen Gate. Without the power of reply the small garrison could have been shot down from the wall, which is little more than a stone's throw from the nearest point of the compound. Shell-fire such as was subsequently used against the Legations would have smashed the buildings into fragments.

All the Maritime Customs staff and their families living in the East City, a mile or more beyond the foreign quarter, the professors and teachers of the Tung-wen-Kuaan, Dr. Dudgeon, Mr. Pethick, the secretary of Li Hung Chang, and others, were forced to abandon their homes and come in for protection. Preparations for defence went on at all the Legations, for it was now inevitable that we should have to fight. A *conseil de guerre* was held, attended by all the military officers, and a plan of defence determined. The palace and grounds of Prince Su, opposite the British Legation, were to be held for the Christian refugees, and an area was to be defended some half a mile long by half a mile broad, bounded by the Austrian and Italian Legations to the east, the street running over the north bridge of the canal to the north, the British, Russian, and American Legations to the west, while the southern boundary was to be the street running at the foot of the great City Wall from the American Legation on the west, past the German Legation on the east, to the lane running from the Wall north past the French Legation, the buildings of the Inspectorate General of

---

228 Francis Dunlap Gamewell, 1857–1950, went to China with the American Methodist Episcopal Mission in 1881.

Customs, and the Austrian Legation. All women and children and non-combatants were to come into the British Legation. Each position was to be held as long as possible, and the final stand was to be made at the British Legation. No question of surrender could ever be entertained, for surrender meant massacre.

On the 10th it was announced that reinforcements were on the way and that they were coming with the approval of the Viceroy and of the Chinese Government, an approval more readily accorded since it was known to the Viceroy that the troops could not come by train. More than one of the Ministers was so confident that they were coming that carts were sent to await their arrival at Machia-pu, the terminal railway station at Peking. One of the foreign Ministers meeting me to-day said, "Thus I have telegraphed to my Government:— Day and night for 15 days the foreign Ministers have been armed to the teeth to protect themselves against the soldiers of the Government to which they are accredited. They are not a Government, they are brigands." His indignation was intensified when he read the disgraceful decree which was issued in the evening. In this no reference was made to the alarming condition of the city which had driven the Europeans under the protection of foreign guards; no allusion was made to the incendiarism at Tung-chau, to the murder of missionaries, to the wholesale massacre of native Christians not at all. But a direct insult was thrown in the face of the foreign Ministers. The movement against which they had unavailingly protested was held up to ridicule by saying that another abusive coolie had been arrested for insulting conduct in the street, and then Government gave its first public official recognition of the "Boxers" by announcing that the notorious chief of the "Boxers," Prince Tuan, had been appointed President of the Tsung-li-Yamên. Prince Ching was superseded but was not removed from the Yamên. One harmless old Chinese, Liao Shouheng, was sent into retirement while four rabidly anti-foreign Manchus entirely ignorant of all foreign affairs were appointed members. The last hope of any wisdom springing from the Yamên disappeared with the supersession of Prince Ching by the anti-foreign barbarian who, more than any other man in China, was responsible for the outbreak.

The following morning most of the Europeans rode to Machia-pu to await the arrival of the foreign troops. They waited, but no troops came, and then rode back past the jeering faces of hordes of Chinese soldiers. Our security was not increased by this fiasco.

Murder of the Japanese Secretary

Soldiers sent to guard the summer residences of the British Legation in the Western Hills left their posts during the night. The buildings had been officially placed under the protection of the Imperial Government. In the pre-arranged absence of the soldiers the buildings were attacked by "Boxers" and entirely burnt to the ground; the soldiers witnessed if they did not assist in the burning. But worse events were to happen that day. In the afternoon news passed through Peking that Mr. (Akira) Sugiyama, the Chancellor of the Japanese Legation, had been murdered by soldiers. He had been sent by his Minister a second time to Machia-pu to await the arrival of the troops. Passing unarmed and alone in his cart beyond the Yung-ting Mên, the outer gate on the way to the station, he was seized by the soldiers of Tung fuh-siang, dragged from his cart, and done to death in the presence of a crowd of Chinese who witnessed his struggles with unpitying interest and unconcealed satisfaction. A "mafoo" in the service of the American Legation waiting at Machia-pu in the vain hope of seeing the train arrive was warned to quit there, speedily and was cursed for being in the service of the foreigners. He rode to the Yung-ting Mên where he saw the foreigner lying dead and mutilated, but was not permitted to enter, and, riding furiously, he came round by another gate and so breathless into the Legation. Mr. Narahara, the second secretary, at once, went to the Yamên, but no attempt was made to recover the body. The heart was cut out and, there is every reason to believe, was sent as a trophy to the savage General Tung fuh-siang himself. No attempt was ever made to recover the body, and the following morning my servant, sent by me to inquire, found his mutilated body roughly covered with earth at the place were it had been murdered. One leg was exposed and children, to the amusement of their elders, were poking at it with sticks.

A decree published after the murder attributed the crime to the action of desperadoes outside the city, whereas it was notorious that the murder was committed by the soldiers of Tung-fuh-siang, the favourite bodyguard of the Empress Dowager. In another decree General Nieh was censured, apparently for his too energetic treatment of the Boxers, but was permitted to retain his command and make amends for his misdeeds. Chao Shu-chiao, who knew well the master he was serving, published his report on the "Boxer" troubles at Chob-hau and on the railway, and with sublime effrontery attributed the disasters, not to the "Boxers," but to the foreign-drilled soldiers of General Nieh. Telegraph communication by every route was cut. Almost, the last of the servants who were not Christians fled from their masters.

On the 12th a deputation, consisting of Chi Hsiu, a member of the Grand Council and newly appointed to the Yamên, Hsu Ching-cheng, the ex-Minister, the "Boxer" leader Chao Shu-chiao, and another Manchu, called upon the British Minister. Chi Hsiu made a long address, his theme being the enduring nature of the friendship between China and England and the duty which China has always recognized as a sacred obligation to protect the members of the Legations who were her guests and the strangers within her walls. Chi Hsiu assured the Minister that the movement was at an end, that all was now tranquil, and that there was no more reason to fear. Yet the very next day Baron von Ketteler[229] himself captured a "Boxer" from amid the crowd in Legation street. He carried the consecrated headpiece, and was armed with a sword. Round his waist he had a belt containing a talisman of yellow paper smeared with mystic red symbols by which he was rendered "impermeable to foreign bullets." And in the afternoon the "Boxers" came down in force from the north of the city and the burning of foreign buildings began.

The cry arose that the "Boxers" were coming. Every man ran to his post, a cordon was established round the foreign quarter and no one was allowed to pass. Guards were on watch at all the Legations, but their numbers, spread over so many posts, were very inadequate, and they were still further reduced by the guards detached for duty at the Pei-tang Cathedral, where, three miles distant within the Imperial City, were gathered in the one great compound Mgr.[230] Favier, the Bishop, his

---

229 Clemens August Freiherr von Ketteler, 1853–1900, was a German career diplomat, fluent in Chinese. The peace settlement required a monument to be erected in his honour. See photo on p. 137.
230 Mgr is an abbreviation of Monseigneur, an honorific title bestowed on senior Catholic prelates by the Pope.

3 | 'THE SIEGE OF THE PEKING LEGATIONS'

coadjutor, Mgr. Jarlin, the missionaries and lay brothers, the sisters of charity, and a vast concourse of Christian refugees, estimated at 2,000, who had fled from the massacre in the country.

A guard of five Austrians was sent to the Belgian Legation. The Austrians with their machine gun commanded the Customs-street leading to the north; the Italians with a one pounder commanded the Legation-street to the east. The British with their Nordenfeldt swept the Canal-street to the north and the North-bridge, the Russians were on the South-bridge, while the Americans with their Colt machine gun had command of Legation-street to the west as far as the court facing the Imperial Palace. The Russians, having no gun, dropped their heavy ammunition down the well.

The Massacre of Native Christians

As darkness came on the most awful cries were heard in the city, most demoniacal and unforgettable, the cries of the "Boxers," "Sha kweitze"—"Kill the devils"—mingled with the shrieks of the victims and the groans of the dying. For "Boxers" were sweeping through the city massacring the native Christians and burning them alive in their homes. The first building to be burned was the chapel of the Methodist Mission in the Hata Mên-street. Then flames sprang up in many quarters of the city. Amid the most deafening uproar the Tung-tang, or East Cathedral, shot flames into the sky. The old Greek Church in the northeast of the city, the London Mission buildings, the handsome pile of the American Board Mission, and the entire foreign buildings belonging to the Imperial Maritime Customs in the East City burned throughout the night. It was an appalling sight.

Late in the night a large party of "Boxers" bearing torches were seen moving down Customs street towards the Austrian Legation. The machine gun mounted was in waiting for them. They were allowed to come within 150 yards in the open street near the great cross road, and then the order was given and the gun rained forth death. It was a grateful sound. The torches disappeared. They had come within a restricted space, and none, we thought, could have escaped. Eagerly we went forth to count the dead, expecting to find them in heaps. But there was not one dead. The gun had been aimed very wide of the mark. Two hundred yards north of the "Boxers" there is a place where 30ft. above the level road the telegraph wires crossed to the station. Next morning they were found to have been cut by the Austrian fire. The only persons who suffered injury were possible wayfarers two miles up the street. There can be little doubt that this fiasco helped to confirm the Boxers in a belief in their invulnerability.

The Tung-tang, or East Cathedral, having been burned, it was clear that the Nan-tang, the South Cathedral, was in danger. Père Garrigues, the aged priest of the Tung-tang, had refused to leave his post and had perished in the flames. But the fathers and sisters at the Nan-tang might yet be saved. Their lives were in great peril; it was necessary to act quickly. A party of French gentlemen, led by M. Fliche of the French Legation and accompanied by M. and Mme. Chamot, rode out at night, and early the following morning safely escorted to the hotel every member of the mission—Père d'Addosio and his two colleagues, a French brother, five sisters of charity, and some twenty native nuns of the Order of Josephine. They were rescued just in time. Scarcely had they reached a place of safety when the splendid edifice they had forsaken was in flames. To the sky wreathed the smoke, a pillar of cloud marking the destruction, not of a faith, but of a nation. This historic pile of great historical interest, the home of Verbiest and Schaal,[231] with its memorial tablet given to the cathedral by the emperor Kang Hsi, was ruthlessly sacrificed. It continued burning all day, the region round it, the chief Catholic centre of Peking, being also burnt. Acres of houses were destroyed and the Christians in thousands put to the sword.

Watch was still kept. Streets within the area to be defended were kept clear. Barricades were thrown up and every preparation begun for the defence which seemed inevitable, though there was still hope that reinforcements would arrive before it was too late. Postal couriers were

---

231 Ferdinand Verbiest, 1623–1688, was an influential Jesuit missionary who arrived in China in 1658 and went to Peking in 1660 to assist Adam Schall von Bell, 1592–1666, in the Imperial Astronomical Bureau. He survived the 1664–69 persecution if Christians and proved his worth the Kangxi, emperor by his superior astronomical calculations compared those of Chinese experts. He transferred western canon manufacturing technology to the Qing and in 1678 facilitated a Sino-Russian treaty which opened trade routes through Siberia.

3 | 'THE SIEGE OF THE PEKING LEGATIONS'

prevented from passing through the enemy lines, and only the scantiest information reached us from outside. During the evening "Boxers" were killed on the North-bridge endeavouring to rush the British sentries.

On the 15th rescue parties were sent out by the American and Russian Legations in the morning, and by the British and German Legations in the afternoon, to save if possible native Christians from the burning ruins around the Nan-tang. Awful sights were witnessed. Women and children hacked to pieces, men trussed like fowls, with noses and ears cut off and eyes gouged out. Chinese Christians accompanied the reliefs and ran about in the labyrinth of network of streets that formed the quarter, calling upon the Christians to come out from their hiding places. All through the night the massacre had continued, and "Boxers" were even now shot redhanded at their bloody work. But their work was still incomplete, and many hundreds of women and children bad escaped. They came out of their hiding-places crossing themselves and pleading for mercy. It was a most pitiful sight. Thousands of soldiers on the wall, witnessed the rescue; they had with callous hearts witnessed the massacre without ever raising a hand to save. During the awful nights of the 13th and 14th Duke Lan, the brother of Prince Tuan, and Chao Shu-Chiao, of the Tsung-li Yamên, had followed round in their carts to gloat over the spectacle. Yet the Chinese Government were afterwards to describe this massacre done under official supervision under the very walls of the Imperial Palace as the handiwork of local banditti.

More than 1,200 of the poor refugees were escorted by the "foreign devils" to a place of safety. Many were wounded, many were burnt beyond recognition. All had suffered the loss of everything they possessed in the world. They were given quarters in the palace grounds of Prince Su,[232] opposite the British Legation. Among them was the aged mother and the nephew of Ching Chang, recently Minister to France, and now, Chinese Commissioner to the Paris Exhibition. The nephew was cruelly burnt; nearly every, other member of the

---

[232] Shan Ch'i, 1866–1922, Manchu and clansman of the Imperial family. Had large estates in Manchuria which were lost to the Russians after the Boxer uprising. He supported modernisation, especially of the police and the monarchy. He later supported the Japanese and his daughter, who adopted a Japanese the name Yoshiko Kawashima, was a notorious spy, executed as a traitor at the end of WW2.

family was murdered. A Catholic family of much distinction—a family Catholic for seven generations—was thus almost exterminated and its property laid in ashes.

It was announced this day that only "Boxers" might enter the Imperial City. The Government was rushing headlong to its ruin.

On the June 16 a party of 20 British, ten Americans, and five Japanese, with some Volunteers, and accompanied by Lieutenant Colonel Shiba,[233] the Japanese military attaché, patrolled the East City, visiting the ruins in the hopes that some Christians might yet be in hiding. But to our calls everywhere no reply was given. Refugees, however, from, the East City had managed to escape miraculously and find their way, many of them wounded, to the foreign Legations, seeking that protection and humanity that was denied them by their own people. As the patrol was passing a Taoist temple on the way, a noted "Boxer" meeting place, cries were heard within. The temple was forcibly entered. Native Christians were found there, their hands tied behind their backs awaiting execution and torture. Some had already been put to death, and their bodies were still warm and bleeding. All were shockingly mutilated. Their fiendish murderers were at their incantations burning incense before their gods, offering Christians in sacrifice to their angered deities. They shut themselves within the temple, but their defence availed them nothing. Every one of them, 46 in all, was in "Boxer" uniform armed with sword and lance. Retribution was swift; every man was shot to death without mercy.

In the afternoon a fire broke out in the foreign drug store in the native city outside the great gate of the Chien Mên. It was the work of "Boxers," done while the soldiers were looking on. In order to burn the foreign drug store and do the foreigners a few pounds worth of damage, they did not hesitate to jeopardize by fire property worth millions of

---

233 Goro Shiba, 1860–1945, of an established samurai family from Aizu, in now Fukushima prefecture, in easter Honshu. A Chinese and English speaker Shiba previously served in China, Britain and the United States as military attaché, observing among other things, the Spanish-American War and the US invasion of Cuba. After the uprising he had a distinguished military career, received a knighthood from the British, and retired, a general, in 1930. He committed suicide in August 1945 following Japan's defeat in World War 2.

3 | 'THE SIEGE OF THE PEKING LEGATIONS'

pounds, and that is what happened. Adjoining buildings took fire, the flames spread to the booksellers' street, and the most interesting street in China, filled with priceless scrolls, manuscripts, and printed books, was gutted from end to end. Fire licked up house after house, and soon the conflagration was the most disastrous ever known in China, reducing to ashes the richest part of Peking, the pearl and jewel shops, the silk and fur, the satin and embroidery stores, the great curio shops, the gold and silver shops, the meeting houses, and nearly all that was of the highest value in the metropolis. Irreparable was the damage done. From the street below the fire spread to the central outer Chien Mên gate, which directly faces the Imperial Palace, and which is only thrown open for the passage of the Emperor. An imposing temple crowns this wall; it was engulfed in the conflagration. The great tiled roof with its upturned gables fell with a crash of falling worlds, while great volumes of smoke spread like a pall over the Imperial Palace foreboding the doom of the Imperial house. It was a sight never to be forgotten.

While the fire was in progress another broke out in the houses at the end of Legation street, and the triumphal archway was consumed. Fear of fire was to be added to other dangers assailing us.

The Chinese Government and the Legations

During the night the Americans, fearing an attack from the street at the back of their Legation, kept the street clear till daybreak. During one of the volleys four of the Tsung-li Yamên Ministers called upon the American Minister. They were blandly assuring him that all was now quiet, that there was no need for further alarm, that great was the tenderness of the Throne for men from afar, when a rattle of musketry was heard which rendered them speechless with fear. They hurriedly went away. Assurances of the Throne's tenderness did not deceive us. Our barricades were everywhere strengthened and defences systematically planned, for rumour was quick to reach us that the relief forces had been driven back to Tien-tsin, and this did not add to the security of our position.

Inside the Imperial City wall, within one hundred yards of the British picket on the north bridge a large Chinese camp was formed. Peking was in a state of panic, all the streets near the foreign quarters were empty, and people were fleeing from the city. There was a run on the banks, and the Ssu-ta-heng, the four great banks, the leading banks of Peking, closed their doors, and paper money was not in circulation. The Palace of Prince Su was occupied by the refugees, and its defence, the most important of all and a vital one to the British Legation, was entrusted to Colonel Shiba and Japanese marines and volunteers.

The crisis was approaching. On the morning of June 19 Mr. Cordes, the Chinese Secretary of the German Legation, was at the Yamen, when the secretaries told him that the allied fleets had taken the Ta-ku forts on June 17. This was remembered when at 4 30 in the afternoon an ultimatum was sent to the foreign Ministers. It was a bolt from the blue. They were to leave Peking within 24 hours.

A despatch, they wrote, has arrived from the Viceroy Yu Lu, forwarding a note which he has received from the *doyen* of the Consular body in Tien-tsin, the French Comte du Chaylard, to say that, unless foreign troops are at once permitted to land at Tien-tsin, the allied fleets will bombard the Ta-ku forts. As this is equivalent to a declaration of war, the Tsung-li-Yamên herewith notify the foreign Ministers that they must leave Peking within 24 hours, otherwise protection cannot be guaranteed to them. They will be given safe conduct and transport.

It was quite in accordance with Chinese custom that a despatch saying that the seizure of the Ta ku forts had been threatened should be sent after the seizure had been effected. What is distasteful to them to say they avoid saying.

A meeting of the diplomatic body was at once held. It was decided to accept the ultimatum. They had been given their passports by the Chinese Government; what other course was open to them? They drew up the following letter and despatched it to the Yamen:–

Pékin, le 19 Juin, 1900.[234]

Altesses et Excellences, Les Ministres étrangers ont reçus avec grand étonnement la note que le Tsung-li-Yamen leur a envoyée

---

234 Peking, 19 June 1900.
Highnesses and Excellencies, The Foreign Ministers have received with great astonishment the note sent to them by the Tsung-li-Yamen of today's date. They know

en date d'aujourd'hui. Ils me savent absolument rien de ce que la note contient au sujet de ce qui a pu se passer au forts de Ta-ku.

Les Ministres étrangers ne peuvent qu'accepter la déclaration et la demande que leur fait le Yamen et se sont disposée à quitter Pékin. II est seulement matériellement impossible d'organiser le départ dans le court délai de 24 heures. Le Gouvernement Chinois doit considérer qu'ilya un grand nombre de dames et d'enfants, et qu'est un très nombreux convoi que l'on doit organiser. Le Tsung-li-Yamen nous dit qu'il nous donnera des sécurités pour la route. Les Ministres étrangers désireraient savoir en quoi consistent ces sécurités, attendu que la campagne est pleine des rebelles.

Nous ne doutons pas de la loyale volonté du Gouvernement Chinois a notre égard, mais, puisqu'il y a des soldats étrangers en route qui marchent vers Pékin pour coopérer amicalement avec les forces du Gouvernement au rétablissement de l'ordre, les Ministres étrangers désirent que ces détachements soient vite prévenus, afin qu'ils puissent se joindre à nous pour partir tous ensemble.

absolutely nothing about what the note contains about what may have happened at Ta-ku forts.

The Foreign Ministers can only accept the declaration and the request made to them by Yamen and are ready to leave Peking. It is only materially impossible to organize departure within the short period of 24 hours. The Chinese Government must consider that their is a large number of ladies and children, and that there is a very large convoy to be organized. The Tsung-li-Yamen tells us that he will give us security for the road. Foreign Ministers would like to know of what these securities consist, as the countryside is full of rebels.

We do not doubt the loyal will of the Chinese Government towards us, but since there are foreign soldiers on their way who are marching towards Peking to co-operate amicably with the forces of the Government in restoring order, the Foreign Ministers desire that these detachments be quickly notified, so that they can join us to leave together.

Foreign Ministers must also request means of transport, carts, boats, and provisions, and also to be accompanied by some of the Ministers of Tsung-li-Yamen.

To settle all these questions, the members of the Diplomatic Corps ask to be received by Prince Ch'ing at Prince Tuan tomorrow, Wednesday, at 9 o'clock in the morning.

The Diplomatic Corps expects an immediate response.

> Les Ministres étrangers doivent demander en outre des moyens de transport, charrettes, bateaux, et provisions, et aussi d'être accompagnes par quelques uns des Ministres du Tsung-li-Yamèn.
>
> Pour régler toutes ces questions, les membres du Corps Diplomatique demandent à être reçus par le Prince Ch'ing at le Prince Tuan demain, Mercredi, à 9 heures du matin.
>
> Le Corps Diplomatique attend une réponse immediate.

Word was passed round that preparation had to be made to leave Peking the following day. Mr. Conger, the American Minister, asked for 100 carts; and his Legation spent most of the night making preparations. No packing was done at the British Legation, for it was there considered inconceivable that China should insist upon sending the Ministers their passports. Only two days before, in the Peking Gazette of June 17, it had been officially announced that the road to Tien-tsin was unsafe. "If," it said, "the Ministers and their families wish to go for a time to Tien-tsin, they must be protected on the way; but the railroad is not now in working order. If they go by the cart road, it will be difficult, and it is feared that perfect protection cannot be guaranteed. The Ministers and their families will therefore do better to abide here in peace as heretofore, and wait until the railroad is repaired." When the decision of the Diplomatic Body became known in Peking the most profound indignation was everywhere expressed at so unworthy a decision and the most profound astonishment that such a course of action should have received the support of M. Pichon, the French Minister, "Protecteur des Missions Catholiques en Chine," and of so humane a man as Mr. Conger, the American Minister; for to leave Peking meant the immediate abandonment to massacre of the thousands of native Christians who had trusted the foreigner and believed in his good faith.

The Murder of Baron Von Ketteler

Early on the morning of the 20th a meeting of the Diplomatic Body was held at the French Legation. No reply had been received from the Tsung-li-Yamen to the request for an audience and the proposition that all the Ministers should go to the Yamen found no seconder. Had it

3 | 'THE SIEGE OF THE PEKING LEGATIONS'

been, carried out, there would have occurred one of the most appalling massacres on record. Two chairs later left for the Yamên. In the first was the German Minister, Baron von Ketteler, who had this advantage over other Ministers, that he spoke Chinese fluently. In the second was the Chinese Secretary of the German Legation, Mr. Cordes. News travels quickly in Peking. Not many minutes later my boy burst into my office—"Any man speakee have makee kill German Minister!" It was true. The German Minister had been assassinated by an Imperial officer. The Secretary had been grievously wounded, but, running for his life, shot at by a hundred rifles, had escaped as if by a miracle. A patrol of 15 men under Count Soden, the commander, went out to recover the body. Fired on by Chinese soldiers from every side, they were forced to retire. Lying ill in hospital, Mr. Cordes made this graphic statement to me:—[235]

> On the afternoon of the 19th of June I was sent to the Tsung-li-Yamên by Baron von Ketteler as on the previous day to demand once more the withdrawal of the Kan-sub troops of Tung-fuh-siang stationed at a distance of a few paces from our posts in the electric light works. The Secretary, who received me, and whom I had known for many years, was extremely nervous. There had been a great change in the position, he said. The foreign admirals had taken the Ta-ku forts, and it would be very hard to keep the Chinese troops in hand. Discussion seemed useless. I left my message for Yung Lu, the Grand Secretary, Commander-in-Chief, and came away. At 5 o'clock the ultimatum of the Tsung-li-Yamên was sent to the Ministers, giving them 24 hours' notice to leave Peking. Believing the note to have been inspired by an access of madness, and hoping that China might still be amenable to reason, Baron von Ketteler sent a note in the evening to the Yamên asking for an interview with the Princes and Ministers of the Yamên at 9 a.m. the following morning.

---

235 In December 1900, Morrison received a letter from Edith Blake, the wife of Hong Kong Governor, Sir Henry Blake. She asked, having read this account of the siege, "Do you not think that Baron von Ketteler having shot the Boxer in the German Legation and making the German Guard fire on the Boxers going though their incantations in the Chinese City ... had a good deal to say to his murder?" Lo, op. cit., p. 153.

The signed receipt of this note is now in the German Legation. On the morning of the 20th, no word having come from the Yamên that the Princes and Ministers would be unable to receive my Minister, Baron von Ketteler, after the conference with the other Ministers, and I set out for the Yamên in two chairs. An armed escort of a non-commissioned officer and four men was ready to accompany us, but the Baron decided that it was wiser to leave it behind, partly because the. passage through the streets of armed foreign soldiers might arouse, excitement, but mainly because the Tsung-li-Yamên knew that the Minister was coming, and would therefore ensure him the protection due to a foreign Envoy. We were both unarmed. Our chairs were accompanied by two Chinese outriders from the Legation. We left the French Legation, where the conference had been held, passed the Austrian Legation, then turned along the Ch'ang-An-street into the Hata Mên-street. Along the raised way in the centre of this street our chairs were carried, one mafo as usual riding in front and the other behind. We passed the Arch of Honour near the Belgian Legation, and were close to the police station on the left. I was watching a cart with some lance-bearers passing before the Minister's chair, when suddenly I saw a sight that made my heart stand still. The Minister's chair was three paces in front of me. I saw a banner soldier, apparently a Manchu, in full uniform with a mandarin's hat with a button and blue feather, step forward, present his rifle within a yard of the chair window, level it at the Minister's head and fire. I shouted in terror, "Halt." At the same moment the shot rang out, the chairs were thrown down. I sprang to my feet. A shot struck me in the lower part of my body. Others were fired at me. I saw the Minister's chair still standing, but there was no movement. One moment's hesitation would have been fatal. I ran, wounded as I was, 50 paces to the north, and turned down the street to the east, a lively rifle fire following me. Looking back I saw the Minister's chair still standing. There was no sign of life. Believing myself to be in the street leading to the Tsung-Li-Yamên, I ran on thinking to report what had happened, and perhaps find protection. But it was not the street. Two men armed with lances

3 | 'THE SIEGE OF THE PEKING LEGATIONS'

pursued me, but fearing I was armed left me. Then I resolved to try and reach the American Mission buildings near the Hata Mèn Gate. Dripping with blood I dragged myself along, often down crowded streets filled with Chinese who witnessed my struggle without pity and without emotion, and without even replying to my question as to the direction. I overheard one man remark, "A foreigner who has got his desserts!" Then, in a quiet road, a peddlar, more humane than his countrymen, gave me the direction, and in half an hour after the murder of my Minister I reached the American Mission, and fell fainting at the entrance. My wounds were dressed, and I was carried back to the German Legation.

All the chair-bearers returned safely to the Legation and both the outriders. One had immediately after the assassination ridden on to the Tsung-li-Yamên, and seeing there a secretary whom he knew had informed him of the murder of the Minister.

No Prince or Minister was at the Yamên, itself a suspicious circumstance, for it was the invariable custom when the Minister could not be present to receive a foreign envoy to send a messenger and request him not to come. That the messenger was not sent on this fatal morning, but the Minister drawn into an ambush, proves the complicity of the Chinese Government in the murder. The people who committed the murder were not brigands or men belonging to the irregular troops, but Imperial banner troops in full uniform. The men detached for the murder took up their position near a police station under the jurisdiction of Chung Li, the military commandant of Peking. Incriminating documents, discovered in a "Boxer" camp, have been found proving the complicity of Chung Li with the "Boxers" and his encouragement of a movement against foreigners, whom it was his province to protect. These were in the possession of the German Legation. Officials of the police station witnessed the murder. They knew well that the man to be murdered was the German Envoy—the Minister, not a private person, for if that had been the intention I would not have escaped. The deed was not done by the "Boxers," for no attempt was made to harm the Chinese who accompanied us, which is quite contrary to the practice of the "Boxers," whose fury is equally excited against the foreigners as against the Chinese who eat the foreigners' rice.

In conclusion, I affirm that the assassination of the German Minister was a deliberately-planned, premeditated murder, done in obedience to the orders of high Government officials by an Imperial bannerman.

Such was the statement of Mr. Heinrich Cordes, the Chinese Secretary. There was no more question about leaving for Tien-tsin.

Later in the day the Yamên, evidently indifferent to the gravity of the position created by the Government, sent an impudent despatch to the German Legation to the effect that two Germans had been proceeding in chairs along the Hata Mên-street, and at the mouth of the street leading to the Tsung-li-Yamên one of them had fired upon the crowd. The Chinese had retaliated and he had been killed.

They wished to know his name. No reply was sent, for it was felt to be a mockery. Only too well the Yamên knew whom they had murdered. Weeks passed before the body was recovered, and it was not until July 18 that any official reference was made to the murder. In the course of the morning a despatch was sent to the Diplomatic Body in reply to the answer they had sent to the ultimatum of yesterday. The country, it said, between Peking and Tien-tsin was overrun with brigands, and it would not be safe for the Ministers to go there. They should therefore remain in Peking. It is difficult to write with calmness of the treachery with which the Chinese were now acting. Four p.m. was the hour given in the ultimatum for the Ministers to vacate their Legations, but the ultimatum had been rescinded, and the Ministers invited to remain in Peking. Thus it was hoped that they would be lulled into a false security. Chinese soldiers were secretly stationed under Cover at every vantage point commanding the outposts. At 4 p.m. precisely to the minute, by preconcerted signal, they opened fire upon the Austrian and French outposts. A French marine fell shot dead through the forehead. An Austrian was wounded. The siege had begun. (To be continued.)

3 | 'THE SIEGE OF THE PEKING LEGATIONS'

Memorial to von Kettler, Peking.
Mitchell Library, Sydney

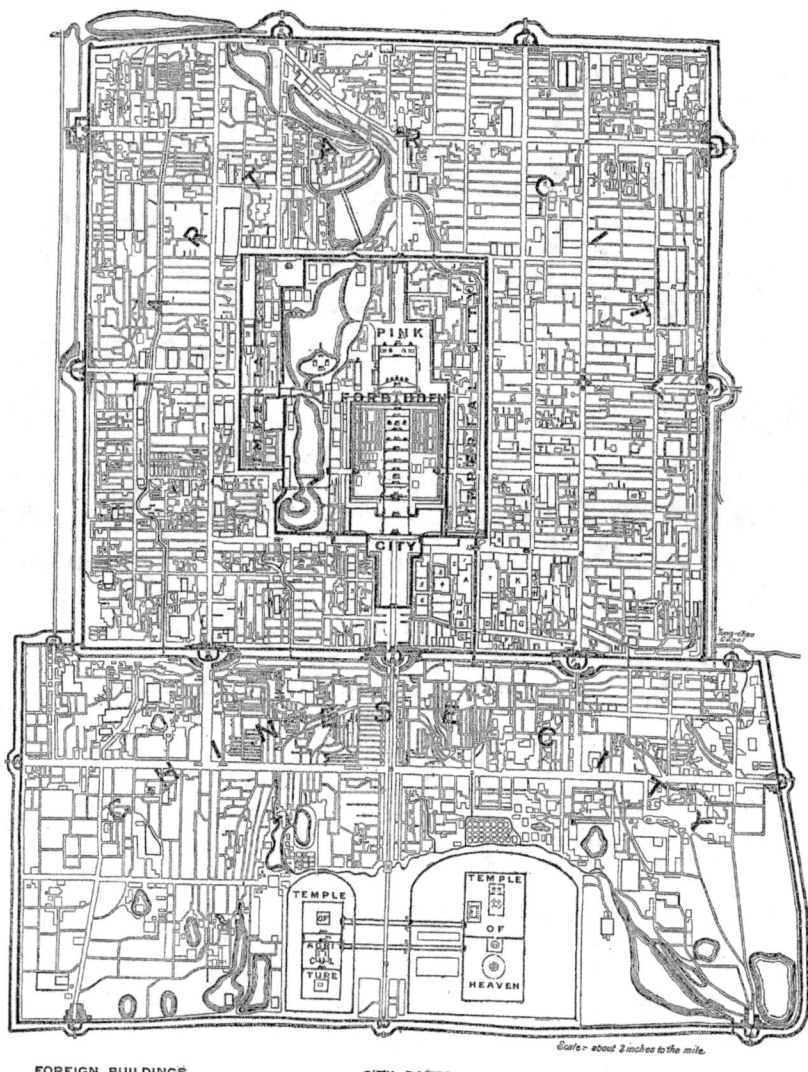

Plan of Peking accompanying 'The Seige of the Peking Legations' article published in The Times on 13 October 1900.

'The Siege of the Peking Legations'

(Continued from *The Times* of October 13)
From Our Own Correspondent, Peking, 14 August 1900[236]

The Strength of the Garrison

At this time (June 20), at the opening of the siege, the total strength of the combined Legation guards consisted of 18 officers and 389 men, distributed as follows:–

> American.— Three officers, Captain Myers in command, Captain Hall, Surgeon Lippett, and 53 marines from the Newark.
> Austrian.— Five officers, Captain Thomann, the Commander of the Zenta, Flag-Lieutenant von Winterhalder, Lieutenant Kollar, two midshipmen, and 30 marines from the Zenta.
> British.— Three officers, Captain B. M. Strouts in command, Captain Halliday, Captain Wray, and 79 men R.M.L.I—30 from ELM.S. Orlando and 49 from Wei-hai-wei.
> French.— Two officers, Captain Darcy and Midshipman Herbert, and 45 marines from the D'Entrecasteaux and Descartes.
> German.— Lieutenant Graf Soden and 51 marines of the 3rd Battalion Kiao-chau.
> Italian.— Lieutenant Paolini and 28 bluejackets from the Elba.
> Japanese.— Lieutenant Hara and 24 marines from the Atago.
> Russian.— Two officers, Lieutenant Baron von Rahden and Lieutenant von Dehn, and 79 men 72—marines from the Sissoi Veliki and Navarin and seven Legation Cossacks.
> Total, 18 officers and 389 men.

---

[236] Published on Monday 15 October 1900, pp. 3–4.

In addition the French sent Lieutenant Henry and 30 men to guard the Pei-tang Cathedral, and the Italians detached one officer, Lieutenant Cavalieri, and 11 men for the same humane mission. To this insignificant force of 18 officers and 389 men of eight nationalities the entire foreign quarter had to trust for its defence. Fortunately several visitors or residents had received military training, and they at once went on the active list and rendered invaluable service. Captain Percy Smith, late of the South Staffordshire, was in Peking on a visit when he was called upon for assistance. Captain F. G. Poole, of the East Yorkshire, who had seen service in Central Africa, was here studying Chinese, as was also Lieutenant Vroublevsky, of the Ninth Regiment Eastern Siberian Rifles. Mr. Nigel Oliphant, who had served in the Scots Greys, was in the employment of the Imperial Chinese Bank. Captain Labrousse,[237] of the French Infanterie de Marine, had only recently left Tongking, his term of service having expired, and was passing through Peking on his way home via Siberia, while Herr von Strauch, a retired officer of the Imperial German Guards, was here in the service of Sir Robert Hart. He had the advantage of speaking Chinese, for he was formerly military instructor to the army of Viceroy Chang Chih-tung. Nearly all the Japanese officers also had the advantage of speaking Chinese. Their military attaché, Lieut.-Colonel G. Shiba, took command at once. Though he had only recently returned to Peking, he knew China well, having been here as a student, and having fought through the Japanese-Chinese war. Colonel Shiba was for some years military attaché in London, and was with General Shafter's army in Cuba. Before returning to Peking he inspected the defences along the North-Western frontier of India. He is an artillery officer. Captain Morita, the assistant to Colonel Shiba, had been in Peking for six years, while Captain Ando, who raised and took command of a very effective body of Japanese volunteers, had only come to Peking two days before the interruption of communications compelled him to remain here.

---

[237] Captain Alexis Jacques Henri Labrousse, 1860–1900, was a French colonial officer. There is a memorial to him in the garden of the French embassy in Peking.

3 | 'THE SIEGE OF THE PEKING LEGATIONS'

Milling around the bulletin boards, Peking, 1900.
C.A. Killie, Mitchell Library, Sydney

Volunteers and Irregulars

A volunteer force numbering altogether 75 men, of whom 31 were Japanese, was enrolled and armed with all available rifles. They added greatly to the strength of the garrison, taking watch and watch like the Regulars, fighting behind the barricades, and never shrinking from any duty imposed upon them.

There was also an irregular force of 50 gentlemen of many nationalities, who did garrison guard duty in the British Legation and were most useful. They were known, from the gentleman who enrolled them, as "Thornbill's Roughs," and they bore themselves as the legitimate successors on foot of Roosevelt's Roughriders. Armed with a variety of weapons, from an elephant rifle to the *fusil de chasse*[238] with a picture of the Grand Prix, to all of which carving knives had been lashed as bayonets, they were known as the "Carving Knife Brigade."

---

238 A light smooth bore flintlock musket the French used for hunting.

They were formidable alike to friend and foe. For, all unaccustomed as they were to the military art—the most experienced of them was he who had once witnessed the trooping of the colour in St. James's Park—they had a habit of carrying the rifle horizontally over the shoulder, so that when they swung quickly round the blade swept into the throat of the man behind. Diversity of language was another difficulty. The opening of the wall on the southern extremity of the British Legation was not a vital point. A sentry selected from the French members of the brigade was usually stationed here. Going one dark evening his rounds, the British officer of the watch stopped here. "Sentinelle," he said, in his best Sandhurst French. There was no reply. Pursing his mouth to convey the correct accent, he raised his voice and repeated "Sentinelle," when a scared voice from the darkness replied, "Begorra! and what the h—'s that?"

Such were the effective forces. They were provided with four guns, an Italian one-pounder with 120 rounds, an American Colt with 25,000 rounds, an Austrian machine gun, and a British five-barrel Nordenfelt, pattern 1887. Rifle ammunition was very scanty. The Japanese had only 100 rounds apiece, the Russians 145, and the Italians 120, while the best provided of the other guards had only 300 rounds per man, none, too many for the siege the duration of which could not be foreseen.

Punctually, then, at 4 o'clock, Chinese soldiers began firing upon us whom they had requested to remain in peace at Peking. And immediately after the Austrian legation was abandoned. No sufficient reason has been given for this abandonment, which was done so precipitately that not an article was saved. It was left to the mercy of the Chinese, and the guard retired to the corner of Customs-lane, leaving west to the Prince's Palace. This involved the sacrifice of Sir Robert Hart's and all the Customs buildings, and hastened the advance of the Chinese westward. As previously arranged, the American mission buildings had been abandoned in the morning, for they were quite untenable. All the missionaries, their wives and families, crossed over to the British legation. Converts to the number of several hundreds joined the other refugees. The captain and 20 American marines returned to the American Legation. By an error of judgement on the part of the captain the mission was finally left in a panic. Almost nothing was saved, and nearly all the stores accumulated for a siege were lost. The British

3 | 'THE SIEGE OF THE PEKING LEGATIONS'

legation was now thronged. Rarely has a more cosmopolitan gathering been gathered together within the limits of one compound. All the women and children were there. All the missionaries, American, British, French, and Russian, all the custom staff, the French, Belgian, Russian, American, Spanish, Japanese and Italian ministers and their families, the entire unofficial foreign community of Peking, with the exception of M. Chamot, who remained in his hotel throughout, though it was in the hottest corner of the besieged area. First of the ministers to come in for protection was M. Pichon, the French minister, though there seemed to be no immediate reason for his forsaking his Legation, and his hasty retreat at the outset of the siege would have discouraged men less courageous than the fine body of marines who formed his legation guard. French volunteers bravely stood by their own Legation and the Austrian chargé d'Affaires and Mme. von Rosthorn,[239] remained there, as long as there was a room habitable. Mr. Squiers,[240] the first Secretary of the American Legation, with Mr. Cheshire, the Chinese secretary and Mr. Pethick, the well known private secretary of Li Hung Chang, stayed by the United States Legation, and the staff of the German legation also kept staunchly to their posts.

Many well-known men were to be seen among the busy community at the British Legation. M. Pokotiloff,[241] the head of the Russo-Chinese bank, whose knowledge of the Far East question is probably greater than any other living man; M. Podzneeff, the greatest living authority on Manchuria; Dr. W. A. P. Martin, the learned professor of the Tung Wen Kuan; Dr. Smith, the author of "Chinese Characteristics", and many others. After 40 years service under the Chinese government, Sir Robert Hart was driven from his home to the protection of the

---

239 Arthur von Rosthorn, 1862–1945, Austrian diplomat and Sinologist. His wife's name was Paula.
240 Herbert Goldsmith Squires, 1859–1911, soldier and diplomat. Appointed secretary of the American Legation in Peking in 1898. He left in 1902 to be Minister in Cuba. Controversy about how he acquired his magnificent collection Chinese antiquities dogged him until his death.
241 Dmitri Dmitrievich Pokotilov, 1865–1908, director of the Russo-Chinese Bank which financed the Manchurian railway, and later (1905–1908) Russian Minister where he was instrumental in negotiating railway concessions, loans, and territorial concessions. age died suddenly of a heart attack, possibly due to natural causes.

British Legation, and all the papers and correspondence and archives of the great department which he controlled left to be destroyed by the soldiers of the government he had served with such unparalleled devotion and fidelity.

Preparing for Hostilities

When the Austrians withdrew from their Legation, the British picket on the north bridge retired to the main gate, where the redoubt was built and the Nordenfelt mounted. Stores were commandeered, shops in Legation Street were stripped. Sniping began and was not discontinued till relief came. Late in the evening, Mr. Huberty James, the professor of English in the Peking University, was killed. He had rendered great service, for it was through his influence with Prince Su, that the palace had been thrown open for the Christian refugees. He seemed to have a blind faith in the Chinese. Prince Su had assured him that Yung Lu had given him his word that no soldier would fire upon a foreigner, and he believed him with the fatal confidence that was his undoing. To cross from the palace to the British legation, he went round by the North bridge, though he knew that the bridge had been evacuated. On the bridge, he was fired at by a soldier at short range, ran back apparently unhurt, and was fired at from another quarter. He raised his hands to show that he was unarmed and fell shot into the canal, where volleys were fired into his body from the water gate under the Imperial city wall. The murder was seen from the British legation, desultory firing continued through the night. One Russian marine was shot dead through the forehead. In the morning, a letter reached the American delegation from one of the captains in the relief column, dated June 14, it was written from a point only 35 miles from Peking. It was a casual chatty letter, which gave no indication that in the opinion of the writer, there was any need for hurry.

At the British legation, fortification began in real earnest, the refugees worked like coolies. Sand-bags were made by the thousand, and posts mounted round the Legation. A way was knocked through the houses to the Russian legation, so that the Americans if they had to fall back could pass through to the British legation. During the day, every Legation was exposed to a continuous fire from surrounding house tops,

3 | 'THE SIEGE OF THE PEKING LEGATIONS'

and in the case of the British Legation from the cover in the Imperial Carriage Park. Chinese put flames to the abandoned buildings and the Belgian Legation, the Austrian Legation and the Methodist Mission and some private houses were burned.

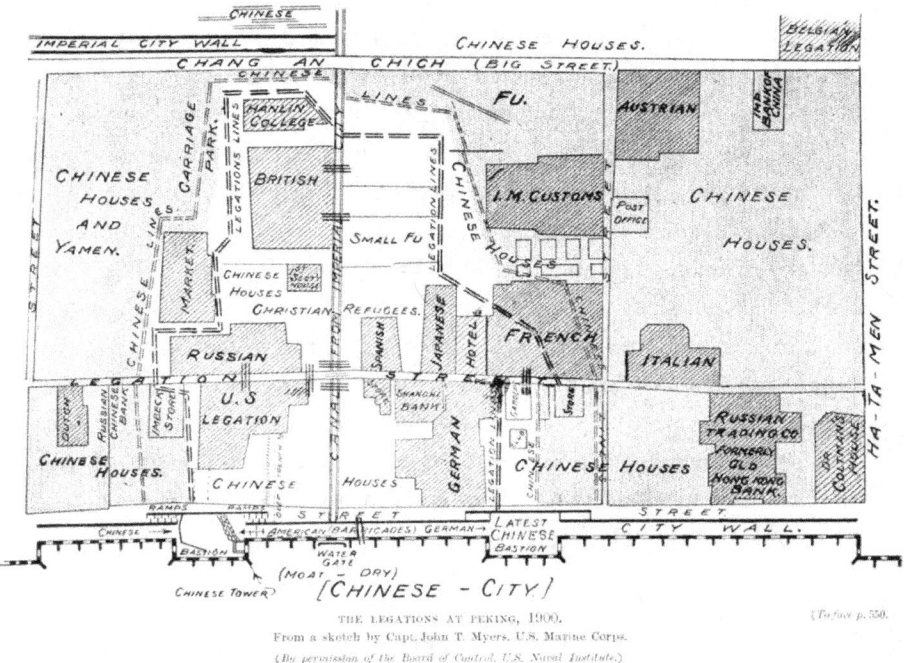

Disposition of foreign embassies in Peking at the time of the Boxer Rebellion.

Sir Claude MacDonald Assumes Command

June 22 opened disastrously. The evening before Captain Thomann,[242] the Austrian commander announced that as the senior officer, he had taken command in Peking. This morning, hearing from an irresponsible American that the American legation was abandoned, he, without taking steps to verify the information, ordered the abandonment of all the allegations east of Canal Street, the detachments to fall back upon the British Legation. There had been no casualties to speak of, none of

---

242 Eduard Anton Thomann Edler von Montalmar, 1853–1900, Capitan of SMS *Zenta*.

the Legations had been attacked, and every commander who received the order to retreat regarded the action as madness. Peremptory orders were sent to the Japanese to abandon the Princes Palace, or Fu (as I shall henceforth call it), and they retired to their Legation. In the British Legation nothing was known of the order when to the amazement of all, the Italians, Austrians and French came running down Legation Street, followed a little later by the Japanese and subsequently by the Germans who recalled their post on the wall and marched without a shot being fired at them down under the wall to Canal-street. Americans and Russians learning that all east of Canal street had been abandoned, saw themselves cut off, though their communication had not even been menaced and retreated precipitately into the British legation. It was a veritable stampede, a panic that might have been fraught with the gravest disaster. Prompt action was taken. Captain Thomann was relieved of his command and Sir Claude MacDonald, at the urgent insistence of the French and Russian ministers, subsequently confirmed by all their colleagues, assumed the chief command. The French and Austrians reoccupied the French delegation, but the barricade in Customs-street was lost. One German only was killed and the position was saved, but the blunder might have been disastrous.

Chinese Incendiarism

It was obvious from the first that the great danger at the British Legation was not so much from rifle fire as from incendiarism, for on three sides the compound was surrounded by Chinese buildings of a highly inflammable nature. Before time could be given to clear an open space around the Legation, the buildings to the rear of Mr. Cockburn's house, were set on fire, and as the wind was blowing strongly toward us, it seemed as if nothing could prevent the fire from bursting into the Legation. Water had to be used sparingly, for the wells were lower than they had been for years, yet the flames had to be fought. Bullets were whistling through the trees. Private Scadding, the first Englishman to fall, was killed while on watch on the stables near by. Men and women lined up and water passed along in buckets to a small fire engine that was played upon the fire. Walls were broken through, trees hastily cut down and desperate work saved the building. It was the first experience

3 | 'THE SIEGE OF THE PEKING LEGATIONS'

Chienmen, Peking.
Mitchell Library, Sydney

of intense excitement. Then the men set to with a will, and till late at night were demolishing the temple and buildings outside the wall of the Legation. Work was continued in the morning, but when it was proposed to pull down an unimportant building in the Hanlin Academy that abuts the Legation to the north, the proposition was vetoed. Such desecration, it was said, would wound the susceptibilities of the Chinese government. It was, "the most sacred building in China," to lay hands upon it, even to safeguard the lives of beleaguered women and children could not be thought of for fear of wounding the susceptibility of the Chinese government! So little do the oldest of us understand the Chinese.

A strong wind was blowing from the Hanlin into the Legation. The distance separating the nearest building from the Minister's residence was only a few feet. Fire the one and the Minister's residence would have been in danger. Suddenly, there was the alarm of fire. Smoke was rising from the Hanlin. The most venerated pile in Peking, the great Imperial Academy, centre of all Chinese learning, with its priceless collection of books and manuscripts, was in flames. Everyone who was off duty rushed to the back of the Legation. The Hanlin had been occupied during the night by Imperial soldiers, who did not hesitate in their rage to destroy foreigners to set fire to the building. It was first necessary to clear the temple. A breach was made in the wall, Captain Poole, headed a force of Marines and volunteers who rushed in, divided, searched the courts, and returned to the main pavilion with its superb pillars and memorial tablets. Chinese were rushing from other burning pavilions to the main entrance. They were taken by surprise and many were killed, but they had done their evil deed. Other great libraries have been destroyed by the victorious invader. What can be thought of a nation which destroys its own most sacred edifice, the pride and glory of its learned men throughout the centuries, in order to wreak vengeance upon the foreigner?

To save the Legation, it was necessary to continue the destruction and dismantle the library buildings. With great difficulty, with inadequate tools, the buildings were pulled down. Trees and dangerous opposition were felled. An attempt was made to rescue specimens of the most valuable manuscripts, but few were saved, for the danger was pressing. Sir Claude MacDonald, as soon as the fire was discovered, dispatched a message to the Tsung Li Yamên, telling them of the fire and urging them to send some responsible officials to carry away what volumes could be rescued, but no attention was given to this courteous communication. The Dutch Legation was burned on the 22nd. The next day Chinese soldiers set fire to the Russo-Chinese Bank, and a greater part of the buildings were destroyed, involving in danger the American Legation. Chinese volunteers were called for. They responded readily, worked with much courage exposed to fire from the wall, and the Legation was saved. All the buildings back from the bank to Chien Mên (the main gate between the Chinese and Tartar cities facing the entrance to the Forbidden City) seemed to be on fire. Then all the customs buildings were fired, so that flames were on every side, and the smoke was tremendous, while the fusillarde was incessant. An Italian and a German died of their wounds The first American was killed, shot from the wall, then a Russian fell. They were dropping off one by one, and already we were well accustomed to the sight of the stretcher and the funeral. Wounded were being brought in from every legation to the hospital. In the British legation, the Chancery had been converted into

3 | 'THE SIEGE OF THE PEKING LEGATIONS'

a hospital. There was a staff of trained nurses and qualified doctors. Dr. Velde of the German delegation and Dr. W. Poole of the British Legation were in charge and did admirable work throughout the siege. Both surgeons had the advantage of previous experience of gunshot wounds, Dr. Velde having been attached to the ambulance in the Turco Greek War, and Dr. Poole, having seen service on the Niger in British Central Africa. First Aid to the Japanese and others in the Fu wounded in the field was given by surgeon Captain Nakagawa, a highly-trained surgeon of Berlin and Tokio, while the well-known Dr. Matignon of the French Legation fearlessly exposed himself throughout the siege, attending the wounded that fell in the defence of his Legation.

Krupp Guns Open Fire

Then a new terror was added to the fears of the besieged, for the Imperial troops mounted a 3in. Krupp gun on the Chien Mên, the gate opposite to the Forbidden City and began throwing segments shells from a distance of 1,000 yards into the crowded Legation. The first shell struck the American Legation, others burst over the British compound, while others crashed into the upper rooms of the German Legation. It was known that the Chinese had ten similar guns in Peking, while we had nothing with which to answer their fire, and no one ever knew where the next gun might be mounted. Immediately all hands dug bomb-proof shelters for the women and children. Rifle fire also played on the Americans from the wall quite close to them at a distance of a few hundred feet only, whence, safely sheltered by the parapet of the wall, men could enfilade the barricade which was held by the Americans on the street running east and west under the wall. The barricade became untenable, and to occupy the wall was a paramount necessity which could no longer be delayed.

Already on the 22nd, the Germans had occupied the wall east of the German Legation, thus cutting off the Chinese troops from the great east gate, Ha-ta Mên, and under Captain von Soden[243] had patrolled the

---

243 Alfred, Graf von Soden, b. 1886, later served as Flügeladjutant (Aide-de-Camp) to the Kaiser from 1904. Later as a Generalleutnant in WW1 he was German Military

wall passed the American legation. On the 24th a party of Germans and Americans, leaving the Austrians and French in charge of the German barricade, advanced again westward along the wall, sweeping the way clear past the American Legation for 200 yards towards the Chien Mên the other great gate on the west. Then the Germans retired to their own barricade, while the Americans retain the position which had been thus gained. At the head of the ramp behind the Legation, they began to build hastily, a covering wall to shelter them from the fire, which was shortly rained along the open surface from the west. The Germans and the American barricades were now distant from each other, about 500 yards. No enemy could live between them, and the security of the American legation was increasingly tenfold. But a great blunder was made at this stage. The Americans built a barricade across the wall from the ramp to the eastern corner of the bastion, leaving the bastion outside their lines. The enemy swiftly seized the advantage offered them. They mounted the wall by the next ramp to the west and under cover of night through an exactly corresponding barricade across the wall to the western corner of the best in. Thus, there were two barricades facing each other at a distance of 80 yards. The Christian coolies worked all night at strengthening the barricade, while small pickets of Germans and Russians were sent to assist the Americans to hold the position which was subsequently held by the British and Russians in conjunction with the Americans.

Down in the besieged area, the enemy pressed upon every side. Again they attempted to fire the British Legation from the Mongol market on the west; but a sortie was made by British Marines and volunteers, and the Chinese were driven from house to house out of the market. The work was dangerous, and Captain Halliday was dangerously wounded, while Captain Strouts[244] had an extraordinary escape, the bullet grazing the skin above the carotid artery. The sortie was entirely successful; some rifles were captured and ammunition, which was more

---

Commander of Brussels. *Der Held von Pekin* (the Hero of Peking) died at Lübek in April 1943 and was buried with full military honours.
244 Captain Bernard Morton Strouts, d. 1900, was an officer with the Royal Marine Light Infantry who commanded the Tientsin Winter Guard, a detachment of Marines stationed in China. Morrison was with him when he was fatally shot on 16 July 1900.

3 | 'THE SIEGE OF THE PEKING LEGATIONS'

precious than silver. The buildings were then fired by us, the fire being kept under control, which cleared a long distance around the west of the Legation.

Fortification proceeded without intermission, and all the defences of the besieged area quickly gathered strength. For the first time in war art was a feature in the fortifications. Sandbags were of every colour under the sun, and of every texture. Silks and satins, curtains and carpets and embroideries were ruthlessly cut up into sandbags. In the Prince's Fu the sandbags were made of the richest silks and satins the Imperial gifts and accumulated treasures of one of the eight princely families of China.

In the Prince's Fu the Chinese made a determined attempt to force their way into the Palace in their frenzy to slaughter the native Christians. In the angle of the wall in the north-eastern court of the Palace they made a breach in the wall and rushed wildly in. But the Japanese were waiting for them. And from loopholes they had made opposite rolled them over like rabbits, driving them helter-skelter back again. Some 20 men were killed, and but for the unsteadiness of the Italians who were assisting the Japanese the execution would have been greater. The Chinese were driven back, but the same evening they threw fireballs and petroleum over the walls and set fire to the building. Flames spread to the splendid main pavilion of the Palace. The Japanese in their turn, were driven back, and the Christians escaped from the burning buildings overflowed from the Fu into all that quarter lying between the Palace grounds and Legation street.

Chinese Treachery

On June 25 a truly oriental method of weakening our defence was attempted by the Chinese. Up to 4 o'clock in the afternoon the shooting of rifles and field guns had been continuous. When suddenly bugles were sounded north, east, south and west and, as if by magic, the firing ceased. It was under perfect control—Imperial control commanded by responsible central authority. The silence abruptly following the fusillade was striking. Then an official of low rank was seen to affix to the parapet of the north bridge near the British legation, a board inscribed with 18 Chinese characters:– "Imperial command to protect ministers and stop firing and dispatch will be handed at the Imperial Canal Bridge." A placard whereupon was written, "Dispatch will be received" was sent by one of the Christian clerks employed in the legation. But when he approached that bridge a hundred rifles from the Imperial Palace gate were levelled at him. The dispatch was never received, the artifice deceived no one. Treachery was feared, vigilance was redoubled. Sandbags were thrown on positions, which during the fire were untenable. So that when at midnight, the general attack was made upon us, we were prepared, and every man was at his post. The surprise had failed. As firing had ceased so it began. Horns were sounded, and then from every quarter a hail of bullets poured over us, sweeping through the trees and striking with sharp impact the roofs of the pavilions. No harm was done, though the noise was terrific. Great steadiness was shown by the men. They lay quietly behind the sandbags and not a shot was fired in reply. It was suggested as an explanation of this wild firing that the shots were to kill the guardian spirits which were known to hover over us. Similar fusillades took place at the American Legation, and at the French Legation, and with the same result. During the armistice the Chinese had availed themselves of the quiet to throw up earthworks in the Carriage Park alongside the British Legation, in the Mongol market between the British and Russian delegations, and at both ends of Legation Street, facing the Americans on the west, and facing the French legation corner on the east.

Complete Isolation

Isolation was now complete, and the enemy's cordon was constantly drawing closer. Every wall beyond the lines was loopholed. Not only was the besieged area cut off from all communication with the world outside Peking, but it was cut off from all communication with the Pei-tang. No messenger could be induced for love or money to carry a message there. Bishop Favier[245] and his guards must have been already hard pressed, for they were exposed to the danger not only of rifle and cannon, but of fire

---

245 At this time Favier was Vicar Apostolic of Northern Zhili, the Vatican's most senior man in China. He was Bishop of Peking.

3 | 'THE SIEGE OF THE PEKING LEGATIONS'

and starvation. The small garrison detached from the guards was known to be inadequately supplied with ammunition. It was known, however, that the danger of the situation had long been foreseen by Monseigneur Favier, who, speaking with unequalled authority, had weeks before the siege, vainly urged his minister to bring troops to Peking. When the crisis became inevitable and Christian refugees poured into the city the bishop endeavoured to buy arms and ammunition, so that there was a hope though a faint one that the Chinese themselves had assisted in the defence. So with stores. Large quantities of grain was stored in the Pei-tang, but whether sufficient for a siege for a garrison of 3000 souls was not known. Their condition was a constant source of anxiety to the Europeans within Legations, who were powerless to help them. Watch was kept unceasingly for any sign of the disaster that seemed inevitable—the massacre and the conflagration.

Towards the evening of the 28th a Krupp gun was mounted in the Mongol market, not 300 yards from the British legation, and fire was opened upon a storeyed building occupied by marines in the south court of the Legation. Fired at short range, the shells crashed through the roof and walls. For now the bombardment continued, but no one was injured, though a crack racing pony in the stables below was killed, and next day eaten. It was determined to capture this gun. So in the early morning, a force consisting of 26 British, ten Germans, ten Russians, five French and five Italians, and about 20 volunteers made a sortie from the Legation to try and capture the gun and burn the houses covering it; but the attempt was a fiasco. The men got tangled up in the lanes so that the reserve line with the kerosene marched ahead of the firing line; there was a Babel of voices, no one knew where to go, the captain lost his head and set fire to the houses in the rear, and the men retreated pell mell. As the British marine described the operation:– "The capt'n 'e sez, 'garn boys, garn, chawge boys, chawge,' against a bloomin' 'ouse wall, 'e waves 'is bloomin' arms in the air and 'e sets fire to the 'ouse be'ind us!" This was a bangle. The Chinese, however, were alarmed and removed the gun. Meanwhile, both French and German delegations had suffered heavily. The German legation was especially exposed and since the soldiers were more than their allies, disdainful of cover, the small band, numbering originally only 50 men, was being daily reduced in numbers. Their commanding officer, Graf Soden, was untiring in his duty, working as he had to do single-handed.

Attack on the French Legation

On the 29th the French delegation was hard pressed. One of their offices, the midshipman Herbert was shot. Reinforcements were hastily sent from the Fu, and the attack was repulsed but some of the outer buildings of the Legation were burned, and the French had to retire further into the Legation. In this siege it was striking what a powerful part petroleum was made to play. Already the French Legation had suffered more severely than than any other Legation; of their 45 men 16 had been killed or wounded. Krupp guns had been mounted not 50 yards to the eastward, and the eastern walls of the pavilions were being gradually and systematically battered into ruins. All day now until the cessation of hostilities shells were pounding into the French Legation, into Chamot's hotel, and from the Chen Mên on the wall, promiscuously, everywhere. Much property was destroyed, but though the shells burst everywhere and escapes were marvellous, few people were hit. Bullets whistled in the Legation compounds. Surgeon Lippett was talking to Mr. Conger in the American Legation when he was hit by a bullet that smashed the right thigh bone. Had the bullet not struck the surgeon it would have hit the Minister. Mr. Pethick was sitting at the window of the American Legation fanning himself when a bullet pierced the fan. A civilian was wounded in the British Legation, and a marine, Phillips, was killed while walking in the compound. A fragment of shell fell on a patient inside the hospital.

A Day of Misfortunes

The cordon was drawn closer. In the Fu nearly one-third of the buildings had been abandoned and the Japanese retired to a second line of defence. Shells were fired by the hundred. On the 29th 70 shells were thrown into the British Legation. The difficulty of holding the Americans and German barricades on the city wall was increasing. The positions were very much exposed. A Krupp gun was brought close to the American barricade. The Russo-Chinese bank and all

3 | 'THE SIEGE OF THE PEKING LEGATIONS'

French Legation, Peking.
Mitchell Library, Sydney

the buildings near were occupied by Chinese troops, the walls being loopholed and lanes barricaded. And all were so close that you could not look through a loophole without being shot at. Yet the American barricade, with its mixed guard of Americans, Russians and British had to be held at all hazards; otherwise the Krupp gun could be brought down the wall and play havoc upon the Legations, the furthest of which—the British—was at its nearest point not 400 yards distant. Still more exposed than the American barricade was the outpost on the wall held by the Germans. At first they had been reinforced by the French and the Austrians, but the needs of the French Legation were equally pressing and the guards were withdrawn and the small picket of British sent to aid the Germans. Already the Germans had lost terribly for the outpost was situated at a distance of 250 yards from the Legation and the reliefs were exposed throughout this distance to fire from a hundred snipers. One hundred yards in front of the German barricade was the Chinese barricade, picturesque with the banners of the army of Yung Lu. Here was mounted a Krupp gun, from which shells burst over the German barricade, seriously wounding two of the six British who were there on guard. On the same day that this happened two Germans on guard at the barricade were shot through the head, stone dead a third was shot through the head, but is still living—a marvellous recovery—a fourth was wounded in the face by a shell, a fifth was shot through the thigh in the same deadly corner. Two men going to relieve guards were shot by snipers, one slightly through the hand, the other fatally through the right leg—he died from tetanus 11 days later; while, to crown the misfortunes of the day, Corporal Robert Goelitz, who wore the war medal given him only last year for an act of heroism in the field at Kiaochau was shot through the head and died instantaneously. Altogether this barrier on the wall cost in the one day four men killed and six wounded. During the night the position was held by eight Germans and three British. In the morning of July 1 the Chinese climbed up the ramp and surprised the guard. The order was hastily given to retire, and the picket, shaken by its losses of yesterday, left the wall. The German non-commissioned officer who gave the order was severely blamed for thus abandoning a position that he had been ordered to hold. Withdrawal left the Americans exposed in the rear. They saw the Germans retire, and in a panic fell back to the Legation, rushing pell-mell down the ramp. Nothing had occurred at the barricade itself to justify the retreat, although two men had fallen within a few hours before. Yet the wall was the key of the position and had to be maintained. A conference was held at the British Legation, and as a result orders were given to return to the post. Captain Myers at once took back a strong detachment of 14 Americans, ten British, and ten Russians, and reoccupied the barricade as if nothing had happened. The Chinese, ignorant that the post had been evacuated, lost their opportunity.

Then the guard in the French Legation was driven a stage further back and M. Wagner, a volunteer, was killed by the bursting of a shell. He was a young Frenchman of much courage and spirt, the Acting Postal Secretary in the Maritime Customs under Sir Robert Hart, with a career opening before him of, much promise. The son of a former Consul-General at Shanghai, he was the first civilian to lay down his life in the defence of women and children in Peking.

A Gallant Sortie

It was a day of misfortunes. In the afternoon the most disastrous sortie of the siege was attempted. A Krupp gun, firing at short range into the Fu (i.e., the Prince's Palace), was a serious menace to our communications.

3 | 'THE SIEGE OF THE PEKING LEGATIONS'

Captain Paolini, the Italian officer, conceived the idea that he could capture the gun if volunteers could be given him and if the Japanese could assist. The Japanese Colonel Shiba readily did so; they forced their way to a rendezvous agreed upon, losing one man killed and two wounded. Their sacrifice was fruitless; they waited, but, the position being untenable, retired.

Meanwhile a party of 16 Italians, four Austrians, two Frenchmen, seven British marines, and five British students, were led by Captain Paolini to the capture of the gun. He conceived that the gun was to the north-east of the Fu, to be reached by a lane running from Canal-street opposite the British Legation eastward. No one knew that this was his conception. One hundred yards up this lane there was a high Chinese barricade; the houses on the north side of the lane were held by the Chinese and loopholed. From a position occupied by Captain Poole's men in the Hanlin the lane could be enfiladed. They were therefore on watch, expecting that the Chinese were to be taken in the rear and driven down the lane into the canal. Close to the barricade there was a hole in the wall of the Fu from which a previous attempt had been made to enter the lane. The Italian captain was ignorant of the existence of this hole. Then to the amazement of the British who were watching it from the Hanlin the men were lined up under the wall opposite and, after waiting a little, Captain Paolini called his men and dashed up the lane. Wildly cheering, they followed him into the death-trap. By the rush they were able to advance some distance before fire was opened upon them. Then rifles from behind the barricade and from the loopholes broke forth. The column recoiled, the men fired wildly into the air, the captain's arm fell powerless, two Italians dropped dead. The men were turning to rush back when they saw the man-hole, and immediately the Italians and Austrians who were leading made a frantic dash for it and fought like wild beasts to burst their way through. One British marine, badly wounded, escaped back down the lane. The five British students, Russell, Bristow, Hancock, Flaherty, and Townsend, acted with admirable self-possession. Projecting slightly into the lane on the opposite side from the man-hole was a house that gave just sufficient cover. There the men stood for shelter, for they were the last of the detachment. Then, all the marines having got safely through, the students fired a volley into the barricade and one man rushed across, then the four fired and another rushed across. In this way all passed unscathed till the last man, Townsend, who was struck just as he entered the hole by two bullets, one through the back of the shoulder, another through the thigh. The Five young men acted like veterans. Bristow showed conspicuous coolness, for in his dash across he picked up a Lee-Metford rifle which a marine had let fall.

Thus by this ineffective sortie our small garrison was reduced by three men killed, one officer and four men and one volunteer wounded. Fortunately it was no worse.

The Native Christians

The gun that was not captured was brought up again next day into play and continued battering down the Fu walls. The enemy were working their way ever nearer to the refugee Christians. Their rage to reach the Christians was appalling. They cursed them from over the wall, hurled stones at them, and threw shells to explode overhead. Only after the armistice, when we received the Peking Gazette, did we find that word to burn out and slaughter the converts had come from the highest in the land.

The Japanese were driven still further back. Already they had lost heavily, for upon them had fallen the brunt of a defence the gallantry of which surpassed all praise. When the siege was raised it was found that of the entire force of marines only five men had escaped without wounds; one was wounded five times. Colonel Shiba early raised a force of "Christian volunteers," drilled them, instructed them, and armed them with rifles captured from the enemy. They made an effective addition to the Japanese strength, relieving especially the tedium of sentry; and they stood up to the barricades without flinching. Many were wounded and some killed. Those of, us who saw these men under fire were favourably impressed with their conduct. Equally impressed were most of us with the courage and coolness under fire of the Chinese coolies. One morning five of them were wounded going up the ramp to the American barricade. Without their assistance our danger would have been increased tenfold. Many were killed and wounded when working under fire. On July 2 Mr. Kojima, an attaché of the Japanese Legation, was killed and also two Japanese marines. On the same day a German

3 | 'THE SIEGE OF THE PEKING LEGATIONS'

marine was shot dead while standing in the First Secretary's room in the German Legation. A coolie was shot in the leg while digging a grave in the British Legation. Shots fell everywhere. Twice within the British Legation a pigeon was struck by a stray bullet.

Every one worked at the defences. One of the Ministers —such was the emulation of all to do something—offered his services to the British officer commanding. He volunteered to keep watch and watch by night, but his offer was hampered by qualifications. He was eager to keep watch, he said, but he was very short-sighted, he could see nothing at night, and he had never handled a gun. His offer was not accepted, but the spirit which prompted him to make it was admired.

A Desperate Counter-Move

At daybreak on July 3, the Chinese barricade on the top of the wall near the American outpost was successfully, stormed by a party of British, Americans, and Russians, under the leadership of Captain Myers, Captain Vroublevsky, and Mr. Nigel Oliphant.[246] I have spoken of the error committed in the construction of the American barricade, which left the width of the bastion outside instead of within the American lines. The two barricades faced each other at the distance of the width of the bastion, which was on the left. Then the Chinese, working with greats cleverness, always keeping under shelter, pushed forward a covering wall across the bastion, until it curved round and reached the left-hand corner of the American breastwork. Here they began erecting a small fort, the centre of which was 25ft from the nearest American picket. The position was intolerable. It was imperative to rush the barricade and drive out the Chinese; nothing else could be done.

An attack was planned for 3 in the morning, and before that hour a strong force of British was sent over from the Legation. The combined force assembled for the attack consisted of 26 British marines under Sergeant Murphy and Corporal Gregory, with Mr. Nigel Oliphant as volunteer, 15 Russians under Captain Vroublevsky, and 15 Americans,

---

246 Oliphant, b. 1874, wrote his own account of the siege *A Diary of the Siege of the Legations in Peking During the Summer of 1900*, London, 1901.

all being under the command of Captain Myers. When asked if they came willingly one American begged to be relieved and was sent below. This left the total force at 56, of whom 14 were Americans. So close were the Chinese that it was only a couple of jumps from our barricade to their fort. There was a rush to be first over, the fort was stormed, and dashing round the covering wall the "foreign devil" charged behind the barricade. Taken by surprise the Chinese fired in the air, fled incontinently, and were shot down as they ran along the open surface of the wall. Captain Vroublevsky and his detachment acted with especial gallantry, for their duty it was to attack the Chinese barricade in the front, while the British and Americans took it in the rear. Two banners marked "General Ma" were captured. Fifteen Chinese soldiers of Tang-fuh-siang were killed outright and many more must have been wounded. Some rifles and ammunition were captured. Then the allied forces, exposed to a heavy fire, retired within what had been the Chinese barricade and employed it against the enemy who had built it. Captain Myers was wounded is the knee by tripping over a fallen spear, two Americans, Turner and Thomas—one having accidentally jumped on the wrong, aide of the barricade—were killed, and Corporal Gregory was wounded in the foot. News of the successful sortie gave much pleasure to the community. Chinese coolies were sent on the wall, and a strongly intrenched redoubt was built there; the camp was made safe by traverses. Unfortunately, the wound of Captain Myers proved more serious than was at first suspected and he was not again able to return to duty. The services of a brave and capable officer were lost to the garrison; his post on the wall was taken most ably by Captain Percy Smith and other officers in turn.

Most of the shelling was now directed against the French and German Legations and Chamot's Hotel. The hotel was struck 91 times and was several times set on fire, but the flame as extinguisher. Work continued there, however hot the shelling, for food had to be prepared there for half the community in Peking, Russians, French, Germans, and Austrians. The energy of Chamot was marvellous. He fed the troops and a crowd of Christian refugees, killed his own mules and horses, ground his own wheat, and baked 300 loaves a day. Shelled out of the kitchen he baked in the parlour. His courage inspired the Chinese, and they followed him under fire with an amazing confidence.

3 | 'THE SIEGE OF THE PEKING LEGATIONS'

British Legation, Peking.
Mitchell Library, Sydney

THE BRITISH LEGATION HARD PRESSED

Then suddenly a new attempt was made to reduce the British Legation. Guns firing round shot, eight-pounders and four-pounders, were mounted on the Imperial City wall overlooking from the north the Hanlin and the British Legation. With glasses—the distance was only 350 yards—one could clearly see the officers and distinguish their Imperial Peacock feathers and Mandarin hats. Adjoining the battery an upper row of stones on the wall was raised to form loopholes for sharpshooters, who could thus enfilade the canal and our communications eastward. Round shot were hurled into the Hanlin and crashed through the roofs of the British Legation. One pierced both walls of the dining room, passing behind the portrait of the Queen. Two came crashing through the wall of a student's room where a few minutes before Sir Claude MacDonald had been standing, watching the preparations being made to bombard us. Another struck the room occupied by a lady who was in bed and fell at her side. Another ploughed through the carts. Three batteries in all, carrying five guns, were mounted on the Imperial City wall where the bombardment could be witnessed by the Empress Dowager and her counsellors, and day after day round shot were thrown from them into the British Legation, into a compound crowded with women and children. This is what his Excellency Lo Fêng-Luh was describing to Lord Salisbury as "giving effective protection to the British Legation."

On July 5 Mr. David Oliphant, of the British Legation, was killed. He was felling a tree by the well in the Hanlin when he was shot by a sniper concealed in a roof in the Imperial Carriage Park, and died within an hour. Only 24 years of age, he was a student of exceptional promise and ability, universally popular, cool and courageous to an unusual degree. He had only recently been given a post in the Chancery in reward for his being the best student of his year. In the afternoon he was carried to his grave amid the booming of guns, followed by a crowd of mourners of 13 different nationalities.

The Chinese Press On

Day by day the Chinese were pressing us more closely. In the Fu they were gradually wedging their way in from the northeast so as to cut the communications between the British and the Legations to the east They burned their way from house to house. Keeping under cover, they set alight the gables within reach by torches of cloth soaked in kerosene held at the end of long poles. If the roof were beyond reach they threw over fireballs of kerosene, or, if still further, shot into them with arrows freighted with burning cloth. In this way and with the use of the heavy gun they battered a way through the houses and courtyards of the Prince's Palace. A daring attempt made by the Japanese to capture the gun resulted in failure. Coolies failed them when they were within four yards of success, and they were forced to retire. Their gallant leader Captain Ando was shot in the throat while waving on his men, one marine was seriously wounded, and one Christian volunteer killed. Captain Ando had come to Peking on a visit only two days before the cutting of the railways. His services were given ungrudgingly. A young man of much ability and of untiring energy, his loss was regretted by the whole community.

By the 8th the position in the Fu was alarming, for the Japanese force had been reduced to 13 marines and 14 volunteers; yet with decreasing, numbers they were constantly called upon to defend a longer line. Reinforcements were sent, them of half-a-dozen Customs

3 | 'THE SIEGE OF THE PEKING LEGATIONS'

and student volunteers and of six British marines. Nothing can give a better indication of the smallness of our garrison than the fact that throughout the siege reinforcements meant five men or ten men. Strong reinforcements meant 15 men. Our reinforcements were counted by ones, not by companies. With this force a line of intrenchment stretching from the outer court of the Pu on the east across the grounds to near the extreme north-west corner was held till the end. In the north-west corner at an artificial rookery were stationed a mixed force of 15 Italian and five Austrians. But the position was an exposed one, and it was difficult to keep the southerners at their posts. They were said to have no lack of spirit, but their *forte* was in attack. They lacked the dull patient courage of sitting behind loopholes cooped up in a sandbag shelter within earshot of the enemy. They were always running away. On the 9th there was a sudden panic, a stampede, and the position was evacuated. The civilian in charge, Mr. Caetani, of the Italian Legation, acted with much coolness, and induced his men to return. Five Austrians were sent away and British Marines put in their places. Ever afterwards a British picket was kept there. The position was one of constant solicitude, for the loss of the Pu would have imperilled the British Legation. A Krupp gun, mounted 50 yards away, had the range and raked the post with shell and shrapnel. To strengthen the breastwork exposure to rifle fire was incurred from 20 yards' distance, while to reach the post required coring a zone of fire which was perhaps the hottest in the whole of the defences. Many men were wounded there, and one Italian had his head blown off. Shell fire finally made it possible to live there. The advanced posts were abandoned, and the sentries fell back to the main picket. No sooner was the advanced post abandoned than it was occupied by the Chinese and the defences we had made were turned against us.

The French and German Legations

Meanwhile, the French and German allegations were being roughly handled, and men were falling daily. At the German Legation shells burst through the Minister's drawing room. Most of the other buildings conspicuous by their height were uninhabitable, but every member of the Legation remained at his post. So, too, in the French legation where the Austrians were, Dr. and Madame von Rosthorn remained by the side

German Legation, Peking.
Mitchell Library, Sydney

of their men. The French volunteers and Dr. Matignon stood staunchly by the Legation, although it was fast tumbling into ruins, their coolness and resolution, being in curious contrast to the despair of their minister who crying "Tout est perdu,"[247] melodramatically burned the French archives in a ditch at the British Legation. Chinese and French were so close that the voices of the Chinese officers could be heard encouraging their men. Chinese were within the Legation itself. Their guns literally bombarded the Minister's residence à bout portant,[248] and the noise of the exploding shells was terrific. Yet the men never flinched. On the 8th the Austrian commander, Captain Thomann, of the Zenta, was killed by the bursting of a shell. He was talking at the time to Captain Labrousse, and Captain Darcy.[249] But they escaped unscathed. Captain Thomann had come to Peking on a short visit and had been detained here by the destruction of the railway. Then still pressing us closer, the Chinese brought a Krupp gun along from the Chien Mên and mounted it behind a wall on the top of the city wall, in a position directly facing the

---

247 "All is lost."
248 "Point blank."
249 Captain Eugène Darcy, 1869–1928, was a French naval officer who fought in the Boxer rebellion. He documented his experiences in *La défense de la légation de France à Pékin*, Paris, P. Challamel, 1903.

3 | 'THE SIEGE OF THE PEKING LEGATIONS'

American barricade, at a distance of 40 yards. Captain Percy Smith and Herr Loesch, a young German officer, were in charge of the barricade, and they had under them the varied force of Americans, British and Russians that had held the position since it was first occupied. Suddenly, the Chinese threw open an embrasure uncovering the gun and fired point blank at the wall in front of them, behind which were the 10 British and two Russians. The shell burst overhead but no one was hit. The gun was in a moment withdrawn. At the second shot, the British fell flat down, the shell burst, they jumped to their feet and fired a volley into the breach. It was quick work smartly and bravely done, but the position could not be held. Before however any casualties occurred, a curious thing happened. At the fifth round when the gun fired a mass of bricks and earth were thrown outwards. A wide breach had been formed by the bursting of the gun or by the wave of concussion, and the gun was silent.

A Day of Heavy Losses

July 11 was a day of many casualties. One German was mortally wounded; one Englishman, one Italian and one Japanese were seriously wounded. Mr. Nigel Oliphant, a volunteer received a bullet wound in the leg, while Mr. Narahara, the well-known secretary of the Japanese legation, wounded by the bursting of a shell suffered a compound fracture of the leg, which from the first gave cause for anxiety. He gradually sank and died on July 24. Mr. Narahara was a brilliant Chinese scholar. He was formally private secretary to Marquis Ito and was present at the peace negotiations in Shimonoseki in 1895. He was universally respected. In a reckless attempt to capture a Chinese banner, three Frenchmen were wounded, one of them, M. Gruingenst, fatally. He was an engineer on the Luhan railway, who had escaped from the burning of the Chang Hsin Tien before the outbreak of hostilities. Chinese banners, indeed, hung temptingly close to every outpost. One morning we are working to find the one waving from the sandbag shelter in the Carriage walk over the very wall of the British Legation. No marine could suffer such an affront. During the day Sergeant Preston, of the Orlando, with two volunteers mounted the wall, shot two soldiers who are on guard behind the sandbags, while his mate seized the flag and hauled it into the compound. On the 11th 18 prisoners were captured by the French in a temple near the Legation. They were soldiers and a Chinese Christian gave information as to their whereabouts. Every one of them was put to death without mercy in the French Legation, bayonetted by a French Corporal to save cartridges. Questioned before death, they gave much information that was obviously false. One man however, declared that a mine was being driven under the French Legation. His story had quick corroboration. As the afternoon of the 13th was closing, a faint attack was made on the Japanese entrenchments in the Fu, then the sound of many bugles was heard from the camps round the French Legation, to be followed in a few minutes by a terrible explosion, and in a moment or two by another; and bricks and *débris* were hurled into the air. It was a dull roar in the midst of the devilish cries of hordes of Chinese shrieking like spirits in hell, the rattle of musketry, and the boom of heavy guns. The mine of which the prisoner had warned us had exploded and burst in entrance into the French legation.

When the first mine exploded, the French Captain Darcy, the Austrian *Chargé d'Affaires*, and two French marines and Mr. Destelan of the Customs was standing over the death-trap. Mr. Destelan and was buried up to the neck, but was rescued unhurt, the two marines were engulfed and their bodies were never recovered. Captain Darcy and Von Rosthorn escaped miraculously. The latter was buried by the first explosion and released unhurt a moment or two later by the second.

Driven out of the main buildings the small garrison (it consisted only of 17 Austrians, with three officers 27 French with two officers, and nine volunteers) fell back a few paces to a line of defence, part of which had only been completed in the afternoon, and securely held the position. It consisted of the chapel, the Pavilion des Étrangers, and a line of earthworks stretching across the Legation garden to the Northern Gate. The buildings they left were set fire to and the ruins were occupied by the Chinese. And when the flames had burned out, Imperial banners were hoisted over the ruins of what had once been the residence of the French minister. And while this tragedy was being enacted in Peking, the Chinese ambassador in Paris was assuring the President that his government was "protecting" the French delegation and "providing its staff with food."

3 | 'THE SIEGE OF THE PEKING LEGATIONS'

Simultaneously with this attack upon the French delegation, the Chinese made a determined assault upon the German Legation, the effective strength of whose garrison numbered only one officer and 31 men. They broke into the Club alongside the Legation and were on the tennis ground when Count Soden and a handful of German soldiers gallantly charged them at a point of the bayonet and drove them out headlong.

Reinforcements of nine Russians and five German volunteers under Herr Von Strauch came up at the double, but their services were not needed. The attack was over. Uniforms of the dead Chinese showed that the attack had been carried out by the troops of Yung Lu reinforced by the savages of Tung-fu-hsiang. Some of the dead were armed with the latest pattern Mauser and the newest German army revolver, some ammunition, of which guards were in much need, was recovered and distributed among the Japanese and Italians. Firing continued around the Legations; every battery open fire; the air hissed with bullets. There was momentary darkness, then flames broke out from the large foreign houses between the German legation and Canal-street. It seemed at one time as if the whole of the quarter would be burned, but the fire did not spread. Heavy rain came on, and the rest of the night passed in quiet.

A Chinese Communication

On July 14, a messenger, sent out on the 10th, with a letter for the troops, returned to the British Legation. He had been arrested by the Chinese, cruelly beaten, and taken, he said to the yamên of Yung Lu, and they're given the following letter, purporting to be written by Prince Ching "and others," addressed to the British Minister. It was the first communication of any kind whatsoever that had reached us from outside for nearly a month.

> For the last 10 days the soldiers and Militia have been fighting, and there has been no communication between us, to our great anxiety. Some time ago we hung up a board, expressing our intentions, but no answer has been received, and contrary to expectation the foreign soldiers made renewed attacks, causing alarm and suspicion among soldiers and people.

Yesterday, the troops captured a convert named Chin-ssu-hei and learnt from him that all the foreign Ministers were well, which caused us very great satisfaction.

But it is the unexpected which happens. The reinforcements of foreign troops were long ago stopped and turned back by the "Boxers," and if, in accordance with previous agreement, we were to guard your excellencies out of the city, there are so many "Boxers" on the road to Tien-tsin and Ta-ku that we should be apprehensive of misadventure.

We now request your Excellencies to first take your families and the various members of your staffs and leave your Legations in detachments. We should select trustworthy officers to give close and strict pretend protection and you should temporarily reside in the Tsling-Li-Yamên pending future arrangements for your return home, in order to preserve friendly relations intact from beginning to end.

But at the time of leaving the Legations there must on no account whatever be taken any single armed soldier, in order to prevent doubt and fear on the part of the troops and people, leading to untoward incidents.

If your Excellencies are willing to show this confidence, we beg you to communicate with all the foreign Ministers in Peking, tomorrow at noon being the limit of time, and to let the original messenger deliver the reply in order that we may settle the day for leaving the Legations.

This is the single way of preserving relations which we have been able to devise in the face of innumerable different difficulties. If no reply is received by the time fixed, even our affection will not enable us to help you. Compliments.

(Signed) Prince Ching and others.
July 14, 1900

Following as it did immediately after the attack on the French legation, which reduced it to ruins, the letter did not lack impudence. "Boxers" had driven back our troops "Militia," not "Boxers," had been attacking us in Peking. The letter was read with derision. It was interpreted as a guileless attempt to seduce the Ministers away from the Legations and

3 | 'THE SIEGE OF THE PEKING LEGATIONS'

massacre them at ease. News we heard subsequently had reached the Chinese of the taking of Tien-tsin city.

It was difficult for his Excellency to "show the confidence" asked for, and to seek the "help" which affection for him promoted the Chinese to offer.

On the 15th the reply was sent declining on the part of the foreign representatives the invitation to proceed to the Tsing-Li-Yamên, and pointing out that no attacks had been made by our troops, who were only defending the lives and property of foreigners against the attacks of Chinese government troops. The reply concluded with a statement that if the Chinese government wished to negotiate they should send a responsible official with a white flag.

Firing continued furiously, the attack being mainly directed against the Fu, where the Chinese had raised their barricades, till they could sweep with fire the palace grounds. On the 15th one of the British students, Henry Warren, was mortally wounded doing duty at the Japanese outpost. He died the same night another victim to Chinese treachery.

Death of Captain Strouts

The morning of the 16th opened with a disaster. Captain Strouts, the senior British officer, was shot while returning from the outpost in the Fu. He was struck in the upper part of the left thigh by an expanding bullet, and died an hour after being brought into the hospital, to the grief of the entire community. Throughout the siege he had acted in a way that won the admiration of all. He was always cool and self reliant and never spared himself, while always considerate of his men. Both Englishmen were buried the same afternoon. It was a mournful gathering that followed them to the grave, officers and soldiers of many nationalities, Ministers and their staffs, missionaries and brave ladies who have shared the discomfort of this unhappy siege. While shells were bursting in the trees, and amid the cracking of rifle bullets, the brave young fellow to whose gallant defence we all owed so much was laid to rest beside the student for whom a career of brilliant promise had just opened.

More Chinese Assurances

While the service was proceeding, a messenger bearing a flag of truce was approaching the gate. A shell burst almost at his feet, the passages in his letter were punctuated by cannon fire directed against the Legation from the wall of the Imperial city. This is what the Chinese were, no doubt, continuing to describe in Europe as giving the: "Legations protection from local banditti." It was a striking evidence of the disregard for the usages of civilised warfare which characterises the nation.

The letter was from "Prince Ching and others." It explained that the reason for suggesting the removal of the Legations to the Tsung-Li-Yamên was that the Chinese Government could afford more efficient protection to the members of the Legations if concentrated than if scattered as at present. As the foreign Ministers did not agree, however, the Chinese would as in duty bound do their utmost to protect the Legations where they were. (While the letter sentence was being read the translator had to raise his voice in order that it should be heard above the crack of the Imperial rifle bullets.) They would bring reinforcements and continue their endeavours to prevent the "Boxers" from firing, and they trusted that the foreign Ministers on their part would restrain their troops also from firing.

A Message from the Outside World

By the same messenger a cypher message was brought to Mr. Conger, the American Minister. It said:– "Communicate tidings bearer." It was in the State Department cipher and had no date or indication by whom it had been sent. Mr. Conger replied in the same cipher:– "For one month we have been besieged in British legation under continued shot and shell from Chinese troops. Quick relief can only prevent general massacre." When forwarding his reply he asked that it should be sent to the address from which the other had come, which address had not been communicated to him. Next day, the Yamên sent him an answer saying that his message had been forwarded and explaining that the telegram sent to him had been contained in a telegram from Wu Ting Fan, the Chinese minister at Washington, dated July 11.

3 | 'THE SIEGE OF THE PEKING LEGATIONS'

This telegram read:– "The United States cheerfully aid China, but it is thinking of Minister Conger. The Hon. Secretary of State inquires after him by telegram, which I begged to be transmitted to him to get his reply." From this, we could well imagine what specious assurances had been given to Mr. Hay by Wu Ting Fang's bland assurances that there had been a most regrettable outbreak on the part of lawless bands in the north of China which the government was vainly struggling to cope with, that the most benevolent protection had been accorded to the foreign Legations and foreign Ministers by the Imperial government, but that help was needed to quell the insurrection, etc. We hoped, however, that the message of Mr. Conger would show the value of such assurances.

Cessation of Hostilities

From July 17 there was a cessation of hostilities; not that men were not wounded afterwards and Christian coolies fired upon whenever they showed themselves, but the organised attacks ceased and the Krupp guns were muzzled. Fearing treachery, however, we relaxed none of our vigilance. Trenches were cut where mines might have been driven. All walls and shelters were so strengthened as to be practically shell proof. Our preparations were purely defensive. On their part the Chinese also continued work at their barricades. From their barricade on the top of the wall near the German legation they advanced westward so that they could fire directly down into the German legation and pick off men going up the steps to the Minister's house. They built a wall with loopholes across Legation-street not 20 yards from the Russian barricade. In nearly every position the enemy was so close that you could shoot into the muzzles of their rifles thrust through the loopholes. The cordon was still drawn tightly around us, and we were penned in to prevent our acting in cooperation with the troops who are coming to our relief. No provisions were permitted to reach us, but a few eggs for the women and children were surreptitiously sold us by Chinese soldiers. All were on reduced rations, the allowance for the 2,750 native Christians whom we had to provide for being barely sufficient to save them from starvation. Their sufferings were very great, the mortality among their children and the aged pitiful. No one could have foreseen that within the restricted limits of the besieged area, with the food supply therein obtainable 473 civilians (of these 414 namely 191 Men, 147 women 76 children were inside the British Legation), a garrison of 400 men, 2,750 refugees, and some 400 native servants could have sustained the siege for two entire months. Providentially in the very centre of Legation-street, there was a mill with a large quantity of grain which turned out 900lb. of flour a day, divided between the hotel and the Legation. One day, the Tsung-li-Yamên insultingly sent us a present of 1000lb. of flour and some ice and vegetables, but no one would venture to eat the flour, fearing that it might be poisoned. Communications now passed almost daily with the Tsung-li-Yamên or with the officials whose dispatches were signed "Prince Ching and others." On July 17, Sir Claude MacDonald replied to the suggestion that the Ministers would restrain their troops from firing upon the Chinese. He said that from the first the foreign troops had acted entirely in self defence, and will continue to do so. But the Chinese must understand that preview of their previous events had led to a want of confidence and that if barricades were erected or troops moved in the vicinity of the legations the foreign guards would be obliged to fire.

In the afternoon, the Chinese replied, reviewing the situation and ascribing the hostilities to the attacks previously made by the Legation guards. They noted with satisfaction that a cessation of firing was agreed to on both sides, but suggested that as foreign soldiers had been firing from the city wall east of the Chien Mên, they should be removed from that position.

Next day Sir Claude MacDonald replied with a review of the situation from the foreign point of view. On June 19 the Yamên had given the Legations notice to quit Peking, and the foreign Representatives had replied pointing out that there were no facilities of transport. The Yamên had then replied extending the time, but in spite of this, fire was opened on the Legations on June 20 and they had been under constant fire ever since from Government troops, a condition of things unparalleled in the history of the world. He alluded to the incident of the board hung up on June 25, the free moving of Chinese troops during the cessation thus caused, and the renewed attacks made after the preparations thus made possible were completed. He hoped that mutual confidence would gradually be restored, but meanwhile he again pointed out that

3 | 'THE SIEGE OF THE PEKING LEGATIONS'

cessation of hostile preparations as well as firing was necessary on the part of the Chinese troops to secure that the foreign troops should cease firing. As for the suggestion that the foreign troops should leave the city wall, it was impossible to accede to it, because a great part of the attacks on the Legations had been made from the wall. He concluded by suggesting that sellers of fruit and ice should be allowed to come in.

CHINESE SYMPTOMS OF ALARM

They were never permitted to come in. It was clear, however, that events were happening elsewhere to cause alarm in the Imperial Court. On the afternoon of the first day of what might be called the armistice M. Pelliot, a French gentleman from TongKing, entered the Chinese lines and to the great anxiety of all was absent five hours. He was taken by soldiers to a Yamên of one of the big generals—he knew not which—was plied with questions which, speaking some Chinese, he could answer, and was sent back unmolested with an escort of 15 soldiers "to protect him against the 'Boxers." This unusual clemency was interpreted favourably. It was clear that the Chinese had sustained a severe defeat and that relief was coming. Next day direct communication was for the first time held with an official of the Tsung-li-Yamên. A secretary named Wen Jui came to the Legation to see Sir Claude MacDonald and was received by the Minister outside the gate, not being permitted to enter. He said that the regrettable occurrences were due to "local banditti," that the Government had great concern to protect the foreigners, that Baron von Ketteler's body had been recovered from the hands of the "local banditti" who had murdered him and been enclosed in a valuable, coffin. He urged that the maintenance of foreign troops on the city wall was unnecessary and that they should be withdrawn. It was pointed out to him that, as we had been very continuously shelled from the city wall both from the Ha-ta Men and the Chien Mên, it would be inadvisable, to retire. Asked to send copies of the *Peking Gazette*, he hesitated a moment and then stammered that he really had not himself seen the *Peking Gazette* for a long time, but he would inquire and see if they could be bought.

He never came back and never sent a *Gazette*. His name was Wen Jui.

When we did obtain copies of the *Gazette* it was interesting to find two items that must have been especially unpleasant for him to have us know. On June 24, by Imperial decree, leaders were appointed to the "Boxers," or "patriotic militia." Among the chiefs was Wen Jui.

The visit of Wen Jui was on the 18th. Up to the time of his visit, though more than four weeks had passed since the assassination, no illusion of any kind whatever had been made in any *Peking Gazette* to the murder of Baron von Ketteler. Then the Empress-Dowager, yielding to her fears, published an allusion to the murder. Will the German Emperor rest satisfied with the tardy official reference to the brutal assassination of his Minister by an Imperial officer?

> Last month the Chancellor of the Japanese Legation was killed. This was, indeed, most unexpected. Before this matter had been settled the German Minister was killed. Suddenly meeting this affair caused us deep grief. We ought vigorously to seek the murderer and punish him.

No more. The date July 18; the murder June 20!

Reassuring News

Yet even in this decree there was a complete *volte-face*. Missionaries who were by the decree of July 2 "to be at once driven away to their own countries" were by the decree of July 18 "to be protected in every province," "to be protected without the least carelessness." The truculence and belligerence of the decrees issued when our troops had been driven back had disappeared; the tone now was one of justification and conciliation. Only one interpretation was possible—that the Chinese had been defeated. Confirmation came the same day. A messenger sent out by the Japanese successfully passed the enemy's lines and brought us the news that we had so long awaited.

From this we learned that General Fukushima with 4,000 Japanese soldiers had arrived at Tien-tsin on June 29, that subsequently 4,000 Russians, 2,000 British, 1,500 French, 1,500 Americans, and 500 Germans had landed, that Tien-tsin city had been taken on the 14th, and that the arsenal was in the hands of the allies. We further learned that a division of the Japanese army had left Hiroshima on July 8 and was expected

3 | 'THE SIEGE OF THE PEKING LEGATIONS'

Russian soldiers manning legation barricades, Peking, July 1900.
Mitchell Library, Sydney

at Tien-tsin on the 20th, and that a relief force consisting mainly of Japanese was to start for our relief immediately. This meant that the relief was actually further from us on July 18 than we had believed it to be on June 18. Yet every one heard the news with satisfaction. The choice of the leader seemed to us an admirable one, for General Fukushima is well known in Peking, having been here for several years as a military student and having taken an important part in the war with China, especially in the preparation of the intelligence reports which were the basis of the plan of campaign. It was he who rode overland across Asia from Berlin to Vladivostok, and who, when he landed in Japan, was received with the honours due to a Moltke[250] returning from a victorious campaign.

By the same messenger a letter was received by the French Minister informing him that he had been decorated with a higher grade of the Legion d'Honneur, that France had sent his passports to the Chinese Minister, and that China had promptly given him new credentials and instructed him to invite assistance from the friendly Republic whose

---

250 Helmuth Karl Bernhard Graf von Moltke, 1800–1891, Prussian field marshal, chief of staff of the Prussian army for 30 years and one of the creators of modern warfare.

Legation in Peking Imperial troops under the command of Yung Lu were at the time blowing up with gunpowder.

The same messenger also brought to the Belgian Minister a despatch from his Consul at Tien-tsin. Do not be uneasy, it said. Be tranquil. If misfortune should happen to him, the interests of Belgium would not suffer; M. de Cartier, who had been Chargé d'Affaires in Peking and was on his way home, had been detained in Shanghai and instructed to act as Minister in the event of his death. This news was very cheering to M. Joostens. Days followed quietly now, though "sniping" did not cease. Several casualties occurred among the garrison. A Russian was killed and an Austrian wounded; an Italian wounded and also a Japanese. In the Fu it was still dangerous for the Christian refugees to move about, and several were hit and two killed. But the Yamên became, more and more conciliatory, until we could gauge the advance of the reliefs by the degree of apology in their despatches. But all supplies were rigorously cut off, and the sufferings of the Christians were acute.

Chinese Messages to the Powers

On the 21st it became known that the representatives of the Great Powers had received despatches from the Tsung-li-Yamên enclosing copies of memorials forwarded by the Throne to the rulers of their respective States. That to Sir Claude MacDonald stated that the Grand Council had on July 3 sent them a telegram to be forwarded from the Emperor of China to the Queen appealing for England's assistance in extricating China from her present embarrassments. The Yamên said that the telegram "had long before been forwarded," and they now sent the Minister a copy. It was a profoundly interesting telegram, especially so because it followed the very day after the promulgation of an Imperial edict which commanded that Christians should be exterminated, extolled the loyal and patriotic services of the "Boxers" in burning out and slaying the Christians, and ordered the expulsion from China of all Christian missionaries.

The telegram proceeded to say that:–

> Lately, on account of enmity between the people and the converts disorderly people have seized the opportunity to

3 | 'THE SIEGE OF THE PEKING LEGATIONS'

commit lawless acts, with the result that all Powers suspected the Throne of supporting the people and being hostile to the converts, and there followed the attack and occupation of the Taku forts. Since then war has been threatening and the situation has become more and more complicated. Now England relies mainly on her trade with China, nine-tenths of which is British. England's action has always been friendly and she does not desire Chinese territory. But this war against all the Powers may end unfavourably for China, and in that case another Power may take the opportunity to seize territory in China. This will prejudice England alike with China. To England alone then China appeals for aid in extricating her from her difficulties.

Presumably some such similar letter was sent to the President of the United States, which called forth the reply:– "United States cheerfully aid China."

Obviously this was to be China's line of defence upon the day of reckoning. Not the Imperial troops had been firing upon the Legations from the Imperial wall and the city wall with shell, and shrapnel, round shot and expanding bullet, but banditti, whom China was desirous to suppress, but unable to suppress. Chinese troops had been "protecting" the Legations and "providing them with food." That these self-same banditti had been belauded in Imperial edicts as loyal and patriotic was a contradiction the power to explain away which might safely be entrusted to the dauntless mendacity of a Lo Feng-Luh or a Wu Ting Fang.

Sir Robert Hart

On the 22nd Sir Robert Hart received a despatch from the Tsungli-Yamên. They naively remarked that it was now one month since they had heard from him, and his silence gave them concern for his welfare. Moreover, a report had just reached them that his house had been burned, but they expressed the hope that he and all his staff were well. Another despatch requested his advice upon a Customs question that had arisen in Shanghai. Sir Robert Hart wrote a dignified reply. For more than a month, he said, he had been a refugee in the British

Legation with all his staff having had to flee from his house without warning; that all Customs records and papers and every paper and letter of value that he had accumulated during a lifetime, had been, destroyed; that not only his house, but some 19 other buildings in the occupation of his staff had been burned with all their contents; that the acting postal secretary had been killed by a shell, and two other members of his staff—Mr. Richardson and Mr. Macoun—had been wounded by bullets. Too proud to admit that they were being slowly starved by the Government he had served for 40 years, he made no allusion to the sufferings of the women and children deprived of the food to which they had been accustomed, and forced to exist on slender rations of rice and horseflesh.

The So-Called Armistice

Meanwhile, the armistice continued, if armistice it can be called where true armistice there was none. Desultory firing continued, and sniping was still the chief pastime at the Chinese outposts. Friendly relations were, however, opened with some Chinese soldiers in the Fu. A Japanese Volunteer established a bureau of intelligence to which the enemy's soldiers had access. One soldier was especially communicative, and earned high reward for the valuable information that he conveyed to us. For a week from July 26 to August 2 daily bulletins based upon this information of the advance of the relief column were posted on the bell tower of the British Legation. An unbroken series of victories was attending our relief forces. They had razed Yang Ts'un to the ground; they won a victory south of Ho-hsi-wu, another at Ho-hsi-wu, a third on this side of Ho-hsi-wu. They fought, again successfully, at Matou on the 29th and at Chang-chia-wan on the 30th. Chang-chia-wan is only some 20 miles from Peking, and hopes beat high that in a day or two the sound of the bugles would be heard.

Letters were given to the soldier to take to the general of the relief column, and a reward offered if an answer should be brought next day, but no answer was ever brought. Our informant had brought the armies along too quickly. He was compelled to send them back. Accordingly on the 31st he made the Chinese recapture Chang-chia-wan, killing 60 of the foreigners; advancing upon Matou he killed 70 foreigners more, and drove them back to An-ping. Next day be drove the foreigners disastrously back to Tien-tsin with a loss of 1,000. The day was equally disastrous to himself. Our informant had killed the goose that lay the golden egg. For a messenger arrived on that day with letters from Tien-tsin, dated July 30, informing us that a large force was on the point of leaving for our relief.

Impudent Chinese Demands

Meanwhile, while our informant was marching our relief backwards and forwards to Tien-tsin, Prince Ching and others were vainly urging the Ministers to leave Peking, but whether they left Peking or not they were to hand over the Christian refugees now under the protection of the Legations to the mercies of the Government, which had issued a decree commanding that they be exterminated unless they recanted their errors. In other communications Prince Ching "and others" urged that the foreign Ministers should telegraph to their Governments *en clair* lying reports of the condition of affairs in Peking.

Two days after the cessation of hostilities Prince Ching "and others" sent a despatch to Sir Claude MacDonald to the effect that it was impossible to protect the Ministers in Peking because "Boxers" were gathering from all points of the compass, and that nothing would satisfy them (the "Boxers") but the destruction of the Legations, and that the Ministers would be given safe conduct to Tien-tsin.

Sir Claude, in reply, asked why it was that protection could be given to the Ministers on the way to Tien-tsin and yet could not be given to them while in the Legations in Peking. Prince Ching "and others" replied:–

July 25, 1900.
From first to last we have never neglected the protection of the Legations, but owing to the fact that the number of rebellious people are daily increasing, we are greatly afraid that something may happen too suddenly to be guarded against and produce a great calamity. This was why we renewed the suggestion for a temporary retirement.

> As to the inquiry what difference there is between giving protection in the city or on the road, and why it is possible to give it in the latter, there is only an apparent discrepancy. For the being in the city is permanent, the being on the road is temporary. If all the foreign Ministers are willing to temporarily retire we should propose the route to Tung-chau and thence by boat down stream to Tien-tsin, which could be reached in only two days. No matter what difficulties there might be a numerous body of troops would be sent, half by water to form a close escort, half by road to keep all safe for a long way on both banks. Since the time would be short we can guarantee that there would be no mishap. It is otherwise with a permanent residence in Peking, where it is impossible to foretell when a disaster may occur. No matter whether by day or by night, a single hour or a single moment's remissness may produce an alarm without time to take precautions. This can readily be understood, and there is no inconsistency involved.
>
> As your Excellency and the other foreign Ministers have to arrange the re-establishment of the status quo, it would seem better to settle matters at Tien-tsin, and we would repeat our request that you will pack your baggage by an early date and name a fixed day in order that we may prepare boats and provisions. Compliments.

In the envelope which brought this letter were two other communications of the same guileless nature.

> On July 24 (said the first) we received a telegram from Mr. Warren, British Consul-General in Shanghai, to the effect that while China was protecting the Legations no telegram had been received from the British Minister and asking the Yamên to transmit to Sir C. M. MacDonald's telegram to Shanghai.
>
> As in duty bound we communicate the above, and beg you to send a telegram en clair to the Yamên for transmission.

Tender consideration was shown for us in the second letter:–

> For the past month and more military affairs have been very pressing. Your Excellency and other Minister sought to telegraph

3 | 'THE SIEGE OF THE PEKING LEGATIONS'

home that your families are well in order to soothe anxiety, but at the present moment peace is not yet restored, and your Legation telegrams must be wholly en clair, stating that all is well without touching on military affairs. Under those conditions the Yamên can transmit them.

The writers beg that your Excellency will communicate this to the other foreign Ministers.

Evasive replies were given to these communications. Further particulars as to the kind of protection that was to be given on the way to Tien-tsin were asked for. Naturally the Ministers said that it was impossible to send a telegram informing the home Governments that women and children were well, in view of the fact that women and children had suffered from being cooped up in the British Legation and from being so long deprived of the food to which they were accustomed. Our position at this time compelled us to temporize. We knew from the alteration in tone of the Chinese despatches that they had suffered defeats and were growing alarmed, but we did not know how much longer international jealousies or difficulties of obtaining transport were to delay the departure of the troops for Tien-tsin.

Tidings from Tien-Tsin

Great, then, was the rejoicing in the Legation when, on July 28, for the first time since the siege began, a letter was received from outside by the British Minister. It was from Mr. W. R. Carles,[251] the British Consul in Tien-tsin, a gentleman of considerable experience in the Consular service. At the risk of his life the courier had brought the despatch through the enemy's lines. When the letter was posted at the Bell Tower there was a rush to read it. It said verbatim and literatim:–

> Tien-tsin, July 22, Your letter July 4. There are now 24,000 troops landed and 19,000 here. General Gaselee expected Ta-ku to-morrow. Russian troops are at Peitsang. Tien-tsin city under

---

251 William Richard Carles, 1848–1929, British diplomat, Sinologist and explorer who traveled extensively in Korea, and Manchuria. He published a book about life in Korea (1888).

foreign government and "Boxer" power here is exploded. There are plenty of troops on the way if you can keep yourselves in food. Almost all ladies have left Tien-tsin. The Consulate is being repaired.

W. CARLES

Men read this communication and then moved away to express their feelings beyond hearing of the ladies. It was amusing to witness the petulance with which the British were forced to admit that this somewhat incoherent production was really written by a Consul still in the British service.

With this document it was impossible to know whether the troops were on the way to Peking from Tien-tsin, or to Tien-tsin from Europe, who were the troops, and how many, or whether the number landed was 24,000 in all or 43,000, while the observation that the troops were coming if our provisions held out seemed to imply that if our provisions failed the troops would return to Tien-tsin.

A day or two later a letter equally instructive was received from Mr. Ragsdale, the American Consul at Tien-tisn. When Mr. Conger had succeeded in deciphering the message extracts from it were posted at the Bell Tower. It began, "I had a bad dream about you last night." It contained not a shred of information for which we were longing, but it contained a superfluous expression of the Consul's wish, "It is my earnest desire that you may all be spared." Equally it was our desire, and this explained our anxiety to receive news of the reliefs.

How the Chinese Kept the Armistice

Though now nominally under the protection of an armistice sniping still continued, especially in the Pu, into any exposed portion of the besieged area. Many Chinese refugees were hit. An Italian, a Japanese, and a German were wounded, a Russian and a German were killed, and another Russian dangerously wounded. An American was wounded; a French marine was killed, but most serious casualty of all, the brave Captain Labrousse, of the French Legation, who had with Captain Darcy stood at the forefront of the defence of his Legation, was shot

3 | 'THE SIEGE OF THE PEKING LEGATIONS'

through the forehead and fell dead into the arms of his comrade only two days before the reliefs marched into Peking.

The Chinese worked on continuously at their fortifications. They built a powerful fort on the city wall commanding the German Legation and another beyond the American Legation. Across the North Bridge they ran up in a single night a stout wall of brick and manned it with sharpshooters. During the siege our men had gained great skill in sharpshooting. Sergeant Saunders especially showed rare skill in picking off the enemy's crack shots. Finding that the Ministers declined to telegraph to their Governments *en clair* that all was well with the Legations, the Tsung-li-Yamên wrote to Sir Robert Hart asking him to send home a telegram in the sense they suggested. Sir Robert replied diplomatically, "If I were to wire the truth about the Legations I should not be believed."

The Chinese and the Native Christians

A malevolent attempt was next made by the Chinese to obtain possession of the refugees who were in our safe keeping. On July 27 they wrote to Sir Claude MacDonald saying that "they hear that there are lodged at the Legations a considerable number of converts, and that, as the space is limited and weather hot, they suggest that they must be causing the Legations considerable inconvenience. And now that people's minds are quieted, these converts can all be sent out and go about their ordinary avocations. They need not have doubts or fears. If you concur, an estimate should be made of the numbers and a date fixed for letting them out. Then all will be in harmony." The reply of the diplomatic body was to the effect that while they were considering the two last letters—one offering safe conduct to Tien-tsin and the other declaring that the converts might leave the Legations in perfect security—heavy firing was heard in the direction of the Pei-tang, which was evidently being attacked in force; that yesterday and last night a barricade was built across the North Bridge, from behind which shots are being continuously fired into the British Legation. The French and Russian Legations are also being fired upon. As all this seems inconsistent with the above letters, an explanation is asked for before further consideration is given to the offer.

Promptly the Yamên sent its explanation. The Pei-tang refugees, it seemed, who were starving, had made a sortie to obtain food. And they had fired upon the people. "A decree," it went on to say, "has now been requested to the effect that if the converts do not come out to plunder they are to be protected, and not to be continually attacked, for they also are the children of the State. This practice (of continually firing upon the converts) will thus be gradually stopped."

Such a callous reply was read with indignation, and there was not the slightest intention on the part of any Minister to leave Peking. Yet on the 4th of August a decree was issued appointing, Yung Lu to conduct the foreign Ministers safely to Tien-tsin "in order once more to show the tenderness of the Throne for the men from afar."

Then the Yamên, knowing that our reliefs were marching victoriously from Tien-tsin, began showing small courtesies to the Ministers. They announced to Marquis di Salvaggo Raggi their grief at receiving news of the death of the King of Italy, and they informed him that Lo Feng-Luh had been appointed by special decree to express the condolences of the Emperor and Dowager Empress. On the death of the Duke of Edinburgh the Yamên made a similar notification to the British Minister, and this gave Sir Claude an opportunity which he did not fail to seize of reminding the Yamên of the strange inconsistency of their action. The presence of Lo Feng-Luh in London engaged in conveying condolences to her Majesty indicated a maintenance of friendly relations which was in no way compatible with the existence of hostilities in Peking, and the continued deprivation extending over two months of the Legations of food. Sir Claude might well have added that he had no reason to think that his Excellency the Chinese Minister in London was inditing his despatches to the Foreign Office sandbagged in his chancery in Portland-place with 12-pounder shells exploding on the bed-room floor, and with the guards under a barricade opposite firing volleys into his family's dwelling rooms.

To our final protest against the shooting which deafened us at night and which, though we did not admit it, accounted as time went on for so many casualties, the Tsung-li-Yamên impudently replied, saying, "With regard to the firing at night it was, as before, the result of mutual misunderstanding. It was more or less on the same footing as the

3 | 'THE SIEGE OF THE PEKING LEGATIONS'

sounding of the evening drum and the morning bell, the daily duty of temple priests. It is really hardly worth a smile."

The Lasy Days of the Seige

On August 10, Friday, a messenger succeeded in passing the enemy's lines, and brought us letters from General Gaselee[252] and General Fukushima.[253] A strong relief force was marching to Peking, and would arrive here if nothing untoward happened on the 13th or 14th. Our danger then was that the enemy would make a final effort to rush the Legations before the arrival of reinforcements. And the expected happened. For the last two days we had to sustain a furious fusillade and bombardment, and our casualties were many. One shell burst in Sir Claude MacDonald's bed-room. But our defences were now admirable and our walls shell-proof. We had seized the Mongol market, and killed the general in command of the Shansi troops who had undertaken to reduce the Legations in five days.

On August 12 the impersonal body "Prince Ching and others" wrote requesting an audience with the foreign Ministers to discuss the preliminaries of a cessation of hostilities. Permission was given and the interview fixed for 11 a.m. next day, but the Ministers never came. At the last moment they were "too occupied," or too frightened, to come. Yesterday passed under a continuous fusillade which increased during the night. Then at 3 on this morning we were all awakened by the booming of guns in the east and by the welcome sound of volley firing. Word flew round that "the foreign troops are at the city wall

---

252 General Sir Alfred Gaselee, 1844–1918, spent his career in the Indian Army where he rose to quartermaster-general. He was chosen to lead the British expeditionary force to break the siege in Peking. He was made a full general in 1906.
253 Baron General Fukushima Yasumasa, 1852–1919, general in the Imperial Japanese Army. Descended from a samurai family Fukushima studied foreign languages of which he was fluent in 10. He fought on the government side during the Satsuma Rebellion (1877) and gained a posting with the army General Staff. He served in Japanese diplomatic mission in Peking and Berlin, the last being the point of departure for an epic horse ride across Russia to Japan. He commanded troops in the Sino-Japanese War (1895) and again before and after the Boxer rebellion in Tianjin and Peking. He also wrote poetry. He featured in popular art, see p. 37.

and are shelling the East Gate." At daylight most of us went on to the wall, and witnessed the shelling of the Great East Gate. We knew that the allies would advance in separate columns, and were on the *qui vive* of excitement, knowing that at any moment now the troops might arrive. Luncheon, the hard luncheon of horseflesh, came on, and we had just finished when the cry rang through the Legation "The British are coming," and there was a rush to the entrance and up Canal-street towards the Water Gate. The stalwart form of the general and his staff were entering by the Water Gate, followed by the 1st Regiment of Sikhs and the 7th Rajputs. They passed down Canal-street, and amid a scene of indescribable emotion marched to the British Legation. The siege has been raised.

Postscript
Peking, Aug 15.

On reading over my narrative of the siege I find that in the hurry and confusion of concluding my report I have omitted one or two things that I had wished to say.

In the first place, I find that I have not in any adequate way expressed the obligation of all those confined in the British Legation to the splendid services done by the Rev. F. D. Gamewell, of the American Episcopal Mission, to whom was due the designing and construction of all our defences, and who carried out in the most admirable manner the ideas and suggestions of our Minister, Sir Claude MacDonald.

To the Rev. Frank Norris, of the Society for the Propagation of the Gospel, our thanks are also specially due. He superintended, often under heavy fire, the construction of defences in the Princes' Pu and in other exposed places, working always with a courage and energy worthy of admiration. He was struck in the neck once by a segment of a shell, but escaped marvellously from serious injury. He speaks Chinese well, and Chinese worked under him with a fearlessness that few men can inspire.

In the second place, I notice that I have not sufficiently recorded the valuable services rendered by Mr. H. G. Squiers, the First Secretary of the American Legation, who on the death of Captain Strouts became Chief of the Staff to Sir Claude MacDonald. He had been for 15 years in the United States cavalry, and his knowledge and skill and the resolution with which he inspired his small body of men will not readily be forgotten.

Finally, writing as an Englishman, I desire to place on record the excellent discipline, steadiness under fire, courage, and eagerness of the non-commissioned officers and men of the Royal Marine Light Infantry, who defended the British Legation throughout the siege and who constantly reinforced the most dangerous outposts. I am but expressing the opinion of every one of the community in the British Legation in saying that our men kept up the best traditions of the British Army.

To-day the Pei-tang Cathedral was relieved. Bishops, priests, and sisters had survived the siege, and, thanks to the wonderful foresight of Bishop Favier, the Christians had been spared from starvation. Japanese coming down from the north of the city relieved the cathedral; French, British, and Russians from the south arrived as the siege was raised. Mines had been employed with deadly effect. The guards had lost five French killed and five Italians. Some 200 of the Christians had perished.

The victorious armies gather in Forbidden City in Peking on 28 November 1900 celebrated their victory.
Public domain

Chapter 4

AN IMPERIAL PROCESSION

At the height of the Boxer Uprising Tsu Hsi, the Empress Dowager, and the Imperial Court fled to Sian-fu[254] in Shannxi province. Sian was one the four ancient capitals of China and the former seat of the Tang Dynasty, among other dynasties. The Court fled because they feared reprisals from the western powers who knew that the Boxer's attempt to kill western officials at the Peking Legations had the active support of the government. The foreign powers would impose a draconian peace settlement on the Chinese Empire for the fact of the rebellion and the aid and comfort the government had given the rebels. It would be Li Hung-chang's melancholy duty, his last for the Empire before he died in November 1901, to negotiate the terms of this punitive treaty.

The article republished here does not deal with treaty matters. Instead it recounts the return of the Imperial court from Sian. And what a journey it was. The first part an Imperial procession on a specially built road, the second part, Tsu Hsi's first trip on a railway. This article allows Morrison to show his readers the extraordinary procedures of the Chinese court, in its almost mediaeval complexity, and the lengths it takes to move about the country, everyone keeping to their allotted place. It is one of the few general feature articles he wrote for *The Times*, one that gives readers a sense of life in China.

254 Xi'an today.

Significant also is that the journey marks a change in attitude towards the railway by the elite and Tsu Hsi in particular. She had hated railways. To her they were the outward manifestation of an inward technological superiority possessed by barbarians from the West. They were also unpopular among ordinary, rural Chinese. The paths they took often meant the destruction of graves and, in a country such as China where the official belief system, Confucianism, placed ancestor worship at the apex of familial duty, the destruction of graves was no trivial matter.

The year 1875 was important for the railways in China. The first operational railway was built that year and it ran between Shanghai and Wusung;[255] it was financed by Jardine Matheson, a British conglomerate in the making, whose fortunes rested on the opium trade. Also that year, Li Hung-chang, a high official who wanted to see China modernise made what was to prove an abortive attempt to Tsu Hsi's backing for railways. He had a short stretch of line laid and Tsu Hsi sat in a carriage that was pulled by donkeys. Much like her contemporary Queen Victoria, she was not amused. This bode ill for the future of railways in China. The line Jardine Matheson financed was built without official sanction. This raised the ire of officialdom, and when a local man was run over and killed there was outcry and the Chinese government moved to teach the foreigner a lesson. The line was closed and within a year the government, after paying compensation, took control. It did so, however, not to operate the railway by to destroy it. The government dismantled the line and dumped the scrap iron and locomotives on the shores of Taiwan to rust. A temple to the Queen of Heaven was erected on the site in Shanghai where the main station once stood. No more powerful a symbol of utter rejection of westernisation was there and it took nearly 20 years for another line to be built, and that only after much lobbying by officials, including the previously unsuccessful Li Hung-chang. Yet progress was slow. As late as 1896, China's railway network amounted to some 370 miles of track. That compared with 182,000 miles in the US, 21,000 miles in Britain and 2,300 miles in Japan.[256]

---

255 Wosong today and more a district than a place. Located to the north of Shanghai on the mouth of the Huangpo River (formerly Wusung River).
256 Spence, op. cit., p. 250.

4 | AN IMPERIAL PROCESSION

By the time Morrison was writing, the global railway industry—encompassing iron, steel, coal, and engineering—was the largest industry in the world. The value of rail stocks on the London Stock Exchange and the New York Stock Exchange dwarfed any other industry or activity, such as banking. In 1900, the rail industry accounted for 50 per cent of the value of *all* companies listed on the London Stock Exchange and some 63 per cent of the New York Stock Exchange.[257] Some of the companies listed on those stock exchanges and others were very active in China, a new frontier for the expansion of their industry. When historians talk about the "battle for concessions" in late Imperial China, rail concessions are very high on the list, along with mining.

Indeed, the railway Tsu Hsi rode on was built and operated by the *Société d'Etude de Chemins de Fer en Chine*, a Belgium company. Its chief engineer, the man pictured in the photograph accompanying the article, was Jean Jadot, a Belgian railway engineer who later became an influential banker in Belgium. Before he went to China he had worked on a railway in Cairo. In China, Jadot was to oversee the construction of the country's main north-south line which passed through central China to the Yangtze River. In all, the line would run for 754 miles (1,200 kms). In 1908, the year of Tsu Hsi's death, the Chinese government would wrest control of the Peking-Hankow line from its Belgium concessionaires. To do this it raised £5 million in London and Paris via a 5 per cent loan to buyout the Belgians. This time, rather than destroy the line, the government kept the railway, and, in spite of official graft, it turned a profit.

Morrison refers to the line as the Luhan railway, a word constructed from the first characters of Luguachio, located near the celebrated Marco Polo Bridge outside Peking, and in the south it terminated at Hankow, hence Luhan. The Empress Dowager changed trains, to one operated by British concessionaires, for her final journey into Peking.

---

[257] Global investment Returns Yearbook 2024 (Summary), Elroy Dimson et al, Zurich: UBS AG, 2024, p. 12 and charts.

'The Chinese Court's First Railway Journey'

(From Our Own Correspondent)
Shanghai, 6 February 1901[258]

The following description of the first railway journey undertaken by the Chinese Court can scarcely fail to be of general interest. I am indebted for its details to the courtesy of M. Jadot,[259] engineer in chief of the Luhan railway,[260] who accompanied the Imperial party from Cheng-ting-fu[261] to Fengtai,[262] and personally superintended the traffic and other arrangements for the journey. Early on December 31st the Court arrived at Cheng-ting-fu, escorted by a large body of cavalry and accompanied by an enormous suite of officials, eunuchs and servants. The baggage was carried by a train of carts, estimated by an eye-witness at 3,000. The eunuchs numbered between 300 and 400, and of cooks and other kitchen servants there were almost as many.

---

258 Published 13 February 1901, p. 8.
259 By his admission, Morrison's source for much that follows was Jean Jadot (1862–1932), Belgian railway engineer and banker. In 1898, Jadot moved from Egypt, where he had developed a tram system for Cairo, to China to join the *Société d'Etude de Chemins de Fer en Chine* as director of works for the Peking-Hankow railway. The Imperial court used a section of this line on their return to Peking from Xi'an. On his return to Brussels in 1906, Jadot was made Director in charge of the Industry Department at the Société Générale de Belgique.
260 This is now known as the Jinghan Railway and is the northern section of the Peking-Canton Railway. In Morrison's time, the line terminated at the Lugou Bridge, precisely 20 miles from Peking—the distance stipulated by the Empress Dowager for railways to terminate from the capital.
261 Today known as Zhengding and located in south-west Hebei province.
262 A district south west of Peking.

Jean Jadot, centre in white cap, inspecting a section of the Peking-Hankow railway c. 1900.

To provide accommodation for such a mass of people was impossible, especially as all the best quarters in the town had already been occupied by the high officials who, with their retainers, had come from the north to welcome the Empress Dowager on her return. For three days the Court rested in Cheng-ting-fu, during which time the scene was one of indescribable confusion; baggage, stacked haphazard, filled every available corner, eunuchs and servants camping around and upon it, stolidly enduring much physical discomfort with the apathy peculiar to Asiatics. Yet, so great was the cold (on the night of January 1st the thermometer stood at 20 deg. cent. below zero) that many of these wayfarers gave way to lamentations and tears. Officials of the lower and middle grades, unable to obtain a lodging, were compelled to pass these days in such makeshift shelter as they could find in the vicinity of the railway station, where swarmed a mob of undisciplined soldiery.

On the second night a fire broke out in the stables of the Imperial residence, which, though eventually checked before much damage was done, added greatly to the general disorder and might well have had serious results, in the absence of all organization and control. The definite announcement of the Court's intention to leave for Pao-

4 | 'THE CHINESE COURT'S FIRST RAILWAY JOURNEY'

ting-fu[263] on the 3rd was received with unmistakable relief by the hungry motley crowd which represented the pomp and pride of Asia's greatest Empire.

From the Yellow River to the railway terminus at Cheng-ting-fu—a distance of about 250 miles the ever-growing Imperial procession had travelled almost continuously in chairs, litters, carts, and on horseback; affording a spectacle which recalled in many of its chief characteristics those of Europe's medieval pageantry as described by Scott.[264] Every Manchu Prince had a retinue of horsemen varying from 30 to 100 in number; along the frost-bound, uneven tracks which serve for roads in Northern China an unending stream of laden wagons creaked and groaned through the short winter's days and on, guided by soldier torchbearers, through bitter nights to the appointed stopping places. But for the Empress Dowager and the Emperor, with the Chief Eunuch and the ladies of the Court, there was easy journeying and a way literally made smooth. Throughout its entire distance the road over which the Imperial palanquins were borne had been converted into a smooth, even surface of shining clay, soft and noiseless under foot; not only had every stone been removed, but as the procession approached gangs of men were employed in brushing the surface with feather brooms. At intervals of about ten miles well appointed rest-houses had been built, where all manner of food was prepared. The cost of this King's highway, quite useless, of course, for the ordinary traffic of the country, was stated by a native contractor to amount roughly to 50 Mexican dollars for every eight yards—say £1,000 a mile—the clay having to be carried in some places from a great distance. As an example of the lavish expenditure of the Court and its officials, in a land where squalor is a pervading feature, this is typical.[265]

---

263 Today known as Baoding, Hebei province.
264 Sir Walter Scott was a romantic novelist of the early 19th century and the originator of modern historical fiction in English.
265 Old habits die hard. Fifty years later, in December 1949, when Mao Zedong made his first visit to Moscow to meet Stalin, he travelled in an armoured carriage with sentries posted every 100 metres along the railway lines. See Frank Dikötter, *The Tragedy of Liberation*, Bloomsbury, London, 2013, p. 122.

The hour for leaving Cheng-ting-fa was fixed by the Empress-Dowager at 9.30 a.m. on January 3. It is significant of the character of this remarkable woman, now in her 69th year, that even in matters of detail she leaves nothing to chance, nothing to others; the long arm of her unquestioned authority reaches from the Throne literally to the servants' quarters. Without creating any impression of fussiness, she makes a distinctly feminine personality felt, and the master-mind which has guided the destinies of China for the last 40 years by no means disdains to concern itself in minor questions of household commissariat and transport. It is impossible not to reflect what such a woman might have been, what she might have done for her people, had there come into her life some accident or influence to show her, in their true light, the corruption, dishonesty, and cold-blooded cruelty of her reign. It is impossible to forget that this woman, now affably discussing with the Belgian railway personnel incidents of the day's journey, is the same who, 18 months ago, gave the orders under which Yuan Chang and Hsi Ching-cheng[266] were sawn in pieces for counselling friendly relations with the hated foreigner.

The departure of the Court by a special train, long since prepared for its reception by the Belgian railway authorities and Sheng Ta-jên, was fixed for 9.30 a.m. in accordance with her Majesty's orders; that Imperial and imperious lady, however, made her appearance at the station at 7 o'clock, accompanied by the young Empress, the Imperial concubine, and the ladies in waiting. The Emperor had preceded her, and upon her arrival knelt on the platform to perform respectful obeisance, in the presence of an interested crowd. The next two hours were spent by the Empress, who showed no signs of fatigue, in supervision of the arrangements for despatching the vast accumulation of her personal baggage, and in holding informal audiences with various high dignitaries, military and civil, on the platform. Amongst, others, she sent for M. Jadot and spent some time in friendly conversation with him, expressing great satisfaction at the excellent arrangements made for her comfort, and pleasure at exchanging the sedan chair for her luxuriously appointed

---

266 Two senior Ching dynasty officials. Yuan was Vice-President of the Court of Sacrifices, while Hsu (Morrison misspells his name) was Senior Vice President of the Board of Civil Office.

drawing-room car. She took pains to impress upon the engineer-in-chief the importance which she attached to keeping the Court's baggage and effects within reach, evincing on this subject much determination of a good-humoured kind. Eventually, after the despatch of four freight trains, her mind was relieved of this anxiety, but it was to be clearly understood that the same personal supervision would be exercised at Pao-ting-fu, for in no circumstances could the impedimenta be sent on in advance to Peking.

There is a touch of feminine nature in this incident which can hardly fail to bring the Empress Dowager into some degree of kinship with her fellow women in other lands; there is also an implied reflection on the honesty of persons in attendance on the Court which is not without significance.

The scene upon the platform was one of remarkable interest. In utter subversion of all accepted ideas in regard to the seclusion and privacy in which the Chinese Court is supposed to live, move, and have its being, there was on this occasion—and indeed throughout the journey —no sign of either attempt or wish to guard their Majesties from observation and intrusion. The crowd, quietly inquisitive but showing no inclination to demonstration of any sort, came and went at its pleasure; Yuan Shih-kai's braves, who to the number of about 1,000 travelled to Peking as the Empress-Dowager's bodyguard, crowded around the Imperial party, invading even their railway carriages. While the ruler of the Empire held audience with some of its highest officials, none of their retainers were employed, as might have been expected, in keeping the people at a respectful distance; the scene, in fact, bore striking testimony to that democratic side of the Chinese character which cannot but impress itself on every foreign visitor to a Viceroy's or magistrate's yamên in the present instance, however, it must have been, for all concerned, a new and remarkable experience.

To the native spectators, the ladies of the Court with their eunuch attendants were as much objects of interest as the foreign railway officials; the Imperial concubine, a lively young person of pleasing appearance, attracting much attention. This lady, gaily clad and with lavishly painted face, bestowed upon everything connected with the train an amount of attention which augurs well for the future of railway enterprise in China, running from car to car and chatting volubly with the ladies in waiting. All the ladies of the Court wore pearls in profusion—those of the Empress being particularly fine—and all smoked cigarettes in place of the time-honoured water-pipe. Herein again, for the optimistically inclined, may be found a harbinger of progress. During the Empress Dowager's audiences, lasting sometimes over a quarter of an hour at a time, the Emperor stood close at her side; invariably silent, generally listless, though his expression when animated is described as conveying an impression of remarkable intelligence. The young Empress has good features, marred, in European eyes, by excessive use of paint; she, too, appeared to be melancholy, and showed but little interest in her surroundings. The Emperor and both Empresses were simply dressed in quiet coloured silks.

The special train in which, punctually at 9.30 a.m., the rulers of China left for their capital consisted of a locomotive and 21 carriages, arranged in the following order:– Nine freight-cars, laden with servants, sedan chairs, carts, mules, &c.; a guard's-van, for employees of the railway; two first-class carriages (Imperial Princes); Emperor's special carriage; first-class carriage, for high officials in attendance (Yung-Lu, Yuan Shih-kai, General Sung Ching,[267] Lu Chuan-lin, Governor Tsen of Shansi,[268] &c.); Empress Dowager's special carriage; special carriages of the young Empress and the Imperial concubine; two second-class carriages, for eunuchs in attendance; first-class carriage (Chief Eunuch), and the, "Service" carriage of M. Jadot.

The special carriages had been prepared at great expense under instructions issued by the Director-General of Railways, Shêng.[269] Those of the Empress Dowager, the Emperor, and his consort were luxuriously furnished with costly curios and upholstered in Imperial yellow silk;

---

267 Song Qing, 1820–1902, was appointed general in 1862, however he was more defeated than victorious in his military career. His last battle was that of Yangcun where in defence of the Boxer uprising, he encountered the allied army *en route* to Peking to relieve the foreign Legations.

268 Cen Chunxuan, 1861–1933, was acting governor of Shanxi at the time of this journey. After this he became governor-general of Sichuan and later viceroy of Liangguang (Guangdong and Guangxi). He was forced into retirement by Yuan Shikai in 1911. He became a republican and supporter of Sun Yat Sen.

269 Sheng Xuanhuai, 1844–1916, a pro-modernisation Qing official important in China's early embrace of railways and telegraphs. He was an advisor to Yuan Shikai.

each had its throne divan and reception room. Heavy window curtains had been thoughtfully provided in the carriages intended for the ladies' use; they were not required, however, as none of the party showed any desire for privacy during the entire journey. While travelling, the carriage of the Empress Dowager was the general rendezvous of all the ladies, attended by their eunuchs, the Empress Dowager spending much of the time in conversation with the Chief Eunuch—of somewhat notorious character—and the Emperor.

At Ting-chau luncheon was served, the Empress Dowager and Emperor eating together in the former's carriage. By her orders special dishes, in great number and variety, were sent to the various high officials in attendance, M. Jadot receiving particular marks of this attention. At 3 p.m. the train arrived at its destination, Pao-ting-fu, and the Empress expressed to M. Jadot her great satisfaction at the punctuality observed. For three days—from January 4 to January 6—the Court rested in Pao-ting-fu.

The Empress-Dowager possesses in a marked degree a characteristic frequently observed in masterful natures; she is extremely superstitious. The soothsayers and astrologers of the Court at Peking enjoy no sinecure; on the other hand, more attention is paid to their advice than that which the average memorialist obtains, and the position of necromancer to the Throne is not unprofitable. On the present occasion the sages in ordinary had fixed the auspicious hour for the Sovereign's return to Peking at 2 p.m. on January 7; M. Jadot was accordingly requested to make the necessary arrangements to this end, and the Empress-Dowager repeatedly impressed upon him the importance which she attached to reaching the Yung-ting gate[270] of the city at that particular hour. To do this, as the engineer in chief pointed out, would entail starting from Pao-ting-fu at 7 a.m., but the determined ruler of China was not to be put off by any such considerations. At 6 a.m. this wonderful woman arrived at the station; it was freezing hard, and a sandstorm was raging violently; soldiers, bearing lanterns and torches, led the way for the chair-bearers, since the day had not yet dawned. The

---

270 Also written as Yongdingmen, or Gate of Perpetual Peace. Constructed by the Ming in 1553, it was the front gate of the outer city of Peking old city wall. This wall was torn down in the 1950s as part of Mao's desire to modernise the city. It was rebuilt in 2005.

scene in all its details appeals powerfully to the imagination. Once more the baggage question monopolized the Empress Dowager's attention; her last freight train, laden with spoils of the southern provinces, preceded the Imperial train by only 20 minutes. It will be realized that the august lady's requirements in the matter of personal supervision of her property added responsibility of a most serious kind to the cares—at no time light—of the railway staff.

An incident occurred at Pao-ting-fu which throws a strong sidelight upon the Empress Dowager's character. The high Chinese officials above mentioned, who travelled in the first-class carriage between the Emperor's special car and that of the Empress, finding themselves somewhat pressed for space, consulted the railway officials and obtained another first class compartment, which was accordingly added to the train. Her Majesty, immediately noticing this, called for explanations, which failed to meet with her approval. The extra carriage was removed forthwith, Yuan Shih-kai and his colleagues being reluctantly compelled to resume their uncomfortably crowded quarters; to these her Majesty paid a visit of inspection before leaving the station, making inquiries as to the travellers' comfort and expressing complete satisfaction at the arrangements generally. At 11.30 a.m., punctual to the minute, the train arrived at Feng-tai, where the Luhan line from Lu-kou-kiao meets the Peking-Tientsin Railway; here the British authorities took charge. The Empress Dowager was much reassured by the excellence of the arrangements and the punctuality observed; nevertheless, she continued to display anxiety as to the hour of reaching Peking, frequently comparing her watch with railway time. To M. Jadot, who took leave of their Majesties at Feng-tai, she expressed again the satisfaction she had derived from this her first journey by rail, promising to renew the experience before long and to be present at the official opening of communication between Han-kau[271] and the capital. She presented $5,000 for distribution among the European and Chinese *employés* of the line and decorated M. Jadot with the order of the Double Dragon, Second Class.

---

271 Now known as Hankou. It, along with Wuchang and Hanyang, were merged to become Wuhan in 1949, a major industrial city on the Yangtze.

4 | 'THE CHINESE COURT'S FIRST RAILWAY JOURNEY'

From Feng-tai the railway under British control runs directly to the main south gate of the Tartar city (Chien-men), but it had been laid down by the soothsayers and astrologers aforesaid that, for good augury and to conform with tradition, the Imperial party must descend at and enter the Chinese city by the direct road to the Palace through the Yung-ting-men.[272] At midday, therefore, leaving the railway, the Court started in chairs for the city, in the midst of a pageant as magnificent as the resources of Chinese officialdom permit. The scene has been described by European writers as imposing, but a Japanese correspondent refers to its mis en scene as suitable to a rustic theatre in his own country. Be this as it may, the Empress Dowager, reverently welcomed by the Emperor, who had preceded her, as usual, entered the city, from which she had fled so ignominiously 15 months before, at the hour named by her spiritual advisers as propitious. Present appearances at Peking, as well as the chastened tone of Imperial edicts, indicate that the wise men were right in their choice. It may be added, in conclusion, as a sign of the times, that the Empress Dowager's sleeping compartment, prepared under the direction of Shêng Ta-jên,[273] was furnished with a European bed. *Per contra*, it contained also materials for opium-smoking, of luxurious yet workmanlike appearance.

~

---

[272] Yongdingmen (Gate of Perpetual Peace), was was once the front gate of Peking's outer city wall. It was built by the Ming in 1553 and destroyed by Mao in the 1950s when most of old Peking's walls and gates were demolished. A replica was installed in 2005.

[273] 'Ta-jen' (daren) is a Qing honorific meaning, literally, big person. It is not his given name which Morrison seems to suggest it is.

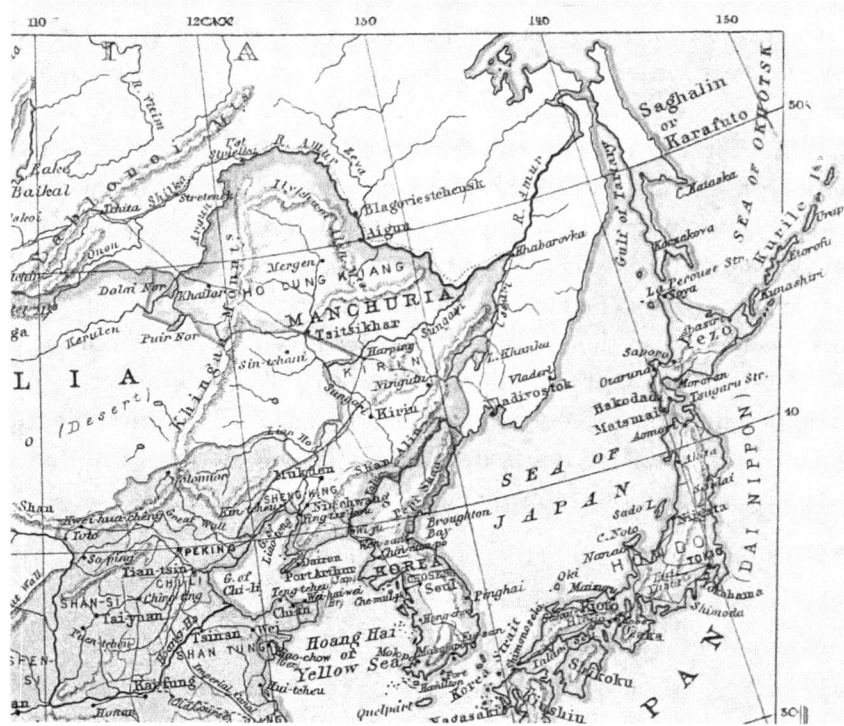

The theatre of the battle (detail). From: *J G Bartholomew, A Literary & Historical Atlas of Asia,* Lindon: J M Dent (n.d.) c. 1910.

Chapter 5

Japan Defeats Russia

In early 1905, Japan inflicted a crushing defeat on Imperial Russia. It was a defeat from which Czar Nicholas II would never really recover and which hastened the end of autocracy in Russia, at least that practiced by monarchs. In 1905, it also ended decisively Russia's 50-year quest to be the dominant power in the Far East in general and in north China in particular. The locus of the fighting was the waters of the Bohai Sea, the gateway to Peking, Tianjin, and the north-east, and the territory around Mukden, Shenyang today, the ancestral home of the Manchu founders of the Qing dynasty.

The war began in 1904 after Japan and Russia were unable to agree on their respective 'sphere of influence' in Korea and north China. The Russian rout started at the end of that year with the ignominious surrender by the Russian's at Port Arthur,[274] a strategic location at the point of the Liaoning peninsular which extends into the Bohai Sea. This setback was followed by two further defeats. In February 1905, Russia lost the Battle of Mukden,[275] the largest land battle the world had ever seen;[276] and then, at the end of May, in a naval engagement in the Straits

---

274 Lushun today.
275 Mukden is the Manchu name for what was subsequently known as Fengtian. Today it is known as Shenyang and is the capital of Liaoning province.
276 In February and March 1905, the two belligerents staged what is thought to be the largest battle the world had ever seen, involving 624,000 combatants. See Kotkin, op. cit., p. 73.

of Tsushima the Imperial Japanese Navy destroyed Russia's Baltic fleet, a fleet that had sailed 18,000 miles from its home waters to secure Russia's dominance of north China.

The Russo-Japanese War was one of the biggest events to take place in China while Morrison was *The Times'* resident correspondent. The war for control of Manchuria, and of Korea was arguably of greater global significance than the Boxer rebellion. Curiously, though, Morrison had very little to do with the day-to-day coverage of the war.

Moberly Bell, *The Times'* manager, devoted considerable resources to covering the conflict, enlisting the expertise of retired army and navy senior officers. As for reporting the War, *The Times* dispatched Lionel James, a 32-year-old, who had covered small wars in India and Africa, and had been with the newspaper in South Africa since 1899.[277] James had also introduced Moberly Bell to the idea of using wireless telegraphy, a new innovation in communication, to transmit his reports of the conflict. The wireless promised much speedier transmission of stories and hence ought to give *The Times* and edge on its competition,[278] or so it was hoped. The deployment of wireless technology for *The Times* was a mixed success. The cost proved astronomical; Moberly Bell calculated that the wireless cost the paper £1 a word,[279] around £80 in today's money. Another limiting factor, journalistically, was that James was dependent on the good graces of the Japanese military, principally the navy. The navy had an interest in delaying the timeliness of James' reports for reasons of battlefield security. Also, unbeknownst to James, the Japanese navy also planned to use wireless to communicate, making the Russo-Japanese War the first in which wireless was used for military and journalistic purposes.

It will be remembered that the first large scale article Morrison wrote for *The Times* was about the trans-Manchurian railway. The prescience of his focus on Russia's ambitions in Manchuria was born out by subsequent events, as was his concluding sentence: "And though

---

277 See Pearl, op. cit., p. 145.
278 Peter Slattery, *Reporting the Russo-Japanese War 1904–05 Lionel James's First Wireless Transmissions to The Times*, Global Oriental, Folkestone, 2004.
279 Pearl, op. cit., p. 145.

nearly every Russian I met on my journey spoke with unconcealed derision of her pretensions, the importance of Japan in relation to the future of Manchuria cannot be disregarded."

Tinged with what we now would regard as racism, the Russians were contemptuous of the Japanese and few could conceive of an 'Asiatic' power capable of resisting their military might. Not for the first time did such arrogance presage a fall. Japan was the poster child of rapid industrialisation at the end of the 19th century. And, as it had with China, Japan outstripped Russia in rapid industrialisation, industrialisation that underpinned its military prowess. The world had marvelled at Japan's defeat of China in 1894–95; 10 years later it was about to do the same.

For five months the Japanese laid siege to Port Arthur, its harbour littered with the pride of the Russian eastern navy, the land-based fortifications pummelled. The Russians surrendered on January 2, 1905 and Marshall Yamagata,[280] a senior Japanese politician, said Morrison should be invited to see the battlefield.[281] He rode with Sir Ernest Satow,[282] Britain's minister at Peking, on a borrowed pony. He recorded the following in his diary:

> Japanese carrying Russian sick on stretchers—much humanity. Russians doing nothing of the kind but witnessing procession … Past all the wrecked fleet burned and perhaps past repairs sight for French creditors a fleet destroyed by incapacity … All British officers spoke contemptuously of the Russian surrender and of the trenches paved with vodka bottles… introduced

---

[280] Prince Yamagata Aritomo, 1838–1922, was the Imperial Japanese Army's inaugural chief of staff and chief architect of the country's military. He twice served as Prime Minister and was a talented garden designer.

[281] "We are much indebted to Dr Morrison, for he counselled us to go to war against Russia never doubting the result," Yamagata said. See Pearl, op. cit., p 147.

[282] Sir Ernest Mason Satow, 1843–1929, known mostly for his role in Anglo-Japanese relations and his scholarly histories of Japan and his seminal *Guide to Diplomatic Practice,* currently still in print in its 7th edition. In 1900, he swapped posts with Sir Claude McDonald, him moving to Peking until 1906 and McDonald to Tokyo.

to Nogi,[283] Ijichi[284] his Chief of Staff and others. All very kind speaking flattering words.[285]

Not quite three weeks later, *The Times* published his account based on that visit. It was an excoriating description of Russian cowardice and incompetence. Morrison methodically and coolly described the scene he witnessed, a scene that in no way supported the contention of Russian General and commander Stössel that the Russian situation had become intolerable. On the contrary, Morrison found an abundance of food, ammunition, medicine and men who could have sustained battle for a further three months on what they had. What they did not have was leadership. Morrison's judgement, highlighted in the headline, was a "discreditable surrender." It reverberated around the chancelleries of Europe. As W. T. Stead, British newspaper editor said, Morrison's story altered Europe's opinion of Russia.[286]

As described above, Japan went on to victory on land and sea in the coming months. By mid-year the Americans were hosting a peace conference at Portsmouth. As part of that settlement the Japanese regained Port Arthur and took control of the railway. They rechristened it the South Manchurian Railway. In 1931, an 'incident' involving the railway, at Mukden, was staged by Japan as a pretext for Japan's full-scale invasion of Manchuria, the Second Sino-Japanese War, and the date from which some say World War II began. The world was no longer cheering the Japanese.

---

283 Count Nogi Maresuke, 1849–1912, general in the Imperial Japanese Army, governor general of Taiwan. He studied military science in Germany. He captured Port Arthur but lost many men. He requested permission to suicide but the Emperor refused. Under Nogi's leadership, "the conduct of the Japanese during the Russo-Japanese Was towards both prisoners and Chinese civilians won the respect, and indeed admiration, of the world." Richard Storry, *History of Modern Japan*, Penguin, London, p. 217. On the day of the Emperor Meiji's funeral, he and his wife committed suicide, in accordance with samurai tradition on the death of one's master.

284 Ijichi Kōsuke, 1854–1917, General Imperial Japanese Army. Chief of Staff of Japanese Third Army (Nogi's). He was the Military Attaché in Britain from 1898–1900.

285 Quoted by Pearl, op. cit., p. 147.

286 ibid.

'Port Arthur from Within: "Discreditable Surrender"'

(From Our Peking Correspondent)[287]

By favour of the Japanese Headquarters I have been permitted to visit Dalny[288] and Port Arthur, and have just returned to Peking. I witnessed the chivalrous courtesy with which the Japanese treated the Russian, prisoners, was present at the triumphal entry into Port Arthur, and joined in the service in honour of the heroic dead. I was allowed much freedom of movement, and was shown the formidable forts; I wandered through the town of Port Arthur; and, in the company of the brilliant officer who commanded the Naval Brigade of the besieging army and is now dockyard superintendent, I was taken in a steam launch to every wrecked ship, both in the harbour and across the entrance.

Strength of the Fortress

No one who has not seen all this can form any conception of the stupendous strength of the positions held by the Russians, or of the incredible heroism displayed in the capture of the forts. Port Arthur was stoutly defended by the Russian soldiers, and for long the resistance was splendid; but the death, on December 13, of General Kondrachenko,[289]

---

287 Published in *The Times* on 25 January 1905, p. 5.
288 Dalny is the Russian version of Dalian.
289 Roman Isidorovich Kondratenko, 1857–1904, is credited with improving and re-organising the defences of Port Arthur after his arrival there in 1903. He took command in the field and successfully repulsed four attempts by the Japanese to capture the port. He was killed in action on 2 December 1904 and 18 days later General

Port Arthur after the Russian capitulation, 1905.

who was responsible for the plan of defence, was as disastrous to the mortal of the garrison as the death of Admiral Makaroff[290] was to that of the fleet.

No foreign officer can explain the reason for the capitulation. Want of men certainly cannot explain it. Surgeon-General Balasheff, when discussing the terms us surrender, affirmed that, of the garrison of 25,000, only 5,000 were effective, the remaining 20,000 being sick and wounded in hospital. General Stössel[291] reduced the number to 4,000 effective, declaring that the hardships had been so intense that only

Stössel surrendered. The Japanese raised a granite cenotaph to Kondratenko on the spot where he died.

290 Stepan Osipovich Makarov, 1849–1904, was the Vice-admiral assigned to the defence of Port Arthur. An oceanographer, Makarov published extensively on naval tactics. He sought engagement with the Japanese navy. In April 1904, in pursuit of Japanese forces his battleship, *Petropavlovsk*, hit a mine and sank. The Japanese recovered his body in 1913 and buried him at the military cemetery at Port Arthur.

291 Anatoly Mikhaylovich Stössel, 1848–1915, fought in the Russo-Turkish War and distinguished himself during the Boxer rebellion with his actions during the Battle of Tientsin in July 1900. He was appointed in August 1903 as commander of the Russian garrison at Port Arthur. He was discharged from the army in September 1906 and court-martialled for cowardice in surrendering Port Arthur. He was sentenced to death, commuted to 10 years imprisonment. In May 1909, Czar Nicholas II pardoned him and he rejoined the army.

5 | 'PORT ARTHUR FROM WITHIN: "DISCREDITABLE SURRENDER"'

28 officers remained unscathed. Yet the Japanese found in the fortress more than 25,000 strong, able-bodied soldiers capable of making a sortie. They were well-clad and well-nourished, and included several hundreds of unscathed officers. Only 200 Russian officers are believed to have been killed or wounded during the siege. In the hospital there were 14,000 cases from all classes of the population, but only a small proportion were wounded. Many of them were suffering from minor ailments, such as rheumatism or scurvy, and there were many malingerers, especially among the officers.

Nor was failure of ammunition the reason for the surrender; for the first indication which the besiegers had that the fortress would fall was the reckless throwing away of small-arm and gun-fire ammunition, which was aimlessly discharged from all the defences throughout two days. Yet, in spite of this, and in spite of the ammunition thrown into the harbour, large quantities remained. Three magazines have been exploded; but the largest magazine of all, that in the torpedo depôt south of the western harbour, has not been touched, and is full to the roof of all kinds of ammunition for the naval guns.

Scarcity of food, again, could not have been the reason for the capitulation; for there was ample food for three months, even if we assume that the supplies would not be replenished by junks from the mainland. The waters teem with fish, and there were 2,000 horses in fairly good condition. No private stores had been commandeered. One large building in the Naval Dockyard contained 6,000 tons of flour untouched, most of which had recently been landed from the British steamer King Arthur; and many private stores were full of provisions. There was also abundance of champagne and other wines and medical comforts. In one store alone more than 4,000 dozen bottles of vodka were looted by the garrison on December 31.

Cold could not have been the reason for the surrender; for the weather was mild and the troops were well-clad with an abundance of warm clothing, while in addition there were large quantities of firewood, stacks of briquettes, and an immense amount of woodwork and scaffolding on large numbers of buildings which wore under construction. In addition there were stacks of coal near the railway and in private houses, and 70,000 tons in the dockyard alone, including more than 32,000 tons of Cardiff coal in the large coal sheds.

The Damage to Buildings

Finally, want of shelter could not have been the reason of the surrender. I know Port Arthur well, having been there four times in the year preceding the siege, and this is the result of the bombardment. Practically no buildings in the whole of the New Town are injured, nor has any injury been done to the fine barracks in Torpedo Bay. No buildings from the dockyard eastward to the sea have been damaged. The Japanese, with rare humanity, directed their fire on the docks, workshops, and the ships in the harbour, wasting little ammunition on the buildings. It is true that the Old Town between the eastern end of the railway and the engineer's residence and the creek were subjected to a severe bombardment; but, even in the midst of the destruction, Clarkson's offices and other buildings remained habitable. Only two shots struck the Viceroy's house, inflicting trifling damage, while one shell exploded near the church. General Smirnoff's and General Stössel's residences and many others round about are entirely uninjured. Practically no damage has been inflicted on any of the many large buildings. On the road to the racecourse there was much destruction, especially at the end of the street which leads to the quay and in which the offices of the *Novy Krai* are. Altogether the number of damaged buildings is so small, especially the number of inhabited buildings, that the success of the Japanese fire could not have been the reason for surrender. Many buildings are marked with the Red Gross; but in only one could I find any appreciable damage, the hospital which is in an exposed position above the railway and in a direct line with the dockyard being struck by one shell. Stories about the Red Cross buildings being wrecked by Japanese fire are admitted by reputable residents to be pure fabrications spread to excite sympathy.

The Ships and Docks

In the harbour three hospital ships are lying, the *Angra*, the *Kamian*, and the *Mongolia*. The first, when, surrounded by warships which were seeking the protection of its emblem, was struck by one-shot, causing her bow to be depressed some feet. She is in no danger of sinking, and the others are unscathed. Many steamers, dredgers and torpedo-

5 | 'PORT ARTHUR FROM WITHIN: "DISCREDITABLE SURRENDER"'

boats were sunk in shallow waters, and can be raised without difficulty. The old docks can easily be replaced, and the new docks, which are under construction, are uninjured. The Bayan is lying on her side in the East Dock and can be repaired, as certainly can the Poltava, the Peresviet, and probably the Retvisan. The Pobieda and the Sevastopol are in a hopeless condition. The prospect of repairing the others is uncertain. Nearly all these ships ware sunk by their own officers; yet they had men, food, ammunition, guns, and sufficient steam coal to take them back to Russia.

The Civilian Inhabitants

Never was there greater demoralization. The condition of the population, as witnessed by the foreign officers, was in no wise deserving of commiseration. The civilian population suffered insignificant injury. There were 500 women in the town, including 50 prostitutes. The junk service was continuous, junks constantly arriving throughout the siege with fresh provisions, sometimes 50 in one day. Many Chinese who remained in the town declared that were well and considerately treated. There were some Sikhs also, who have strange stories to tell of Russian incapacity.

Praise and Blame

All accounts agree in condemning General Stössel, who, if he had not been checked by the resolution of General Kondrachenko, would have capitulated weeks before. All accounts agree in condemning the majority of the Russian officers, who had more fear of the failure of other comforts than of ammunition. All accounts praise the courage of the Russian rank and file, who were in too many cases shamefully commanded by their officers. All accounts agree that no man who ever held a responsible command less deserved the title of hero than General Stössel.

[Immediately following Morrison's dispatch excoriating Stössel, *The Times* printed the following]:

General Stössel's Last Proclamation
Chifu, Jan. 23

A passenger who arrived to-day has brought a copy General Stössel's final proclamation. The General first reviews the glorious record of the garrison, and next refers to the slow, irresistible tightening of the Japanese cordon, to the ceaseless rain of great shells which nothing could withstand, and to the exhaustion of the resisting power of the fortress. The proclamation then proceeds:– "It is apparent that further resistance is merely daily murder. It is the duty of every commander to avoid a useless sacrifice of his men's lives. It is not hard to die for one's country, but I must be brave enough to surrender." In conclusion General Stössel says that the fortress has done its work, as there is no longer a fleet to be protected and a vast Japanese army has been crushed and, kept from joining the enemy opposing General Kuropatkin. He thanks the officers, soldiers, and civilians for their devotion, and announces his surrender "with full consciousness of the sacred duty I am performing."

General Stössel's last act on leaving Port Arthur was to kneel down, say a short prayer, and kiss the ground he had held so long.

Chapter 6

THE FUNERAL OF THE EMPRESS

The Dowager Empress, Tsu Hsi, died on 15 November 1908. A year and one day later, 16 November 1909, she was interred in the Eastern Hills outside Peking in a magnificent tomb that had been constructed years before to receive her remains. The ceremony for this event began on 9 November, and the procession of her catafalque through Peking provided Morrison with an opportunity to pen a feature article about the obsequies surrounding her final journey.

In the article, Morrison leaves the reader in no doubt that the Dowager was the real power in the land during her lifetime. He contrasts the splendour of her funeral with that of the Emperor Kuang Hsu, the man who tried to reform China but failed. "[T]he mounted troops were more numerous and better turned out, the police were noticeably smarter, and the pageant as a whole was in many respects more imposing." Morrison later in his article estimates that, to the aggrandisement of the Tsu Hsi's 'face', twice as much was spent on her funeral than on the emperor's.

*The Empress Tsu Hsi's catafalque carried through Peking,
photographed by Morrison, 9 November 1909.*
Mitchell Library, Sydney

*Funeral procession for Tsu Hsi,
photograph by Morrison, 9 November 1909.*
Mitchell Library, Sydney

'China: The Funeral of the Empress Dowager'

(From Our Own Correspondent)
Peking, 9 November 1909[292]

To-day, November 9, at 5 a.m., was the hour of good omen chosen by the Astrologers for the departure of the remains of her late Majesty the Empress-Dowager from their temporary resting-place in the Forbidden City for the Mausoleum prepared for her at the Eastern Hills. To meet the convenience of the foreign representatives, it was arranged that they should not go to the Forbidden City at that early hour, but should await the procession at a pavilion erected for them near the North East Gate of the city.

The arrangements for the procession and the part taken by the Diplomatic Body were generally similar to those of the funeral of his Majesty Kuang-hsu,[293] but the mounted troops were more numerous and better turned out, the police were noticeably smarter, and the pageant as a whole was in many respects more imposing. But for those who, in May last, witnessed the late Emperor's funeral, the scene to-day lacked one element of its brilliantly picturesque effect—namely, the bright sunshine which on that occasion threw every detail and distinctive note of the cortége into clear relief against the grey background of the Palace walls. To-day was cold, with lowering clouds, and the long delay which preceded the appearance of the catafalque at the point where the

---

292 Published on 27 November 1909, p. 7.
293 Kuang Hsu, 1871–1908, died a day before Tsu Hsi. After her coup, he was confined to a residence in the Forbidden City and not seen again. In all likelihood he was murdered, as analysis of his remains in 2008 indicated large quantities of arsenic in his bones.

Diplomatic Body was stationed had an inevitably depressing effect on the spectators.

The catafalque was borne by 84 bearers the largest number which could carry this unwieldy burden through the city gates. Beyond the walls, the coffin was transferred to a larger bier, borne by 120 men. In front walked the Prince Regent, the Bodyguard of Manchu Princes, and the members of the Grand Council, attended by the Secretariat Staff. Behind rode first a smart body of troops, followed by a large number of camels whose Mongol attendants carried tent-poles and other articles for use in the erection of the "matshed palaces" in which the coffin rests at night at the different stages of the four days' journey to the Tombs. Behind the Mongols were borne in procession the gaudy honorific umbrellas presented to the "Old Buddha"[294] on the occasion of her return from exile at Hsianfu[295] in 1901; all these are to be burnt on the 16th inst.[296] when the body is finally entombed. Following the waving umbrellas came a body of Lama dignitaries, and after them a contingent from the Imperial Equipage Department, bearing Manchu sacrificial vessels, Buddhist symbols and embroidered banners. Conspicuous in the *cortége* were three splendid chariots with trappings and curtains of Imperial yellow silk, emblazoned with dragons and phoenix and two palanquins similar to those used by the Empress-Dowager on her journeys in state; these also will be burnt at the Mausoleum. Noticeable figures in the procession were the six Chief Eunuchs, including the notorious Li Lien-ying[297] and the short handsome attendant who usually accompanied the Empress's sedan chair. The spectacle, as a whole, was most impressive; no such pomp and circumstance, say the Chinese, has

---

294 The nickname she was called by Chinese and foreigners alike. She had many names. In this article she is also called Tsu Hsi and Yehonala, her Manchu clan name.
295 Xi'an.
296 Abbreviation for *instante mense*, the current month.
297 Li Lianying, 1848–1911, entered the Forbidden City as a eunuch in 1856, named Li Jinxi. He was renamed Li Lianying in 1869 by the Dowager Empress when he entered her service. He became the most powerful member of her court, controlling access to her and manipulating court appointments. Noted for his corruption and scheming, he retired after Tsu Hsi died. His grave in Peking was destroyed during the Cultural Revolution in 1966. The epitome of the corruption and decadence of the late Qing.

6 | 'CHINA: THE FUNERAL OF THE EMPRESS DOWAGER'

The diplomat corps pays its respects to Tsu Hsi, 9 November 1909.
Mitchell Library, Sydney

marked the obsequies of any Empress of China since the funeral of the Empress Wu (circa A.D. 700), with whom, if the annals record truly, hundreds of attendants were buried alive.

The police arrangements attracted general attention by their remarkable efficiency, which many Chinese attribute to the present Empress-Dowager's constant fear of assassination. Every closed door along the route of the procession was closely guarded by soldiers and special precautions were taken against bomb-throwing. The street guards were numerous and alert, and the arrangements generally characterized by discipline and decorum. There was little confusion in the *cortége*, and none of the unseemly shouting usual on such occasions.

The Mausoleum

Ninety miles away, in a silent spot surrounded by virgin pine forest and backed by protecting heights, are the Eastern Hills towards which, for the next four days, the great catafalque will make its way along the yellow sanded road. There stands the Mausoleum, originally built by the faithful Yung-lu for his Imperial mistress, at a cost which stands in the Government records at eight millions of taels (about £1,200,000). It is close to the "Ting Ling," the burial-place of her husband, the

Emperor Hsien-feng. To the west of it stands the tomb of her colleague and co-Regent, the Empress-Mother (Tzu-an), and on the east, that of the first Consort of Hsien-feng, who died before his accession to the Throne and was subsequently canonized as Empress. During her lifetime, and particularly of late years, Yehonala took great interest and pride in her last resting-place, visiting it at intervals, and exacting the most scrupulous attention from those entrusted with its building and adornment. On one occasion (in 1897), when practically completed, she had it rebuilt because the teak pillars were not sufficiently massive. After the death of Yung-lu, Prince Ching became responsible for the custody of the tomb and its precious contents—the sacrificial vessels of carved jade, the massive vases and incense burners of gold and silver which adorn the mortuary chamber, the richly jewelled couch to receive the coffin, and the carved figures of serving maids and eunuchs who stand for ever in attendance. After the last ceremony at the tomb, when the Princes, Chamberlains, and high officials take their final farewell of the illustrious dead, and when the present Empress-Dowager with her attendants and the surviving Consorts of the Emperors Hsien-feng and Tung-chih have offered the last rites in the mortuary chamber, the massive stone door of the tomb will be let down and the resting-place of Tsu-hsi closed for ever.

Funeral Expenditure

The cost of the late Emperor's funeral has been officially recorded, with the nice accuracy which characterizes Chinese finance, at 459,940 taels, 2 mace, 3 candareens, and 6 li.[298] As the cost of a funeral in China closely reflects the dignity of the deceased and the "face" of his or her immediate relatives, these figures become particularly interesting when compared with the cost of the Empress-Dowager's funeral, which is placed at 1¼ to 1½ million taels. Rumour credits the Regent with an attempt to cut down this expenditure, which he abandoned however at

---

298 One tael is the equivalent of 50g of silver; a mace is one tenth of a tael; a candareen is 1/100 of a tael, and a li is 1000th of a tael.

6 | 'CHINA: THE FUNERAL OF THE EMPRESS DOWAGER'

the last moment in the face of the displeasure of the powerful Yehonala clan. That the "Old Buddha's" magnificent funeral was appreciated by the populace of Peking is certain, for to them she was for half a century a sympathetic personality and a great ruler.

Chapter 7

Morrison's Last Hurrah

With his series *Across China and Turkestan*, Morrison comes full circle in his Chinese adventure. He set off from Peking on 15 January 1910. The journey took six months and he arrived in London on 25 July where he was to stay until his return to Peking, via a short stop in Moscow, in early March 1911. His journey across China was similar in length that which he took from Shanghai to Rangoon in 1894. That journey formed the basis for his book *An Australian in China*. For the 1910 journey, some 3,760 miles were covered in 174 days. He was accompanied by Ah Heng and they didn't walk but rode horses. In this series Morrison's endless curiosity is in evidence, his fascination with personality, his keen eye for detail, his geopolitical sense of the far west's importance. Sadly it did not result in a book, this was despite theurging of friends for him to produce one, and his dissatisfaction with the editing his dispatches had received by *The Times*.

At China's far western frontiers the empire bumped up against the Russian Empire, an empire, as we have seen, that was bent on expansion and, until 1905, been spectacularly successful at it.[299] Both the Chinese and Russian empires had conquered new territories. Indeed the Chinese name for its far western province is Xinjiang or New Territory, which became part of the Chinese empire in the 18th century. Frequent uprisings by the conquered peoples were met with severe reprisals by

---

299 See Introduction, pp. 54–56.

the Qing government. The most recent uprising, for Morrison, was the one between 1862 and 1878. It was put down brutally by General Tso Tsung-tang[300] and the scale of the destruction he visited upon the area was still visible when Morrison traveled Xinjiang 35 years later.

He is one of the greatest curses that have ever blighted China. His expedition was a calamity as great as the inundation of the Yellow River. Yet he is glorified not as a scourge who reduced a whole province to a desert but as hero.[301]

The Muslim uprising that Tso put down also prompted intervention from Russia that sensed weakness in the Qing. Russia invaded Xinjiang and occupied much of the fertile Ili valley region. In a rare instance of giving up conquered territory, Russia withdrew from the area after signing the 1881 Treaty of St Petersburg, which ceded to Russia 18,000 sq miles of western Ili and assorted trade benefits.[302]

On both sides of their border the Russians and Chinese ruled over Turkic peoples—Qazaq, Tatar, Uzbek, Uyghur (they had migrated to the far west from the Mongolian plateau in the 9th century),[303] Azerbaijani, Kirghiz, Turkish and Astrakhan to various degrees. It was a place to where internal exiles were sent and in Urumchi Morrison would meet an old Boxer rebellion adversary, Duke Lan (Zailan), with whom he had his photograph taken.

His account of his journey across Chinese Turkestan would win praise from colleagues and friends. William Rockhill,[304] an old friend and then the United States ambassador to the Russian Empire at St Petersburg, urged Morrison to write a book based on his journey.

---

300 See n. 67 for biographical details.
301 Pearl, op. cit., pp. 200–201.
302 Paine, *Imperial Rivals*, op. cit., p. 161.
303 See F. W. Mote, *Imperial China 900–1800*, Harvard University Press, Cambridge, 1999, p. 35.
304 William Woodville Rockhill, 1854–1914, was a renowned US diplomat who was influential in drafting the US Open Door policy on China. He was an authority on China and its international relations, especially with Tibet. He spoke and wrote Tibetan and had a lengthy correspondence with the 13th Dalai Lama. Among his many diplomatic postings, he was US ambassador at Peking from 1905–1909 after which he was appointed Minister to Russia and then Minister to the Ottoman Empire. In 1914, with Morrison's help, he was made an advisor to Yuan Shikai but died en route to China in Honolulu. He published extensively on Tibet and China.

> I have read and am carefully measuring, your articles on your journey through Turkestan; they have interested me greatly, but they are too short. I hope you will bring them out fully elaborated and with your usual array of facts, dates, figures, etc. etc., in volume form. You will really be rendering a service to China as well as the rest of the world, for we all have—except you and a very few others,—a most incorrect and imperfect idea of the present condition of the Chinese Empire.[305]

Morrison was not at all happy with the way *The Times* handled the 12-part series, which began publication on 5 March 1910 and concluded on 26 September, 1910. On 25 August, he wrote to the new proprietor of *The Times,* Lord Northcliffe (A. C. W. Harmsworth) in part to accept an invitation from the proprietor to meet in Paris. He looked forward to the meeting and said he hoped to convince the new owner that the best interests *The Times* "cannot be served by wrecking the work of the correspondent in Peking."

Morrison contrasts the way he was treated on his journey—"everywhere I travelled I was treated like a Minister"—with the treatment of his copy "condensed to telegraphic brevity" for the newspaper. "It is the policy of the paper to prefer belated reports by mail (i.e. correspondents' letters) to prompt dispatched by cable. I think the policy is a wrong one."[306]

Northcliffe wrote a supportive reply. "They are nice people there" at *The Times* but they had forgotten the paper had been created by editors of the calibre of John Thadeus Delane[307] "who would not keep articles waiting a minute."[308] But Morrison was not to write another long series for the newspaper again. Just over a year after he returned to Peking, he had resigned.

One thing Morrison took with him on his journey through western China was a camera. The Morrison Collection at the Mitchell Library in Sydney is rich in the photographs he took during the journey, especially

---

305 Lo, op. cit., Rockhill to Morrison, 8 September 1910, pp. 545–546.
306 ibid., Morrison to Northcliffe, pp. 544–545.
307 J. T. Delane, 1817–1879, the greatest of the paper's 19th century editors.
308 Lo, op. cit., Northcliffe to Morrison, p. 547.

the stages from Kuldja (known as Yining today) through the mountain passes to Russian Turkestan (today Kyrgyzstan).

From The Times *of 31 August 1910.*

'ACROSS CHINA AND TURKESTAN'
I. PEKING TO HONAN

[*This article is the first of a series by our Peking Correspondent, who is travelling across China and Turkestan towards the railway at Tashkent.*]
Sianfu, 31 January 1910[309]

On January 15 I left Peking on the first stage of a journey along the great highway of Central and Western China. As far as Chêngchow[310] I travelled by the Peking-Hankau trunk line, and there changed on to the transverse line which joins the city of Khaifeng[311]—the capital of the province—with Honanfu,[312] one of the historic capital cities of China. At Honanfu, known for centuries as Loyang, I left the railway and followed the course of its projected extension to Sianfu,[313] the capital city of Shensi Province. Greatly is this extension to be desired. From Chengchow to Honanfu is a distance of 72 miles; from Honanfu to Sianfu the projected extension would be 260 miles. Its route has already been surveyed and an estimate made of its cost by Mr. D. P. Ricketts, the newly-appointed engineer-in-chief of the Northern Railways. A patriotic movement was started to provide local funds for its construction, so that it might be independent of foreign capital, but the effort has been a failure. Up to the present only a paltry £50,000 has

---

309 Published 5 March 1910, p. 5.
310 Zhengzhou is the capital of Henan province.
311 Kaifeng, is a large city in east central Henan.
312 Luoyang was renamed Henanfu (which Morrison transliterates Honanfu) during the Qing dynasty but regained its former name in 1912. Luoyang today has a population of 7 million. It is the earliest of the four ancient capitals of China—Xi'an, Nanjing and Peking being the other three.
313 Xi'an is the capital of Shaanxi province.

been promised. Chinese capitalists who can, by fairly safe investment, obtain from 12 to 24 per cent per annum are reluctant to provide capital yielding under Chinese management a doubtful 5 per cent.

Other sources are, however, available. Treasure to the value of millions sterling is hoarded in the Palace at Peking, and the time may come when some of this abundance may be put to a profitable use. The Railway Administration may yet have power to devote the surplus earnings of the productive railways of China—and those that are productive pay very handsomely indeed—to the building of new railways. Further, there is the unexpended balance of the £1,500,000 subscribed by British investors for the construction of the Shanghai-Hangchow-Ningpo Railway. Up to the present the provinces have used on this railway only a comparatively small proportion of this loan, and have built the section of the railway from Shanghai to Hangchow[314] mainly with their own money. The main portion of the whole loan has been transferred to China, but the amount actually used for the purpose for which it was subscribed is so small that the provinces have expressed their ability and their desire to refund to the British the whole amount so expended. Whether the struggle to induce the provinces to employ this money for the purpose for which it was subscribed will continue, or whether a compromise will be agreed upon and the money be employed for the building of some other railway, remains to be seen. Should the latter alternative be adopted there is no line for which it could be more profitably employed than for the extension of the Honan Railway westward to Sianfu.[315]

The Effects of Railway Construction

In no other land has railway construction so great a future as in China. Improved means of communication is the crying need of the country. In the *loess*[316] country of Central China the roads are exceptionally bad, and as the bridges are never repaired there is steady deterioration in

---

314 Hangzhou is the capital of Zhejiang province.
315 Xi'an, today. It was one of ancient China's capital cities.
316 A deposit of fine yellowish-grey loam which occurs extensively from north-central Europe to eastern China.

road communication, and a consequent steady increase in the cost of living. In normal times, when the road is at its best and prices are at their lowest, freight from Honanfu to Sianfu by heavy cart is equivalent to a fraction less than 5d.[317] per ton per mile; during the rains traffic is occasionally suspended for eight weeks at a time, and even the slightest fall of rain causes delay owing to the tenacious character of the mud which forms the roadway. What railways can do for China is evident from the Peking-Hankau trunk line. The growth of prosperity along its route is quite extraordinary. Round every station the settlements have extended, the houses are of a better type, and the inns, go-downs, warehouses, and coal yards have been greatly improved.

Coal is abundant.[318] In the province of Shansi, which lies parallel to the course of the railway as far as the Yellow River, is the greatest undeveloped coalfield in the world. In several places branch lines run from the main line to the coalfields, and their construction has been immediately followed by an improvement in the general conditions. Farmers within reach of the railway in country that formerly grew enough only for its own needs can now sell their produce in the great markets of Peking, in the north, and at Hankau, on the Yang-tsze. No one who has seen the change which is taking place in the country served by this railway can long remain pessimistic as to the future of China.

The Peking-Hankau Railway is for its length one of the most productive trunk lines in the world. Even under inefficient control, and with a wastage and leakage that would be the dismay of European railway authorities, it pays handsomely. The most important engineering work connected with it is the Yellow River Bridge, a fine structure 10,000ft. in length, a *chef d'oeuvre* of the distinguished Belgian engineer Jean Jadot.

The greatest difficulty the management has, to contend with is petty pilfering and the, nightly thefts of ring-bolts and plates; no less than 60,000 bolts per month and 10,000 plates per annum are stolen from the railway. There is no adequate means of dealing with the offence;

---

317 This is an abbreviation for 5 pence/pennies. There were 12 pennies to a shilling, 20 shillings to the pound sterling, making 240 pennies to the pound.

318 It has been estimated that coal reserves in Shanxi amount to 260 billion metric tons— about a third of China's total coal reserves. Its annual production exceeds 300 million metric tonnes, making it China's leading coal producing province.

no law was provided by the ancients to meet the theft of screw-bolts. Malefactors escape unscathed, though the police know where their plunder is stored. The steel, being much superior to the native product, is turned into razors and scissors, hoes and ploughshares, and other articles. The receiver of stolen goods, protected by the police, can find a ready market for his industry.

The Danger from Floods

Similar losses occur nightly on the Belgian built railway from Khaifeng to Honanfu, and a recent accident, involving the death of a European, which was due to the weakening of the line in consequence of such thefts, has compelled the foreign engineers in charge to close the line to traffic except during the hours of daylight. This line runs near the Yellow River, and consequently its existence is precarious. China is confronted with no greater danger than the failure to keep this river within its present bed; sediment is brought down in vast quantities, so that its water is constantly rising, and the Chinese know no, other moans to keep the water within its banks than by raising the banks above the level of the water. The great river flows for many miles through country which is on a lower level than its own bed. No planting is being done along the banks; on the contrary, all timber, shrubs, and grass are ruthlessly stripped from the soft soil, and every day the great catastrophe is drawing nearer when the river will break from its present channel and its waters will pour across the thickly-populated country to the sea, causing death and destruction incalculable. Such a catastrophe nearly occurred during a cloud-burst in June, 1906 near the city of Khaifeng, which lies 26ft. below the level of the river that flows a few miles to the north.

One difficulty of railway construction in China is the absence of trustworthy data as to rainfall and floods. Owing to the denudation of the country and the felling of all timber, rainfall is very capricious, and floods of uncontrollable violence may occur. Every railway in China has had this experience; every year there is still great damage done on the Peking-Hankau Railway from this cause; washouts may extend, not for one or two miles, but for fifty or a hundred miles. The railway from Khaifeng to the Peking-Hankau Railway had no sooner been completed than it was completely destroyed by unexpected floods and had to be relaid. On the section from the main line to Honan the most important bridge on the railway was destroyed last year. A cantilever bridge, the largest of its kind yet constructed in China, is now being erected in its place by French engineers under the supervision of the engineer-in-chief, who is also a Frenchman. There is much tunnelling on this section through the *loess*, the longest tunnel having a length of 500 metres. In the projected extension to Sianfu there will also be much tunnelling.

On the Chinese railway the traveller notes many unaccustomed things. No one is in uniform except the railway police. Station-masters, clerks, and coolies are all mixed together in the crowd. There is an infinite multiplication of *employés*, each of whom distrusts the honesty of the other—a reasonable distrust, for in China public office is rarely a public trust. There is not one native conductor, but a band of three, an arrangement which would suggest to the stranger efficient protection against "squeezing." To the resident, however, it betokens that the illegitimate profits of the calling have to be divided among three and not pocketed by one only. Every difficulty is put in the way of the passenger desiring to purchase a ticket. The crowd crushing at the window at Peking clamouring for tickets while the ticket-seller is chatting pleasantly with half-a-dozen of his friends behind the closed window is a spectacle which affords constant amusement to the Westerner. But China is only in an early stage of railway management, and allowances must be made for inexperience.

*Seven-storied Pagoda of Pinchow, 4 February 1910
(Binzhou, Shaanxi, bordering Gansu).*
Mitchell, Library, Sydney

II. HONAN TO SIANFU

(From Our Peking Correspondent)
Sianfu, 31 January 1910[319]

I left Honanfu on the morning of January 18. The distance to Sianfu is 260 miles. My things were carried in two Chinese carts, each drawn by three mules. There was abundant room in each for my two servants, who could thus travel comfortably—as comfort is understood in China—sheltered from the wind and snow. My native groom and I rode strong, white ponies. The road enters an open country of dull grey colour, timbered only where trees have been planted round the graves, and with no imposing structure to arrest the eye. At the first inn, where hot cakes were being sold, my men rested for an *alfresco* meal. There was a temple here and I went across to see it. The priest politely invited me into the guest-room. He probably did not expect me to enter, but I did so, and found in a small room some 20 men smoking opium or drowsing after the debauch. And it was the priest who had supplied the opium and the opium pipes. Could the Buddhist faith as exemplified in its degraded ministers in China sink much lower?

Along the road—and this is characteristic nothing is being repaired. It is the national failing to spend nothing on repairs, to build and then leave the building to fall gradually into decay and ruin. Nor is anything cleaned, and the squalor that is a feature even of the Imperial palace in Peking is most extraordinary. A few miles out of Honanfu there is a fine stone bridge of five arches; but the piers are falling away, the parapet has disappeared, and the flagstones with which it is paved have great gaps and hollows, so that the cart rumbles and crashes and bumps across it in a way that would break any but a Chinese springless cart. To repair is no one's business. There is abundant traffic on the road. Numberless coolies with carrying poles are met, the loads either triced[320] up close to the pole or hung low just above the ground. In the disengaged hand a crutch is carried, on which to support the weight when halting. Huge bundles of cotton and small but weighty packages of cash and copper

---

319 Published 7 March 1910, p. 5.
320 To pull or haul with a rope.

Entrance to the Imperial palace, Xi'an, c. 1910.
Mitchell Library, Sydney

cents, the cumbrous currency of this country, are carried. Pedlars with knick-knacks, coolies wheeling barrows, carts with small cast-iron wheels, carts with oxen, mules, or ponies, open carts, barrows, wheeled and drawn, with rude sails ready to be set should the wind be favourable, and long camel trains moving noiselessly along but for the dull clanging of the bell on every leader, throng the road. Camels travel chiefly at night, an old custom due to the difficulty of passing in the long, deep *loess* cuttings through which the road runs from time to time. The traffic is almost continuous, such traffic indeed as might be expected on the first section of the great highway that leads from railhead and modern civilization away to the west of the Empire. The chief products under transport are cotton and cottonseed, hemp, vegetable oil, and hides of many kinds. Every day a train of opium carts travelling under official protection and with armed escort passes by. The people's desire to suppress this traffic is shown by the deliberations of recent Provincial Assemblies to be in advance of that of the Government. Goats, sheep, and cattle are numerous, while everywhere are the noisome pigs, the scavengers, the export of which from China is now engaging the attention of a great British steamship company.

7 | 'ACROSS CHINA AND TURKESTAN'

On the fourth day out we reached the Kuan Yin Tang, the Hall of the Goddess of Mercy, a fine temple which is, however, in a filthy state. Its two sexagonal towers are used as a common lodging-house. In this degraded temple the goddess herself and all her female attendants are represented with the smallest of small feet. Frescoes of considerable force and even of beauty adorn the walls of this decaying building, which the expenditure of a few hundred dollars would restore to its pristine glory. A few cents would make it clean, but the cents are not spent. It is no one's business. Opium is smoked in the dirty rooms.

The Foot-Binding Evil

All the women met with, old and young, have mutilated feet. Imperial decrees exhort the people to discontinue the practice, and some enlightened people have done so. But the custom in these central provinces is practically universal. Chinese writers in English journals speak of the custom as having been already abandoned, but nobody who travels in the interior of the Empire is yet able to note any apparent improvement. Nevertheless there is some improvement. The anti-foot-binding society founded by the energy of Mrs. Archibald Little[321] has been untiring in its efforts to reduce the evil. It has accomplished a great deal. Some high officials have publicly stigmatized the custom, which the ruling race [the Manchus] have never practised, but I doubt whether, all told, in spite of all the work done by Mrs. Little and other philanthropists, 5 per cent of the women of China are blessed with natural feet. I believe that the feet of 95 out of every 100 females in China above the age of eight are mutilated. Yet the practice must cease if China is to take her due place among civilized nations. A powerful stimulus to the movement is given in the regulations issued by the Ministry of Education on January 14, for the control of girls' schools in China. In these it is ordained that no girl shall be admitted to school who dresses

---

321 Alicia Ellen Neve Little, 1845–1926, women's rights campaigner whose 1885 novel *Mother Darling* raised the issue of women's unequal marital rights subsequently alleviated by the Married Women's Property Act of 1893. She lived in Chongqing in the 1890s and in 1896 founded the Natural Foot Society (Tien Tsu Hui) to campaign against foot binding.

in foreign clothes or has unnatural feet. It is one of the wisest regulations yet issued in China, and will have more effect than any number of exhortatory Imperial edicts. In this province of Shensi feet are bound more tightly than in other provinces, the foot being compressed into an unsightly peg—a hideous deformity that adds enormously to the burden of the people.

It is pleasant travelling along the road. Everywhere the foreigner is treated with civility and deference. The carters are a hard-working, industrious class. There is little friction and little quarrelling, although carts occasionally get locked in the deep gullies and ravines. There is no made road other than that cut in the friable *loess* by the continuous passing of iron-tired carts. Heavy laden carts pass by in endless procession. It would be an ideal route for a railway. No wonder the people who have seen the advantages of the railway to Honanfu are eagerly awaiting the day when the work will be begun. Every day I am asked, "Have you come to survey the railway?" and I am questioned as to how it will come and by what route, and when is it to be begun. There is a universal desire for railway communication, and the Government could do no greater service to the people of these provinces than to begin the construction at once. Railways will enrich, the country; they will remove many of the people's burdens. They simplify the currency, they assist in the maintenance of order by the easy transport of troops, they teach the people the value of time and punctuality, they help to break down the provincial barriers and make the people one. Perhaps to some extent the anticipated coming of a railway, which will kill the present cart traffic, may account for the shocking condition of the native inns. With railway extension in the air, there is no inducement for the innkeeper to spend money on the upkeep of his hovel. Nothing is repaired; their filth and squalor are amazing. In the inn yard the well has its mouth below the level of the soil, so that water which is spilt may flow back into the well and carry with it the surface drainage. A doctor must notice the prevalence of consumption. To the universal habit of expectoration on the floor, the exclusion of air, and the absence of drainage this prevalence must be due.

7 | 'ACROSS CHINA AND TURKESTAN'

A Primitive Currency

Currency on this route is primitive to a degree. Lump silver only is used and copper cash. Coined money is not current. Even in Honan city, which is distant only two days from Peking, lump silver, the same cumbrous currency that has been used for centuries, is still employed. It is cut into small pieces by hammer and chisel. Every town and even village has its own weights and scales, and there is no pretence at uniformity. Two forces are, however, working towards an improvement—the increase in the number of post-offices and the sale of stamps and money orders in dollars,[322] and the extension of the railways and the use upon them of the dollars and subsidiary coinage. In other parts of China dollars are being more widely used. I speak with some knowledge, for I have crossed China from Peking to the Tong-king [Vietnamese] frontier, and through the south-western provinces of Yunnan and Kweichow back to Shanghai, and used nothing but dollars.

On the seventh day we reached the natural fortress of Tungkwan, built on a ledge between high terraced hills. We had left Honan Province and entered the province of Shansi. Three provinces meet here, for Shansi is on the other bank of the Yellow River. From deep sunk roads shut out from all view the traveller emerges into this important gateway with its view of the broad river junction, where the Yellow River receives its most important tributary from the west. Along this branch (the Wei River) the road continues to Sianfu. Next day we reach Hua Yin Miao,[323] one of the finest temples I have seen in China. It lies within an enclosure comparable to the Temple of Heaven in Peking, and has splendid halls, courts and pavilions. Yet what a ruin! The roofs have decayed or fallen in, the triumphal archways are tottering. Barbers and beggars frequent the pavilions. I have seen no more striking evidence of decay. Truly Buddhism in China is sadly deteriorating. A village has gown up around

---

322 The 'dollar' referred to is probably the Chinese silver dollar that began to be minted in China in 1889. It was designed to replace the use of Mexican dollars and the Spanish silver dollar (pieces of eight) that had hitherto formed the basis of reliable exchange. Copper coins, called 'cash', were used for small transactions.

323 This is the Great Temple at Mount Hua Shan. It was built in Qing dynasty or earlier as a gateway for pilgrims ascending Hua Shan, a revered mountain in Taoism.

this splendid temple. Every inn in the village keeps prostitutes, a large portion of whose earnings is the perquisite of the priests.

The village and the temple lie under the shadow of that range whose culminating peak is Huashan, one of the five sacred mountains of China. A loft crag rising above the rugged pinnacles with precipitous cliff facing the west, it is a mountain well fitted to inspire a superstitious people with a belief in its sacredness. It is lit by the sun's rays when all the mountains below it are in darkness.

An avenue of willow trees have been planted along the highway west from Tungkwan, but it is quite neglected. Planted by the Governor-General Tso Tsung-tang[324] on his march westwards to recover Chinese Turkestan from the Mohamedans, and extending throughout most of the way to Kuldja, it was one the most imposing avenue in the Empire, but it is disappearing rapidly. Trees are falling or are being felled, and it is no one's business to plant new ones in their places. At Tungkwan[325] the Court, in its flight from Peking in 1900, after traversing the province of Shansi, crossed into Shensi, and pursued its way to Sianfu. The road is low and marshy and undrained, and long detours have to be made through the unfenced fields. Such trespass is suffered without protest. A farmer whose land borders the highway may discover any morning that a cart road has been opened through his field. He suffers the damage with the resignation of fatalism.

Westwards from Tungkwan the country is a vast persimmon orchard, and in the autumn when the rich scarlet fruit is ripe the country is lit with a glorious wealth of colour. The spectacle is one of the most beautiful in the world.

Huachow,[326] a ruined town, was the scene of the outbreak of the Mahomedan insurrection of 1861, which caused widespread destruction of life and property, led to the devastation of Shensi, Kansu, and

---

324 See n. 67 for his details.
325 Tongguan is a town and county in eastern Shaanxi, on the Yellow River and Wei River. The Tong Pass is in this county and has played a pivotal role in Chinese military affairs since its construction in 196 AD.
326 Huazhou has been absorbed into Weinan City, Shaanxi. The uprising engulfed western China and precipitated, in 1871, the Russian occupation of the Ili valley and surrounding terrain. See Paine's *Imperial Rivals: China, Russia and Their Disputed Frontier*, pp. 117–125.

7 | 'ACROSS CHINA AND TURKESTAN'

Kashgaria, and was not suppressed till 1878. The town, one of the numerous market-places along the high road, has grown up, again outside the West Gate, and is a busy community. Further west at the foot of the hills is Lin-tung Hsien, famous for its hot springs, near which the rich people of Sianfu have built summer villas. This is the burial place of the first Emperor of the Chin Dynasty, Shih Huang-ti,[327] who built the Great Wall of China and burned the classics. The river Wei is in full view to the north. An easy ride of 20 miles, during which a wide branch of the river is crossed by a stone bridge one-third of a mile in length, then across the fields past numberless grave mounds, and the traveller enters under the stately gate towers of the ancient city of Sianfu.

A bridge over the Wei River (?) near Hsien yang (Xianyang) about 40li (20 km) west from Xi'an. Xianyang was the first capital of a unified China under emperor Qin Shi Huang in 221 BC.
Mitchell Library, Sydney

---

327 Qin Shi Huang, 294–210 BC, founder of the Qin Dynasty and unifier of China after the Waring States period. Declared himself China's first emperor.

III. THE CITY OF SIANFU

(From Our Peking Correspondent)
Sianfu, 31 January 1910[328]

Sianfu is one of the most famous cities in China. For long periods it was at different times the capital of the Empire under dynasties which reigned in China during 23 centuries. Its walls, 12 miles in circumference, and its lofty gate towers are as imposing as those of Peking. They were built in the early years of the reign of the founder of the Ming dynasty (1368–1399), and are in excellent condition. For centuries it has been known as the Western capital. Its population is variously estimated at from a quarter of a million to one million, the lower figure being the more trustworthy. Within the walls is a large Mahomedan population, and there are a dozen or more mosques, one of which claims to be the most ancient in China. From time to time within the last few years they have received visits from religious teachers or emissaries from Constantinople.

In Sianfu the late Empress-Dowager and Emperor stayed while Peking was in foreign military occupation. The palace in which they found refuge was a former residence of the Viceroy of this and the adjoining province of Kansu. It had remained unoccupied since the Viceroy had transferred his residence to Lanchow.[329] The palace is shown to visitors, who wonder why such fine halls and pavilions should be so filthy and neglected.

The Governor of the province, En Shou, is a courtly old Manchu of the old school, dignified in appearance, but ill-fitted to be the ruler of a province seeking guidance along modem lines. But he has powerful connexions and retains office at his own pleasure, for is not his daughter married to Prince Tsai Chen, the eldest son of Prince Ching, the President of the Grand Council? A former Governor was Tuan Fang,[330] who subsequently rose to be Viceroy of the metropolitan province,

---

328   Published 8 March 1910, p. 5.
329   Lanzhou is the capital of Gansu province.
330   Tuan Fang, 1861–1911, Manchu bannerman, Viceroy, was Governor of Hebei from 1901–04, then Hunan 1903–05, finally Viceroy of Liangkiang in 1906, and 1909 as Viceroy of Zhili.

where he had experience of the capriciousness of high office under an Oriental despot. His sudden dismissal from office last November, when apparently in high favour, was nowhere more regretted than in this province. He was Governor here during the Boxer outbreak and during the stay here of the Imperial Court after its flight from Peking. Every missionary in the province speaks of him with gratitude. During the persecution he acted most honourably and humanely. At the risk of punishment for disobedience of the Imperial orders he rescued every foreigner in the province. Tuan Fang is one of the chief authorities on ancient Chinese bronzes, and his private collection is the finest in the Empire. It was enriched during his tenure of office here. Treasures are constantly being found. No other portion of China offers such a rich field for archeological research. The city contains many interesting objects. In the north-west corner of the parade ground in the Manchu city is the famous stone with the impress of the hand of the Empress Wu Tze-tien. The Pei-lin, the Forest of Tablets, contains the greatest collection of historical records on stone, pictorial and otherwise, in the Empire. Within the enclosure is now housed in a shabby little pavilion the Nestorian Tablet, which was hurriedly removed there from its former position outside the city after the departure of the enterprising Dane who secured a replica of it for the Metropolitan Museum of New York. It is one of the most famous Christian monuments in the world, and, despite the constant paper rubbing to which it is subjected, is in good preservation. Erected in 781 A.D., the tablet testifies to the many establishments that the Nestorians then had in China, for the Syrian apostle had arrived in Sianfu in 635.[331] For two centuries they enjoyed religious liberty, but they were proscribed in 845. The monument was unearthed in 1625, and the first account of it was published by the Jesuit Semedo[332] a few years later. It is certain that

---

331 The stele recorded 150 years of Nestorian missionary activity beginning with the arrival of Alopen, a Syriac-speaking Christian monk in 635 AD.

332 The Portuguese Jesuit Alvaro Semedo, 1585–1658, was named procurator of the China mission in 1636. He died in Canton in 1658. He wrote an account of the discovery of the Xi'an Nestorian monument (most likely around 1625) and his influential history of China was first published in Portuguese in 1641, in Spanish in 1642 and then in multiple languages thereafter.

further excavations, scientifically conducted, would unearth other evidences of the Nestorians in China.

The Military Spirit

The ancient city is awakening. The spirit of militarism and of Western education is abroad. Though a Tartar general's command, the military forces of the city are unimportant. It is to acquire more importance in the future. The building has begun outside the East gate of what will be one of the four chief military schools of the Empire. Already there is an excellent military preparatory school, with clean well-kept buildings and facilities for instruction along modern lines. Teachers are Chinese who have gone through a course of military training in Japan. There are 200 students. Every schoolboy in Sianfu is given daily drill, and the effect upon the physique and smartness of the boys is quite noticeable.

Probably the greatest change observable in modern China is the honour shown now to the formerly despised military profession. In many ways is honour shown: in improved pay with consequent improvement in discipline and higher *esprit-de-corps*, in the high commands sought for by Imperial Princes, in the revolution which has reversed the corresponding ranks of civil and military officials and has awarded to the military a scale of dignities compared with the civil that a few years ago would have been deemed impossible. Military rank may come to supersede civil rank in the aspirations of the ambitious. Soldiers now are proud of their uniforms, they keep their rifles clean, they are smart and respectful—always, of course, comparing them with the Chinese soldiers as we knew them a few years ago. Soldiers now demand that they be treated with consideration by their own authorities. Officers travel on the train first-class; the rank and file will not suffer themselves to be herded as before like cattle in open trucks; they now require covered carriages in which they can sit with comfort. It is a noticeable change. The contempt which the regular soldier displays for the untrained brave is not less than the contempt entertained by the foreigner for the same slovenly object.

The city is rich in its schools—its higher school and its normal school being unusually fine. They are modem style, well built, with clean commodious class rooms. But the city is poor in teachers. More teachers, and teachers of a higher class, are badly needed. The Chinese do not realize the importance of securing the best teachers. Unlike the Japanese, who engaged the best teachers that money could procure, the Chinese are contented if the teachers are a little superior to the taught.

Japanese School Teachers

In the many schools of the city there are only three foreign teachers, and they are Japanese. Some time ago there were 14 Japanese. Speaking no Chinese they teach by writing the ideographs on a blackboard—as unstimulating a way of giving instruction as could well be devised. There is a widespread desire to learn English, and at most of the schools English is taught, but it is of an elementary kind and quite unserviceable. It is taught by Chinese who have received a meagre training in Shanghai or in Japan. There is also a police school where police are trained on modern lines. Dressed in semi-foreign uniform and armed with *bâtons* they are stationed at blue sentry-boxes throughout the city. They are civil and do their duties well, and are an immense advance on the old system.

Sianfu has for many years been a centre for missionary activity. Adam Schaal came here as far back as 1622, and resided here until he was called to Peking, where he assisted in the preparation of the calendar for the last Emperor of the Ming Dynasty. At present the Catholic Mission belongs to the Order of Franciscans. There is a French Bishop, the well-known Monseigneur Gabriel Maurice,[333] and he is assisted in the city by one American Father and one Irish Father and by a number of native priests, some of whom have been trained in Rome.

Protestant missionaries carry on a successful work. They have excellent schools and their medical work is known throughout the province. At present there are four medical missionaries here and one lady doctor, and the relief they give to suffering cannot be overestimated. They belong to the Baptist Missionary Society. There is also a branch of the Scandinavian Alliance Mission of America, which carries on

---

333 Auguste-Jean-Gabriel Maurice, 1862–1925, Bishop of Shensi.

an active and successful mission work in the provinces of Shensi and Kansu. It is affiliated to the China Inland Mission.

The Provincial Deliberative Assembly[334] met here, as in other capital cities, on October 14, and the sittings continued for the statutory 40 days. The good sense and decorum which were characteristic of the first meeting of these Assemblies were also conspicuous here. I visited the Assembly while in session and was much impressed. They appeared to have been accustomed to such deliberations for many years and not, as was the fact, for a few days only. Sixty-six members constituted the Assembly, of whom 16 were residents of the city and 10 were elected in the country. Daily reports were published of their proceedings. The question of opium was the chief topic of discussion, and there was complete agreement as to the necessity of dealing with the opium evil.

Shensi Province is backward in its support of the anti-opium movement. It lags far behind the adjoining province of Shansi, where under the enlightened Ting Pao-chuan[335] there has been complete suppression of poppy cultivation. Complete suppression there and the consequent sixfold increase in price has enabled this province, where the cultivation was greater than in any previous year, to reap a rich harvest. Lack of co-ordination of this kind among the provinces is a serious hindrance to the suppression of the evil. In the streets itinerant preachers warn the people against the use of opium; on the other hand, the Government wants money, and the people can in this province most easily pay their taxes with opium.

---

334 The provisional Deliberative Assembly (1910–1912) was an attempt by the Imperial Qing government to reform itself into a constitutional parliamentary monarchy. Members were appointed and charged with drawing up a constitution by 1916. Its deliberations were overtaken by the 1911 Revolution which precipitated the collapse of the dynasty.

335 Ding Baoquan, d. 1919, was the last Qing governor of Shanxi (1909–1911) who retired from public service after the fall of the Qing.

IV. THE ANTI-OPIUM CAMPAIGN IN KANSU

(From Our Peking Correspondent)
Lanchau, 23 February 1910[336]

Kansu,[337] the most distant and the most backward of the 18 provinces of China proper—a province for many years past steeped in opium—is making an effort to come into line with other provinces in enforcing the suppression of the opium evil. Already considerable progress has been made. Opium can be obtained, of course, though its price is much greater than before; but the opium divans are closed and there is no public smoking. The extent of the evil is recognized, and the impoverishment of the province is attributed in large part to the widespread cultivation of the poppy. Experiments conducted by Chinese experts in the agricultural school here, founded by the Taotai Peng Ying-chia,[338] have shown that other products, such as cotton, hitherto uncultivated, grow well in this climate. Poppy is planted in Kansu at the end of this month. Opportune, therefore, is the issue of the following excellent official proclamation which is posted throughout the city, where it is being read by the thousands thronging the streets on the occasion of the lantern festival.

A Drastic Proclamation

The proclamation reads:–

This Proclamation is issued by the Acting Provincial Treasurer of the Province of Kansu in the matter of forbidding the use of opium.

For a long time opium has been doing great injury. Nothing wastes men's time more than opium, it creates sickness and poverty, it prevents labour, it brings ruin to the home. Frequent

---

336 Published 8 April 1910, p. 5.
337 Known today as Gansu.
338 Peng Yingjia was governor of Gansu from 1906–1911, a province he had worked in for many years.

Imperial commands bave been received forbidding the use of opium. Its use must be abandoned now for ever.

Last summer we forbade the growing of any poppy in the future. The Government was determined that the cultivation of the poppy in all the provinces should cease at the end of the first year of Hsüan Tung (February 9, 1910). Intimation to this effect was conveyed to all the provinces in the Empire.

Before the introduction of poppy cultivation was Kansu as poor as it is now? Why with the introduction of the poppy did it become poorer, not richer? And why should it be useless to grow in its stead grain and cotton, potato cud beetroot?

A despatch just received from the Viceroy of Szechuan states that the importation of opium into Szechuan is henceforth forbidden. Every other province will act in the same way. If Kansu cannot export its opium, where will be the profit from growing poppy?

Before the use of opium was forbidden the Government collected opium taxes to the amount of 20 million taels annually and yet it was not satisfied. Now it sacrifices without regret so great a revenue because it desires that this evil nay be removed from the people and the country become strong.

People of Gansu, do not seek small profit and forget great danger! When famine comes, can you satisfy your hunger with opium? Even at this moment you are threatened with famine. Obey the Imperial will and you will escape the anger of Heaven. Take warning, abandon opium quickly, tear up the evil by its roots.

All local authorities have been ordered everywhere to inspect the fields and see that no poppy is grown. You shall not grow poppy again! Should any man disobey and grow even one poppy plant he will be punished without mercy and the plant he has sown will be uprooted.

All other provinces are under similar orders. Tremble and obey!

7 | 'ACROSS CHINA AND TURKESTAN'

Hung Tsu Miao, overlooking the Ho River, Gansu, 16 March 1910.
Mitchell Library, Sydney

Possible Effects

Such a proclamation as this is bound to be followed by a large reduction in the area of opium production. There will be a rise in price and a consequent reduction in the individual amount consumed and a marked decrease in number in the users of the drug. The Taotai tells me that in anticipation of the suppression there are families in the city long habituated to its use who have laid in sufficient opium to last them for three years. They are in hopes that before that time the anti-opium movement may have collapsed and that old times may return. But there is no mistaking the general desire of the people to be rid of the habit. There is widespread suffering and destitution owing to the failure of the harvests, and the lack of foodstuffs is attributed in large measure to the planting of the poppy instead of cereals. For three years the harvests have failed. Last summer there was severe drought and the present outlook inspires much anxiety. No rain has fallen since October 16 and the snowfall has been quite inadequate. At present 7,000 to 8,000 destitute are being fed daily by charity in this city, and the number may rise to 30,000. Public kitchens have been organized in six centres and one hot meal of grain is issued daily. Relief has been sent from the coast, and missionaries and others are already carrying succour to the country districts near Lanchau where suffering is greatest. The province has been tried greatly; for last year was also a bad year for tobacco. Kansu tobacco is famous throughout China, it is the most important product of the province, but it is feeling severely the competition of the foreign cigarette, the importation of which into China is attaining such amazing proportions.

In Yunnan and Shansi, to speak of the two provinces where poppy cultivation was suppressed most drastically, suppression was followed by harvests such as had not been known for many years, a coincidence which impressed upon the superstitious the belief that their action had the approval of Heaven. Should a similar phenomenon be observed in this province—and by the doctrine of chances it is probable after these years of drought and bad harvest that there will be a change—further anti-opium proclamations will be superfluous.

7 | 'ACROSS CHINA AND TURKESTAN'

V. INDUSTRIAL DEVELOPMENT IN KANSU

(From Our Peking Correspondent)
Lanchau, 24 February 1910[339]

On January 31 I left Sianfu, the capital of Shensi province, and in 18 marches I was in Lanchau.[340] No incident marked the journey; there is little on the way to interest the traveller. Kansu is the poorest of all the provinces of China and the most inaccessible by reason of its defective communications. Devastated by Mahomedan insurrection in the years from 1861 to 1878, it has never recovered from the ravages to which it was then subjected. The ruins everywhere of what were once thriving towns and villages impress the traveller with a sense of the horrors of insurrection in China. Insurrection means extermination of the vanquished—no quarter to old or young, to man or woman. Loss of life during the great insurrection amounted to millions, and even in the short insurrection of 1896 the destruction of life was appalling. The province now needs repeopling, but in the absence of communications the work is difficult. It is a treeless province. There has been universal destruction of timber. Even the fine avenue of willows and poplars planted by Tso Tsung-tang between the two capitals is fast disappearing. Deforestation is profoundly affecting the climate. When rain falls it falls with such violence that it scars the face of the country, which is everywhere covered with soft *löess* of varying thickness, with no vegetation to bind the soil together.

From Sianfu to Lanchau

The road between the capitals is 450 miles in length. Its highest point is 8,700ft., in the difficult pass of the Liu Pan Shan. Transport charges are excessive. For example, the currency is silver in lump or Chinese cash. One dollar's worth of cash weighs 8lb. On 16s. worth of cash freight amounts to 6s. Yet engineers say that a railway could be built between the two points without great difficulty. It is the most essential railway

---

339 Published on 8 April 1910, p. 5.
340 Called Lanzhou, today. It is still the capital city of Gansu.

in China if China is to develop her western territory. Along the road the people are very friendly. Their villages are mostly of mud, all the better buildings having been destroyed either by the Mahomedans or by the Imperialists.[341] Many are cave dwellers, and the hills are often honeycombed. Everything about them indicates poverty.

At only one village had I any difficulty. We were marching late in the dark, and I had sent my groom on ahead to find me an inn, as he had often done before. He entered the village, and finding the large inn door closed, he called out to the people to open it. But his Peking speech is not easily understood in Kansu, and no one answered him. Then he knocked, and to his dismay the crazy door fell down. Immediately there was a row. The innkeeper and his vociferous spouse shouted out their wrongs. Every one came into the street to hear; the whole village was roused. When I arrived it seemed like a demonstration in my honour. As is the custom, a dozen people together told me what had happened. I soon satisfied every one by first examining the damage and then paying compensation in full I paid one hundred cash (rather more than twopence), and my generosity was approved. The structure thus damaged reminded one of the jerry-built houses familiar to students in Edinburgh, where it is on record that a lodger once complained to his landlord that the ceiling in his room had fallen down. "But how do you account for that?" asked the landlord. "Somebody in the next flat sneezed," replied the lodger. "Good Heavens!" said the Landlord with some heat; "you people think that because you pay 25s. a month rent you can carry on as though you lived in a Roman citadel."

Tranquillity now reigns in Kansu, and order is maintained along the highway by a ridiculously small number of men. Each hsien village has a few police armed with batons, dressed in semi-foreign uniform, and stationed in blue sentry-boxes. They are the most civil of men. Distance from the coast and from newspapers gives free play to the imagination. Rumours of the most astonishing kind find credence. Nearly every day I was asked if Russia and Japan were again at war, while only last evening an intelligent member of the local gentry came to ask my opinion upon two serious items of information. First, why had 200,000 French soldiers

---

341 The Chinese.

7 | 'ACROSS CHINA AND TURKESTAN'

Wayside shrine with praying-wheel, 25 February 1910.
Mitchell Library, Sydney

been landed at Kuanchaowan and, secondly, why had the comet come? I suggested that perhaps the comet had landed the 200,000 Frenchmen at Kuanchaowan, and he admitted that this was an explanation that had not occurred to him. Chinese are astonishingly vague about numbers. Two thousand men handled by the Chinese chronicler soon become two hundred thousand men. Thus the accounts of the battles and victories of Tao Tsung-t'ang, with the numbers given of the opposing forces are known now to be almost ludicrously exaggerated.

Education: Belgian Influences

But there is progress in Kansu. An important factor is the extension of the post office, which runs courier lines through the province and gives a cheap and efficient service, amazing to the Chinese. One foreigner is in charge of the post offices of the two provinces, and it would be difficult to overpraise the good work that is being accomplished. In Lanchau the progress is most marked. Seven years ago there were no schools in this city—no schools, that is to say, except antiquated schools for teaching the classics. Now there is a good provincial college or high school, a military school with 300 cadets, a normal school, middle schools, and a number of preparatory schools. And at all the teaching is on Western lines. The Berlitz system is used, and the excellent textbooks and school-books and educational appliances, maps, and charts and diagrams attractive coloured pictures issued m such profusion from the Commercial Press in Shanghai—are found in every school in the city. But there is the lack of teachers that is so often noted.

There were three Japanese teachers in the high school, but their work was a failure, and they were removed after one year. With one exception there are no other foreign teachers. English is taught by two Chinese who are quite incompetent. One is a native of Hong-kong and is the official interpreter of the Viceroy and the Director of Telegraphs. His English is deplorable, and that of his fellow instructor not less so. But French is well taught. A cultured Belgian missionary, Père van

Dijk,[342] gives a thoroughly good French training to 80 Chinese students, among whom have been the sons of viceroys and other high officials. French has come to be regarded here as the more aristocratic language, the language of diplomacy. At present it is also the more useful, owing to the fact that most of the industries conducted here for the Chinese have been entrusted to Belgians.

Belgian influence in the capital is quite considerable. It has made itself felt for many years, largely through the influence of one man. One of the best known figures in China was Paul Splingaerd,[343] the Fleming, who was for 16 years employed by the Chinese as a Customs Commissioner and director of the Bureau of Foreign Affairs at Suchau on the western frontier of the province. He married a Chinese wife, and was much trusted by the Chinese, and deservedly. More than three years ago he died in Sianfu, when on his way back to Lanchau from Belgium, whence he was bringing for service under the Chinese engineers and mechanics to reopen the old woollen mill, start candle and soap factories, build laboratories, found a school of mining, and develop the copper and gold mines found at three days' distance from Lanchau, on the road to Sining. On his death, his eldest son (who is a red button Mandarin) succeeded him, and he is now in this city conducting the various enterprises in which his father had interested the Chinese.

Industries

The woollen mill which was founded by the Governor General, Tso Tsung-tang, in the eighties, when eight Germans were employed in it, and, which was closed for years, has been repaired, its old machinery patched up, new machinery imported from Belgium, and under a Belgian director with half-a-dozen Belgian assistants it has been reopened and is turning out cloth of several kinds. Some 80 Chinese workmen are employed. Under the German *régime* the mill was saddled

---

342 Louis van Dyck, 1862–1937, was appointed Bishop of the archdiocese of Suiyuan (now part of Inner Mongolia) in 1915.

343 Paul Splingaerd, 1842–1906, ran a fur and wool trading business in Mongolia and was recruited by Li Hung-chang in 1881 to serve as customs inspector at the far western Chinese city of Jiuquan—known as Suchau (sometimes Suchow) by Morrison.

Laingchow, twin pagodas inside Antingmen, 4 March 1910.
Mitchell Library, Sydney

with the maintenance of thirty Chinese Deputies, whose voracity ate up all the profits so that after a while the mill had to be shut down. For a time it was used as an arsenal. Now its outlook is better and it promises success, despite official interference, unskilled workmen, and imperfect raw material—an inferior hairy wool, not to be compared with the beautiful product from Australia—bad water (for the mill has been erected on the other side of the city from the river whence the water has to be carried), impure native phosphates, and inferior coal containing much sulphur. At an official depot in the main street near the Viceroy's yamên the cloth is sold. It is coarse, rough, and strong, and will, it is hoped, be used for the clothing of the soldiers in the western provinces. On the occasion of the recent review of the military school all students and their instructors wore uniforms made from this cloth. It costs 5s. the yard of 4ft. width. At present the output is 200ft. to 250ft. the working day, but it will soon be increased to 500ft.

In the north-west corner of the city is the old Mahomedan quarter. It is an enclosure of largo size, in the centre of which Tso Tsung t'ang erected the Examination Hall and buildings. By the present progressive Taotai Peng Ying-chia these have now been turned into a hive of activity. Here are the mining and agricultural schools, the former with a well-equipped laboratory under a Belgian chemist and metallurgist, the latter under Chinese experts who have a large area of garden in which to experiment. There are 200 students in all, and they receive an excellent training. With his mining class of 40 students all of whom have been taught French by Père van Dijk, the Belgian professor is shortly leaving for the copper mines, three days distant, which are now being opened and developed for the Chinese with modern machinery by Belgian engineers.

In the same quarter are the soap and candle works and the various industries founded by the energetic Taotai, where Chinese are making foreign chairs and tables, carpets, satin, silk, and gauze, cotton cloths, and lacquer work. There is a small tannery producing excellent leather, made on the spot into bags and foreign boots and chair coverings. Glassblowing is taught by Chinese from Szechuan, who have themselves been taught by Japanese. In all some 350 boys and men are employed. Technical instruction is given to a number of natives of this province, who, it is hoped, will extend instruction inland. The work is of great utility.

The Yellow River

To the same Taotai is due the improvement in the roads of the city. Good macadamized roads made under German supervision extend from the Viceroy's yamên to the south-east and west gates of the city. To him also is due the building of the bridge across the Yellow River, a work of great practical utility much appreciated by the people. The bridge is 710ft. in length in five spans. Designed by an English engineer in the employ of the German firm who had secured the contract, it was constructed by the American Bridge Company of New York and erected by an American engineer born in China, assisted by foremen who had been trained in similar work on the northern railways. It was opened last year. A curious circumstance noted by the superstitious was that a few days before the opening of the new bridge the old pontoon bridge in whose place it was being constructed was swept away by the current, which here in confined banks rushes past the city with great velocity.

The bridge cost approximately £25,000 (165,000 taels). Charges for transporting the material from the nearest railway to Lanchau came to an equal amount. The entire cost was defrayed from the estate of the notorious Tung Fu-hsiang, the "Boxer" General, who left on his death two years ago 400,000 taels in the Provincial Treasury. "By the consent of the relatives," as the euphemism terms it, this money has been devoted to works of public utility. In his estate were also a large number (said to be 12,000, but Chinese figures are very untrustworthy) modern Mausers and Mannliehers, which are now stored in the arsenal inside the city. The troops themselves, though belonging to thee regular modern army under the Ministry of War, are armed actually with single shot 1888 Mausers.

At present the river is icebound and can be crossed by the heaviest carts. In the spring the first steamer is to be placed on the upper Yellow River. Constructed by the Belgian firm Cockerill, it is now in Tientsin. It will be taken in sections to Kuei Hua Ch'êng, west of Kalgan, and at the river port near by will be put together and launched on the river. It is a small river steamer or launch of 12-knot speed, and is expected to make the up river voyage to Lanchau in 13 days and the down river voyage in nine. There are several rapids and shallows, but the project of placing shallow draught steamers on the river will, it is believed, be proved by this experiment to be practicable. A Belgian engineer has surveyed the river with this object. All these things, small in themselves, are evidence of satisfactory progress. They receive the full approval of the Provincial Assembly as well as of the authorities.

The Viceroy

Kansu has recently received a new Viceroy, Chang K'êng, his predecessor having been removed for having—such was the official reason—memorialized the Throne urging that the province was not yet ripe for the establishment of any measure of constitutional government. Chang K'êng is a Manchu, whose family belong to Nanking, but who was himself born in this province. He is 68 years of age, feeble, almost decrepit, but an amiable patriarch of good character, who has made a kindly impression upon the people. He was a noted General in the time of Tso Tsung-tang, well versed in the literature of the bow-and-arrow period of military science. His strength lay in his ability to show by quotation from the classics that the enemy's tactics were not in accordance with the military precepts laid down in the time of Confucius. Eleven years of his life have been spent as Tartar General of Ili, and from that distant post he has lately been transferred to the Viceroyalty of the two provinces of Shensi and Kansu.

By far the ablest and most progressive official in the province is the Taotai Peng Ying-chia, the president of the Provincial Bureau of Foreign Affairs and of other offices. Only 46 years of age, he is bound, if his health permits, to reach high office. His career has been an interesting one. A native of Mukden, he was in office in Chih-li province at the time of the Boxer outbreak. He acted well, as many missionaries whose lives he assisted to save can testify. During the military occupation he was arrested by Count Waldersee,[344] and was for 40 days in prison in daily expectation of death. Liberated by the interposition of Bishop Favier, who knew him well, he acted as one of the secretaries of Li Hung Chang during the peace negotiations. He represented China in various negotiations for the settlement of Christian indemnity claims. In Manchuria he arranged with the Presbyterian missionaries a settlement satisfactory to all, and with Monseigneur Choulet[345] he drew up the agreement for the payment of indemnity for the destruction of Christian property which became the basis of settlement of similar case elsewhere. For his, services then, he was decorated by the French Government with the Cross of the Legion of Honour. Four years ago he was appointed to Lanchau, and now he has been called back to Peking. Few officials have served their country better.

---

344 Alfred Ludwig Heinrich Karl Graf von Waldersee, 1832–1904, Field Marshall, Commander of Allied expeditionary force that put down the Boxer uprising. He arrived after hostilities had ended and was mostly engaged in 'pacification' work. In Peking he reportedly slept in the bed of the Empress Dowager in the Forbidden City.

345 Marie-Félix Choulet, 1854–1923, arrived in China in 1880, named Vicar Apostolic of Southern Manchuria and Titular Bishop of Zela in February 1901. Resigned due to ill health in 1920 and died in Newchwang (Yingkuo) in 1923.

Tsai Shen Maio, Urumchi, April 1910.
Mitchell Library, Sydney

VI. THE NEW DOMINION

(From Our Peking Correspondent)
Urumchi, Sin-Kiang, 5 May 1910[346]

To most of your readers the name Urumchi will not be familiar. It is equally unfamiliar to the Chinese, who designate officially the capital city of the new Dominion as Tihuafu, while to the common people it is universally known as Hungmiaotzu,[347] a name derived from a conspicuous red temple in the neighbouring mountains. Russians and Turkis alone speak of it as Urumchi.

Origin and Growth

Four years after the suppression of the Mahomedan rebellion an Imperial edict, issued on September 5, 1882, constituted all that vast territory lying between Mongolia on the north and Tibet on the south and between China proper on the east and Russia, Central Asia, and India on the west into a province under the title of the New Dominion or Sin-kiang, with the capital at Urumchi. It was given a Governor, a Provincial Treasurer, and a Provincial Judge, and there was introduced the same general mechanism of government employed in each of the other 18 provinces of China proper. The inauguration of the new regime was entrusted to the Hunanese General Liu Chin-tang, who had proved himself the ablest of the generals, under his fellow provincial Tso Tsung-tang, the Commander-in-Chief in the campaign of reconquest. Liu had himself drawn up the scheme off reorganization. Since then there has been peace in the province, giving it time to recover in some measure from the ravages of the insurrection. Its population is increasing rapidly, both by natural growth and by immigration from other provinces. Last year 40,000 immigrants passed through the Chia-yu-kuan barrier,[348]

---

346 Published on 13 June 1910, p. 7.
347 During the Qing this was also another name for Urumchi. Also known as Dihua and Tihwa.
348 This is the Jiayuguan Pass, built c. 1370, and is one of the famous fortified gates of the Great Wall of China in Gansu province. It was known as the First and Greatest Pass Under Heaven, and it was an important staging post for traders.

Chia-yu-kuan (Jiayuguan City, Gansu), March 1910.
Mitchell Library, Sydney

A chantou man and Mohammedan boy near Urumchi, 24 April 1910.
Mitchell Library, Sydney

while considerable numbers are continually entering the province by the northern routes from the provinces of Shansi and Chihli. Few other cities in China are growing more rapidly than Urumchi. Last year its population increased by 10,000. Fifteen years ago the space within its walls was almost empty; now the city is thickly peopled from gate to gate with Chinese, while a still larger area outside the wall contains a busy population of Mahomedans of the three main classes—Chantous, or Turkis, who are Mahomedan subjects of China, a Mahomedan Chinese, and Russian Mahomedan subjects from, Russian Turkestan.

With the increase of population and of cultivation there is a noticeable change in the climate. Year by year it is becoming milder. Grain crops grow now which a few years ago the seventy of the climate prevented from ripening. With the growth of population the revenue is increasing and, though the province still derives financial assistance from the other provinces to the amount of £375,000 annually, the time cannot be far distant when it will be self-supporting. Up till now with the exception of the land tax the province has been exempt from taxation such as is levied in other provinces. Corruption is becoming more difficult. Contributions forwarded for its maintenance from other, provinces are being applied more to the needs of the province and less to the personal enrichment of the officials entrusted with their distribution. A new spirit is animating the province, a spirit that manifests itself in improved education along more modern lines in improved methods of finance, in an improved army and police, and in the movement for the suppression of opium.

Currency and Schools in Urumchi

In Urumchi material progress is to be noted in almost every direction. There is less currency confusion than is usual in a Chinese city. Government one-tael notes of limited number are issued by the Provincial Treasury, and have a fixed rate of exchange of 400 red cash. The eight chief Tientsin houses also issue notes of the same value, which are guaranteed by the eight firms conjointly and are accepted with confidence. In addition many shops issue their own one-tael notes, which are not accepted with confidence. Coined silver of various denominations is current, the largest being a half-tael. Copper coins are also issued of the value of ten red cash. The rate of exchange remains fairly constant throughout the province.

Three or four years ago there were no modern schools in the capital. Now there are schools of many kinds—preparatory schools, a middle school, a high school, law school, school of agriculture, and a military school of 140 pupils who are undergoing a preparatory training of three years. Mahomedan boys are admitted to this school. English is taught by two enterprising Chinese, one of whom at least speaks an English that no Englishman could understand. Pupils are many, but competent teachers are few. At present in the whole province there is only one foreign teacher, a Japanese in the military school at Ili; and he is leaving on the expiration of his contract. For two years Mr. Hayashide, a Japanese gentleman, was engaged as teacher in the law school and in the military school, but on the completion of his engagement at the end of February he returned to Japan.

Formerly the New Dominion, owing to the difficulties of access, was one of the least favoured of the provinces by the official class. Officials regarded their sojourn as a modified form of exile, and while here devoted all their energies to the acquisition of wealth; but there has been a marked improvement, and the higher officials of the province have as high a sense of the responsibilities due to the people as have their colleagues in other provinces—though that is none too high.

The Suppression of Opium

The Governor, Lien Kuei,[349] is a Manchu of good repute who has set himself the task of suppressing opium throughout the Dominion. Difficulties are greater than in other provinces, but the evil is being combated all along the line. Cultivation is forbidden under penalty of six months' cangue[350] for the farmer and forfeiture of the land. Men are punished if their wives smoke. Opium appliances are destroyed wherever

---

349 Liankui served as governor of Xinjiang (1905–08) overseeing a 'restive' frontier characterised by Muslim unrest and Russian territorial encroachment.
350 A broad heavy wooden frame or board worn round the neck like a kind of portable pillory as a punishment in China.

7 | 'ACROSS CHINA AND TURKESTAN'

Hadas (Khazak) tents and sheep near Ili valley, western China, 1910.
Mitchell Library, Sydney

found. The sale of opium is forbidden under penalty of forfeiture and of a fine 60 times greater than the value of the seizure. Smuggling entails the same heavy penalty. Only to-day 17 officials were dismissed from office for being opium smokers. Drastic measures like these are having their effect. No one pretends that smoking has been entirely abolished or its cultivation entirely suppressed; but there is no question as to the sincerity of the provincial Government in enforcing the Imperial regulations. Opium last year sold for 80 red cash the one ounce weight; it is now sold clandestinely at its weight in silver, and this price places it beyond the reach of a large body of those who formerly were addicted to the habit. From the frontier of Kansu to Urumchi I saw no opium being used, nor could any be bought along the way. Recently there has been disturbance in the district around Ku Cheng, and a demonstration made by the farmers against the enforcement of the prohibition. In that district last year permission was given to plant the poppy, an indulgence which the Governor is determined to discontinue this year. Wheat and Indian corn are being distributed gratuitously and sown in place of the poppy. Much credit is due to this far-away Government for the support it has given to this national movement.

In his work the Governor receives strong support from the next two highest officials, the Treasurer and the Judge. The Provincial Treasurer,

Wang Shu-nan,[351] a native of Chihli, is a well-informed and scholarly man who is now engaged in the compilation of a comprehensive gazetteer of the New Dominion containing a mass of information concerning the country, its people and products, its customs and history. Nine volumes have already been published, and others are being rapidly prepared. They are published in the Provincial Printing Office, and to the student of Central Asia will be of much value and interest. Already the Treasurer is well known as an author. He has published a history of Greece, a history of European wars, and a Chinese manual on the ethnography of the peoples of Europe. Progressive also is the Provincial Judge, Jung Pei, a Manchu. Assisted by a foreign official nominated by the Postal Secretary in Peking, he has established a branch of the Imperial Post Office, and hopes within one year to have a mounted courier service along all the main routes of the Dominion. Two lines are already open. From Chia-tu-kuan, in the Great Wall, to Urumchi, a distance of 1,033 miles, the mails are now delivered regularly in nine days six hours. To Chuguchak,[352] otherwise known as Tarbagatai, the distance, 543 miles, is covered by the couriers regularly in four days 18 hours. The new service will in time entirely displace the old costly and defective postal service. Postage is double the Chinese postal rates, which are by far the cheapest inland rates in the world.

Distinguished Exiles

Among the more progressive men in the province are two exiles. The Imperial Duke Lan, who accompanied the Court in its flight to Sianfu and by the terms of the Protocol was subsequently banished to the New Dominion as punishment for the part he played in the Boxer rebellion, has been here for more than ten years. He has always protested that he was unjustly punished, that he was always friendly to foreigners, and

---

351 Wang Shunan, 1851–1936, co-authored the *Xinjiang Tuzhi*, Illustration gazetteer of Xinjiang, a monumental 116-volume work documenting Xinjiang's geography, politics, ethnic groups and customs. After the fall of the Qing he worked on the *Draft History of the Qing*.

352 Known as Tacheng today; Morrison uses the Kazakh name. It is close to the Dzungarian Gate, an historic pass linking to China and Central Asia.

that the affixing of his name to Boxer proclamations, the offence for which he was exiled, was done under orders of his superiors. Certainly since his arrival here he has shown no evidence of anti-foreign prejudice. He is much esteemed by the officials and the people, is treated as a high official, lives in good style, and is on terms of intimacy with the Russian Consul. Fond of sport, of the country, of guns and horses, he has country cottages both near Urumchi and in the noble mountains to the south, whose snow-clad heights are the most beautiful object within sight of the city. Time hangs heavily on his hands, and he finds his chief pleasure in photography. He is now 55 years of age. The wish of his life is to return to Peking before he dies.

Here also in Urumchi is the Peking editor, Peng Yi-chung, whose name is known to every newspaper reader in the Empire. Of all writers to the Chinese Press he was the most fearlessly outspoken, and perhaps the most violent. He is exiled here for ten years on the charge of having drawn his revolver and fired upon the police official to whose office he was taken when arrested on a charge of sedition. At present he acts as tutor in the family of one of the local officials.

Quite close to the central tower in the Manchu city of Urumchi, lying behind the ancestral temple of the Hunanese, is a market garden, upon which formerly stood the residence occupied during his exile by Chang Yin-huan.[353] On this spot he was executed in July, 1900. Formerly Minister to the United States and later Minister of the Tsungli Yamên, Chang Yin-huan was regarded as the most prominent Cantonese in the Empire. He represented China at the Queen's Jubilee in 1897, and was given the G.C.M.G.[354] In September, 1898, all Peking was astonished to hear of his arrest on the charge of complicity with the reformer Kang Yu-wei. What process of trial he underwent is best known to the Chinese. Exiled to Urumchi he arrived here early in 1899. In July, 1900, while the relief expedition was marching to Peking, his execution was

---

353 Chang Yinhuan, d. 1900, was a Qing diplomat who negotiated territorial treaties with Russia, negotiating the present China-Kazakhstan boarder, ceded parts of Tarbagatai to Russia, helped resolve the Ili Crisis (1871–1881) through the Treaty of St Petersburg (1881) where Russia returned land it had taken in the Ili valley in exchange for favourable trade privileges.
354 Grand Commander of the Order of St Michael and St George.

Morrison with Duke Lan (second from the right), Urumchi, 24 April 1910.
Mitchell Library, Sydney

ordered by the Empress Dowager. It is said that he was taking a midday meal with the Governor when the latter received a peremptory mandate to put his guest to death. Chang Yin-huan met his death philosophically. A matshed was hastily erected outside his front gate, and he was beheaded by a blacksmith in the afternoon. Eyewitnesses tell of the crowds that collected on all the adjacent housetops and walls to witness the tragedy. Two years later, in deference to the representations of the American and British Ministers, all his honours were posthumously restored to him—a great consolation to his family, and, the Chinese say, to the victim also, who is now one of the most honoured of ghosts.

Another distinguished exile, the Marshal Su, Chevalier of the Legion of Honour, commander-in-chief of the troops in Kwangsi province along the French border, died here last August. His policy of disbanding large bodies of troops, casting them adrift unpaid, and pocketing the moneys transmitted for their maintenance led to one of the most serious of Kwangsi rebellions. No one can question the justice of the punishment of this guardian of the Heir Apparent.

7 | 'ACROSS CHINA AND TURKESTAN'

Foreign Trade

The bulk of the foreign trade of Urumchi, unimportant as it is compared with the foreign trade of 100 Chinese cities, is naturally with Russia, and is in the hands of Russian Asiatic Mahomedan subjects, several of whom have amassed large fortunes. The head of one house, the headquarters of which are in Kazan, began business here 20 years ago with a capital of £200, and now is known to possess a capital of not less than £200,000. The favoured trade route with Russia is by Tarbagatai, called by the Russians Chuguchak, a Chinese frontier town 18 stages from Urumchi and Semipalatinsk, the Russian town ten stages from the frontier. Transport is by carts and camels. Exports are mainly wool, cotton, hides, skins, and furs, and imports are iron ware and iron bars, glassware, brass ware, cheap porcelain, coloured prints of gaudy colours, and many other articles. Trade is governed by the regulations embodied in the Ili frontier treaty of 1881. The Chinese contend that this treaty is one-sided; they have given notice as provided by the treaty, and next year will begin in Peking the negotiations for its revision. Questions of China's sovereign rights will then be submitted, and attempts made among other concessions to obtain the removal of the Russian military escorts attached to the Russian Consulates. Here the Consular guard consists of one officer and 36 mounted men.

In Urumchi one Englishman has made his home. Mr. G. W. Hunter,[355] of the China Inland Mission, is one of the most widely travelled men in the province. Of fine physique, well equipped with a knowledge of Chinese and Turki, he works untiringly as an evangelist and *coloorteur*.[356] Already he has visited nearly every important centre in the new Dominion. He takes rank with the most distinguished and tactful pioneer missionaries sent by England to China. His work deserves the special support of all those interested in mission work.

---

355 George W. Hunter, 1861–1946, was a Scottish missionary and formidable linguist. He arrived in China in 1889 and spent his first two years studying Chinese language. In 1906 he moved to Urumqi where he spent the next 40 years. He translated the Gospels into Kazakh and the Bunyan's *Pilgrim's Progress* into Uyghur among others.

356 French for pedlar.

VII. THE JOURNEY TO URUMCHI

(From Our Peking Correspondent)
Urumchi, Sing-Kiang, 5 May 1910[357]

From the nearest point on a Chinese railway to Urumchi is a distance of 82 regular stages, while the nearest point on a Russian railway is 28 stages distant only, and there is no comparison as to the difficulty of transport. From the south of China the shortest route is by India, the Karakorum Pass, and Kashgaria. Two Chinese are here now who have just come by this route. Their father was a Major-General Chen, who was dismissed from his command in Kwang-tung[358] and banished to the New Dominion, where he died last year. His sons have come to recover the body and return with it to China.

From Peking to Urumchi was exactly 100 lays on the journey. There were no difficulties, there was no unpleasantness of any kind. Every one was civil and friendly. This is now the common experience of those who travel in inland China. West from Lanchau, the capital of Kansu province, the journey is divided into three main sections, terminating respectively in Suchau, Hami, and Urumchi, each of 18 stages. The first section, Lanchau to Suchau, is divided further into three sections of unequal length the termini of which are Liangchau, Kanchau, and Suchau. In the first section is the highest pass on the whole route, the Wu Shi-ling, 9,875ft. It presents no serious difficulties to cart transport. Liangchau is the centre of a well-watered, fertile district, supplied with excellent coal and formerly thickly inhabited, but now disfigured by countless ruins. Villages in ruins are the characteristic feature of an immense area of this province. Be it remembered that the former population of Kansu in the lifetime of men now living was estimated at 30 millions: its present population is certainly less than six millions. There is no reason why the province should not recover its former prosperity as the Yang-tsze provinces have recovered and as Yun-nan province has recovered. This year harvests round Liangchau have been exceptionally good and the prosperity is great. Liangchau is the furthest post of the China Inland

---

357 Published on 14 June 1910, p. 5.
358 Kwangtung is a region in north-east China encompassing Manchuria.

7 | 'ACROSS CHINA AND TURKESTAN'

Mission in Kansu province. In its neighbourhood are the headquarters of the Belgian Mission to Kansu and the residence of Mgr. Otto,[359] the learned successor of Mgr. Hamer,[360] who was murdered at Kwei-hua-cheng in 1900.

Kanchau, the next important city to the west, is also prospering. Noticeable here is a superb temple, 13 centuries old, containing a reclining image of Buddha, 113ft. in length. Many convicts transported to the Imperial post roads are sent to this city. In chains, with their feet often confined in wooden blocks or chained by neck and ankle to an iron crowbar, they are an object of pity to the traveller who is aware that they may be guilty, but who knows also that, while they have in every case confessed their guilt, in every case the unwilling confession has been extracted from the poor wretches by torture.

View from Splingaerd's yamen looking north, Suchow (Jiuquan), March 1910.
Mitchell Library, Sydney

---

359 Hubert Otto was later Vicar Apostolic of Northern Shaanxi.
360 Joseph Hamer, 1840–1900, was a Catholic missionary and Bishop in Inner Mongolia and northern China who, during the Boxer rebellion, was captured, tortured and executed by rebels at Xiwanzi (modern day Chahar), Inner Mongolia.

Paul Splingaerd

Both Liangchau and Kanchau held out against the Mahomedan insurrection. Suchau, on the other hand, was captured by the Mahomedans and recaptured by the Chinese. Abundant evidences of the struggle still exist. This is the city in which resided for 16 years the Belgian, Paul Splingaerd, whose Chinese name, Lin Tzu-mei, is a household word in Western China. A remarkable man was Splingaerd. Of humble origin, he came to China in 1864 as servant of a Belgian Lazarist missionary, Père Verbiest, who died one year later at the mission station near Kalgan. He married a Chinese Christian woman, who bore him 20 children, four of whom are nuns. He had the gift of tongues and spoke Chinese and Russian and several other languages. Employed by the German Legation in Peking he was attached to Baron Richthofen[361] as interpreter and accompanied the great geologist in his travels in China. Subsequently he entered the Chinese service and was stationed in Suchau as adviser and Russian interpreter in the frontier Customs. Here he remained until 1895.

In the Boxer year 1900 he was in Lanchau with the Commercial Mission despatched by the King of the Belgians under Colonel Fivé. Imperial orders had been sent to the Viceroy to put to death all foreigners in the province. Splingaerd was warned of the arrival of the telegram. He went at once to see the Viceroy, was admitted, and was able to persuade him that the telegram was a forgery and to stay his hand. Some days later a second order was received countermanding the previous order. No foreigner in Kansu lost his life. Splingaerd died in Sianfu in 1906.

For some time Suchau was the residence of one of the early missionaries to China, Frère Benoit de Goes. Entrusted by the Viceroy of India and by his Superiors of the Society of Jesus with a mission to discover a route overland to Peking, de Goes left Agra on October 2, 1602, arrived in Yarkand, November, 1603, and remained there one

---

361 Ferdinand Freiherr von Richthofen, 1833–1905, coined the terms "silk road" and "silk route" to describe China's overland trade with central Asia and Europe. He was a traveller and scientist who held professorships in geology and geography at a number of German universities.

year. Continuing his journey he crossed the desert and reached Suchau at the end of 1605. Here he learned that Ricci and other Jesuits were already established in Peking. He informed Ricci of his arrival, and the Superior sent to welcome him and assist him in his mission that Cantonese missionary who was the first Chinese ever admitted into the Society. But de Goes, already weakened in health, lived only a short time after his arrival. They met in March, 1607, and the valiant traveller died on April 11. No record can be found of his stay in Suchau, nor has any trace been discovered of his place of burial.

Hsing Hsing-hsia, April 1910.
Mitchell Library, Sydney

An Historic Frontier Gate

A short day's stage from Suchau is the historic frontier gate of Kia-yu-kwan, a "fortress" in the ruined mud rampart to which in its earlier course near Peking has been justly given the title of "great." Here Dr. Stein made one of his most important discoveries. He traced near Kia-yu-kwan the junction of two defensive lines of widely different age and purpose, the earlier one built to protect the belt of oases along which Chinese expansion was moving westwards to Turkestan, and another at right angles to this, of much later date, through which passes the present Kia-yu-kwan gate, for the opposite purpose of closing the Central Asian trade route at a time when China had resumed its traditional attitude of seclusion. The fortress is now mainly a Customs barrier. It has no garrison and is undefended except for heaps of stones stacked along the walls ready to be used in the repulse of robbers.

Six days further west is Ansichau, a desolate town ravaged by sandstorms of extraordinary violence. Five stages still further west, near Tunhwanghsien,[362] are the Grottoes of the Thousand Buddhas, where Dr. Stein[363], and more recently Professor Pelliot,[364] obtained some of the richest archaeological treasures, art relies, books, and manuscripts acquired in recent years. At Ansichau stores are laid in for the desert journey to Hami, on the fifth day, by the pass of Hsing Hsing-hsia the road enters the New Dominion. A new form of defence is seen here small cairns of stones piled to represent the images of soldiers are dotted over the hill sides. The commander of the handful of badly-armed guards on duty at the pass denied, however, that he drew pay for these mannikins as soldiers on the active list. Such happy means of enrichment are now impossible. Six stages further the road reaches the small oasis of Hami, a prosperous, fertile, well-irrigated Chan-ton state whose Prince has authority, under Chinese supervision, over 1,950 Chan-tou families.[365] Chinese authority is maintained by a Ting, or Sub-Prefect, and by 800 Chinese soldiers armed with old-type Mausers under a brigadier. Every three years the Prince is expected to proceed to Peking for audience. An enlightened man, he has shown courtesy to many travellers,

---

362 Today known as Dunhuang.
363 Sir Mark Aurel Stein, 1862–1943, was a Hungarian by birth, British by adoption. Stein was one of the foremost archaeologists of central Asia of his time. His greatest discovery was made at the Mogao Caves, known as "Caves of the Thousand Buddhas", near Dunhuang in 1907. He discovered a printed copy of the Diamond Sutra, the world's oldest printed text, dating to AD 868, along with 40,000 other scrolls. He took 24 cases of manuscripts and 4 cases of paintings and relics. They are housed in the British Library.
364 Paul Eugène Pelliot, 1878–1945, was a French sinologist best known for his explorations of Central Asia and his discovery of many important Chinese texts such as the Dunhuang manuscripts. He followed Stein, who had bought manuscripts from Abbott Wang, but unlike Pelliot, Stein knew no Chinese. Pelliot spent some weeks examining the ancient and mediaeval manuscripts in the Abbott's possession and selected what he regarded as the most valuable. They are now at Paris in the Bibliotèque Nationale.
365 Chantous (*chan tou* means 'turbaned heads') was the catchall the Chinese applied to Uyghurs, Kazakhs, and other Turkic groups in Western China.

especially to English travellers, to whom he mentions with gratitude the generous action of the Indian Government a few years ago in sending back to China ten natives of Hami who, on their return from the pilgrimage to Mecca, were stranded destitute in Bombay.

Another section of 18 stages, largely at first through alkaline deserts with cultivation and habitations only round the stages, lies between Hami and Urumchi. The most important town on the route by which I came is Guchen, the terminus of several trade routes from North China and Mongolia. Here, in a separate walled town built in 1887, are gathered the remnants of all those Manchu families from Urumchi, Ili, and Barkul who escaped destruction during the Mahomedan insurrection.

Chantou family, Hami, 8 April 1910.
Mitchell Library, Sydney

VIII. KULDJA[366] AND THE REGION OF ILI

(From Our Peking Correspondent)
Kuldja, 27 May 1910[367]

More than 20 years ago Colonel Mark Bell,[368] who had recently made a remarkable reconnaissance journey from Peking to Kashgar, characterized the distant Chinese bases of Tarbagatai, Kuldja, and Kashgar in the absence of good communications as "dissevered limbs of China," and he contrasted the strength given to the Russian Empire by her Cossack military frontier settlements with the weakness of the Chinese frontier settlements and the perpetual danger to the Chinese Empire arising from that weakness. What he wrote is true to this day. China is awakening to a sense of the importance of these distant settlements, but so far her efforts to improve them have been confined to the creation of a local branch of the regular army and to the establishment of elementary schools and police; she has done nothing to improve the communications, nothing to link up by railway or even by metalled road these distant portions of her Empire.

THE RUSSIAN OCCUPATION OF KULDJA

Kuldja, from where I am writing to you, was from 1871 to 1882 the most advanced Russian outpost in Central Asia. It can at any moment become so again. Its recovery by China by the threat of war was one of the most amazing instances of successful bluff on record. No such bluff could be successfully attempted a second time. The Powers are now too well informed of the true military strength of Western China. It is amazing now to read the preparations that Russia in 1881 deemed necessary to enter upon a campaign against China, and astonishing to read the fears expressed by General Kaufmann as to the issue of a

---

366 Now known as Yining.
367 Published on 25 June 1910, p. 7.
368 Mark Sever Bell, VC, 1843–1906, was born in Sydney and served in the Royal Engineers. In 1887 he travelled from Peking to Kashgar. Morrison took a similar route. His account of the journey was published by the Royal Geographical Society in February 1890.

7 | 'ACROSS CHINA AND TURKESTAN'

A view of Kuldja, April 1910.
Mitchell Library, Sydney

struggle with the redoubtable General Tso Tsung-tang, the Hunanese who had commanded the army of extermination whose march across Western China through a country defended only or mainly by unarmed villagers has been the theme of such extravagant praise. "The history of the advance of Tso Tsung-tang's 'Agricultural Army'," says Wells Williams, "would, if thoroughly known, constitute one of the most remarkable achievements in the annals of any modern country." [369]

As a matter of fact the more it is known the more groundless appears the praise lavished upon the achievement. Even more than in 1871 Kuldja is at the mercy of Russia. In the Boxer year, 1900, it was virtually re-occupied by the 500 troops of all arms despatched from the Russian frontier to strengthen the Consulate guard. The region is practically undefended and it must continue to remain derelict until China connects it by railway with her Empire. The nearest point on the Chinese railways is 2,820 miles distant by road from Kuldja, while

---

369 Samuel Wells Williams, 1812–1874, was an American Sinologist, missionary and diplomat. He was an interpreter with Commodore Perry's expedition to Japan in 1853–1854, an event that presaged the 'opening' of Japan, and wrote an account of the Chinese empire, history, geography and people, called *The Middle Kingdom*. New York: Charles Scribner's Sons, 1907.

Hassas (Kazakhs) near Tarbagatai, 18 May 1910.
Mitchell Library, Sydney

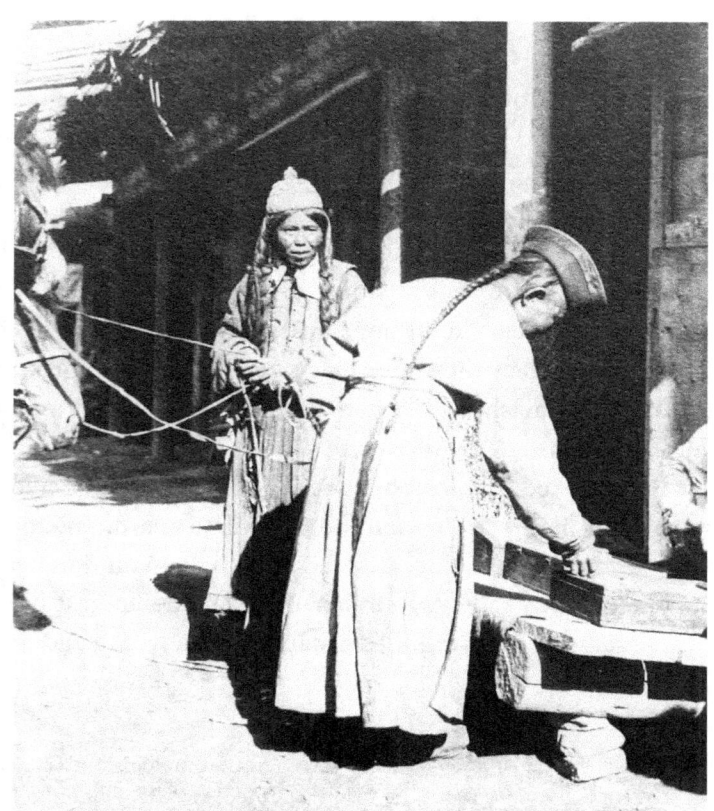

Mongols in Kuldja, man and woman, 20 May 1910.
Mitchell Library, Sydney

it is certain that before many years the Russian railway system will be extended right up to the frontier, which is one day's march from the Chinese headquarters.

The Journey from Urumchi

From Urumchi, the capital city of the New Dominion, to Kuldja is a distance of 582 miles. The road is available for cart traffic throughout the year, subject, however. to long delays m the summer, when the labyrinth of rivers flowing down from the Tien Shan, none of which are bridged, are swollen by the melting of the snows. The road passes generally through a fertile, well-cultivated country, occasionally through long stretches of deep sand. For some distance it passes by the Sairam Noz at the base of pine-clad mountains, and descends by the Talki pass through country as beautiful as Switzerland into the basin of the Ili. Rather more than 100 miles from the capital is the granary of the capital the fertile oasis of Manas, famous for its rice fields, its vineyards, and its orchards. Continue along the main road a further distance of 113 miles and the town of Hsi Hu[370] is reached. Here the main road bifurcates, one branch going north-west to Tarbagatai (called Chuguchak by the Russians) and the other continuing to Ili.[371] At the village of Tahoyen, midway between Hsi Hu and Kuldja, there is another road, not available for carts, which from the main road runs over the mountains direct to Tarbagatai. Whoever holds Hsi Hu holds all the roads to Tarbagatai and Kuldja from the capital of the province, and it was in the hills commanding this point that the Russians stationed their advanced outpost during the occupation of Kuldja. China has no troops at Hsi Hu. She has a badly armed detachment at Tarbagatai; her main force is in the region of Kuldja.

Kuldja is the name of a town close to the river Ili. It takes the place of a town of the same name, now buried in the Ili River, which was destroyed by the Mahomedans in 1865. By foreigners the name has been applied to the district. It is somewhat confusing, but there are

---

370 Xihu now lies on the Lianhuo Expressway connecting Urumqi to Ili (Yining).
371 Tacheng town, Tacheng prefecture.

three towns quite separate from each other which are vaguely termed Kuldja by the foreigner. On coming from the capital the road, bending from the north into the Ili valley, reaches first the thriving town of Sui-ting-hsien, a busy mart with a rapidly increasing population of Chinese, adorned with one striking temple, the memorial temple to Chin Hsün, the General who recovered for China the territory lying between the capital and Kuldja, and who was the first Tartar General of Kuldja after its evacuation by Russia. There is a high military officer in Sui-ting, a Chen tai, whose command is held from the provincial Governor and is independent of that of the Tartar General. A body of ragged provincial levies, badly armed, represents the might of China.

An Incompetent Commander

Sui-ting-hsien is 30 miles from the Russian frontier. Five miles southwest from the city is a new city built 15 years ago, called Hsin Cheng, a well laid-out town with broad streets, unmetalled, with large yamêns and marked business activity. This is the headquarters of the Tartar General, the seat of the new military school, and the depôt of a newly created branch of the modern army of China. It is the chief stronghold of the region, but is built in an indefensible position. A military spirit is abroad in the town, and the sounds of bugles, the tramp of soldiers singing patriotic choruses as they march, and the voices of drill instructors are heard all day long. Officers in smart uniforms, proud of their uniform and their sword, swagger about the streets. It is a quite new movement, and promises well. It originated in the time of the last Tartar General, the excellent patriarch who was recently appointed Viceroy in Lanchau, and is continued by his successor, a courteous gentleman of the old school named Kuang Fu, who complains of the costly legacy and trouble therewith associated bequeathed him by his predecessor. Kuang Fu is not a General of whom any country would be proud. No other country but China would think of appointing such a man to such a post. Appointments of this kind make progressive Chinese despair. Here you have a post of extreme importance, requiring for its command an officer trained, in the knowledge of modern military science and such men are to be found in China's modern army—and China selects for this command only a month ago, for a second term

7 | 'ACROSS CHINA AND TURKESTAN'

of office, a doddering old gentleman of 67, a Mongol Bannerman, who can neither read nor write, who knows nothing of military things, but is believed, being a Bannerman, to have an hereditary instinct for war, who was with Chin Hsin 37 years ago, and has spent since nearly all his official life in this region, yet during all that time has not even inspected the routes across the mountains connecting the points on the frontier under his command. Such a warrior held indecision by the Russians, inspires contempt for his country.

The Troops

Nominally his force consists of one regiment of Infantry, 2,004 men, one regiment of Cavalry, 1,117 strong, two batteries of Field and one battery of Mountain Artillery, in all 568 Artillery. Actually the strength of his force is:- Infantry, 1,400; Cavalry, 700, with only 100 horses; and 200 so-called Artillery, unprovided with horses or guns. Two batteries of six 37mm. Krupp mountain guns are locked away in the military school. They have been here for 15 years. Locked away in the Chentais Yamên in Suiting are 12 57mm. Creuzot fired guns sent here by the Provincial Governor before the arrival of the Krupp guns. Rifles are of various patterns—Mamuers, 1871, 1878, 1887, some imported, some made in the Hanyang Arsenal, and Mannlichers, to which were added four years ago, in order to assist in the confusion. 150 Japanese rifles of a totally different bore. Cartridges are imported in small quantities from Urumchi and some are made by hand. There are no machine guns, but there is a band. There are no Engineers, no transport, no Army Medical Service, no arsenal and no magazine, but there is a new military school of 300 cadets, where one foreign instructor, a Japanese, is employed under a two years' engagement. There is also a police school. No foreign language is taught at either school, and none of the Chinese instructors have been educated abroad.

Troops are mainly recruited locally, but the officers come from other provinces. Difficulty is found in retaining men from other provinces. Pay given is less than that promised. Expense of living is greater than in any other town of China, and the men desert in large numbers.

The Provincial Revenues

Thus a beginning has been made, and the keenness of the officers and men is promising. Lack of adequate funds is urged as an excuse, why more has not been done. Theoretically provincial contributions towards the upkeep of the now Dominion amount in all to £375,000 per annum, of which sum £300,000 are claimed by the Tartar General for the maintenance of his frontier defences. It is his grievance that a steadily increasing proportion of this contribution fails to reach his treasury and that reforms are crippled by this want of means. The whole question of the provincial revenue and its allotment is now being investigated by a competent delegate from the Ministry of Finance, at present stationed in Urumchi. Much is hoped for as the outcome of the negotiations, which begin next year, for the new frontier trade treaty with Russia. Taxation is very light and the people's wealth is growing rapidly. There can be no question of that. The prosperity of the Kuldja region is unmistakable. Shopkeepers and traders from North China are coming here in rapidly increasing numbers, and more and more are accompanied by their wives and families. The population is multiplying rapidly both by natural increase and by immigration. This year the increase has been so great that it has outrun the relative food supply and led to greatly increased prices.

The Races of the Region

There are many races in this region, but there is little intermingling, and tribal characteristics are being preserved. There are Chinese of the "Great Religion" (Buddhism) from North China, mainly from Tientsin, and to a man members of the Tsai-li-hui Secret Society; there are Chinese of the "Small Religion" (Mahomedans), known to foreigners as Tungans, originally drafted here from the Mahomedan centres of Western China; there are Manchus, who speak only Manchu, of two classes—Solons and Shibos—descendants of military colonists from Manchuria, who were transferred here in 1764 after the destruction of Ralmuk[372]

---

[372] This refers to the Kalmyk people, a branch of the Oriat-speaking western Mongols, nomads who roamed what is today western China, Mongolia, Kazakhstan, and Russia.

7 | 'ACROSS CHINA AND TURKESTAN'

sovereignty. Comparatively few modern Manchus reside here; they are mostly of the official class and speak Chinese, not Manchu. Seven miles from Kuldja on the way to Hsin Cheng there stand the ruins of the former prosperous, Manchu city of Bayantai, which before the rebellion contained a population exclusively of Manchus variously estimated to number from 50,000 to 150,000. In 1865 the city was destroyed by the Mahomedans, and every man and most of the women and children were slain. None of these could speak Manchu. Yet the language is still used by Solons and Shibos. All official intercourse between the Russian Consul and the Chinese requires the employment of Manchu as a means of communication. Despatches sent by the Consul are written in Manchu and Russian; the Chinese reply in Chinese and Manchu. Thus a language which has long disappeared in China and Manchuria is preserved in the valley of the Ili.

Then there are various races of Mahomedans, most numerous of whom are the Taranchis,[373] descendants of colonists transplanted from Kashgaria, and Hasas or Kassaks,[374] not to be confused with Cossacks. There are Russian Mahomedan subjects from Andijan,[375] Kazan, and Tashkent, among whom are the wealthiest traders, and there are many branches of Mongols. By natural increase the Mahomedans are increasing more rapidly than the Chinese. They are cleaner and healthier, and have finer physique, living more in the open air, and their women are not, as are the Chinese, deprived from childhood of the powers of healthy locomotion. Natural increase is aided by a constant influx of Chantous from less favoured districts.

Four of these groups comprised that Dzungar Khanate, which was defeated and then exterminated by the Qing in 1757-8 in what is known as the Dzungar genocide.

373 The Taranchi (Taranqi) were a Turkic Muslim group who were forcibly resettled in the Ili Valley. They supported the Muslim uprising in the mid-19th century and were harshly dealt with.

374 Kazakhs.

375 Andijian is located in eastern Uzbekistan and was the birthplace of Zahiriddin Muhammad Babur, the Muslim chief who invaded northern India, subjugated the Hindus, and founded the Mughal empire in the early 16th century.

Our inn-yard at Kuldja, 28 May 1910.
Mitchell Library, Sydney

The Christian Community

In Kuldja there is a small Christian community whose history is one of more than usual interest. Readers of the entertaining narrative of Abbé Hue will remember his frequent references to the persecution of the Christians in the reigns of Yung Cheng[376] and Chien Lung,[377] when Christians from every province in China who refused to apostatize were sent in exile to Ili. At first they were branded on the cheek, a punishment which was afterwards discontinued; otherwise they were not unkindly treated, and were allowed a considerable measure of liberty, but were forbidden to return to China. For more than a century the community remained without, a pastor, but in 1861, after the joint occupation of Peking, the Bishop of Shensi, Mgr. Chiais, sent a native priest to seek the descendants of the faithful. On the outbreak of the Mahomedan insurrection in 1863 the priest disappeared. He was murdered by a guide whom he had trusted, and the Christians were again without a pastor.

---

376 Yongzheng, 1678–1736, unlike his father Kangxi, was wary of the Christians and promulgated tough measures against them.
377 Qianlong, 1711–1799, rebuffed the invitation by Lord Macartney in 1793 to trade, noting "our Celestial Empire possesses all things in prolific abundance and lacks no product within its own borders." His persecution of Christians was more rigorous than his father.

7 | 'ACROSS CHINA AND TURKESTAN'

During the insurrection the community was much reduced in numbers. Some of the men were killed, many, of the children and a number of the women wore carried off by the Musulmans.

Russia occupied the region in 1871, and prevented any further massacre, and compelled the restitution of some of the women. But Russia did not favour the establishment of any Roman Catholic missionary, and it was not until after the restoration of the region to the Chinese in November, 1882, that a foreign missionary was allowed to come here. At the end of that year Père Hendricks, a Dutchman, arrived from Europe, and he was able to report with pride that the community, which numbered some 150 persons all told, had not forsaken the religion for which their fathers had made such great sacrifices, but had remained good Catholics. One year later three missionary priests, sent overland by the Bishop of Kansu, arrived here and established their mission. They were Père Steeneman (Dutch), now the superior of the mission, Père De Deken (Belgian)[378], the famous traveller, who accompanied Bonvalot[379] and Prince Henri d'Orléans, on their journey across Tibet, and subsequently died in the Congo, and Père Janssons (Dutch), the first superior of the mission, now a *curé* in Holland. They belonged to the congregation of Schent, near Brussels. Work has continued from that time. The community is small, but numbers some members of good standing, among them being the larges oil millers of Suiting, descendants of Catholics exiled a century and a half ago, from Kueichow in South China.

---

378 Constant Pierre-Joseph De Deken, 1852–1896, participated in the 1889 expedition in Turkestan, funded by Prince Henri, whose goal was to reach Shanghai via Tibet and Tongking (Vietnam) becoming the first Europeans to visit Tibet. A Chinese speaker, he acted as interpreter. He died in Congo from ill-health.

379 Pierre Gabriel Èdouard Bonvalot, 1853–1933, was a French explorer in Central Asia and Tibet. The expedition, which he lead to Tibet was financed by Prince Henri of Orléans.

IX. FROM KULDJA ACROSS THE TIEN SHAN TO AKSU

(From Our Peking Correspondent)
Aksu, 11 June 1910[380]

Far Western China, or the province of the New Dominion, is divided laterally into two main portions by the mountain range of the Tien Shan and each division is named from its relation to the range, as the Pei-lu, or northern highway, and the Nan-lu, or southern highway. The northern division terminates westwards in the territory of Kuldja, the southern division terminates in the territory of Kashgar, in each case the point of departure being Urumchi—the centrally situated capital city of the province. To reach Kashgar from Kuldja the best road lies through the adjoining Russian territory. It is a round-about road available for cart traffic. Entering Russian Turkestan at Kuldja, it passes by Vierny to Narin and thence, crossing the Turgat Pass, re-enters Chinese territory and proceeds direct to Kashgar city.

To the traveller who would remain in Chinese territory two routes are open. Should he wish to avoid the crossing of the mountains he may return to Urumchi by the northern road and then bend back to Kashgar by the southern road, a journey available for cart traffic and invariably selected by Chinese officials, for whom time is never an object when proceeding from one post to the other. Or he may follow the short direct route over the mountains by the Musart Pass, the southern terminal of which route is the city of Aksu on the southern highway. For many centuries this route has been followed by Far Western traders. By this pass the pilgrim Hsuan Chuang[381] returned to his native country from his mission to India in the seventh century. Long before the Mahomedan insurrection this was the most important of China's western frontier trade routes. By this pass could the only possible junction have been effected had an attempt been made, as the Russians feared, to unite the

---

380 Published on 31 August 1910, p. 4 with map.
381 Xuanzang, a Buddhist monk, made a 17-year journey to India in search of authentic Buddhist texts; he accumulated 657 Sanskrit texts which he brought back to China in AD 645.

7 | 'ACROSS CHINA AND TURKESTAN'

Crossing the Aksu River, June 1910.
Mitchell Library, Sydney

Mahomedan forces of Kashgar under Yakub Beg with the Khurgiz and other Mohomedan insurgents of Kuldja, whose hostility to Russian trade had compelled the Russian occupation of Kuldja in 1871. When Russia, therefore, occupied Kuldja, she did not fail to occupy also the Kuldja entrance to the pass, and the evidence of her occupation, the log cabins used as barracks, remain to this day.

An Ancient Way

At the best of times the route is a dangerous one for pack animals. As the only available pass between two of the outlying portions of her empire it would be reasonable to expect that China would take some measures to improve its condition and minimize its perils. But China's ways are not the ways of other frontier Powers. "Every year the road is repaired; it is now in good order," the chief Chinese military commander, the Tartar General of Kuldja, had confidently informed me only a few days before. But he had never visited the road himself, nor had any of his officers, and I question whether the road is now in any better condition than it was in the seventh century.

There is no difficulty about engaging transport. Every few days throughout the year caravans of horses and donkeys leave from both terminals. Payment is made in roubles, and despite the mortality among the animals the rates are not excessive, ten to twelve roubles being paid for each pack animal carrying two hundredweights. The distance is 347 miles, divided into 13 stages, the dangerous crossing being on the eighth day, and the difficult fording of the river on the ninth. My own experience during my ride across the pass was an agreeable one. Travel in the mountains was a welcome change to the sweltering heat of Kuldja, confined as the city is in a basin among the mountains only 2,050ft. above sea level. My caravan drivers were Russian Andijani and as it was the season of rich pastures their animals were sleek and fat and in fine fettle. These caravan men are a good class of hardy, independent men, past masters in their calling. Largely they are Russian subjects from Russian Turkestan, provided with Russian registration certificates renewed every six mouths, for which they are requited to pay the equivalent of one guinea per annum.

Ili and Tekes

On the first day out from Kuldja city the broad river Ili has to be crossed by a ferry. We had a long wait at the crossing, for the ferry was on the opposite bank, and the current was running like a mill-race. With infinite labour the ferry was towed by horses made fast to it by their tails upstream to a point from which it could drop down by the current to our landing. Before crossing the weary boatmen rested to take breath; but, my native guard wire excited and would give them no rest. "Here is the foreign great man waiting," they shouted, "and waiting, and yet you who have neither fathers nor mothers sit there and idle."

Finally when the ferry did push out into the stream it swung past our landing so swiftly that the rope failed, and before the clumsy boat could touch the bank it had been swept half a mile down stream. So we had our wait for nothing. Then we marched up the bank to another ferry a day's journey higher up the river, and having spent the night in a Taranchi village, we crossed the next day and began the ascent of the watershed lying between the Ili river and its chief affluent, the Tekes River.

By the fourth day we had crossed the watershed among glorious pine woods, having slept one night in a beautiful glade fragrant with flowers where the partridges called us in the morning, a second night

7 | 'ACROSS CHINA AND TURKESTAN'

by a mountain stream in a primitive water-mill kept by an aged Mongol, and the third night in a Turki inn in a Mongol encampment of tents and log cabins grouped round the Lamasery of Hunokai[382] in the valley of the Tekes. It was a surprise to find so imposing a lamasery in such a region. It seemed is if it might have been bodily lifted from Mongolia and re-erected in these steppes. Large enough to shelter within its compound the entire village, it was five years in building, having been completed in 1899, the year before the Boxer outbreak. Four hundred Lamas are attached to the temple.

The Tekes valley consists of rich agricultural land, well and permanently watered. It supports a nomad population scanty in numbers of Hasas (Khurgiz) and Mongols, who live in tents and not in permanent dwellings. On its wide pastures graze vast numbers of horses, sheep, and cattle. No attempt is made: at cultivation. The fine country is being wasted. One can easily understand why Russia desired permanently to retain this valley apart from its advantageous position strategically. Some day, it will yield rich harvests to the husbandman. Had the Russian occupation become effective it would long ago have been dotted with farmsteads.

The Musat Pass

There is a ferry across the Tekes River in charge of the Mongols, and one march from the river on the edge of the pine woods are the log cabins of the advanced Musart Pass left from the Russian occupation. At this point the Northern Musart River emerges from a narrow rocky defile. Up the valley of the river among the pine woods the path winds high up the mountains until the stage is reached and shelter found in wretched log-cabins roofed with turf that have been in ruins for years. The ascent of the Musart Pass begins at this stage. From the north side the summit is reached after a steep climb of 13 miles; on the south side the descent down the mighty Japarlik glacier is longer and more

---

382 The lamasary (or Honghuapai Lama Temple) is an historic Tibetan temple near the boarder of Kazakhstan. Morrison saw the reconstructed monastery. The original was built in the 17th century and destroyed by the Qing in their defeat and subsequent genocide of the Dzungar people in 1755–1759.

Musart Pass, on the Japarlik Glacier, June 1910.
Mitchell Library, Sydney

gradual. The dividing ridge is 12,000ft above sea level. The descent down the glacier is the chief danger. Covered with débris the surface is broken into millions of tiny tent-shaped knolls, the origin of which, says Merzbacher,[383] is to be attributed to peculiar melting processes. Deep crevasses yawn on each side of the irregular and slippery track which zigzags down the glacier. The way is strewn with the skeletons of dead pack-animals. Containing walls 3,000ft. high rise -on each side of the glacier. The glacier itself is gradually shrinking, melting into the valley down which runs, in a wide bed of gravel in many channels, the lower Musart River. It ends in an abrupt fall of 350ft. In the precipitous ice-face steps have been cut, and down these the laden animals are passed singly with much care.

On a shelf in the adjacent mountain wall is the stage of Mazarbashi, where some Turkis from the plains are stationed to repair the road and render assistance to the traveller. But they work under no skilled direction and they are paid nothing for their labour; the repair of the road is a Turki obligation. It is an ill-organized service, the most inefficient possible. Neglect of the pass is cited as striking evidence of national decadence. Traders require uncommon fortitude to face its dangers, and their losses in transport animals are very great, but as there is no alternative direct route across the mountains they are forced to come this way. They carry on a trade of considerable importance, easily capable, were the road improved, of ten-fold increase. A few hundred dollars a year spent with knowledge would make a great improvement, but the dollars are not spent. China derives a considerable revenue from the traffic, but she gives nothing in return. Pitiful it is to see the hardships imposed upon these hardy traders, and pitiful to see the Chinese tea-gatherers levying burdensome tolls upon a trade conducted in spite of Government neglect.

---

383 Gottfried Merzbacher, 1843–1926, led an expedition in the area in 1903, and produced a meticulous survey of the Tian Shan mountains. His ethnographic worked ranged over the Caucasus and Central Asia.

The Town of Aksu[384]

Twenty miles south of the glacier, where the containing walls converge, a substantial barrier has been thrown across the valley, and here, by the double gateway, sit the Hunanese tax gatherers. This is the barrier of Khurgan.[385] The busy town of Kuchar[386] is five stage's distant on the main road east of Aksu. The town is of interest to Englishmen because it is the place of exile of Safder Ali Khan,[387] the deposed Mir of Hunza, who here in straitened circumstances, far away from his people, makes a precarious living as a wine dealer. A belt of sand desert 20 miles wide encircles the oasis of Aksu, one of the most prosperous districts in the Nan-lu. There are two towns ten miles apart, old Aksu, the Turki town and residence of the Aksa Prince, a crowded insanitary mass of irregular tottering mud-houses, built along tortuous, undrained alley-ways; and new Aksu, a Chinese walled town, in which reside the Chinese officials and Chinese traders from North China. Both towns swarm with Turkis. Goitre is conspicuous among them. A handful of old-style Chinese braves are sufficient to preserve order. In accordance with a policy everywhere enforced in Western China no soldiers are recruited from Mahomedans, but Turkis are admitted to the police. In that case, in accordance with the rule applied to all native official in Chinese employment they are required to adopt Chinese dress. In Aksu, as in all other towns in the New Dominion, the best stocked shops are those belonging to merchants from Tientsin, who have to transport their goods by cart or camel back across the whole width of China. In both cities the busiest houses are the pawnshops, which in every case are owned by Chinese. Turki earnings readily find resting-place in these houses of usury. British interests are represented by one Hindu trader and by some Afghans, the senior of whom is the British Aksakal, or White Beard, the deputy of the British Consul in Kashgar. Russia has also and Aksakal.

---

384 Aksu today is the capital of the Aksu Prefecture.
385 Kurgan is known in Chinese as Huoergaosi, it is important for cross-border trade between China and Central Asia.
386 Kuche or Kuqu, is an ancient site of Buddhist culture on the Silk Road.
387 Mir Safdar Ali Khan (reign dates 1886–1891) fled to China after conquest of Hunza and Nagar States by British Forces in December 1891.

7 | 'ACROSS CHINA AND TURKESTAN'

Musart Pass, 5 June 1910. It connects Aksu with Yining (Kulja).
Mitchell Library, Sydney

X. FROM AKSU TO KASHGAR

(From Our Peking Correspondent)
Kashgar, 22 June 1910[388]

In Aksu I engaged two broad-wheeled light carts to carry my servants and things to Kashgar while I continued on horseback. The distance is 322 miles, divided into 18 stages, which we covered in less than ten days. It is a flat country consisting of saline wilderness and sand dunes with dead scrub and gnarled trees deeply embedded in sand, rare habitations and brackish water alternating with splendid irrigated lands, well timbered, producing richly, and thickly peopled. Land is being steadily recovered from the desert, cultivation is spreading, and the rainfall increasing. At regular intervals there are horse stages where those provided with a Government order can obtain extra horses. In the New Dominion these stages are invariably entrusted to Hunanese, who find in the opium pipe some consolation for the dreariness of the lives which they have to live among a people of whose language they are entirely ignorant. Opium is grown across the Russian border and is smuggled into the Dominion in kerosine tins provided for the purpose with a false bottom. Its price is greater than its weight in silver and is rising rapidly, so that the stage men are put to straits to purchase what they require. It is the starved horses that suffer.

Privileges of the Hunanese

This monopoly of the post stations is another of the special favours shown to the natives of the province of Hunan. In the reconquest of the New Dominions the two Generals who took the leading part were both Hunanese. One of them was the first Governor of the reconstituted province. Their troops were mainly Hunanese braves. Generous in its conception of what it owes to them the Throne has ever since shown the Hunanese marked favour in the new province, giving them the monopoly of the tea trade and of the post stages and selecting them to fill 80 per cent of the official posts in the Dominion. They own

---

388 Published on 31 August 1910, p. 5.

7 | 'ACROSS CHINA AND TURKESTAN'

On the way to Kashgar, June 1910.
Mitchell Library, Sydney

most of the pawnshops. They are the *likin*[389] officials, the magistrates, and tax-gatherers. They form the majority of the "expectant" officials of the province, that is to say, the officials who have purchased rank and the right of office and are waiting for a vacancy to enter upon a career of official plunder. They are a bad type to be sent to a new province, for they carry on the traditions of the reconquest and bleed the people unmercifully. The most arrogant of Chinese, they have a profound contempt for the Turkis, contemptuously describing them as "submissive to oppression and incapable of gratitude." They refuse to learn Turki. Recently, however, China appears to have realized that discrimination in favour of this class has not been a wise policy. They are being gradually deprived of the special privileges previously accorded them, and during the last few years the higher officials have not been Hunanese.

---

389 A Chinese provincial transit duty or tax.

Halfway between Aksu and the city of Kashgar is the oasis of Maralbashi,[390] the meeting place of main roads from Yarkand[391] and Kashgar, a fertile, well-irrigated, well-timbered district, teeming with people, with numberless mosques, none of which, however, are worthy of a passing glance. It is curious to observe such an admirable system of irrigation existing alongside such crudely-built dwellings of wood and mud of such primitive architecture. Currency along this road is less confusing than in other parts of China. Russian rouble notes are chiefly in use, the rate of exchange being reasonably constant, while the Chinese currency has a stability of exchange greater than is met with in any other province. "Dragon notes" issued by the provincial Government of the value of 400 red cash are everywhere current, as well as silver coins minted in Kashgar. Russian subsidiary coinage is also in circulation.

The City of Kashgar

Long avenues of willows and poplars lead to the double city of Kashgar, where are gathered together the most numerous mass of people in all the New Dominion. As is the case in so many of the cities of Chinese Turkestan there are twin cities several miles apart. Old Kashgar, the Turki city, has a population of 110,000 overspreading a wide area outside the city wall. The new Chinese city is much less thickly peopled. Within its walls are the yamêns of the provincial Commander-in-Chief and of the Prefect, and the business houses of the Chinese merchants.

In the old city, in a commanding position, is the beautiful residence of the British Consul, Mr. George Macartney.[392] The ample quarters

---

390 This is the Uyghur name (the Chinese know it as Bachu Xian). It is located in Kashgar Prefecture. In 1937 it was the scene of fighting between Soviet forces who defeated Ma Hushan (1910–1954), a Hui Chinese Muslim warlord who was executed by Mao for counter-revolutionary activities.

391 Known as Shache in Chinese it was a major trade, cultural and political hub on the southern Silk Road.

392 Sir George Macartney, 1867–1945, arrived in Xinjiang in 1890 as interpreter for Francis Younghusband's expedition across China to India. He remained there until 1918. Macartney first proposed what is known as the Macartney-MacDonald line as the boundary between China and India in Aksai Chin (today somewhat under strain).

7 | 'ACROSS CHINA AND TURKESTAN'

Kashgar in the distance, 21 June 1910.
Mitchell Library, Sydney

of the Russian Consul-General, Mr. Sokow, are near the river bank. Only within the last few days has Mr. Sokow received his well merited promotion as Consul-General. He is the second successor of the famous Consul General Petrovsky[393] who opened the Consulate in 1882, and was for many years so dominating a force in Kashgar that he was popularly styled the King of Kashgar. Times have changed since then. Russian prestige in Chinese Turkestan gained nothing by the war with Japan. At the Consulate there is a Cossack guard of 60 well-mounted men from Orenburg, with two officers. There is a branch of the Russo-Chinese Bank, a Russian post office, and a Russian Customs office for facilitating the passage of goods through the Customs station on the frontier. There is a large colony of Russian Asiatic subjects, and the registration and passport fees which they are required to pay, graduated from one guinea per annum upwards, must defray a large percentage of the cost, if not the

---

Macartney was born at Nanjing and was half-Chinese; his godfather was Chinese politician Li Hongzhang. His father, Halliday Macartney, was a kinsman of Lord George Macartney, the 18th century British diplomat who petitioned the Emperor Qianlong, unsuccessfully, to open China to foreign trade; his mother was a near relative of Lar Wang, one of the leaders of the Taiping rebellion.

393 Nikolay Fyodorovich Petrovsky, 1837–1908, was the Russian consul-general in Kashgar from 1882 until 1902.

entire cost, of the Russian establishment. Intercourse with the Chinese is held chiefly through the intermediary of the frontier officer, the Tung Shang, a native of Kansu province, who has held his post for 13 years and speaks Russian, having been a student at the Chinese Russian school in Urumchi. Relations are friendly and only recently all outstanding cases have been amicably adjusted.

There are many British subjects from India, including a number of Shikarpuri moneylenders,[394] but the chief British centre is Yarkand, not Kashgar. British trade struggles manfully against many obstacles, not the least of which is the barrier interposed by the Government of India, whose enlightened frontier policy modelled on that of the Kingdom of Tibet requires that the trade routes across the Himalayas and Hindu Kush shall not be made easily passable for fear they may facilitate possible foreign invasion. Impassable roads are to be regarded as heaven-sent barriers against foreign invasion. That China should neglect her roads is not surprising, but for India to do so in pursuance of a settled policy is inconceivable.

Of one section of our Indian traders we have no reason to be proud. The Shikarpuri moneylender is the curse of every country he visits. Formerly there were 600 in Kashgar, but Consular action has reduced their numbers by one-half. They are losing ground as the natives are becoming more intelligent. To recover a debt they will shrink from no barbarity. English officials have recommended their expulsion, just as colonies of them have been expelled from Russian Turkestan and from Afghanistan. The Chinese could deal with them by forbidding the natives to deal with them—a course to which it has been made known there would be no objection on the part of the Indian Government. Far, however, from being subjected to such measures, the usurers are actually protected by the Chinese officials, who borrow money from them and in return for lenient treatment in their own case connive at the extortion they practise on others.

In both cities of Kashgar are branches of the Swedish Protestant Mission. They began work here among the Mahomedans in 1892 and

---

394 The Shikarpuri moneylenders were an historic network of Sindhi Hindu traders and financiers from Shikarpur (modern day Pakistan) who played a curial role in financing central Asian and Afghan trade from the 17th to 20th centuries.

among the Chinese in 1900. The missionaries are excellent linguists. They are provided with passports, obtained through the French Legation in Peking, in which they are described as members of the religion of the Lord of Heaven—that is to say, the Catholic religion— but when the Swedish Treaty is ratified they will have suitable passports issued by their own Legation.

German Interests

No other nations have any interests here with one notable exception. In a circular recently addressed by the German Consul in Tien-tsin, North China, to Turkish subjects in Kashgar, in reply to a petition sent by an Armenian carpet weaver resident in Khotan, named Piranantz, the Consul informed them that his Government had, at the request of the Turkish Government, undertaken the protection of Turkish subjects in China. Kashgar being within his district, he desired to know the names and addresses of all Turkish subjects, and he requested them to communicate with him, and he pledged himself to give them all necessary assistance. There are known to be 14 Turkish subjects in the Taotai's district of Kashgar, and there are no doubt others. Formerly France, by an informal arrangement with Turkey, gave protection to Turkish subjects in China. Last year Piranantz applied for registration as a British subject, but his request was refused. In view of the increasing intimacy of relations between the Mahomedan subjects of China and their co-religionists of Turkey and the extension of the Pan-Islamic movement the action of the German Consul calls for notice, especially as China has recently announced that she will not recognize protection given by a treaty Power to subjects of a Power having no treaty relations with China.

Twice on my journey across China I met emissaries from Western Islam. One was a native of Tunis, sent to visit the Mahomedans of Kansu. He was a French subject and had a French passport. The other was an Arab, who had travelled direct from Constantinople to inspect the mosques of the Pei-lu. He also was provided with a French passport. Increasing numbers of Chinese subjects, both Chinese Mahomedans and Turkis, make the pilgrimage to Mecca. There are Hadjis in every village of Turkestan. Usually four or five men make the journey together. North of the Tien Shan they go and come by the Russian railway through Tashkent and Transcaspia, invariably proceeding to Constantinople before going to Mecca. South of the Tien Shan a large number make the outward journey by the Russian railway from Andijan and return by Bombay and the Karakorum Pass over the Himalayas. Seventy pounds sterling covers the cost of the round trip.

Incompetent Officials

The Chinese officials maintained in this distant region are even for China singularly ill chosen. The chief civil official is the Taotai, whose circuit is the largest in the Empire, extending in one direction to Aksu and in the other to Keria.[395] Its holder is an Anhui man who first cane to the province at the time of the reconquest in 1878. He is 69 years of age, and is the worst type of the traditional Chinese official. Feeble and decrepit, he is sprightly compared with the district magistrate, a Hupeh man of 79 in his second childhood, whose experience in the province also dates from 1878. The poor old fossil has magisterial control over 300,000 people.

Neither of the aged military commanders has any modem training. The provincial commander-in-chief is a military Mandarin of obsolete type whose title is an empty one. There are no modem troops. Troops are the old-fashioned provincial braves, and their effective strength bears no reasonable proportion in fact to their numbers on paper. Nominally there are seven squadrons of cavalry, whose men provide their own horses, six battalions of infantry, and one battery of artillery with two guns. One of these guns was used in the reconquest in 1875, and has apparently not since been cleaned. There is also an old Hotchkiss gun. Arms are of varied pattern. They are mostly Tower muskets cut down to carbine size; there are some Mausers of the 1871 model and some of more modern type, and some Remington rifles. No doubt in time modern drilled troops, properly armed and accoutred, will be sent here. At present the military display is not one calculated to strike terror into the heart of China's warlike neighbours.

---

395 Keriya town today.

XI. KASHGAR

(From Our Peking Correspondent)
Kashgar, 3 July 1910[396]

Kashgar has a large population which is increasing with great rapidity, as, indeed, is the population of all Far Western China. There is progressive increase in the area of cultivation and a marked improvement noticeable even within the last five years in the mildness of the climate. By climatic changes, trade routes closed for centuries are being reopened. Trees grow rapidly; and infinitely more trees are being planted, for the timber is marketable and the natives now grow trees for marketable purposes. In the time of Yakub Beg[397] trees were taxed, with the result that the timber was destroyed to evade payment of the tax. Rain then fell at rare intervals, and after evaporation a saline incrustation was left on the soil, highly prejudicial to plant life. Now in the warm season it rains quietly and frequently, and there are no longer complaints of saline deposits. Never have the rice fields of Kashgar been planted so widely as this year. The territory is unusually rich in fibre-producing plants. One despised shrub growing in unlimited quantities was recently found to contain all the essentials of jute. Properly developed fibre cultivation gives promise of great possibilities, while equally promising is the extended cultivation of cotton and of silk. This rich and fertile country, where millions of people live, their tranquil and uneventful lives in their fertile oases, never set back by the ravages of famine or of epidemic, is a vast market where alone compete the goods of the two rival but now friendly Powers of Central Asia, Russia and England. Yet how unfair is the competition.

Obstacles to British Trade

Russia fosters her trade, and, as her trade relations develop, her former influence is being re-established. She builds roads up to the frontier.

---

396 Published on 24 September 1910, p. 4.
397 Yakub Beg, 1820–1877, was a Khoqandi ruler of Yettishar (Kashgaria) during his invasion of Xinjiang from 1865 to 1877. He held the title of Atalik Ghazi ("Champion Father"), although he appears to have been an unpopular leader. He died suspiciously, either of poisoning or suicide.

She encourages China, she even compels China, to continue these roads to Kashgar. But the Indian Government glories in the badness of the awful roads which Indian traders, trying to sell British manufactured goods, have to surmount, in order to bring their wares, to market. It is incredible that in these days of strenuous competition British manufacturers, whose goods are thus excluded, should submit to such treatment. Captain Shuttleworth, the competent Indian frontier officer who was in charge of the British Consulate during 1908–1909, writes in his trade report:

> If more routes were opened to the trade with India, trade would benefit to an enormous extent. Military considerations have prevented such routes being opened before. Yet it seems undesirable to stifle trade and prevent its proper expansion for fear of a possible invasion by a route which could be destroyed at selected points in a few minutes.

And Mr. Macartney, writing with still higher authority in 1908, after referring to the abundance of money among the Turkis, "whose wealth has increased to an extraordinary degree," and the increasing use made of it to purchase goods of foreign origin, adds:–

> Indian trade must remain handicapped so long as it is confined to the Ladakh route, the longest, the most elevated, the most inhospitable, and for the shortest season opened of all the three main thoroughfares between India and Chinese Turkesten.

Russian trade with Kashgar increased from £163,000 in 1882, when the Consulate was established, to £589,000 in 1905, but it has since suffered temporary decline to £457,500 in 1909. Last year British trade, which amounted to 44 lakhs of rupees in 1908, showed an ominous decrease, cotton niece goods imported from England being some two-thirds less than in the previous year.

Exports of native production enter Russian territory duty free. Imports from Russia into Chinese Turkestan are exempt from *likin* when imported and owned by Russian subjects, but are subject to these dues when imported and owned by Chinese subjects. British imports enjoy similar immunity. Russian piece goods are aided by what is called a bounty, but what is really a refund of the duties paid upon

7 | 'ACROSS CHINA AND TURKESTAN'

A market in Kashgar, May 1910.
Mitchell Library, Sydney

the raw materials and part of the machinery used in their manufacture on their importation into Russia. Russo-Chinese trade relations across the frontier are governed by the St. Petersburg Treaty of February 24, 1881, by the provisions of which China was permitted to reestablish her authority in the greater part of Kuldja. which had been occupied by Russian troops since 1871.

Recently the commercial clauses of this treaty have been denounced by China, who had, unfortunately for herself, been prevented from denouncing them, as the treaty provides, ten years ago, at the end of the previous decennial period, owing to the Boxer outbreak. Negotiations for their revision begin next year, and promise to be long and difficult. Two main features of the treaty objected to by the Chinese are —first, the stipulation in Clause XII which grants the right of free trade, both in exports and imports, to Russian subjects in the new dominion as far as the Great Wall; and, secondly, the vagueness of the wording by which "*localité*" can be claimed by one side to mean the town only and by the Russians to mean the whole Consular district.

Communications with Russia

The treaty protects the Russian subject, and thus covers all the goods in his possession. Equality of treatment has to be given to British subjects, but the provision bears hardly upon the Chinese, and permits their being undersold in their own territory by foreigners. Russian trade and British trade are, however, in no sense on an equality. Russia has a serviceable cart road from Russian Turkestan right to Kashgar city, the Chinese having been compelled to make their section of the road and throw a bridge over the Kashgar river. The bridge, by the way, is now in ruins. It was built by a Russian contractor, and did not last one season. Russia thus facilitates trade, and when the new railways are built her trade will have still greater advantages. A reference to the map shows this. At present the two chief main routes to Kashgar from Russian Turkestan are—first, a route available for pack animals only from the railway at Andijan by Osh and Gulcha, entering Chinese territory at Irkeshtam,[398] and thence in five stages reaching Kashgar city; and, secondly, the important cart road which leaves the Tashkent-Orenburg Railway a few stations north of Tashkent at Kabulsai, runs by Pishpek, Tokmak and Kutemaldi, on the Lake Issik Kul, to Narin, a total distance of 544 miles, and thence enters China by the Turgat Pass, reaching Kashgar city in ten stages. All Russian officials travel this way. They can travel the whole way in tarantass.[399] East of Tokmak is Vierny, a city connected by cart road with Kuldja in the one direction and with Semipolatinsk in the other. Vierny will be the future junction of the Central Asian Railway with the Siberian Railway. At Vierny the future Tashkent Railway will be linked with the projected railway running from the Kuldja frontier to Semipolatinsk and Omsk.

While Russia is steadily developing her trade routes with Chinese Turkestan and excluding British manufactured goods by prohibitive tariffs, the policy of the Indian Government is a reverse one, and, by discouraging British trade, is indirectly fostering Russian trade. Russian

---

398 Irkeshtam (Erkeshtam) is the westernmost border crossing in China. It is one of two border crossings between Kyrgyzstan and China, the other being Torugart some 165 km (103 miles) to the northeast. Andijan, Morrison's objective, is in Uzbekistan.
399 A four-wheeled horse drawn Russian carriage without springs.

Turki subjects can pass freely into India without passports, but British Indian subjects cannot enter Russian Turkestan without passports, for the *visé* of which fees have to be paid to the Russian authorities. Which is the more businesslike policy? Russians tax the subjects to whom they give protection, and thus maintain an establishment that is almost self-supporting. At present no fees are collected from British subjects in Chinese Turkestan, not even registration or passport fees, the Indian Government, no doubt, feeling, diffidence in taxing traders already burdened by the badness of communications. To collect debts due to Shikarpturi usurers, and to do so with infinite trouble, knowing often that the debt is cruelly unjust, and then to hand over the money without deduction of fee is the height of misdirected Government generosity. Yet the British community would gladly pay Consular fees, and our Consulate, which will now presumably be raised to a Consulate-General, could be made largely self-supporting. At present we do not possess a Consulate building, but rent the finest site in the whole city. For some paltry £8,000 this site can become British property, but the condition of our Indian finances will not permit of such an expenditure. So one fine morning we may find that the property has been purchased over our heads by some Russian trader.

The British Consul

No one can write from Kashgar without paying his tribute of praise to the British representative in this far distant spot. Mr. Macartney has rendered conspicuous service to his country. His knowledge of frontier questions is unique. His name is a household word in Western China. Throughout Chinese Turkestan our Consul is known as the British official whose action in bringing about the liberation of the slaves captured from States under the protection of the Indian Government by Kanjuti slave raiders[400] led directly to the abolition of all slavery in the province. For years he had to contend against the powerful Russian Consul General Petrovsky. His action in the Boxer year is believed

---

400 The Kanjutis (also known as Hunzakuts or Burusho people) come from the Hunza Valley, Pakistan, and were known in the 18th and 19th centuries as slavers in the Pamir mountains and southern Xinjiang.

to have prevented the Russian occupation of Kashgar. In 1900, at the time of the Boxer outbreak in North China, the ever active Russian Consul-General made a bold attempt to induce a Russian occupation of Kashgar. He reported that a similar outbreak was imminent in Kashgar, that there was danger to life and general insecurity, and he called for a large increase in the strength of his Consular guard. It is on record that at the same time the British representative was reporting to the Indian Government that everything was tranquil and there was no danger of outbreak. The policy of M Petrovsky did not receive the support he had hoped for. On the ground, however, that frontal communications were threatened, the Consul-General obtained from the Chinese the right to station an outpost at Tashkurghan,[401] in Sarikol, 64 miles within the Chinese border, for the protection of the mails, and this outpost has remained there since.

Exceptional gifts are required to fill adequately the post of British Consul in Kashgar. A knowledge of Chinese is essential, for the Chinese officials, unlike the English officials in India, speak their own language only. Equally essential is a knowledge of Turki, the native language of Turkestan, of Hindustani, the language of intercourse of Hindu traders; of Persian, which is the language of the office, and also of Russian. To an observer it would seem essential that the Consul should be given an assistant from the Chinese Consular service. More and more the Chinese are impressing their influence upon the province, and as the province is now subjected to the same system of government as that established in China proper, it is much to be desired that our Consul should have the assistance of one conversant with affairs in China proper.

China's foreign relations in Kashgar are at present satisfactory. It is curious to find China still preserving the fiction of being the joint suzerain Power over the protected Indian State of Hunza. The deposed Thum of Hunza[402] is an exile in Chinese territory. At the installation of his half brother as his successor China claimed the right to take equal

---

401 Tashihu'ergan is an historic town near the Tajikistan, Afghanistan and Pakistan boarders. It is located in the Sarikol (Pamir) region.
402 The Thum (or Mir) of Hunza is the hereditary ruler of Hunza Valley in the Karakoram Range of Gilit-Baltistan, Pakistan.

part in the ceremony and sent two officials, one civil and one military, to represent her. Permission was given them to be present as spectators. They subsequently reported that they had carried out their instructions. Hunza still pays tribute to China. Every January four or five Kanjutis from Hunza appear before the Taotai in Kashgar and present him with a small ingot of gold weighing less than one ounce. Then they perform the kowtow to him as the representative of the Emperor of China. For such a service they are rewarded in the same generous manner as is rewarded the decennial tribute mission from Nepaul.

Main street of Ku Ch'êng tzu (Gaochang, Turpan, Xinjiang), 20 April 1910.

XII. KASHGAR TO ANDIJAN

(From Our Peking Correspondent)
Andijan, 12 July 1910[403]

Kashgar city is 132 miles from the Russian frontier town of Irkeshtam, which again is 174 miles from Andijan, the nearest Russian railway station. The distance between the two places is divided into 15 stages, but travelling quickly with excellent horses I covered the distance in a little over eight days. Transport charges are equivalent to £10 10s. the ton. The first stage is Minyul, a village 30 miles from Kashgar, where in a grove of poplars is the famous tablet commemorating the restoration of China's sovereignty in 1878. Here China maintains in wretched mud-hovels a garrison of 30 ill-kempt braves from Hunan and Kansu armed with ancient muzzle-loaders. Petroleum is found at the second stage and coal is being mined at the third. At various places along the route are the ruins of forts erected at the line of the reconquest.

Foreign Garrisons

Recent travellers have reported that there was observable in Turkestan some disquiet on the part of the Russian authorities at the apparent recrudescence of China's military activity in the territory along the frontier. But such reports are not reconcilable with the facts as I saw them. They are as unfounded as similar reports of China's military activity along the Yunnan frontier of Burma. The Chinese chief frontier fort on the main route from Kashgar to Andijan is at Ulugchat,[404] 27 miles from the frontier. Another smaller fort called Yegin is 13 miles nearer the Russian boundary. On all maps of Central Asia Ulugchat is given prominence, its name being set out in type worthy of a frontier stronghold. I examined it accordingly with some care. It is a mud fort situated in a basin on the right bank of an unbridged river, the Kizil

---

403 Published on 26 September 1910, p. 5.
404 Ulugchat came under Chinese (Qing) control after the Dzungar genocide in the mid-18th century. It is located on the Pamir trade route connecting Kashgar to the Fergana Valley (Uzbekistan/Kyrgystan).

Su,[405] and is commanded by mountains on all sides. Inside the fort there is complete disorder. Everything is rotting. Windows are blocked with broad sun-dried bricks. There are ruined stalls, but no horses. Of the four Chinese who hold this frontier post and represent the majesty of China, two at the time of my visit were weeding in the fields, another was washing some onion-sprouts, and the fourth, clad only in a Jersey and pants, was playing the banjo at a cake-stall in the street. No one was in uniform. All were ragged and unkempt. Their arms, which I saw in one dirty room, were rusty old tower muskets-emblems of authority, not weapons of offence. Outside the camp in four Khirgiz tents were the 15 Khirgiz who constitute the second line of defence. They are armed with similar tower muskets cut down to carbine size, and are employed as cavalry patrols. Two filthy ponds of surface water provided the garrison with water. The courageous Khirgiz drink this water unboiled and unstrained, the less courageous Chinese dare not do so.

I am no military expert and my opinion is given only for what it is worth, but I formed the opinion that this frontier stronghold would fall before the resolute attack of three old ladies armed with broomsticks. There could be no better illustration of the neglect which is characteristic of China's frontier policy. Other countries employ smart serviceable soldiers on their borders. China alone sends to her frontier the most wretched of her ragamuffins. Every foreigner who enters China by this route forms his first impression of the Chinese Empire from witnessing the garrison of this frontier post. Every Kashgarian or Andijani who crosses the frontier—and they do so by thousands—has on the one hand the object lesson of Russian strength and military pride and on the other the demonstration of China's weakness and military inefficiency.

At Yegin, a stage nearer the frontier on the other side of the river from the main road, is the second fort referred to. I found it open to all comers. It was occupied by a solitary brave, whom I had some difficulty in rousing him from his opium sleep. And though I succeeded in awakening him, I could not obtain from him any other military information than is conveyed in these words, "I have no opium to sell,"

---

405 Kezilesu River is fed by the glacial met from the Pamir, Tianshan and Kunlun mountains and runs for 900 km within China.

and having repeated this irrelevant declaration twice he rolled back to sleep and I left him.

A pleasant ride of 12 miles over the mountains leads the traveller to Irkeshtam, the Russian frontier post and Customs station, built in 1884 on a steep ridge overlooking the broad river. The post is exactly on the border, its site is well selected, and the small garrison of 25 Cossacks is quite strong enough to preserve order among this unwarlike people.

In Russian Territory

Russian transit trade, imports and exports, passing this barrier on camels, horses, and donkeys, averaged last year throughout the year one thousand pounds a day. Two routes lead from the frontier across to the Russian railway, the winter route by the Terek Dawan and the longer, the summer route, by the Alai. It was necessary that I should travel by the latter. Two passes of 11,000ft. have to be crossed, but they are not difficult. After crossing the first pass, the Tuan Maran (1,200ft.), you descend into the Oxus basin. There is a large traffic. On the way there are splendid pastures with profusion of flowers, picturesque encampments of Khirgiz, abundance of flocks and herds, camels, yaks, and horses, and the most varied scenery of river and snow-clad mountain. The second pass is the Taldek. At its eastern end is the Khirgiz encampment of Sariktash, whence the road branches off to the Murghabi post on the Pamirs, 120 miles distant.

At Sariktash[406] the traveller sees the first evidence of the work of the famous Colonel Grombehevsky,[407] the Russian explorer and frontier officer, whose intrigues and promises in Hunza in 1888 led indirectly

---

406 Sariktash, or Sarik Tash Daban, is situated near the Pamir mountains in Tajikistan near the Afghan-Chinese border.
407 Bronislav Ludwigovich Grombchevsky, 1855–1926, was a Polish officer in the Imperial Russian Army and an explorer/spy, famed for his participation in the, so called, Great Game. Grombchevsky traveled extensively in the Far East and Central Asia during the period 1888–92. He is regarded as the Russian counterpart to the British military-explore Francis Younghusband. The two rivals famously met in 1889 when they were exploring the Raskam Valley in Xinjiang for their respective governments. Grombchevsky rose to the rank of Lieutenant-General but was cast down in the aftermath of the 1917 Bolshevik revolution. Exiled to Siberia he was assisted in escape

7 | 'ACROSS CHINA AND TURKESTAN'

Khirgiz tents on the Tuan Muran where we passed the night, July 1910.
Mitchell Library, Sydney

to the extension of British authority over that territory in 1891, just as the activities of Dorjief[408] some years later were to lead to the British expedition to Tibet, though certainly not to the extension of British authority over that kingdom. In 1893 Grombchevsky continued to Sariktash from Gulcha, a distance of 68 miles, the cart road which had already connected this important military post with Osh, a prosperous town on the main road, 30 miles from Andijan. The road was built in order to enable the Governor-General of Tashkent, Baron Vrevsky,[409] to drive over the pass in a three-horsed carriage. A tablet on the summit of the pass, 11,800ft. above sea level, commemorates the achievement. Orders for the construction of the road required that its minimum gradient should be one in seven. It is still in fair condition, but is not

---

by the Japanese. He ended up in Poland where he died in poverty. See Peter Hopkirk, *The Great Game*, Oxford: OUP, 1991, pp. 457–458.

408 Agvan Dorzhiev, 1853–1938, was a Buryat Mongol buddhist monk, and diplomat, born in eastern Siberia. He was the Dalai Lama's envoy to Russia and met Czar Nicholas II. Later, in 1913, he signed a treaty at Ulaanbaatar, asserting Tibetan and Mongolian independence from China. His attempt to reconcile Buddhism and Soviet communism failed and he was executed in Stalin's purge in 1938.

409 Baron Alexander Vrevsky, 1804–1859, a general and statesman who led the conquest of Central Asia for Imperial Russia, first in the Caucasus and then in what is today Uzbekistan and Kyrgyzstan.

used for carts. It is worthy of note that this road was built along a road available for artillery which had been hastily constructed in 1880 between Gulcha and the Pamirs, when preparations on so elaborate a scale were boing made for the threatened war with China. The road winds through a country of exceeding beauty. Gulcha, the Russian military station, lies in one of the most beautiful valleys in the world. Past the cantonment flows a river difficult to ford in the summer, but once it is crossed there is an excellent cart road leading through a well-peopled, richly cultivated country to Osh and Andijan. Much of the country is tilled by Khirgiz, who are relinquishing their nomad habits and becoming settlers, abandoning the tent for the permanent dwelling. At Osh the traveller ends his journey and takes the Russian stage to Andijan.

Chinese Courtesy

In concluding this brief sketch of a journey across the Chinese Empire, I wish to return my thanks to the Chinese authorities for the willing help that was given me, for their unfailing friendliness and their constant courtesy. Throughout my ride of 3,760 miles, occupying 174 days, between the Chinese railway and the Russian railway, I met with nothing but kindness. I cannot recall a single disagreeable incident. I was entertained by native Princes, by Viceroys and Governors, and Tartar Generals. I met all manner of people, from the humblest carter to the most powerful mandarin, and by all I was treated with equal civility, friendliness, and respect. I found, as I have always found in my travels in China, that I was well treated because I belong to a country which is known to sympathize with every movement in China that has for its object the advancement of the people, the encouragement of education, and the extension of liberal ideas, of methods of truth and justice and fair dealing. To me the suggestion is preposterous that British influence is waning in China. On the contrary, I think that British prestige has never been higher than at present. Certainly I have never seen on any previous journey more abundant evidence of good will towards an English traveller. Only twice on my journey was I asked for my passport, and on each occasion almost apologetically, the magistrate in each case offering to save me trouble by coming to see it himself.

7 | 'ACROSS CHINA AND TURKESTAN'

At Kuldja I first learned the death of the King by observing the military flags half-mast, and immediately afterwards hearing a Chinese read to a crowd of his fellows from a copy of the local newspaper posted by the Tartar General's yamên the sympathetic message from the Wai-wu-pu[410] announcing the death of the "Emperor of the great British nation." By no possible chance could the authorities in that far distant outpost of the empire have anticipated that the evidences of mourning would be seen by an English traveller.

I desire also to express my thanks for the courtesy shown me and for the help given me by every Russian official whom I met on my journey. Especially to Mr. Sokow, the distinguished Russian Consul-General in Kashgar, are my thanks due. He took infinite pains to save me from all trouble at the frontier. He even wrote to the station-master at Andijan telling him what tickets I wanted for myself and my Chinese servant. This is only one of the many striking evidences of the change in Central Asia, where British and Russian relations, often so embittered in the past, have been succeeded by relations that are to an unusual degree cordial and sympathetic.

---

410 Chinese Foreign Ministry.

Yuan Shikai, first President of the Republic of China.
Mitchell Library, Sydney

Chapter 8

THE END OF IMPERIAL CHINA

"How did you go bankrupt?" Bill asked.
"Two ways," Mike said. "Gradually, then suddenly."
This dialogue from Hemingway's *The Sun Also Rises* pithily describes the demise of the Manchu dynasty. From the first substantive sign of revolt[411] in early October, 1911, with an armed revolt at Wuchang,[412] it took less than three months for 2,100 years of imperial rule in China to collapse.

While the end was quick, change had been brewing for a number of years. From 1903, reformers had their hands securely on the levers of power and Tsu Hsi had acquiesced to their plans. China initiated comprehensive changes to its government, especially, and society more widely. But as Alexis de Tocqueville observed of France's ancien régime before the French Revolution,

> ... experience proves that the most perilous moment for a bad Government is that in which it begins to reform itself. The ills borne patiently because they seem to be inevitable appear insupportable when once the idea is conceived of getting rid of them.[413]

---

411 There had been an abortive revolt in Canton earlier in April, but it petered out in confusion.
412 Today part of Wuhan.
413 Alexis de Tocqueville, *The Ancien Regime and the Revolution,* trans by John Bonner, New York: Harper & Brothers, 1856.

And so it proved with the Ching dynasty. Morrison gave detailed coverage of the rebellion and political negotiations that resulted in the abdication of the Manchus. He had scoops, for example, on the timing of the impending abdication, and he conducted an interview with Yuan Shih-kai, the smart money's candidate to wield power after the Manchus. He did not, however, write the 'big piece', the article that rang the changes and reflected on the momentous developments he was witnessing. The time to have written such an article would have been soon after, but by that time his mind was elsewhere and he was soon to start talks about joining Yuan Shih-kai's government.

The uprising began on October 10, a day still celebrated by the Republic of China on Taiwan as its national day. It was preceded by a similar uprising in Canton in April that had proved abortive. Throughout the course of the year, there were assemblies at provincial level discussing political reform. Representatives of the foreign Imperialists wanted China to retain the Manchus at the head of a form of constitutional monarchy. This was based along the British constitution with the Emperor as head of state and a parliament led by a prime minister as the law-making body. The other form of government, promoted by the Republicans who had widespread support, was the complete overthrow of the Manchus, and an end to dynastic government, and its replacement with a Chinese republic headed by a President with executive powers.

In the end, in an exquisitely Chinese way, it was the Empress Dowager, with the infant Emperor P'u Yi at her side, who by Imperial edict abolished the monarchy and decreed "the establishment of a constitutional government on a republican basis." She said that she and the Emperor would retire to "a life of leisure" to watch "with satisfaction the glorious establishment and consummation of the perfect Government."[414]

The victors were not, however, in the giving vein. The depth of antipathy towards the Manchus was underlined in the Republican Manifesto, proclaimed by Dr Sun Yat Sen, the Hawaiian-born Chinese leader of the political reform movement, on 5 January 1912 and published in *The Times* the next day:

---

414 Pearl, op. cit., p. 242.

8 | THE END OF IMPERIAL CHINA

We now proclaim the ... overthrow of the despotic sway of the Manchu dynasty and the establishment of a Republic. The substitution of a Republic for a Monarchy is not the fruit of transient passion but the natural outcome of a long-cherished desire for freedom, contentment and advancement. We have borne our grievance for 267 years with patience and forbearance ... The policy of the Manchus has been one of unequivocal seclusion and tyranny.[415]

Sun Yat Sen, revolutionary and leader of Kuomintang.
Mitchell Library, Sydney

---

415 'Charges against the Manchus', *The Times*, 6 January 1912, p. 6. This carries the full text of Sun's 'Republican Manifesto'.

Within days of issuing this manifesto, Sun had been elected in Nanking as the provisional President of the Republic of China and then just as quickly stepped down from that office in favour of Yuan Shikai. As John King Fairbank, observed:

> The points on which nearly all patriots agreed were that China must have a parliament to represent the provinces, that the country must be unified to forestall foreign intervention, mostly probably by Japan, and that Yuan, a military organiser known as a reformer, was the one man with the ability, experience and prestige to head the government.[416]

Yuan was all those things, especially at the beginning. He has a real claim to be the founder of the modern Chinese military, and he was instrumental in the reforms after the Boxer rebellion, especially reforms to education and the civil service. He co-authored the policy document that lead to the ending of the ancient civil service examinations system. He had hands-on governmental experience. When he was viceroy of Chili, and Grand Councillor (1901–1909), he emphasised the training of a modern army, education for the people (he reformed elementary and middle schools and universities in his jurisdiction), and good local government; in 1907 Yuan authorised elections for the city council of Tientsin, among the first ever conducted in China.[417]

But it was in military affairs where he excelled and from where he ultimately drew his power. As the accompanying article by Morrison testifies, Yuan was the driving force behind the creation of the modern Chinese army, a development that he began in 1895 in the wake of China's comprehensive defeat by Japan in the first Sino-Japanese War. He modelled the training of the army on the German army, Europe's largest and most feared. He required his instructors to learn German. This army of 5,000 became the nucleus of the Pei-yang Army which, by 1905, was fully formed, with its officers still loyal to Yuan.

Morrison had chartered Yuan's rise since he had arrived in China in 1897. In his writings about Yuan, he clearly rated him as the best person

---

416 Fairbank, op. cit., p. 162.
417 See Spence, op. cit., p. 247–249.

to lead China after the Manchus. He was correct as well to focus on the Army. Was it not Mao, himself, who later said, "political power grows out of the barrel of a gun?" When Morrison interviewed Yuan on 20 November, soon after Yuan had become Prime Minister, Yuan had spoken in favour of retaining the monarch in ceremonial role. Loyalty might have been the prime motivation for his comment, however he added a warning to those who would overthrew the monarchy: "If the Revolutionaries should succeed in overthrowing the present dynasty," Morrison reported him as saying, "another revolution might take place headed by the Conservatives, having for its object the restoration of the Monarchy."[418]

And so it came to pass that after three years as the Republic's president, Yuan sought, in late 1915, to restore the monarchy. Under the guise of a specially organised Representative Assembly he abolished the Republic, and created in its place the Empire of China, of which he would be emperor. To demonstrate that he still retained a sense of irony, Yuan chose as his reign name Hongxian (constitutional abundance).

His death in June 1916 brought an end to the dreams of monarchy. His military legacy lived on, however, in the army officers he had trained and welded into the leadership of the Pei-yang army, such as General Feng Kuo-chang,[419] General Wang Shih-chen,[420] General Ts'ao K'un,[421] and General Tuan Ch'i-jui.[422] All deserted Yuan when he tried to become

---

418 'Yuan Shih-Kai on the Crisis', *The Times*, 21 November 1911, p. 8.
419 Feng Guozhang, 1859–1919, was known as the Bulldog of the Zhili Clique, which he led after Yuan Shikai's death; he was briefly President (1917–18). He was one of Yuan's leading protégé's and supported his attempt to restore the throne in 1916. His influence waned after his resignation in 1918 and he died shortly after.
420 Wang Shizhen, 1861–1930, was one of the three outstanding figures in the Beiyang Army. Chief of Staff to Yuan Shikai, was acting Premier, War Minister and Interior Minister. Retired from politics in 1920.
421 Cao Kun, 1862–1938, was a prominent Beiyang warlord; he served as President (1923–24) but his rule was undermined by corruption. He rose under Yuan was was a key figure in the Zhili Clique.
422 Duan Qirui, 1865–1936, was a dominant Beiyang warlord and significant political figure. He was a trusted general in Yuan's Beiyang army and was appointed prime minister after Yuan's death in 1916. He fought the Zhili-Anhui War (1920) where he opposed Cao Kun.

emperor. All became warlord politicians in north China, promoting instability and all were unable to forge a working relationship with the emerging Nationalist Kuomingtang (KMT) government in Nanking.

'THE NEW CHINESE ARMY: ITS QUALITIES AND DEFECTS'

(From Our Own correspondent)
Peking, 6 October 1911[423]

The modern Army of China dates from 1895, and owes its beginnings to an experimental force of 5,000 men organized by Yuan Shih-kai, and trained by Western methods, which was stationed at Hsiao Chan (a camp one day's march south-west of Tientsin), immediately after the conclusion of the disastrous war with Japan. Yuan Shih-kai may claim to be the creator of China's modern Army. He showed what Chinese troops could become with proper training. Instead of the ill-fed, ill-clad, opium-smoking braves of the old type, Yuan formed an efficient, well-trained force, recruited from a good class of men from the rural districts of North China, and guaranteed by the local authorities. Under his care soldiering tended to become an honourable instead of a despised calling.

In November, 1903, the Board of Army Reorganization was established with the object of remodelling the Chinese Army on a uniform standard of efficiency, and reorganizing it throughout. On April 16, 1906, an Imperial Edict ordered the creation within ten years of 36 divisions of modern drilled troops to be distributed among the 22 provinces of China, to which was subsequently added a Guards division in Peking. An Edict of June 1, 1907, provided for the hastening of the original scheme, and for the establishment of the full number before the end of 1912. There is, however, no possibility of this scheme being completed within the time decreed.

---

423 Published 21 October 1911, p. 5.

A Decree of September, 1909, raised the whole status of the military profession in China, formulated corresponding ranks between military and civil officials, and reversed the old order which gave the civilian precedence to the military. By this new relative position a captain ranks with a prefect, a major with a taotai, a colonel with a provincial Judge, and so on. To English officers travelling in China the change is of material importance. They, will no longer have to complain of the comparatively unimportant rank in the Chinese hierarchy to which they were entitled by their foreign military rank, when a captain, for example, was regarded as of considerably lower rank than a district magistrate. A Decree of July 15, 1909, proclaiming the Emperor as Commander-in-Chief still further enhanced the prestige of the Army.

General Staff

On the following day another Decree created a General Staff, the functions of which were enlarged and its powers extended by the Edict of May 8, 1911. The General Staff is now independent of the Ministry of War. It is under the control of an intelligent young Prince, Tsai Tao,[424] full brother of the Regent, who passed two years at the Nobles' School in Peking, and has travelled in Europe. His chief counsellors are Lieutenant-General Fang Kuo-chang,[425] who was China's first Military Attaché in Japan, and was afterwards Director of the Nobles' School, and two Brigadiers, Ha Han-chang[426] who accompanied Tsai Tao on his mission abroad, and Liang Pi,[427] a Manchu, both of whom were educated in Japan, and are regarded as the most highly trained officers in the new Army. Japanese-trained officers are in charge of each of the six sections of the General Staff. In the coming manoeuvres the commanders of the opposing forces are both Japanese-trained.

---

424 Zai Tao, 1887–1970, was a Manchu nobleman and member of the Qing imperial family, the younger half-brother of the Kwang Hsu (Guangxu) emperor. A military reformer and racing horse breeder.

425 See note 380.

426 Ha Han-Chang, 1877–1951, a lesser member of the Zhili clique, Ha served under Yuan in logistical and staff roles.

427 Morrison here appears to be referring to Liangbi, 1877–1912, a prominent Manchu loyalist and military reformer. He was assassinated in 1912 for opposing the Republic.

8 | 'THE NEW CHINESE ARMY: ITS QUALITIES AND DEFECTS'

New Army soldiers, 1906.
Mitchell Library, Sydney

Feng Kuo Chang, Beiyang army general and later president.
Mitchell Library, Sydney

Ministry of War and Japanese Influence

There is a Minister of War, who has a seat in the Cabinet when military affairs are under discussion. The present occupant is a Manchu named Yin Chang,[428] who was trained for some years in the German and Austrian Armies, and has twice been Minister to Berlin. He accompanied the Regent, Prince Chun, on his expiatory mission to Germany. His sympathies are naturally with the country in which he was educated. On the other hand the sympathies of the bulk of the officers under his command, their instincts and training, are to a marked extent Japanese. More than 700 Chinese officers trained in Japan hold command in the Chinese Army, and there are still 80 in Japan completing their training. Japanese teachers in China itself are much reduced in number. There were 60; there are at present seven only—namely, one in Canton, one in Wuchang, and five in Paotingfu, of whom two will return to Japan before the end of the year, their places not being filled. There are three or four German instructors, but no British. Practically all the teaching in the Army and in the military schools is in the hands of Chinese who have been trained in Japan. The Army is modelled on that of Japan. Japanese influence is paramount. Chinese educated in Japan acquire to a surprising degree the Japanese characteristics, especially that of secretiveness. They continue in China the intimate relations formed among themselves when at school in Japan. They are well trained as a rule; it is becoming a saying that unless you are trained in Japan you have little prospect of promotion in the Chinese Army. Appointments are now made from "foreign-educated" officers; the old practice of elevating men to high military commands who were Chinese scholars or Imperial favourites, destitute of military training, has been largely abandoned. About 30 of the officers have been educated in Germany, another 30 in France, one or two in Belgium, two at West Point (the brother of Dr Ch'en Chin-tao[429] and the nephew of Wen Tsung-yao, the Assistant Resident in Tibet), but none, to my knowledge, in England.

---

428 Yin Chang, 1859–1928, a Manchu of the White banner clan, German-trained military officer and fluent in German. He had close ties to Yuan.

429 Chen Jintao, 1871–1939, a Yale-educated PhD in economics, was Yuan's finance minister and later worked for the KMT in financial advisory roles.

8 | 'THE NEW CHINESE ARMY: ITS QUALITIES AND DEFECTS'

The Chinese modern forces consist of (1) the Lu Chün, or field army, under the Ministry, of War, a permanent force; and (2) the Hsun Fang Tui, or patrol army, the so-called provincial troops, a temporary force which will disappear (if the programme is carried out) in four years.

Revolutionary army in Hubei, 1911.
Mitchell Library, Sydney

THE LU CHUN

The Army scheme provided, as I have said, for the creation of 37 divisions before the end of 1912. Theoretically the strength of a division is 12,512 men (758 officers, 10,436 men in the fighting line, and 1,328 noncombatants) and 54 guns. Of the 37 divisions, 15, including the Guards, have been more or less organized, and in addition there are 17 mixed brigades of varying strength, including the Tibet garrison, which is really a portion of the incomplete Szechuan division.

Assuming that the effective strength is the paper strength, and that no man is absent, the total strength amounts to 240,815 men. Careful investigation, however, shows that these numbers are far beyond the real numbers, and that the actual strength consists of 180,000 foreign-drilled men with 162 batteries of mountain and field artillery, each of six guns. Of this number 160,000 are combatants, who have received a more or less efficient military training. Foreign-drilled troops are now quartered in varying strength in each of the three provinces of Manchuria, in each of the 18 provinces of China proper, and in the New Dominion, including Kuldja and Kashgaria, and preparations are in progress for stationing in the future 2,000 men in Mongolia, barracks to accommodate this number being now under construction in Urga. It is this non-existent Mongolian force which is airily described in Russian papers as two divisions of 100,000 men. With, the exception of the metropolitan province, where there are five divisions, and Kirin, where nominally there are two (very imperfect) divisions, no province has more than one division and one mixed brigade.

W. T. Y. Ting, Colonel in the New Army, 15 November 1906.
Mitchell Library, Sydney

8 | 'THE NEW CHINESE ARMY: ITS QUALITIES AND DEFECTS'

Protection of Frontiers

As an indication of China's indifference to the adequate protection of her frontiers, I may mention that it has been estimated that 10 armed Europeans could capture the chief fort on the Tongking frontier; while I found the garrison of Ulugchat, the first fort on the Chinese side of the main route route to Russian Turkestan, to consist of four men, of whom on the occasion of my visit two were weeding in the fields, another was washing onion sprouts; and a fourth was playing the banjo in the main street of the village. On the Yunnan frontier of Burma there is on paper a strength of 13 battalions, not of the Lu Chün, but of the Provincial troops, each nominally 301 strong, armed with Mausers of the 1884 pattern. In Burma British belief in Chinese strength on the, frontier is almost ludicrously exaggerated. It disregards the difficulty with which Chinese troops could be brought to the frontier—the mountainous country, the immense distance from any base, the lack of reserve ammunition, the absence of transport. In Burma this belief is understood to be based upon the report of a police officer who, expecting to find Chinese armed with bows and arrows, was surprised to find them carrying Mausers. His glowing description of Chinese military efficiency is said to have been inspired by the wish to arouse the Indian authorities from their alleged lethargy.

Reports of China's strength in Tibet also require revision. A large body of troops is not required, for they have only to deal with a semi-barbarous people armed with obsolete weapons. The force sent into Tibet, detached, from the Szechuan incomplete division, consisted of 2,000 men in all, including two battalions of infantry, some cavalry, "some miscellaneous mountain guns, and some engineers. It operated at a prodigious distance from its base. People indeed are apt to forget how great are the distances in China. Not to speak of Tibet, the distance to the capital of Kansu province" by the shortest route from the nearest railway station is 28 marches. Kuldja is 120 marches from the nearest arsenal.

Manchus and Chinese

It is worthy of note that of all the officers in the Chinese Army less than three per cent, are Manchus. Among the high commands in Peking there are very few Manchus. There are so few available that nearly all the senior officers in the First Division—the Manchu Division—are Chinese, the commander being a Shantung man of the old school. In the Guards, which was founded primarily as a Manchu division, but is now open to all classes, most of the officers are Chinese, not Manchu.

Finance

It is estimated that each division costs, broadly speaking, £275,000 per annum, and the total expenditure on the Army is nearly £8,000,000 per annum. Military expenditure is met haphazard. There is no War Budget, but a Budget in some form will be submitted at the next session of the National Assembly. Difficulties of finance are always being reported, but financial methods in China pass Western comprehension. There is, of course, great wastage, but incomparably less than in the time of Li Hung-chang and the war with Japan.

Merits and Defects

In the Lu Chün it is still easy to point out a multitude of defects, but there is continuous effort towards improvement. There is a steady growth of military spirit, a steady uplifting of the profession of arms. Sons of high Chinese Princes and officials are proud to hold commissions and to swagger about in uniform. There is an improvement in the moral of the troops—a better esprit de corps. The men take pride in their uniforms and are careful of their arms. Comparatively speaking, they are smart where they used to be slovenly. A better class is recruited. Opium-smoking is non-existent. The discipline is improving—there is indeed excellent material.

Then the men are being paid, and this is a condition which did not always exist. Disaffection and mutiny in the Chinese Army in the past have in every case been traceable to the peculation of the men's pay. Experience has taught the danger of this; so that if squeezing does

8 | 'THE NEW CHINESE ARMY: ITS QUALITIES AND DEFECTS'

continue, as inevitably it must continue, it is in other directions than in the pay of the soldiers.

There is an improvement in the training of medical officers, but there is still a great deficiency in numbers, and there is also lack of veterinary surgeons. Officers show marked ability in field engineering work, and they are excellent topographers. The great difficulty in the Army has been the inefficiency of the cavalry, which are really mounted infantry. Horses are inadequate in numbers, and are not well looked after. The artillery is under-horsed, and has the immense defect of want of uniformity. Krupp guns, or guns of the Krupp pattern, are mainly in use, either imported or made in the arsenals of Shanghai and Hanyang. Next in number come the Japanese Arisaka guns; the sixth division is armed with Canet guns, and there are three batteries of Vickers-Maxim guns. There are also Greussen guns and Danish machine-guns. As an example of confusion critics can point to the first division, which is armed with three different types of guns—three batteries each of Arisaka field guns, Greussen field guns, and Krupp mountain guns. So, too, with the rifles. The arms used have been purchased from almost every country in Europe. There is an infinite variety of Mausers, Japanese rifles, Mannlichers, Winchesters, and other arms, but the prevailing type is the Mauser 1888 pattern. Next to the Mauser is the 30-year Meiji rifle, which has been used largely since the war. These to a considerable extent are discarded Japanese rifles of 6.5 bore re-bored to 6.8; and this latter is to be the standard bore of the Chinese rifle, no matter what the pattern.

There are many arsenals, two only of which (at Hanyang and Shanghai) approach the European standard. But the inherent defects of an army which has no uniform drill, no uniform gun, no uniform rifle, no uniform ammunition, no military budget, no military roads, deplorable lack of communications, do not require labouring. The Army cannot yet be regarded as a modern army, although it has made great progress since it was first created.

Discipline

Will the Army remain loyal? That is the problem of the future. The Provincial Troops (Hsün Fang Tui) have shown greater loyalty than the Lu Chün, and on two occasions have been called in to suppress mutiny among the modern troops, one a serious mutiny in 1910 in the Kwangtung mixed brigade, which was partly disbanded in consequence, and an earlier mutiny in November, 1908, in the Anhui mixed brigade, which has since been reconstituted. Still more recently, when there was the riot in Ch'êngtu, and fears were expressed for the loyalty of the troops, confidence was felt that the position could not become very serious because of the presence in the city of the Hsün Fang Tui.

The explanation is found in the fact that in great part the Hsün Fang Tui are recruited from the old braves, who were rarely natives of the province in which they were stationed. But in the case of the Lu Chün the men are recruited locally and serve in their natal province, economy being the guiding factor in this new departure.

Hsün Fang Tui

All provincial troops—that is to say, the old style miscellaneous troops of every province—are being reorganized. Some are being drafted into the modern Field Army; the remainder are being incorporated into the Hsün Fang Tui, who will police the country in time of peace, and will form the second line of defence in time of war. With two exceptions they have no guns—they are Cavalry and Infantry only. They are under the command of the Provincial High, authorities, by whom they are paid.

This organization comprises the camps, which to the number of many hundreds are scattered about all over the Empire. Of these some 650 may be described as reformed, the remainder are unchanged. The strength of the camps varies from 30 to 250; the battalion in its full, strength numbers 301 men. On paper the total strength of the reorganized Hsün Fang Tui will be 276,981; actually their present strength is 120,000 divided among 22 provinces, with a superficial area of 4,250,000 square miles and a land frontier of 11,000 miles.

Chapter 9

MORRISON'S LIFE IN CHINA AFTER JOURNALISM

Morrison as depicted in the New York Times, August 1912.

T he greater part of this book concerns itself with Morrison's time as journalist in China from 1898 until early 1912, however, it would be remiss of me not to provide a sketch of the remaining years of his life.

It was by no means certain that Morrison would remain in China after he decided in April 1912 to leave *The Times*, "heartily sick of my work [and] unsettled because no hope of advancement."[430] He wrote to George Buckle, *The Times'* editor, in May "I wish to start a new life—I want to do things, not always recording what is being done by others."[431] He was, however, if not broke, a man who was asset rich and income poor, and Morrison, like the caricature of the careful Scott, was a man conscious of income and expenditure. He considered returning to Australia

---

430 Pearl, op. cit., p. 255.
431 Lo, op. cit., pp. 800–802.

where friends had encouraged him to think of a political career, an opportunity, if he had pursued it, that would almost certainly have taken him into the Federal parliament. He also considered selling his prized asset, his Library into which he had poured many thousands of pounds. It was one of the greatest collection of books, manuscripts and maps concerning Asia in existence. He thought it might be worth £40,000, a considerable sum in those days, and there were interested buyers in China, Japan and the United States.[432]

His concerns about money were heightened by his decision to marry. He was 50 years of age and had proposed to and been accepted by Jennie Wark Robin, 23, a New Zealander whom he had recruited in London the previous year as his secretary. They were to marry in England on 26 August, 1912 and enjoyed a happy and fruitful marriage that produced three sons, before Morrison's early death in 1920 and her own in 1923.

His departure from the The Times was bitter. Morrison had hoped for a generous *ex gratia* payment for his years of service but instead The Times, while regretting "losing one of [its] greatest ornaments,"[433] demurred and offered him instead its profound thanks and the cost of passage (£73) to London from Peking.[434] But while he was remonstrating with The Times about the terms of his departure he was involved in negotiations about his employment by the Chinese government. These occupied at least the June and July of 1912 and resulted in him formally accepting the position of Political Advisor on 1 August of that year for a remuneration and benefits of £5,000 a year for five years.[435]

The man who reported the news became the news. Around the world Morrison's appointment was lauded in the press. He made the cover of

---

432 Nearly £4 million in today's money. When he came to sell it in August 1917 he sold for £35,000 equal then to £2 million underling the effects of wartime inflation on the value of the pound.
433 Lo, op. cit., *The Correspondence of G. E. Morrison*, pp. 807–808, Buckle, editor of the paper to Morrison, 20 June 1912.
434 Pearl, op. cit., p. 261.
435 About £295,000 a year in today's money. Lo Min Hui-Min, *The Correspondence of G. E. Morrison II 1912–1920*, Cambridge, Cambridge University Press, 1978, publishes the letter from Tsai Ting Kan, Yuan's English Secretary, appointing Morrison and detailing the agreement, pp. 3–5.

Jennie Wark Robin. She married Morrison in August 1912.
Mitchell Library, Sydney

the *Illustrated London News* (31 August, 1912) and the *New York Times* devoted a whole page of its August 12 issue to a portrait of the man:

> Here is a unique man in a unique job, and his success or failure may affect the whole future of the Far East, and, incidentally, of other nations of the world. It can be said of Dr Morrison that no man has had greater opportunities of learning the truth about the new movement in China which has brought about the downfall of the youthful Emperor, and the establishment of the the republic. For thirteen years past he has had his home in the Chinese capital, travelling largely from province to province. He has helped to make, as well as record, history.[436]

The media hyperbole[437] that greeted his appointment was not entirely mirrored in the reaction of Morrison's friends and informants in Peking. They questioned his upbeat assessment of China's republican future, and his ability to effect change. Dr Douglas Grey, of the British Legation in Peking, wrote to Sir Ernest Satow, a former British ambassador to China and Japan, in the days following the announcement.

> He is quite the most optimistic foreigner out here as to the future course of events. It will be interesting to see how he gets on as servant instead of hitherto an independent unbiased observer who every now and then gave Yuan the benefit of his reflections.[438]

Dr Grey proved prescient. Morrison's first attempt to make a difference was in the way China raised foreign loans, a source of finance that was crucial to the central government's functioning. Morrison's intervention ended in failure. Hitherto a six-nation consortium, comprising Britain, France, Germany, Japan, Russia and the United States, were the lenders

---

[436] James M. MacPherson, 'The Canny Scot Who Advises China's President', *New York Times*, 12 August 1912, p. 62.

[437] Not, for once, that the Australian media could be accused of that. The *Argus* in Melbourne carried a very short notice of his appointment noting, "satisfaction is expressed at the appointment which is most popular among all classes of Chinese." 'Chinese President. Appointment of Adviser. Dr. Morrison Selected.' *Argus*, 3 August 1912, p. 25.

[438] Lo, *Correspondence II* op. cit., p. 5 note 4. Grey wrote to Satow on 8 August 1912.

9 | MORRISON'S LIFE IN CHINA AFTER JOURNALISM

to China, with the powerful Hongkong & Shanghai Bank (which Morrison regarded as a German bank on account of the preponderance of German nationals on its board of directors) as the linchpin. Morrison, soon after his appointment, proposed that an all-British consortium, led by Birch Crisp & Company, assume the lead role in financing a £10 million loan with the participation of other British banks. He saw this as serving British interests and China's as well. Disaster ensued. By October that year the deal was dead. The British Legation, headed by Sir John Jordan, hitherto a 'friend' of Morrison's, turned frosty and he strongly opposed his plan. China backed down. By April 1913, the Consortium, now reduced to five after President Woodrow Wilson withdrew US involvement, provided Yuan with a £25 million loan. He used it to finance the 'Second Revolution' of July-September 1913, Yuan's largely successful attempt to consolidate his power through the eradication of the Sun Yat Sen's Kuomintang. Unfortunately for China, Yuan's policy cemented the country's north/south divide, with the latter becoming the base for the Kuomintang and the north for rent-seeking warlords.

The other big policy issue Morrison got involved in was the separation of Outer Mongolia from the Chinese Empire. Its distance from Peking had meant that Outer Mongolia historically was not as closely supervised by the Qing government as was Inner Mongolia which today still remains part of China. Imperial Russia promoted Outer Mongolian autonomy which it saw as a way of consolidating its influence in a territory it had effectively occupied since the beginning of the century. By the beginning of 1914 agreement had been reached to hold a tripartite conference, Mongolia, Russia, China, to settle the issue; the foundation of the talks was based on China as the 'Suzerain Power' in Mongolia. This was not a position China was able to sustain. In the early 1920s Mongolian communists, with Russian/Soviet support, had taken control of the country and in 1924 the Mongolian People's Republic came into being, with the Soviet Union as the suzerain.

Morrison, who even as a journalist was happy to have a public role, took to the business of advocacy well. In London on his annual visits he was a loyal supporter of Yuan's and an optimistic booster of China's prospects. He started to practise the dark arts of media management, quite early on, offering Reuters, a news agency, payment for the carriage of Chinese government statements, and their correspondent the 'exclusive' drop on announcements. He also intervened directly with the dispatches British journalists were sending to London. The *Daily Telegraph*'s correspondent B. L. Simpson[439] who wrote under the name of 'Putnam Weale', was of particular concern, especially his reporting about the assassination in March 1912 of Sung China-jen, a rising start of Sun Yat-Sen's Kuomintang, and a leading opponent of Yuan's in China's fledgling parliament. Sung was newly elected and a fervent proponent of democracy. He was opposed to Yuan. His assassination would end the cooperation Sun had extended to Yuan since the latter assumed the presidency.

In speculation about who ordered the assassination, the finger of suspicion pointed to the government and, in particular, to the prime minister, Chao Ping-chun. Putnam Weale had the temerity to write what everyone was saying:

> There is not the slightest doubt that he was shot to order. The time when the Government of China by assassin and dagger was possible is long past: the resumption is such methods must inevitable precipitate civil strife.[440]

Morrison said that while Putnam Weale's telegrams "carry very little weight" he recommended that the staff of the Chinese Telephone and Telegraph Administration should warn him about their power to deny him use of their service, and that the British Minister, Sir John Jordan, should be encouraged to have a word with Weale to moderate his stance. Morrison was assiduous in his defence of his employer and would lobby the Fleet Street press on his visits to London. He was not above 'leaking' either. In June 1914 he sent the editor of the *North China Daily News*, the leading English-language newspaper in China, translated copies of letters purportedly sent by Sun Yat-sen to the prime minister of Japan,

---

439 Bertram Lenox Simpson, 1877–1930, was a British author and journalist and was the *Telegraph*'s correspondent from 1911–1914. In 1912 he told *Telegraph* readers that Morrison's appointment that it would be short lived. Morrison was ill-disposed towards him. Simpson died in suspicious circumstances in Tianjin.

440 Lo, op. cit., *Correspondence*, vol. 2, Morrison circulated his report with a memorandum of advice to Admiral T'sai Ting-kan (1861–1935), pp. 114–118.

9 | MORRISON'S LIFE IN CHINA AFTER JOURNALISM

seeking Japanese support and advice for China's modernisation efforts. "Do not disclose the source," he requested.[441]

Inwardly, however, Morrison was disappointed with his job and, for a many who had spent a considerable time observing and writing about the Chinese, he found the negotiating of cultures difficult. William Rockhill, a friend and senior US diplomat wrote, in August 1913,

> I am sorry your work is not proving satisfactory, but with Orientals one must expect just what you are finding. I also recall old Sir Robert [Hart's] remark that what success he had had with the Chinese was the result of his persistent efforts in a given and never changing direction—or words to that effect ... [442]

Morrison was nothing if not determined and he embraced the idea of keeping to a "given and never changing direction". His marriage prospered and in relatively short succession he and Jennie produced three boys—one every two years—although neither of them would live to see them reach their maturity.

For Morrison the years of WWI in China were initially dominated by Japan's attempt to subjugate China. Japan moved decisively in the early months of the war to take control of Germany's major asset in China: Shantung province and its important port of Tsingtao. At the same time the Japanese envoy in Peking Hioki Masu[443] submitted a list of 21 Demands to a severely shocked President Yuan during an audience in January, 1915. The demands, grouped under five headings, called for the redesign of the Chinese government including the army and police, preferment for Japan in Manchuria and Shantung, and would, if accepted, have placed China under Japanese control. The Yuan government's initial response was flat footed, weak and acquiescent. When news leaked Peking allowed the Japanese, who released a pared down version of their demands and briefed sweet reasonableness, to set the tone of coverage. Morrison had to fight to get a copy of the Demands but by the end of February he was able to give a copy to fellow

---

441 ibid., Morrison to F. L. Pratt, 10 June 1914, letter and Sun translations, pp. 323–328.
442 ibid., Rockhill to Morrison, 31 August 1913, pp. 213–214.
443 Hioki Masu, 1861–1926, was a diplomat who served as Minister in Peking from 1914–1917. He was ambassador to Germany from 1920–1924.

Morrison with his three sons in 1917: Ian (1913–1950) left; Alastair (1915–2009) right; Colin (1917–2001) being nursed.
Mitchell Library, Sydney

9 | MORRISON'S LIFE IN CHINA AFTER JOURNALISM

Australian journalist W. H. Donald[444] who was covering for *The Times'* correspondent at the time. Publication helped turn opinion in China's favour and earned Morrison the enmity of the Japanese.

The criticism Morrison was most often subjected to was his faith in Yuan and the rosy outlook for China he propagated, especially on his visits to London and elsewhere abroad. Yet he was no fool; he was a gimlet-eyed realist and this is amply underlined in a letter he wrote in July 1915 to Liang Shih-yi,[445] secretary-general of the presidential office until Yuan's death in 1916. Liang wanted Morrison to engineer the publication of an article he had written seeking international support and opposition to Japan and its predations in China. Morrison bluntly refuted these arguments ("in serious questions ... interchange of views cannot be too frank and open") and then offered his explanation for why the world had given up on China. It is a model of 'speaking truth to power'.[446]

> China must think of the present, of the danger confronting her, the danger of shutting her eyes to the facts, the danger of looking to others for help that efforts of her own should render unnecessary ... As the President has repeatedly proclaimed, China must look to herself for her own salvation ... What Japan has done [reform itself] China ought to be able to do. What Siam [Thailand] has done China ought to be ashamed not to be able to accomplish. Siam had her great lesson in 1883. That year its capital was on its knees before the French fleet. She profited by

---

444 William Henry Donald, 1875–1946, known as Donald of China, was born in Lithgow, NSW, and worked in Asia from 1903 for the *New York Herald*, *The Times*, and the *Far Eastern Review*. He was close to Sun Yat Sen and Chiang Kai-shek, negotiating the latter's release from capture by Mao's communists in the so-called Xi'an Incident of 1936. He survived Japanese capture in the Philippines during WW2 and died in Shanghai in 1946.

445 Liang Shiyi, 1869–1933, was a Cantonese who rose to prominence towards the end of Qing dynasty and became an important power broker in Republican circles. He was a founder of the Bank of Communications (still extant), among other enterprises. Corrupt, the eminence gris of Yuan's support group, he later became Prime Minister, 1921–22, and an advisor to Zhang Zuolin, a warlord, in Manchuria before his death in Shanghai.

446 Lo, op. cit., *Correspondence*, vol. 2, Morrison to Liang, pp. 429–446.

that lesson. With the help of foreign assistants she put her house in order. Her struggle extorted the sympathy and admiration of the world. In 1907, within 14 years of her great humiliation she had recovered her political, judicial, and financial freedom ...

In 1860 Peking was occupied by foreign troops. What did this lesson profit China? Writing in 1896 Lord Curzon ... lamented the fate of China, 'who in the last fifty years has lost Siam, Burma, Annan, Tonking, part of Manchuria, Formosa [Taiwan] and Korea. And since 1896 Lord Curzon has not failed to observe that China has lost in all but name sovereign control of South Manchuria [to Japan], of North Manchuria [to Russia], of Outer Mongolian [to Russia] and of Outer Tibet. Her control of Ili and of Kashgaria has become shadowy. Her sovereign control of Fukien and Shantung has been gravely infringed, she has lost her fiscal freedom, her telegraphic freedom, her financial freedom.[447]

How can a country expect the benevolent sympathy of the world which after all these years has no modern representative government, no civil service, no security of office, no strategic railways, whose territory is traversed by railways voluntarily conceded, policed by the military of powerful neighbours, a country without a revenue system, without any simple system of taxation, without industries, without public works, a country which does not possess a single mile of modern high road, whose cities have the most primitive form of government known, a country which has no education system, although education is the basis of national strengths whose Minister of Education is innocent of all knowledge of Western education, whose Minister of Finance has no knowledge of Western finance although the the financial problems of China are probably greater than any other country. Good finance is the very essence of good government ...[448]

---

447 ibid., pp. 436–437.
448 ibid., pp. 438–439.

I am writing to you the truth because you are a Chinese of high standing and because I am in Chinese employ. I cannot conceive that it is my duty because I am a so-called adviser to say nothing but sweet words and falsely encourage my employers in the belief that things are going well with China when as a fact the situation is one fraught with the gravest possibilities. I believe that what Japan has done China ought to be able to do. I believe that in shutting their minds to the disagreeable facts the Chinese are drifting into danger from which escape as an independent nation will be impossible. I believe that the only hope of salvation lies in ceasing unworthy and pusillanimous make-believe, in ceasing to cry out for help which will not be given and in looking at the situation bravely in the face and honestly attempting to profit from the blunders of the past.[449]

Liang was unsettled by the letter; he told Morrison it kept him awake for two nights. It was translated into Chinese for further distribution. This astringent and cogent analysis of China's ills, however, does not seem to have had a marked effect upon Republican officials or Liang's subsequent career.

In any event, it was 'events' which overtook the urgency of Morrison's apologia and one event in particular, the attempt by Morrison's boss, Yuan Shikai to revive the Chinese Empire with him at its head, a self-styled Emperor, what Morrison was to dub "this mad scheme"[450].

In August 1915 a group of eminent men formed an association to push for the restitution of the monarchy in China, following its analysis of the failure of parliamentary democracy that had been operating since 1912. The group, called the Ch'ou-an hui, or Peace Planning Society, lighted upon a memorandum written by Francis Goodnow,[451] Yuan's American Legal Adviser, called 'Republic and Monarchy in China' which argues that monarchy rather than democracy was better for China at this stage

---

449 ibid., pp. 441–442.
450 ibid., p. 454. Morrison's letter to Sir John Jordan.
451 Francis Goodnow, 1859–1939, was a political scientist and legal authority and Yuan's legal adviser from 1912–14. He left China to return to Johns Hopkins University.

Advisors to Yuan Shikai, c. 1913. Morrison in second row, second from right. Francis Goodnow, centre front row, the 'Legal Advisor' whose memo was used in support of Yuan's restoring the monarchy.
Mitchell Library, Sydney

9 | MORRISON'S LIFE IN CHINA AFTER JOURNALISM

of its development.[452] Pressure, real or confected, increased and soon after the establishment of the Society provincial authorities and military governors were instructed to 'consult the people' as to their opinions of monarchy. Unsurprisingly an enthusiastic response was reported to Peking and 'unanimous people's deliberation' was reached in early November. The Consultative Council established by Yuan to handle the plebiscite following the faux consultation petitioned him to yield to the 'unanimous wishes' of the people and accept the Imperial throne. Yuan, who described himself as a 'mere citizen' said in December it would be wrong to reject 'the will of the people' and authorised preparations for his enthronement on February 9, 1916.

Yuan's plans were poorly received. In Yunnan there were threats of succession if he went ahead, threats that would be repeated in the coming weeks from other provinces. He hesitated and temporised. He sent Morrison on a fact-finding mission to the Yangtze River, taking in Hankow, Nanking and Shanghai. Morrison submitted his memorandum on February 9, the day originally slated for the enthronement but one that Yuan had already let pass.

> I met no man devoted to the interests of China who did not speak with indignation of the action of Your Excellency's Government in forcing despite all advice to the contrary the issue [monarchy] which has thrown the country in rebellion …
>
> Everyone in China has long known that the messages dispatched from the provinces to Peking urging Your Excellency to ascend the throne were in most cases if not all cases prepared by a small body of advisers in Peking and forwarded to the Provinces to be retransmitted to Peking…
>
> The State is in great danger. In only one way can this danger be averted and that is by the definite abandonment of the monarchical restoration until after the conclusion of the present war and the will of the people can be ascertained, by the immediate institution of constitutional assemblies, the calling

---

452 I mostly follow Lo, op. cit., pp. 450–453 in the following narrative.

of Parliament and the creation of a responsible Cabinet with a responsible Prime Minister.[453]

The president's response to this lesson in civics is not recorded but by the end of February Yuan cracked under the pressure of opposition and postponed his enthronement indefinitely. For the unhappy Yuan this was not the end of his problems; to the chorus of opposition from antimonarchists was added complaints from his own supporters who felt abandoned. Yuan died on June 6 and writing soon after, Morrison was generous, if measured, about Yuan. He said he recalled many "endearing qualities of the famous ruler, his generosity, his kindness, his loyalty to his friends, his consideration for others." He went on,

> The most striking characteristic as I observed then of his relations with foreigners was his caution, his unwillingness ever to give full confidence, his inevitable withholding of the essential fact. Thus he could never be given a well-balanced judgement because he never submitted the full facts of the case … I fancy this will always be the difficulty in rendering effective service—this inveterate distrust of the foreigner.[454]

Morrison was less diplomatic with Lady Beatrice Brownrigg, a friend from him journalism days who had repatriated to England.

> Yuan Shih-kai solved the difficulty about his retirement in the best possible way by dying. His mad ambition to become Emperor not only wrecked his own career, but very nearly wrecked his country.[455]

The period of almost continuous rebellion in China during the 19th century had forced the ruling Qing dynasty to decentralise the military. This resulted in the generals in charge of provinces wielding much power and influence where earlier civilian authority held sway. With Yuan's modernisation of the military, after the first Sino-Japanese War of 1895,

---

453 ibid., excerpts from pp. 486, 488, 489.
454 ibid., p. 535, Morrison to Ts'ai Ting-kan. Ts'ai had been Yuan's English Secretary and considering writing a biography of the late president.
455 Lo, op. cit., Letter to Beatrice Brownrigg, 10 July 1916, p. 537.

many of the regional generals commanding provincial garrisons were his men. Grateful as the nation might have been, Yuan's death initiated the rise of China's military governors, soon to be designated War Lords and the period of their ascendancy, Warlordism. From this point until Morrison's untimely death in England in 1920 the government he served would be buffeted by power struggles between the two men who assumed political power after Yuan's death: Li Yuan-hung,[456] Yuan's largely unsighted vice-president since 1912, and Tuan Chi-jui,[457] prime minister and a man in a hurry.

Since the middle of 1914 the issue of China joining the Alliance against Germany see-sawed between those who supported and those who opposed it. Throughout 1916 Morrison was assiduously in his prosecution of the case for Chinese participation. For him the prize was a seat at the table after Germany's defeat and the prospect of reclaiming Germany's 'concessions' in China, notable Shandong province and its important port Tsingtao. While China remained cool to the idea there was little pressure for it to join the Alliance, but once it raised the prospect of joining, Japan emerged and as an intractable opponent. At the commencement of hostilities Japan, with Britain, moved to eject the Germans from Tsingdao. The Japanese wished to make their occupation of the port permanent, a point underlined by the 21 Demands given to Yuan in 1915. From the time of Yuan's death until the end of the year Morrison lobbied on behalf of China. He lobbied leading Japanese politicians during a summer holiday in Japan (a visit that produced another lengthy memorandum) and leading Fleet Street figures in

---

456 Li Yuanhong, 1864–1928, occupied positions at the top of Republican politics from 1912 until 1923, serving either as president of vice-president. He seems to have possess a mix of integrity allied to indecision. He trained at the Tianjin Naval Academy and saw action in the 1895 was with Japan; he was military governors of Wuchang at the time of the revolution in 1911 and sided with Sun Yat-Sen which made him an attractive candidate for vice-president when Sun gave way to Yuan in 1912. He clashed with Duan Qirui, prime minister over joining the allies in the War.

457 Duan Qirui, 1865–1938, trained in military academies under Yuan. He was nicknamed the "Tiger of Anhui" and a leader of the Anhui faction in Republican politics. He was three times Premier from 1916 until 1926, although he lost real power when defeated by Cao Kun, another warlord and protégé of Yuan, in the Zhili-Anhui War (1920). His motto: "China needs strength, not talk."

Morrison seated with Ishida Mikinosuke, right, August 1917. Ishida advised Baron Iwasaki on the purchase of the library and remained in charge of it until 1934.
Mitchell Library, Sydney

London to make China's case in their columns. By the February of the following year (1917) Morrison was urging Premier Tuan Chi-jui to accept "with alacrity" the offer by the Americans to join them in severing diplomatic relations with Germany. Eliding the issue of Shantung and Tsingdao, he highlighted to Tuan the prospect of taking back the German concessions in Hankow and Tientsin. He also held out the prospect of China regaining tariff autonomy by declaring that all non-treaty Powers pay customs duties. It would take until August 1917 for China to declare war on Germany and Austria-Hungary. Unbeknownst to Morrison or his Chinese employer, Britain and France had agreed to Japan's condition for admitting China into the Allies, namely that Japan be allowed to assume control of Germany's concessions in China as part of any peace settlement after the War. This seemingly small concession would prove one of the most consequential side agreements struck during WW1, albeit through the application of the law of unintended consequence. When it became known during the Versailles peace treaty process it sparked mass demonstrations in China, especially Peking, in an event that would become known as the May 4th Movement—a movement that irreparably damaged the government of Duan, galvanised the Kuomintang under Jiang's leadership who soon forged an alliance with Soviet Russia, and is seen by historians as a defining moment in the development of Chinese political consciousness, one strand of which was the embrace of Marxist-Leninist ideology.

That was all in the future, and a future that Morrison would not see. By mid-1917 he had two issues on his mind: the fate of his library; and, having extended his appointment as Political Adviser for another five years, he planned a six-month sabbatical that would take him south, to Australia and New Zealand.

In the early decades of the 20th century there were not many great libraries rich in works about Asia. There was the British Library in London, the Bibliothèque Nationale in Paris, Harvard University Library in the US, and there was Morrison's library. He built the collection from the mid 1890s up to when he sold it in August 1917, controversially to a Japanese aristocrat and scion of the Mitsubishi zaibatsu, Baron Iwasaki for £35,000, the equivalent today of more than £2 million. It is housed in Tokyo and known as the Toyo Bunko, or

Oriental Library (not as Morrison had stipulated in the sale document, The Morrison Library).

The library is multi-lingual, with works in more than 20 languages. It consists of 20,000 volumes, 4,000 pamphlets, 2,000 maps (the earliest date from 1565), 41 editions of Marco Polo's travels, including the first Italian edition of 1494 together with the first English, German and French editions. It has the manuscript of the dictionary taken to China in Lord Macartny's ill-fated mission to the Qianlong emperor in 1792, early Chinese-Latin dictionaries and exquisite examples of late 17th century Chinese printing on rice paper.

The sale was controversial. His library had been a landmark, perhaps more known about than used, but still there was sadness among Chinese intellectuals that it was leaving Peking, and especially for Japan, a country that promoted feelings of admiration and loathing in equal measure. Morrison pleaded necessity. He was 55 and had a young family he needed to provide for; the money raised would provide him with financial independence.

> The library will remain a kind of monument, not to my learning, for my learning does not amount to a row of pins, but to my instinct as a collector."[458]

In November 1917 Morrison left Peking for a six month visit to Australia and New Zealand. He wanted to see if Australia was where he might relocate in the future. He was not, however, encouraged by what he heard from fellow-passengers on the S.S Aki Maru from Hong Kong, especially a Scot called Soutar who had spent time in Melbourne.

> Tells me of the separation of Capital and Labour and the gulf between employer and employed. A policy of retaliation. No sympathy. Each exacting all he can and each insisting on his rights. He emphasizes the general incompetence and unwillingness to learn.[459]

---

458 Quoted in Pearl, op. cit., p. 344.
459 ibid., p. 346.

9 | MORRISON'S LIFE IN CHINA AFTER JOURNALISM

Morrison sailed down the east coast of Australia stopping in the manner of a Royal Progress. At Brisbane he met the Governor ("revolting luncheon"), at Sydney it was luncheon with the Governor-General, whose his wife affected not to know him as asked what he did for a living, and finally to Melbourne where he was feted and "greatly pleased" by being made an honorary member of the Melbourne Club. At the end of December he spoke to a congregation at Wesley Church in central Melbourne. The second Conscription referendum had come and gone; opponents had won, and Morrison had defence much on his mind.

> This favoured island still in swaddling clothes, nursed by the Mother Country [Britain], where 5 millions of people live in luxurious indolence, the largest undefended area in the world's surface today, the most defenceless of all countries, a country believed by the majority of its inhabitants to be not worth defending, the riches prey that can fall under the domination of an aggressive neighbour of a victorious enemy.[460]

His main concern was Japan. His initial enthusiasm for Japan (at its height during the war with Russia in 1904–05) soured. He still admired Japan's response to the West with its embrace of western industrialisation, education and military and political structures, but Japan's embrace of militarism had, he felt, more in common with Germany than it did with the Allies. Moreover it had done little to assist the Allies, of which it was nominally one. And it had a large 'surplus' population which had to go somewhere. He raise his concerns directly with W M "Billy" Hughes,[461] prime minister, and anyone else who would listen. He carried anti-Japanese sentiments with him to New Zealand

---

460 ibid., p. 351.
461 William Morris Hughes, 1862–1952, was born in London to Welsh parents; he emigrated to Australia when he was 22 years old. He was powerful in the New South Wales Labor Party and elected to first Federal Parliament in 1901 where he remained a member until his death. He was Prime Minister, 1915–23, and split with Labor over compulsory military service (conscription) while retaining the premiership. He fought and lost two referendums on conscription and lost. He was influential in conservative politics in the 1930s, leading the United Australia Party, a forerunner to the Liberal Party, but losing the leadership to Robert Menzies in 1939. He promised Morrison a knighthood, which he didn't deliver, to Morrison's regret.

where he was, in the words of his biographer, subjected to a "dreary round of interviews, speeches, lunches, dinners, and receptions."[462] On his return to Melbourne he met Billy Hughes[463] again and gave a tub thumping speech on the prospects for China to the Commercial Travellers Association. He spent Christmas with his sister and her husband, Justice Henry Higgins,[464] although he deplored the meal, commenting that "no wine was offered, and no whisky, and there was found only one bottle of soda-water in this parsimonious house—a shocking dinner."[465]

An outbreak of plague in China provided Morrison with and excuse to cut short his Australasian tour. He was in Peking by May 1918 and found the political situation there dispiriting. Parliamentary elections were for both houses of Parliament were about to begin and by mid-year there were to be elections for President. These elections marked the decisive break between north and south; the Kuomintang repudiated the results and set up a competing administration based in Canton. As for the Presidential election

> There are three candidates now in the field. The one most likely to be elected is Hsu Hsi-chang, who ... was one of Yuan Shih-kai's staff at his camp near Tienstin. He rose under the Manchus to be the first Viceroy of Manchuria ... To the foreigner he appears to have every possible disqualification for such a post ... The other two candidates are the Acting President, Feng Kuo-chang and Tuan Chi-jui, the present Prime Minister. Either of them would make a less unworthy President than Hsu. It is difficult to believe that with the reassembling of Parliament

---

462 ibid., p. 353.
463 Memorably described as "opposed by one half of the people and cordially disliked by the other half." ibid., p. 354.
464 Higgins was President of the Commonwealth Court of Conciliation and Arbitration in 1907 when he ruled in the Harvester case about fair wages. He ruled that workers needed and adequate 'basic wage' which must be enough to support the wage earner in "reasonable and frugal comfort." A landmark rule it that still resonates today.
465 ibid., p. 358.

9 | MORRISON'S LIFE IN CHINA AFTER JOURNALISM

strife will cease in China. For a large section of the people of China will still regard the election as illegal.[466]

In the run up to the president's inauguration—Morrison was correct, Hsu won the contest—Morrison was still applying himself to the political problems China faced. In September he wrote Tsai Ting-kan,[467] Yuan's former English Secretary now in Shanghai, that he planned to advise Hsu to seek the assistance of the United States in mediating between the Peking government and its rival Kuomintang administration in Canton. The US was the first country to recognise the Republic of China and it was the country that brought China into the war. He pushed ministers to state publicly their support for the Balfour Declaration on a home in Palestine for Jews (they did) and recommended to an Australian cabinet minister that Australia should appoint a High Commissioner to visit China to understand the importance of the China market (he didn't). As the year drew to an end Morrison accepted Hsu's invitation to be part of China's team at the Paris Peace talks, the so-called Treaty of Versailles.

Before he left for Europe, on what would turn out to be his last voyage, Morrison returned to a subject that had animated him and stoked his ire since he first visited China in 1893: the scourge of opium. He was never blind to Chinese complicity in the opium trade. But his sights were levelled on the Japanese in a lengthy article he wrote, ('From a Correspondent'), for the *North China Daily News* titled "The Japanese Opium Trade with China: A scandal calling for instant and drastic repression."[468] The headline is more argumentative than the article which is a cool, thorough description and analysis of the Japanese-controlled trade of distribution of opium and morphia in China. Extraterritoriality, he noted, protected Japanese dealers from arrest by the Chinese who would have to notify the Japanese consul of their intention to arrest; the product was imported through ports controlled by the Japanese, either through both ownership or the staffing of Maritime Customs with Japanese nationals.

---

466 Lo, op. cit., p. 682.
467 ibid., pp. 697–698, Morrison to Tsai, 14 September 1918.
468 Published on 17 December 1918. Full text in Lo, pp. 723–726.

His battles with Japan were to continue when in the spring of 1919 and now in Paris for the Peace conference the delegations got down to the real business of treaty making. The Chinese went to Paris wanting to roll-back Japan's relentless incursions into Chinese lands and sovereignty. They wanted the repudiation Japan's infamous 21 Demands of January 1915 which led, amongst of things, to its occupation of Tsingdao in Shantung province, and they wanted the return of previously alienated territories. On the latter, Morrison said in a 1917 interview with *The Age*, Melbourne, China's declaration of war on Germany and Austria would enable the Chinese to rewrite the terms of trade and investment in China.

> After the war, China will have new treaties in which she will be able to make very much better terms than before.[469]

On both counts China failed. To agreement Japan obtained from Britain and France about the fate of German concession in China was added the powerful, and determinative, voice of the United States. Morrison, now in London and very ill, dictated the following to his friend Howell Gwynne, the editor of the *Morning Post*, a conservative daily newspaper, and godfather to Alastair.

> President Wilson completely befooled the Chinese. In order to buy off Japan's opposition to the League of Nations[470] which did not include words stipulating for national equality, he made a bargain, and in return for Japan's not pressing her claim, he undertook to support in their entirety all Japan's claims in regard to China. The result has been that Japan has obtained in China far more than ever she could have hoped for and more than she would have accepted as adequate. Now the President is endeavouring to cajole the Chinese into believing that he

---

469 'Australia and China. The Possibilities of Trade. Dr. G. E. Morrison's Emphatic Advice,' *The Age*, 19 December 1917, p. 12.

470 The League of Nations was Wilson's proposal for a supra-national body to oversee world peace and order, a precursor to the United Nations today. He persuaded many to joint but failed to convince the US Senate which refused its consent to the treaty.

9 | MORRISON'S LIFE IN CHINA AFTER JOURNALISM

was their champion throughout but that the opposition of Mr Lloyd George[471] and the French was such that in order to save his precious League of Nations he had to yield.[472]

Morrison was hospitalised in June and was out by June 21. He and Jennie had rented a cottage in Sussex, Forrest Row, and there they went. He was clearly concerned about his health and he had reason to be: he had lost nearly 20 per cent of his body weight since the beginning of the year. In July he was back in London to consult Dr Ernest Young, another doctor, and received a more plausible diagnosis: pancreatitis. It gave him much confidence. A further consultation produced irritation in the patient and in August he wrote to Dr Young saying he was giving up all medicines in favour of self-treatment, comprising fresh air and diet control. August found him in Edinburgh seeing a range of doctors the best of whom confirmed the pancreatitis diagnosis. He then booked himself into Duff House, Banff, an upmarket sanatorium where one 'dressed' for dinner. He stayed there until October. He continued to lose weight.

He wanted to return to Peking. That was simply impossible. His health continued to deteriorate. Jennie was shocked when she saw him, emaciated and weak. Back at home he was shunted from one doctor to another. Attempts were made to supplement his failing pancreas with extracts of pig pancreas, to no good effect. Amidst this desperate quest for certainty and cure, he managed to keep active and inquisitive. He read voraciously and rekindled (had it ever died?) his enthusiasm for book collecting, focussing this time of Defoe's *Robinson Crusoe*, and restocking his Peking library with a shipment of 1,400 volumes. In March, 1920, feeling somewhat better, he and Jennie took a house in Sidmouth, Devon, in the belief the sea and the air would help. From Sidmouth he kept up correspondence with friends and received visitors. But he continue to lose weight, was susceptible to chills, and confessed to his *Diary* in May that since he left Paris fourteen months before "it has been one long drawn out suffering, the one long deferred hope that wrings my heart and then gives place to hopeless despair."[473]

---

471 British prime minister and leader of the UK delegation.
472 Lo, op. cit., Morrison to Gwynne, London, 9 May 1919, pp. 755–756.
473 Pearl, op. cit., p. 407.

Morrison was dying. During these last weeks his thoughts were much with his young wife, still only 31 years old.

My dearest Jennie

I was lying in the easy chair in the court yard thinking of you always thinking of you when your kind note came. It is impossible that sometimes I shall not feel dispirited when I think of how unworthy I am of you and when I contrast your bright your life with what I see of myself. Oh God how I love you. I never knew before what it was to love and worship as I love and worship you my dear. What can I do to make you happy, that is all I think about, and make you contented and show you my devotion.

May God bless you always my dear and shield you and guard you from all harm and give you all the happiness in the world.

Ever your loving
Ernest[474]

George Morrison died on May 28, 1920 with Jennie by his side. Jennie died in 1923—fulfilling a fortune teller's prophesy that she would marry a famous man and die young—leaving three boys, Ian, Alastair and Colin, in the care of a governess.

Ian followed his father and was a correspondent for *The Times*; he died covering the Korean War in 1953. He was the basis for Mark Elliot, the war correspondent, who has an affair with a Chinese doctor in Han Suyin's autobiographical *A Many-Splendoured Thing*, 1952. Alastair read economics at Cambridge and was an expert on south east Asia; he ended up as an intelligence officer in Canberra, Australia. Colin, like his brothers, was educated at Winchester, and attended Cambridge University. The boys are buried with their father and mother in Sidmouth, Devon.

---

[474] Lo, op. cit., p. 821. Lo's magnum opus he gives this as Morrison's last letter.

An Australian Odyssey

Chapter 10

A Pleasant Excursion

By the time Morrison was born in 1862, virtually all of the major explorations of the Australian continent had been conducted. From the earlier explorations beyond the Blue Mountains, west of Sydney, by Lt John Oxley RN, to John Eyre's 1840 explorations of Australia's red centre, to Dr Ludwig Leichardt's 3,000 mile journey across northern Australia in 1844 and his ill-fated 1847 attempt to travel across the continent from east to west, little of Australia remained unvisited by the white man. Ill-fated too was the attempt in 1861, a year before Morrison's birth, by Robert O'Hara Burke and William John Wills to traverse the continent from the south to the north from Melbourne to the Gulf of Carpentaria and back again.

In the 20th century Leichardt and Burke and Wills became models of Australians' encounter with the outback, as the wilderness is known. Patrick White, Australia's Nobel Prize winning author, made Leichardt's story the basis for *Voss* his novel of outback anomie;[1] Sydney Nolan, the celebrated painter, produced a series of images of Burke and Wills lost in a wilderness of unsparing bleakness and hostility.[2]

In contrast Morrison grew up in the warm afterglow of the explorers' achievements. The difficulties and privations they faced were secondary to their achievements—the maps they made, the agricultural land they

---

[1] Published in 1957 by Eyre & Spottiswoode.
[2] Nolan returned again and again to the theme from 1948 to 1975 for the series now in the Tate Gallery, London.

identified, the mineral deposits they discovered—Victorian optimism had not yet succumbed to late 20th century doubt. So it is very much with that understanding that we need to approach Morrison's account of his 2,043 mile journey across the continent.[3] He saw himself as the heir to Oxley and Eyre, not to Burke and Wills; indeed the route he took was a modified version of their route of return, and he got back … on his own. In his 'Reminiscences' he says of the trek:

> Roughly speaking, it was my intention to follow the route taken 21 years before by the Burke and Wills expedition—that most disastrous of all Australian expeditions when every member of the party perished except one.[4]

In the account that follows he does not even mention their name; for that matter he does not mention any other explorer either. Morrison was 20 years old when he set out from Normanton and tuned 21 during the walk, still a medical student at the University of Melbourne, as well as an aspiring explorer and writer. He tells his story with the bluff nonchalance of a young man who regards the task described as no more than a *petite rien* while the rest of us are left to marvel at his achievement.

While staying at Winton, a settlement, really an outpost, 184 miles south of Normanton, he wrote to his mother:

> The experience I have gained in former trips has been of great value to me. Mine is no feat—*no feat of endurance*—only a pleasant excursion. I am as free as a lark.[5]

Since leaving school Morrison had used the long holidays that coincide with the Australian summer to undertake explorations. Each was more ambitious than the previous one; each feeding his desire that someday he would do something "great".[6] His first was to walk from Queenscliff on Port Philip Bay to Adelaide, the next was to sail down the Murray River from Albury to its mouth in South Australia, and, the one after that, a sea voyage off the north coast of Queensland that resulted in

---

3 3,288 kilometres.
4 'Reminiscences,' p. 386.
5 Cyril Pearl, *Morrison of Peking*, Sydney: Angus and Robertson, 1967, p. 30.
6 See p. 3, this volume.

a multi-part exposé of the use of Pacific Islander labour, known as *kanakas,* in the Queensland sugar cane fields. All of these had been published in a sister paper of *The Age* called *The Leader*, a weekly. *The Age*'s proprietor, David Syme was impressed by his series about the cane fields and *Across the Australian Continent* is the first of Morrison's journalism to be published by that newspaper. Syme would go on to commission Morrison to explore New Guinea and published his series of articles that flowed (not entirely successfully) from that expedition.[7]

Morrison's description of his walk across Australia could have served as a primer for Dorothea Mackellar's 'My Country'. A "wilful, lavish land" indeed; one moment, he is enduring temperatures well above 100 degrees Fahrenheit, the next he is wading chest deep for mile upon mile through a lake formed after 72 hours' nonstop rain. About the only test Morrison did not face was bushfire.

There is of course a darker side to this trek. Although he did no know it at the time the 1880s in Queensland were a time of increased conflict between the aborigines and settlers.[8] Morrison writes of "wretched blacks" who are "shot without mercy" as British settlers clear the land not only of scrub and vegetation but of indigenous Australians as well. "I was at a station whose owner is said to have shot more blacks than any two men in Queensland." Morrison's evident distaste at the treatment of aborigines throws into relief his decision to travel unarmed. His chosen profession was medicine. He sought to be a healer and, though he was capable of violence in self-defence (he attempted to kill the men who were trying to kill him during the Siege of the Legations in Peking in 1900), he was by nature pacific, thoughtful, and a supporter of the underdog. Tempting as it is, however, to cast Morrison in more liberal light, one cannot forget that he was a man of his time, a staunch believer in the benefits of empire and its civilising effects on colonised countries. When he comes to remember his trek across Australia in his

---

7 ibid., p. 5.
8 A chastening account of the settlers' war against aborigines in general and Queensland's aborigines in particular is given by David Kemp, *A Free Country, Australians' Search for Utopia 1861–1901*, Melbourne: The Miegunyah Press, 2019, pp. 174–188.

'Reminiscences',[9] it is the signs of economic development he recalls with enthusiasm rather than the plight of the "wretched" aborigines.

The country Morrison traversed in 1883 was not a nation state; it was a group of independent British crown colonies. Since the 1850s, when effective self-government was devolved from London to the colonies they had met periodically in the intercolonial conferences. These meetings discussed economic matters, mostly, such as tariffs and trade, the gauge of the railways; they were always fractious and often inconclusive. One gets a glimpse of the separateness that colonial Australians felt from, Morrison's account of his walk, and what he felt on entering Victoria after his trek through the wilderness of the interior.

> [I]n my own colony, it was a perfect picnic. Instead of immense tracts of country owned by one man, and given up to sheep, there were a succession of beautiful little farms, each with its haystack, its neat little cottage, its substantial fence, and its scene of vigorous activity. Ploughing was in full swing, clearing and grubbing. The beautiful hilly country, seemingly so fertile, and supporting so excellent a class of people, pleased me beyond measure. Certainly, I thought, my colony may be the smallest, but it is the healthiest and most beautiful of them all.

---

9 'Reminiscences,' p. 386.

'Across the Australian Continent on Foot'[10]

by George Ernest Morrison

It had long been a wish of mine to cross Australia. Lying in bed in Port Mackay with two crippled knees, I first resolved to do the journey on foot. When I heard on all sides of the long stages between stations and the impossibility of travelling without at least two horses, I decided to go alone, and when every-one croaked to me that the blacks would kill me, if the floods did not drown me, I swore I should go unarmed. Fever I had to fear as well as blacks; quinine would be required to combat the former; a telescope might forewarn me of the latter. My telescope was stolen from me in Cooktown; my quinine, by accident, was thrown away at Thursday Island. Of all things none was more likely to be useful than a compass, yet mine was utterly destroyed in New Guinea. What could I argue from these things, but that fever would pass me unharming, blacks would never endanger my life, nor would I ever be in a situation from which there was no escape but by the use of the compass. At Normanton,[11] when I gave out my intention of strolling over to Melbourne, people professed to think me mad. The rainy season was impending, and many signs, especially the comet, pointed to its

---

10 *The Age*, Saturday, 19 May 1883, p. 2.
11 Normanton was founded in 1868 and is situated at the Gulf of Carpentaria, some 3,250km (2,000 miles) due north of Melbourne. It is located in the vicinity reached by the ill-fated expedition (1860–61) of Burke and Wills in their attempt to traverse Australia from the south to north and back again.

being earlier than usual. "How reckless," said one; "so insane," put in another; "it's suicide," added a third. The elderly landlady of the hotel grew eloquent as to the dangers which awaited me. She was no cur she assured me, but she wouldn't be game to tackle such a walk. Fearing an attack of nervousness I hurried out of Normanton to an hotel 15 miles on the road to Cloncurry.[12] Five teams were camped here. It rained with unpromising severity the better part of two days, and as the next house was 75 miles away I had just to wait patiently.

On Friday evening, the 22nd December, the sky was clear for the first time, and starting at once I was 30 miles on my way before it came on to rain again. The teams hesitated, and have been there ever since I fancy. This long stage is much dreaded by the carriers. It lies through country lightly timbered with the gutta-percha[13] tree, the stunted bastard box, and the cooliebar,[14] a district said to swarm with blacks, and annually subject to inundation. When I was half-way through there came on a violent tempest of wind and rain. The track became a bog and the knapsack got so soddened with water that I groaned under its weight. It was not safe to rest. The accounts I had heard of the track when flooded made me tremble to sit down, so I wearily struggled on through water and mud up to my knees, forgetting the dangers of this dismal, gloomy country in the fatigue of walking. Suddenly the wind died away, the sun shone out through the clouds, the rain stopped, and in a little while I came to where no rain had fallen at all. It had been merely a local storm. The following morning I came to two huts and a stockyard, the cattle station of Veno Park. Two stages of 25 miles each through a country whose monotonous flatness is occasionally relieved by richly wooded sand hills, bring you, the first to a cattle station, the second to a public-house. Spear Creek, which has been on your left hand, is now lost sight of. The Sanby is crossed, and you are on that immense plain which stretches to the Flinders River. Between the Cockatoo waterhole, 3 miles beyond the Sanby, and a low hill called

---

12 Cloncurry is 420 kms south of Normanton. It takes its name from its eponymous river which was named by Robert Burke after his cousin, Lady Elizabeth Cloncurry. It lies to the east of Mt Isa.
13 A tree rich in latex.
14 More commonly spelt coolabah, a widely distributed eucalyptus.

10 | 'ACROSS THE AUSTRALIAN CONTINENT ON FOOT'

Route of Burke & Wills 1860–61, from A Literary and Historical Atlas of Africa and Australasia, *London: J M Dent, 1913. This is the route Morrison mostly followed.*

Fort Brown, within 3 miles of the Flinders there is a dead waterless flat, almost bare of trees, which is buried some feet under water during the rainy season. Carriers tell me 30 feet, and I can well believe it, for the high gums on the banks of the Flinders have drift timber in their very topmost branches. I had a mate when crossing this plain, an old man who sought my company out of nervousness. He was mounted on a poor wretched moke[15] which had a fistula between its shoulders that was sickening to look at. Yet he was very proud of his horse and was quite disgusted because the only bid he could get for horse, saddle and bridle when he put him up for sale was 19s.[16] Locomotion was so painful to the horse that hobbles would have been superfluous. His only fault in the eyes of his owner was that he was not a mare. When buying flour for my mate and myself I asked him how much should we require; 6 lb. he replied. "Surely," said I, "6 lb. of flour will not be enough for you and me for three days"—we were 81 miles from the next house—but he begged of me to trust him for that. Borrowing the loan of the kitchen he baked a damper of the weight and hardness of a stone. We had no knife strong enough to cut it. I constantly passed teams now till I got into Cloncurry. Water and grass were abundant, and with the £30 a ton for the 250 miles from the Norman to Cloncurry, they had made satisfactory profits. I went some miles off the road to see the first sheep station. The Guy country seems ill adapted for the sheep, though horses and cattle thrive wonderfully, but here, over 200 miles from the coast, the sheep does splendidly on the open downs with Gidya[17] ridges, which stretch away to the N.W. of Cloncurry. Between the Norman and Cloncurry I saw neither kangaroos, emus nor wild dogs, though the latter abound. There wore native turkeys in score, and every pool of water swarmed with wild fowl. Kites were more plentiful than crows, and you never stopped for a meal but the trees near became grey with kites waiting for you to leave that they might swoop down upon the scraps. The wretched blacks are

---

15 In Britain a moke is a term for a donkey; in Australia is was used to describe an inferior horse.
16 19 shillings; there were 20 shillings to the pound.
17 Gidya is the name the Wiradjuri people of NSW give to Acacia implexa. Morrison found it useful when making a fire.

shot without mercy.[18] One night I was at a station, whose owner is said to have shot more blacks than any two men in Queensland, when the mailman came in and reported that he had seen a black prowling about the stockyard. Loading his rifle Mr —[19] at once sallied out after him, but came back in an hour quite disappointed that though he could pick up the tracks by the stockyard, it was too dark to follow them. Alligators are said to swarm in Spear Creek, as the Norman river is called above Normanton; I hesitate to give the dimensions of the largest that has been seen.

Cloncurry is situated in a slightly elevated upland, in the centre of a pan-shaped depression, surrounded by a rim of low hills. The adjacent country is very rich in minerals.[20] Payable gold has been got here for many years. Bismuth, antimony and manganese are found. There is a hill of iron, and a supposed largo deposit of coal; but copper is the most abundant of its minerals. There is a mine of nearly virgin copper, so pure indeed as to be at present, owing to the absence of firewood, unworkable. This mine lately changed hands for £23,000, so there seems good reason for believing that the copper has a real existence. From Cloncurry my route lay to Winton.[21] A publican in town kindly drew

---

18 "The white man came and shot game and trespassed anywhere without permission. When a white man took up land or a station, he expected the blacks of that locality to move back into other territory, unconscious that this would be an unpardonable violation of tribal laws, and involve immediate deadly warfare with the adjoining tribes. Rarely had any white man attempted to learn a dialect or understand the customs of this peculiar people and those who did had no power to direct the course of events. So wars began between the two races and have continued with little intermission to the present time." Archibald Meston, March 1895 (Former Protector of Aborigines, Qld), "The Black War in Queensland," *Royal Historical Society of Queensland*, 23 October 1958, p. 115.

19 It is possible that Morrison is here disguising the identity of Alexander Kennedy, a Scottish immigrant pastoralist, and "the man who lead to the destruction of the tribes of North West Central Queensland", according to Iain Davidson in a study of the late 19th century anthropologist Walter Roth. *The Roth Family, Anthropology, and Colonial Administration*, eds Russell McDougall and Iain Davidson, Routledge, London, 2008, p. 127.

20 Here, Morrison describes the mineral riches of what is today Mt Isa, due west of Cloncurry.

21 The town was named in 1876 after Winton in Dorset. It was the first home of Qantas, an airline.

me a diagram by which I was to find my way to a hut on the McKinlay River, 104 miles distant. That map I keep as a curiosity. A distance of 9 miles was made to appear twice as long as one of 22 miles, a trifling inaccuracy which caused me unnecessary anxiety and torture. The first night I could not sleep from fear that I had taken a wrong turning. In the morning I started to go 35 miles without knowing whether there was water on the track, or even water where I was making to. My water-bag holds two quarts and a half, but the day was so hot—the thermometer registered 130 deg. in the shade of the hut I refer to— that by midday, although I had hardly wet my mouth, the water was all evaporated. Still I kept moving, but at half-past four I just knocked up. It came upon me most suddenly. Without any warning I was seized with an irresistible desire to throw off all my clothes. I had no wish in the world but to lie down. I camped under a tree. The anxiety of mind, for it was but a chance if water was within 13 miles of me, added to my thirst, and I suffered torments. All through the night I lay naked on my back, my tongue contracted to a point, my body hot and feverish, my brain reeling. Just as day dawned I staggered to my feet, but which way was I to turn, to the right or the left? In a brief intermission of my confusion I recollected that I had turned off to the tree to the right; but during the night I had got my head where my feet should have been, and I actually tried to pick up the track by walking away from it. But Providence watched over me, and set me on my way. I was so dazed that the track became more blurred and indistinct every minute. A wide plain now stretched before me, and a belt of timber at its further end gave me hope. I reached the creek and threw down my knapsack, and followed up and down the sandy bed for a weary distance, but it was as dry as the Sahara. On again, and another plain, with another belt of timber was to cheer or disappoint me. The creek was drier looking and sandier than the first one. I was throwing myself down in despair, when my eyes lit on a beautiful pool of water under the shade of a weeping ti-tree. The reaction quite unnerved me. I rested and drank all day. The mailman came up in the evening and gave me information about the country ahead. The contrast struck so forcibly. There were richly grassed instead of arid plains; creeks no longer dry and sandy, but sparkling with water, and plantations of timber, healthy and vigorous, not a parched and stunted forest. The twin parallel channels of the Williams River meander through a country as beautiful as an English park. Then a vast plain extends to the horizon, where, dancing grotesquely in the sun, is the timber marking the course of the Fullarton River.

Two days' walk from here is the McKinlay River, which drains an immense area of rolling downs. I was tracing up this river, cutting from one point of timber to another, and wondering whether the hut was above or below me, when I saw a man on horseback driving cattle. I drew nearer and nearer to him, and long before I could see his face I recognised the wild war song which had so often inspirited me in my voyage to the islands. This was a young Kanaka, a kindly nice lad, from Motualava,[22] beguiled from his home—one of the most beautiful islands of Polynesia—to tend cattle, to do fencing, to mix with gins, amid all the sultry dreariness and cheerlessness of the most utterly wretched district of the Never Never.[23] The manager of this cattle station was in Cloncurry, and the South Sea Islander was in sole charge. I was taken very unwell when with him, and for three days the Kanaka showed me the greatest kindness and attention. Leaving now the McKinlay River and steering diagonally over to its first sandy billabong, I traced it up till I came to an out station. In this stage of 30 miles I was two days without eating anything, during which I suffered much from thirst. The next stage was 25 miles over the ranges in which the Diamantina takes its source. The heat was something fearful, there was an entire absence of animal life, a faintly marked track which turned and twisted to every point of the compass and continually ran out, and no water, though billabongs and sandy creeks were crossed by the hundred. The only excitement that sustained me in my weakness was the fear of blacks— the wild kalkadoons[24] who are so greatly feared in the hills. At the head waters of the Diamantina a sheep station was being formed where the

---

22 Today known as Mota Lava or Motalava, it is a constituent island of Vanuatu. Morrison had visited it for a series he wrote a series of article about the use of Pacific islanders (known as kanakas) in the Queensland sugar cane industry.
23 Morrison's use of "never never" to describe to outback pre-dates by 16 years its use by Bancroft Boake, 1866–1892, who used the phrase in his posthumously published (1898) poem 'Where the dead men lie'.
24 When Morrison was traversing this part of western Queensland there was an undeclared war between the Kalkadoon (properly Kalkatungu) and settlers. This lasted from late 1870 until 1890 with the defeat of the Kalkadoon at Battle Mountain.

countless billabongs resolve themselves into one of the finest rivers in Australia, a river which shall perpetuate the name of Lady Bowen.[25] The Diamantina from its source trends away to the north-east, and then bends round in tho shape of a shepherd's crook. I was on it for 113 miles, having it for 50 miles on my left, then crossing it at Dagworth station, and having it on my right for 57 miles, till its junction with the Western at Elderslie,[26] one of Sir Samuel Wilson's[27] properties. Both here and at Dagworth[28] there was immense activity. Two or three years hence they intend having 300,000 sheep at Elderslie and a proportionate number on Dagworth. Fencing, tank sinking and building were proceeding with marvellous activity; wages are very high; any unskilled man can earn 30s. or 35s. a week;[29] he will be well fed, as a vegetable garden is now an essential part of a large Queensland station. I was out of the country where men are content to exist on salt beef and damper. The money spent by the squatters hereabouts chiefly finds its way into the public houses of Winton, a rising township on the Pelican Waterholes, near the Western River, placed on a high flat, with not a tree near it. The telegraph line is being extended from here to Cloncurry. Vinden[30] station, another magnificent sheep run, is 15 miles out of Winton. Fifty miles further is

'The Black War in Queensland', *Royal Historical Society of Queensland*, 23 October 1958, p. 171.

25 Lady Diamantina Bowen (née di Roma) was the wife of the first governor of Queensland, Sir George Bowen. An aristocrat from the Ionian islands she gave her name not only to a river but also to Roma, a town in Queensland, west of the capital Brisbane.

26 Wilson acquired that 3,108 sq km (1,200 sq miles) station before 1878. A decade later it had doubled in size.

27 Samuel Wilson, 1832–1895, an Irish Australia who settled in Melbourne in 1852, and had large land holdings in the three eastern states, producing £100,000 ($14.3 million) a year by the mid-1870s. From 1861–1881 he was active in Victorian politics, sitting in both the Legislative Assembly and Legislative Council at different times. Wilson Hall at the University of Melbourne is named after him. He returned to Britain and was Conservative MP for Portsmouth. He died in London.

28 Dagworth was established in 1876. Its chief claim to fame is that A. B. 'Banjo' Patterson worked on it, and it is there that he wrote 'Waltzing Matilda'. Christina Macpherson, daughter of the station's owner, wrote the music.

29 Approximately $235 in today's money.

30 *Vindex.*

10 | 'ACROSS THE AUSTRALIAN CONTINENT ON FOOT'

Evesham station.[31] Then there is a break in the open downs, and you pass through a lot of Gidya scrub country, through Maneroo station to the Thomson River—at this early stage, a trickle of peculiar white water which I stepped across.

The day after crossing the Thomson I was overtaken by an old gentleman on horse back whose companionship I found so agreeable that we travelled on together for 75 miles. He was a toothless darkie,[32] a native of the Gold Coast of Africa, a cook by profession, and one of the kindest, most considerate men it had been my lot to meet with. He would ride on ahead and open the gates that I might not break my stride. He would stint himself of water if the day were hot that I might have the more. And this is how we fell out. We had to go one day 25 miles carrying water. Though parched with thirst he would not take his share. Not to be outdone I also refused any water, and being annoyed I vowed that we must part. I am glad of an opportunity to record my sense of this darkie's kindness. John Smith was his name, and he was the first black man ever seen in Iceland, having been there when a boy on board a Dutch man-of-war which was taking Prince Henry of the Netherlands round the world. The Thomson River we left some distance on our right, two stations being situated on creeks running into it. On the Bimerah Creek is Bimerah sheep station, which, like all Fairbairn's[33] stations, is being rapidly improved on a princely scale. Twelve miles further there was a sudden change. The water in the Emu Creek was stinking; the fish were rotting in the mud, and the crows were in hundreds. Up to this creek grass had been in abundance. Not till I was overtaken by rain, 250 miles further on, did I again come to any. Now I had to pass through the downs and Gidya scrub, which had been the characteristics of the country for the last 600 miles, till

---

31 A property of 800 square miles, which in 1895, supported 200,000 sheep.
32 A casual racial slur which, in this case, can been seen more as descriptive of the man's colour than pejorative.
33 Sir George Fairbairn, 1855–1943, like Morrison, was born in Geelong. He managed sheep and cattle stations in Queensland for his father, pioneering the use of wire-netting to keep out kangaroos, of which Bimera was just one. He returned to Melbourne in the early 1880s to get married and run the family businesses.

in three days I walked into the township of Jundab.³⁴ There is a store here, a saddler and public house, and there will be other houses shortly. I shall chiefly remember it, because of the splendid dam of water in the Thomson and because of the interesting fact that every man in the township was more or less drunk. All were lost in drunken amazement at my prodigious walk. I was now an experienced swagman. My swag was carried New Zealand, or knapsack, fashion. The tucker, spare shoes, socks and shirts, some reading matter and a hammock, the matches, baking powder and canvas basil were rolled up in a single blanket, and the whole then enveloped in a strip of oilcloth and borne on my back, being kept by straps passing over the shoulders. In this way only could I secure the untrammelled use of my arms. The swag was seldom less than 20 lb.; above this its weight varied according to the distance I had to carry tucker. I seldom travelled by night; the heat of the day never troubled me. Indeed, it is my favourite boast that I have yet to see the day that is too hot for me. My own dress was cabbage-tree hat, flannel shirt, and tweed trousers; afterwards replaced by moleskins, and a knife belt and sheath. Boots I wore two sizes too large, and as I always cut the stiffening out of the back before using them, I escaped that soreness of heel which has troubled me on my former walks. Upon arriving at a station I went straight to the store, bought what rations I required, and camped by the most convenient water. The greatest hospitality was always shown me at stations where I was known, but I made it a rule to be as independent of all help as possible. When I had decided to camp I spread the oil cloth, and having lit a fire put on my salt beef to boil in the billy. By the time it was done, and the quart of tea made, I had a Johnny cake³⁵ or flatjack ready for cooking on the raked out coals. The former differ only in size and are distinct from a damper in that they are cooked on the hot embers, whereas a damper is baked in the hot ashes with hot embers outside. No wood that I have seen can equal the Gidya for giving the very ash and ember most valuable to us. A johnny cake made with baking powder is a most delicious scone—the very best

---

34 Jundah, which means 'woman' in the local Kuungkari aboriginal dialect, is 1,100kms south of Normanton, located on the Thomson River.
35 A Johnny cake is a quick bread, or damper, made from wheat flour. Morrison cooked his on a bed of hot coals. A skillet also can be used.

baking powder is Eno's fruit salt.[36] Or course, I did not restrict myself to these two articles of diet. I would vary them with apples and rice, sago or arrowroot, and occasionally with beef tea and potatoes. Preserved potatoes, when prepared in the water in which you have boiled your meat, are most delicious. Soda is an excellent baking powder; the johnny cake becomes a beautiful yellow, so that you can imagine you are eating bread made with milk, butter and eggs. At the stores—every station has its store—flour was 9d. to 1s. per pound, rice 1s., apples and potatoes 1s. 3d., and meat, though most of the stations do not charge for it, was 3d. to 6d a pound for salt beef.

But to return! No one in Jundah could give me any lucid information where water might lie in the next 65 miles. It is the uncertainty which predisposes to the fever of the palate. With the river in sight on my left, and never more than 5 or 6 miles from me, I knew that I could always get water by turning off to it. This, then, was well enough. But the least intoxicated man in Jundah was most positive that there was one stage absolutely without water for 18 miles. He had offered to fight anyone who contradicted him, yet his statement passed unchallenged. I therefore inferred that he was speaking the truth. If, then, I had been thirsty, had turned off 5 miles to water and found none this 18 miles, it would have gone hard with me. As it happened, my anxiety was uncalled for. At several places in the 35 miles cattle tracks crossed the path, and by following them I was always brought to water, but so stale and filthy that it gave me severe griping pains in the stomach, which interfered much with my walking. For a greater part of this distance my way lay through a corner of a vast cattle run owned by two men, and in extent larger than Yorkshire and Durham.

On the 15th of February I came to the most interesting river in Australia. Fifteen miles above this, the Thomson had joined the Barcoo. Wading waist deep through the combined stream, I passed half way to admire the glorious reaches of the river opened up above and below me, and the high banks crowned with magnificent timber. Every description of wild fowl floated idly on the unruffled surface of the current, and it

---

36 Today used as an antacid for upset stomachs, rather than scone making. It is a mix of sodium carbonate, sodium bicarbonate and nitric acid.

was idleness which reigned supreme over the encampment of blacks in the timber on the opposite bank. I was so delighted with seeing Cooper's Creek at last that, despite an empty tucker bag, I must need camp for the night on its margin. Seven miles from the crossing I reached a cattle station, and 28 miles further another. The sky now became overcast, the sun was rarely visible, and everything foreboded rain. I rested a day or two and went on. A slight drizzle fell persistently. Not heavy enough to keep me awake, it made all my things sodden. There was no sun to dry them, nor had I sufficient patience to steam them before a fire. Once I lost my box of matches, and calling at a house to replenish them was given as a favor 19 lucifers. These had to last me two days, sleeping out in the meantime. I cannot imagine any severer trial for one's nerves than when hungry, with no food cooked, nor any house within a day's walk, to have to light a fire in wind or rain with your last match.

On the 23rd of February the Thargomindah and Windorah mailman served me a dirty trick. While I was camped for lunch he and another man came up to me, both well mounted, and driving pack horses. It was a hot, sultry, thirsty day, and I had a larger stock of water than usual, having filled my two quart billy as well as my water bag. These men asked me for a drink, and, before I could stop them, they had emptied my billy of all but a cupful, though they were within 2 miles of water on horseback, while I was over 28 from it on foot. I made it a rule of my walk never to ask or accept a drink from any traveller, whether on foot or horse back. It gave me satisfaction to be independent even in this. The same evening of my meeting with the mailman a foot traveller overtook me and we camped together. We made an excellent break-wind, lit a roaring fire, for we were once more in Gidya country with abundance of firewood, and calmly settled ourselves for the night. But we were not long asleep before the slight drizzle which had forewarned us was succeeded by a heavy pelting rain that knew no ceasing. One could hardly believe the effect of that rain. In the morning our camp was on the only dry ground within sight. For 15 miles we did not see land. The track was a clearly defined channel between the bushes. The creeks were running into a very strong current, and we were so often in water up to our armpits that I travelled with nothing on but my shirt We reached shelter, there to be detained for three days. It rained for seventy-six hours at one stretch. In five days nine inches and thirty points fell. Dams were burst everywhere.

The whole country into Thargomindah has become a vast series of swamps and flooded creeks. Buckling to it, every danger vanished at my approach. Wading through swamps and swimming creeks with long distances to carry food, I yet experienced no fatigue; the dash of excitement kept it away. Where the swamp extended for miles it was but natural that in threading my way among the trees, with no guide but the sun, and water often to my breast, I should wander from the track, but a wide cast on the dry ground would as surely discover it to me. When the water was in motion, centipedes in hundreds and an occasional snake constantly floated across the path in unpleasant proximity. The snakes I saw in my walk were more varied than numerous. On the red Mulga ridges I killed several Mulga[37] snakes—a finely marked brown snake nearly 6 feet in length. When I was at the head waters of the Diamantina, a black passed me, trailing after him a snake 9 feet 6 inches long, and as thick as a cable. It is a kind of rock python, which often attains a length of 12 or 15 feet. The black would have me to believe that it was not deadly. It is a man's duty to kill every snake he can. I have killed the brown snake, the tiger snake, the poor harmless carpet snake, and a black snake with a blue belly. There were many I had no means of identifying, not the least interesting being an active little fellow, which was disturbed by my coming, and commenced to wriggle about in a moat fantastic way. Just as I turned for a stick it made one spring off the track and vanished down a hole not large enough to introduce your two smallest fingers. Many anecdotes of snakes were told me. People so unkindly take advantage of one's credulous inexperience.

The Bulloo I crossed in a boat; a deep wade then put me on the track to Hungerford. At Thargomindah I had laid in such a large supply of flour and beef that for 75 miles I was absolutely independent of everyone. Timber and water wore abundant. By this time I had trained myself to do with very little water. I could walk 25 miles without wetting my lips. The Corellas flock to water at sundown, the thirsty traveller need but be guided by them, and he will infallibly be brought to water. The Paroo was greatly swollen. I had been told to be careful, as the bed

---

37 Another term for a King Brown snake, a deadly viper.

of the river is thickly timbered with the Ypunyah.[38] The stream was not less than half a mile wide, and you cannot see the opposite bank till quite close to it. But caution was unnecessary. I walked slap in, and crossed without difficulty. Hungerford is across the river. The boundary between New South Wales and Queensland passes through the centre of the town. The hotel is in Queensland, where the licence is less; the store is in New South Wales, where there is free trade.[39] I had done with Queensland. Drinks were now 3d., and mutton was to take the place of beef. In crossing the Paroo, 20 miles below Hungerford, I waded in a careless way into the stream, with my heavy swag on my back. Gradually it got deeper; it came over my waist; it reached my breast, my chin then was in the water; the next moment I went out of my depth altogether. The current in among the lignum bushes was very strong, and being impeded with my swag and boots I was a long time floundering about before I could get into my depth again. The experience was of use to me. I stripped and found a passage among the trees; then, returning for my things, I swam over with them in comfort.

Not till I was 100 miles below Hungerford did I overtake the flood waters of the Paroo and wade through the last of the swamps. There were public houses now every 10 or 20 miles into Wilcannia. Away out in that wretched country of clay pans and sand ridges, with its uninteresting scrub, its vast flats of saltbush and occasional stretches of barren hills, I suddenly came on a beautiful lake which wandered away to the east till its outer margin was hidden. For a little while I felt enthusiastic about the country I was in, but having to toil for some hours through heavy sand my misplaced enthusiasm was turned into ridicule. The scene constantly opening before me seemed the very incarnation of dreary desolation. These days were very lonely. Weak and fagged, and badly in need of a spell, I could not rest till I was in Wilcannia. I got in an hour after the telegraph had closed on Easter Monday; it was Wednesday before I had the means of buying any food. With no

---

38 A species of eucalyptus.
39 In colonial times each state operated a separate system of tariffs and taxes. New South Wales was 'free trade', believing that the fewer tax impediments to trade the better. Goods in free trade jurisdictions were often cheaper than in protectionist states, such as Victoria.

money in my pocket, and camped on the flat below the hospital, where those vagrants who I have knocked down their cheques in the hells of this town rest till recuperated enough to start away with their swag, my experience of Wilcannia was not a cheerful one. Another young fellow was in a similar predicament to myself, but he knew a Chinese cook at one of the hotels, and twice sponged a supper. On the second evening another of us camped there was put in the lockup and got a fortnight. Another had been living on this flat for months; no one knew how he lived; he hadn't a sixpence. On the Wednesday I got money and gave a farewell *al fresco* feed to all the tramps and vagabonds, after which I left on the 70 mile track. At the end of the 70 miles is Mount Manaro station,[40] situated in the hollow of the enclosing hill. The way lies through vast clay flats of saltbush and mallee, interspersed with sedges of mulga, boree, leopard woods and sandal wood. The walking is heavy, and there is one stage of 23 miles without water. Above Ivanhoe the country is comparatively picturesque. Immediately after leaving it I got into the endless saltbush plains, the few clumps of box and pine on which can be seen such an incredible distance. The large box which gives its name to the One Tree Plain[41] can be seen 20 miles off. There are public houses every 10 or 12 miles. The landlady of one of them poses in Melbourne society as a squatter's wife. Up here she is known as the Scrub Turkey. I travelled now very rapidly. From Hay I passed through Deniliquin, Echuca, Rochester, Elmore, Heathcote and Kilmore, reaching Melbourne on the 21st of April. While in my own colony, it was a perfect picnic. Instead of immense tracts of country owned by one man, and given up to sheep, there were a succession of beautiful little farms, each with its haystack, its neat little cottage, its substantial fence, and its scene of vigorous activity. Ploughing was in full swing, clearing and grubbing. The beautiful hilly country, seemingly so fertile, and supporting so excellent a class of people, pleased me beyond measure. Certainly, I thought, my colony may be the smallest, but it is the healthiest and most beautiful of them all. This fact I have left to the last. I came 1700 miles through the interior of Australia without seeing

40 Mount Manara (not Manaro) Station is situated at Ivanhoe in NSW.
41 One Tree is situated on the Cobb Highway today. It was founded in 1882. The eponymous tree was blown down in a storm on New Year's Eve in 1897.

a kangaroo. My only objection to writing this account of my walk was a natural one. If it had never been written many people might think that I had done something wonderful. They will read this and see that any one who cared to take the trouble and give up four months of his time could have done the walk more quickly than I did, more easily, and with less discomfort to himself.

Memoirs

Chapter 11

Morrison's Life

Morrison dictated his 'Reminiscences', as he called this attempt at memoir, to his wife Jennie after taking up his position as Political Advisor to Yuan Shikai, President of the newly-formed Republic of China, on 1 August 1912. He married Jennie on 26 August 1912 so, given that the manuscript credits his wife as the transcriber, I take that to be the *terminus post quem* for its composition. More than that is difficult to say as he does not refer to the 'Reminiscences' in his letters or diary.[1]

The 'Reminiscences' take the story of Morrison's life from his birth in Geelong in 1862, until 1899 when he was about to embark on a trip to Korea for *The Times*. Along with his diaries and letters, all of which are housed at the Mitchell Library in Sydney, the 'Reminiscences' is one of the key starting points for anyone who wants to write about Morrison and, indeed, have been an important source for biographers and writers about him. I have not edited Morrison's text in any accepted sense of that word; the text is reproduced with all his quirks and non-standard elements intact, as typed by Jennie and corrected by him. What I have

---

1 Professor Lo says the 'Reminiscences' were started in 1911 when Jennie was his secretary, although most unusually for him he offers no substantiation. Jennie was hired in London in September 1910. Morrison did not return to Peking until March, 1911, by which time he was busy with the Chinese Revolution that would overthrow the Manchu Qing dynasty. The attribution of 'transcription' to his wife argues for a date after August 1912.

done is to make it a more approachable document for the reader by adding notes for the sake of clarity, and details of persons he mentions where I have been able to identify them.

As a memoir, its chief value lies in it being Morrison's account of his life and travels. It is a key source for anyone who wants to study Morrison's biography and has been much relied upon by his biographers. He is not, it must be said, a man given to much self-refection or introspection; it took his impeding death in May 1920 for him enter those waters. He is, however, a gimlet-eyed observer of the world (an excellent characteristic for a journalist) and an astute observer of character, as his assessment of Li Hung-chang, the leading Chinese statesman, demonstrates. His account of the Catholic church's ill-judged but, in the short term, successful attempt to place its bishops at the highest points of administration in China goes part of the way to explaining the suspicion in which the authorities hold it today. Morrison writes well and oftentimes humorously about his adventures and the events he witnessed, no more so than in his account of his subterfuge in crossing into Yunnan, southern China, in 1896 with a forged documents adorned with a pressing from the lid of a Van Houten's cocoa tin (it produced an impressive seal); Italy's failed attempt to jump on the bandwagon and secure territorial concessions in China; or, of Britain's ham-fisted negotiations in 1898 to expand its position in Hong Kong through a 99-year lease of New Territories adjacent to Kowloon in an account where his pursuit of truth outstrips his desire to support British interests.

The memoir ends with Morrison about to visit Korea. We know from his letters that he was hugely impressed by Japanese rule in Korea and the rapid industrialisation that it caused on the peninsular. Only later in his life would his attitude towards Japan change but that would have less to do with its treatment of Korea than its designs on territory in China.

I have reproduced some of the earlier footnotes of key figures to avoid unnecessary page turning.

'Reminiscences'

dictated by G. E. Morrison to his wife
ML MSS. 312/32

I was born in Geelong, Victoria, Australia, on the 4th of February 1862. My father, George Morrison, the son of a small farmer, or factor on the estate of Altyre,[2] in Morayshire, was one of seven brothers, five of whom, educated at Aberdeen University became well-known teachers. Four brothers, one of whom was my father, all living at the same time, held the Honorary LLD of the university.[3] One became Principal of the Glasgow Academy;[4] another was rector of the Free Church Normal School in Glasgow;[5] a third became the first principal of the Scotch College in Melbourne.[6] My father became principal of the Geelong College, while a younger brother[7] held for many years the post of Vice Principal of the Scotch College in Melbourne.

My father had a distinguished university career, winning in his final year the two chief scholarships of the University. He had an unusual memory, was an excellent shot, and in many respects was the best mimic I have ever known. For many years after he left Scotland he was remembered both at the university and in his native Morayshire, by this

---

2 An historic estate which, for the past 800 years, has been the seat of the Cumming clan.
3 An LLD is a Doctor of Laws.
4 Donald Morrison, died 1899. He was rector of Glasgow Academy for 38 years.
5 Also known as the Free Church Normal Seminary. Thomas Morrison died in 1898 after 46 years' service.
6 Alexander Morrison, 1829–1903, was the second principal of Scotch College, Melbourne, and the driving force behind the school's establishment.
7 Robert Morrison, 1835–1908.

remarkable gift. In 1857 he went out to Australia as assistant master at the Scotch College in Melbourne, of which an elder brother was the principal. Here he married in 1859 a Yorkshire lady[8] to whom he had become engaged before leaving home, my mother going out alone when quite a young girl on board one of the old sailing clippers. From shore to shore, the voyage, a fast one in those days, was 84 days.

Shortly after marriage, my father moved to Geelong on the shores of Corio Bay, 45 miles south[9] of Melbourne, one of the healthiest and most delightful towns in Victoria with a climate like that of the Mediterranean. Here he lived for the rest of his lifetime, and here were born to him five sons and three daughters, I being the second child but the eldest son. He opened a private school, which grew to be the largest of its kind in Australia. It had the standing of a Public School, and has since become a Public School. It was known as the Geelong College. Our holidays were spent 20 miles away at Queenscliff at the Heads, the entrance to Port Phillip Bay. We may not have been hard students but we lived healthy, happy lives, giving more time to outdoor play than to study. At my father's college I remained until 1880. In 1881, I entered Melbourne University as a medical student, and there I remained during 1881 and 1882. My tastes were those of the nomad. I loved books of travel; I love to travel alone. During the Christmas holidays. I followed my bent, each year travelling further afield.

In the vacation at the end of 1880 I walked from Queenscliff, at the Heads, round the coast of Victoria and South Australia as far as Adelaide, a distance of 652 miles. No incident marked the journey— it was only a walking tour. In Adelaide I had an experience, for, fired with a desire to see foreign countries I endeavoured to ship as a seaman on board a sailing ship bound for South America. My attempt failed. Had it succeeded, the whole course of my life would have been altered. I returned to Melbourne by steamer.

---

8   Before leaving from Australia, Morrison had become engaged to Rebecca Greenwood, 1838–1932, of Haworth, Yorkshire. She went to Australia before Morrison on a clipper that, from Gravesend, took 140 days to reach Melbourne. They were married in Melbourne on 4 February 1859. Pearl, op. cit., pp. 3–4.
9   More accurately south-west of Melbourne.

The young adventurer, Morrison c. 1880.
Mitchell Library, Sydney

During the year 1881, having been paid seven guineas[10] by the Melbourne *Leader* for the diary of my walk around the coast, which was published as *The Diary of a Tramp*,[11] and having made £10 by preparing the vocabulary of a Latin grammar[12] written by my uncle, I purchased a canoe and spent all my spare time in learning how to handle it. Every Saturday and Sunday used to find me in my canoe on the Albert Park lagoon, near Melbourne. With practice I was able not only to stand up in the canoe and paddle, but I could even balance myself standing on its rounded deck. To my canoe, which was built on the model of the Nautilus associated with the name of Warrington Baden-Powell,[13] I gave the name of the hero of my youth, the African traveller, Stanley. At the end of the year, having passed my first year's examination, I took the canoe by train to Albany[14] on to the Murray and launching the tiny craft, I paddled 1,555 miles down the Murray to the sea and then continued up the arm of the sea, known as the Coorong, parallel with the sea coast, to the coaching stage called Cockatoo Wells. By a curious coincidence I arrived at Cockatoo Wells on the 4th of February 1882 having on the same day of on the previous year arrived at the same spot when on my tramp around to Adelaide. The keeper of the shanty was a man who had spent some time in Spain. His stories thrilled my imagination, and for years I looked forward to the day when I might repeat his experiences. As fortune would have it, some years later I was able to see Spain even more intimately than he had done. Then having sent my canoe by coach to Robetown[15] and thence by steamer to Melbourne, I walked back to Geelong, 347 miles.

---

10 The equivalent of about $1,200 today.
11 Published in *The Leader* in four weekly instalments beginning on Saturday 1 May 1880, on page 1 of *The Leader* supplement.
12 The uncle was Alexander who, in addition to being headmaster of Scotch College, taught Latin and published *A First Latin Course,* a book widely used in Australian schools.
13 The brother of the more famous Robert Baden-Powell who founded the Scouts, Warrington, 1847–1921, was a lawyer and canoeing enthusiast who designed canoes and founded the Sea Scouts.
14 Here, he means Albury.
15 Now known as just Robe.

11 | 'REMINISCENCES'

This was quite successful journey for the account published from week to week in the Melbourne *Leader* more than paid for its expenses. I fear, however, the journey was more interesting and less tedious than the account thereof. Before the narrative was finished. Mr. G. A. Syme,[16] the Editor, repeatedly assured me that everyone was tired of it. It was wearisome, he said and monotonous.

At the end of 1882 I failed in my second professional examination. I failed in the subject of *Materia Medica*.[17] That I was unjustly plucked I have no shadow of doubt, but I bear no grudge to the examiner—on the contrary, his error was one of the fortunate episodes of my life.

Disgusted with my failure at the university. I decided, with the few pounds that I had saved to go away and gain some experience of my own country. From Melbourne, I had an exciting passage on the steamer Leura to Sydney. It was the stormiest passage I have ever known. Grave anxiety distressed the friends and relatives of the passengers because the Leura encountered one of the worst storms on record on the coast of Australia and a senseless report and found currency that the steamer had founded. From Sydney I went in the steerage on the Governor Blackall to Brisbane and along the coast of Queensland, to Port Mackay.

It was my intention to ship on a schooner engaged in the South Sea Island labour trade. At various ports where labour schooners were lying I tried to secure a berth, but without success. At Port Mackay, however, I was more fortunate. Here I shipped as an ordinary seaman onboard the brigantine "Lavina", Captain Smith, engaged in the South Sea Island labour traffic, recruiting Kanakas in the New Hebrides and Banks' group[18] for work on the Queensland sugar plantations. Commonly the traffic was called the slave trade, but it could not correctly be described as slave trade. Severe regulations control the traffic and each schooner carried a government agent or supervisor whose duty it was to see that

---

16 George Alexander Syme, 1821–1894, born at Montrose, Scotland, emigrated to Australia in 1863. Graduate of Aberdeen University in theology. Occasional editor of *The Age*, which his brother David edited, but mainly editor of *The Leader* (1863–1885) which was *The Age's* 'country journal', and the newspaper that carries Morrison's first journalism.

17 *Materia medica* is a Latin term used into the 20th century to describe what doctors now call pharmacology—the use of medicines and their effects on the body.

18 Vanuatu today.

the regulations were complied with. Poorly paid and often exposed to danger, the post of Government agent did not attract a superior class of official. With or without his connivance, there was systematic evasion of the regulations. Scandals increased, until eventually the government intervened, and for a time the traffic ceased.

We left Port Mackay on June 1st, 1882, and returned 100 days afterwards, on Sept. 8th. My account of the voyage called "A cruise on a Queensland slaver,"[19] by a "Medical Student", was subsequently published in the columns of the "Melbourne *Leader*".[20] Before leaving Melbourne, I had seen Mr. David Syme,[21] the famous proprietor of the Melbourne *Age* in the office of his brother, Mr. G A Syme. Mr. David Syme said that an account of the South Sea Island labour traffic would be welcome that the truth was desired because no one believed "that old liar, ———". In this irreverent way, he spoke of ——— of the New Hebrides, a famous missionary preacher, who had for years vehemently attacked the labour traffic as a criminal agency for the extermination of moral ruin of South Sea Islanders.

On my return to Port Mackay, after a stay of several days, I took passage again in the steamer "Ranelagh" for Cooktown. We left at midnight. The steerage is in the forepart of the steamer. All the previous night I had worked without rest finishing my report for the Melbourne *Leader* and was very tired. The steerage was crowded with miners going to a rush at the Palmer River gold diggings, but I found one empty berth and being very tired I turned in. Some hours later I heard a noise, which sounded like the chain running out of the hawse pipe. It only

---

19 This exposé consisted of seven instalments and was published in *The Leader* on: Saturday 21 October 1882, 28 October, 4 November, 18 November, 25 November, 2 December, 9 December. It is one of the earliest examples of investigative journalism in the English-speaking world.
20 'Melbourne' did not feature in the title of *The Leader*.
21 David Syme, 1827–1908, newspaper proprietor. Born at North Berwick, Scotland, emigrated to Australia (by way of the Californian goldfields) in 1851. He joined his brother Ebenezer is acquiring *The Age* for £2000 in 1856. He built *The Age* into a formidable voice in the development of Victoria and Australia. Outspoken on the need to protect Australian industry from foreign competition placing him in opposition to the 'free trade' advocates in Sydney. A campaigning proprietor especially in areas of social justice. A close friend of Alfred Deakin, 2nd Prime Minister of Australia.

half awakened to me. I thought we'd come to anchor in Bowen. I woke up to see the miners leaving the cabin, and I said to myself, we will have more room next day, and I turned over and went on sleeping, when suddenly I was awakened by a loud voice calling me, "Hey, mate, are you going to stay there all night with the ship on the rocks, and orders out for everyone to come aft?" I looked out, and saw that the water was over the cabin floor. I ran quickly up on the deck, and I could see the land quite close, the sea was calm, and I knew that if the worst came to the worst, I could swim ashore, so I came back to the cabin, put all my things together and brought them up on deck. When I left the cabin the water was well above my knees, but there was no danger and no need for excitement. We were taken ashore in the morning and waited until another steamer called to take us north.

The Ranelagh had a curious experience. This was its third voyage and its second shipwreck. On both occasions one of the passengers on board was the honourable P. Perkins,[22] a brewer from Brisbane and a member of the Legislative Council of Queensland. It is on record that sometime later, Sir John Robertson,[23] the lieutenant governor of New South Wales, a man well known for the bluntness of his speech was in Sydney and went to the shipping office to engage a passage on board the steamer Coogee bound for Brisbane running down the list of passengers his eyes caught his eye caught the name of Perkins. He'd be damned. He jerked out if he'd travel with that blank Jonah, and he abruptly left the office without taking his passage. His prescience was providential. The ship ran on the rocks, and there was great destruction and loss of life. It was one of the bad shipwrecks of the coast of Australia.

From Bowen I went on to Cooktown finding there cheap accommodation in an inferior public house in the lower end of town, kept by a lady affectionately known to her fellow townsmen as "Everybody's

22 Patrick Perkins, 1838–1901, an Irish catholic from Tipperary survived three shipwrecks, but died peacefully at Hawthorn, a eastern suburb of Melbourne. He made a fortune in the Victorian goldfields, started a brewery in Castlemaine, translated to Queensland where he had real estate, mining and brewing interests. His beer brand Castlemaine XXXX lives on to this day.
23 Sir John Robertson, 1816–1891, was five times the Premier of New South Wales from 1860–1886. He was never Lieutenant Governor. A rare error by Morrison.

Annie". While I was here, the missionary schooner "Ellengowan" came into port, having onboard the well-known New Guinea missionaries, the Reverend W. G. Lawes,[24] and the Reverend James Chalmers. I longed to see New Guinea, I asked them to let me go back with them to Port Moresby and offered to work my passage for I was sufficiently competent, my experience on the brigantine having given me the necessary knowledge. Moreover, work on a fore-and-aft schooner like the "Ellengowan", where the sales are handled from the deck requires less seamanship than I had acquired on the brigantine. The kind missionaries consented and leaving in a few days, we sailed across to New Guinea. The beauty of this voyage is deeply impressed upon my memory. I was at the wheel when the schooner has sailed down the coast, threading its way among the coral reefs running before the trade wind to Port Moresby. The captain was a native of Finland, named Liljeblad.[25] No difference was named made between me and the sailors. I berth with the men, kept watch and regularly took my trick at the wheel.

At Port Moresby I left the scooter, and stayed for a few days with the missionaries. Then, in the company of Mr. Chalmers, I went for a trip in the mission boat along the coast as far as Aroma where I saw the famous chief Kaopina, a man of giant stature, who when we will walk in together and came to a creek that had to be forwarded, would pick up Mr. Chalmers in his arms and carry him like an infant. Returning to Port Moresby, I would inland on a visit to a bird shooter's party conducted by Andrew Goldie.[26] The naturalist who had formed an unrivalled collection of orchids, the fish, birds and insects of New Guinea. After

---

24 William George Lawes, 1839–1907, an English missionary, was, with his wife and children, the first European resident in Papua. He published *A Grammar and Vocabulary of Language spoken by Motu Tribe, New Guinea*, in 1885. James Chalmers, 1841–1901, a Scot, who joined him in New Guinea was less a scholar than an explorer/missionary.

25 Frederik Hillel Liljeblad, 1849–1924, master mariner in the British Merchant Navy 1882–1914. He piloted the British squadron of warships during the 1884 declaration of the British protectorate of New Guinea.

26 Andrew Goldie 1840–1891, a Scot, was encouraged by the great botanist Ferdinand von Mueller, the creator of Melbourne's Royal Botanic Gardens, to go to New Guinea in search of flora and fauna. From the late 1870s he made his home at Port Moresby where he continued his studies in natural history and trade in exotic species of plants and birds.

some delightful days with him, I returned to the Mission Station, and as there was no other means of returning to Australia. I took passage in a Chinese junk engaged in the *bêche-de-mer*[27] trade and on the eve of returning with its season's catch to Cooktown.

Its Captain, a Cantonese named Ah Gim, had, while I was in Port Moresby, been married with much ceremony to a Raratonga woman, the widow of a native preacher, who had been brought to New Guinea by Dr. Lawes. Fervent had been the protestations of Mr. Ah Gim that he would uphold the missionary cause wherever he might be. On board the junk, when I knew him better I said to him one day: "So by and by you're going to become a missionary?" Pinching up his eyes he said, "You think me blank fool?" By this I judged that he would remain a sailor. There were 17 of us cooped up in the small junk, 12 Chinamen, two New Guinea natives, a Raratonga woman, a Maltese hybrid, and myself, and we were 23 days making the port we were bound for.

The Captain took no observations. He had a compass, and he travelled as he said, by dead reckoning. The distance across was 430 miles. When finally we sighted the Australian coast, the Captain reckoned we were abreast of Cairns, 80 miles south of Cooktown, and promised us a pleasant run before the trade wind at Cooktown. As a matter of fact we were 120 miles north of Cooktown beyond the Ninian group of islands,[28] and we had tediously to beat our way down the coast against the wind until we finally reached our destination.

Following a suggestion that reached me in Cooktown, I decided to go to Hongkong, and endeavour to enlist in the Hongkong Police. Fortune prevented me. The steamer "Euxine" in which I proposed to take passage for Hongkong refused to take me for any price within my means, so I was compelled to abandon the project. I was able to buy a passage only as far as Thursday Island. There I determined to take a steamer to Normanton[29] on the Gulf of Carpentaria, and to make an attempt that I had long contemplated, and had only temporarily abandoned because of the impossibility as I was told of travelling in

---

27 Sea cucumber is a popular delicacy in East and Southeast Asian cuisine.
28 The Barrow Islands.
29 Founded in 1868 as Norman, renamed Normanton in 1872. Home to nearly 1,400 persons in 2021.

the Gulf during the rains, to cross the Australian continent on foot from the Gulf of Carpentaria to Melbourne.

Two passengers were on board—one whom I was in later years to meet in China: the other, Frank Gaylord, an agent of Barnum and Bailey's circus, was on his way to the Northern Territory to purchase for a sideshow the six most hideous blacks obtainable for money, after which he was to proceed to Bangkok to take delivery of a white elephant that was not white, purchased on a previous occasion for the same enterprising showman.

At Thursday Island, although a stranger with no other claims upon his hospitality than that I knew his friend Mr. Chalmers, I was invited by Mr. Chester,[30] the police magistrate and ruler of the island, to stay with him until my steamer left for Normanton. Mr. Chester had a beautiful garden in which the prisoners worked. Outdoor exercise of this kind was found to improve the morale of the prisoners. Sentences, therefore, were apt to vary with the season and the amount of work required in the garden.

From Thursday Ireland I went by a small steamer to Normanton, arriving there on Tuesday, December the 19th 1882, and at once prepared for my journey. Every hour was precious for the rainy season was close at hand, the sky was already threatening. At the general store, I purchased a rough swagman's outfit, a Panama hat, heavy boots and corduroys an oil cloth and a blanket, a billy belly and a quart pot, and the evening of the same day, I started on my walk. It was my hope to reach Melbourne before the end of April. The distance was 2043 miles. Roughly speaking, it was my intention to follow the route taken 21 years before by the Burke and Wills expedition—that most disastrous of all Australian expeditions when every member of the party perished except one. My journey was accomplished without difficulty, other than that involved in constant physical exertion. If nothing else, my walk proved how great had been the progress of colonisation in the interior during the years

---

30 Henry Majoribanks Chester, 1832–1914, police magistrate for Thursday Island. In 1883, on the orders of Sir Thomas McIlwraith, he sailed to Port Moresby, and claimed for the British crown the 'unoccupied' eastern half of New Guinea. His actions were disowned by the British government until after the German annexation of the north east of the island in 1884.

that has elapsed since the Burke and Wills party met with its disasters. I travelled alone and unarmed, like any ordinary sundowner. Except on rare occasions I slept in the open. I was never molested, and I reached Melbourne, within the time appointed, having covered the 2043 miles in 123 days, including all stoppages. My route lay through Cloncurry, Winton, Hungerford, Thargomindah, Wilcannia and Echuca.

In Melbourne I arrived in perfect condition on April the 21st, 1883. At the request of Mr. David Syme, the Editor Proprietor, I wrote an account of my walk for the Melbourne *Age*. The narrative attracted some attention. It occupied four and a half columns of close print comprised 6000 words, and Mr. Syme paid me for it £4.10.0. At this time, much attention in Australia was being directed to New Guinea. I had freely expressed with my wish to return there. My desire was communicated to Mr. Syme and hit his fancy.

The result was that I undertook to return to New Guinea with the grand eloquent title of Special Commissioner of the Melbourne *Age*, but without any pay and without the remotest prospect of obtaining any. I was young and inexperienced and ardent. I cared nothing for money. I had a firm belief in my own future. I could not believe in the possibility of my failing and against the advice of my friends, I accepted a responsibility for which I was unfitted. My journey was ill-conceived and ill-prepared. The two companions whom I picked up promiscuously in Cooktown were not suitable helpers for a traveller. The two Australian natives whom I took with me from Cooktown were also ill fitted for travelling in a country like New Guinea.

Starting from Melbourne on the 6th of June, I reached Port Moresby in the middle of July, when I encountered every kind of difficulty. I do not care to dwell upon these disagreeable months of my lifetime, and I have destroyed every paper that I had in connection with my journey, and endeavoured to a face from my memory or recollection of it. Very ill at the time I'm only partly responsible for the series of articles on my journey subsequently published. The narrative I wrote was called 'My Failure in New Guinea'. But the exigencies of the newspaper required the adoption of a less modest title. I had no copy to speak of.

As might have been foreseen, my journey ended in disaster. On the 3rd of October, while travelling in the highlands, about 120 miles from Port Moresby. I was separated from my men and was marching alone

Group portrait, Morrison (2nd from right, back row) and his classmates and teachers in Edinburgh, 1886–7.
Alexr. Ayton, Edinburgh / Mitchell Library, Sydney

leading a horse, when, as I emerged from the woods into some high grass, I was treacherously struck down by two spears, one of which entered the hollow of my right eye, missing the eyeball by a hair's breadth, and the other struck me in the abdomen. The points of the spears remained in the wounds. They were sharp pointed wood. Through the devotion of one of my men, I was enabled to get back to the coast, badly lamed with the point of one spear in my body, and the other point wedged in the back of my throat, between the first and second cervical vertebrae. My voyage back to Melbourne, defeated and wounded, was the most disagreeable experience in my lifetime.

It seemed to me as though I had been lamed for life. The point was in my throat for 169 days, and was then extracted without chloroform, through my right nostril, by the leading surgeon of my time in Australia, Mr. , afterwards Sir Thomas, FitzGerald.[31] The other point remained in

---

31 Sir Thomas Naghten FitzGerald, 1838–1908, Irish, arrived in Melbourne in July 1858. He was reputed to be a brilliant surgeon, noted for his diagnostic skill, who rose to the top of medical practice in colonial Australia.

my body 260 days.³² In the meantime, I had gone home to Edinburgh to continue my medical studies when it was cut out from the extra peritoneal tissue above the external iliac artery by Professor John Chiene,³³ the professor of surgery in the University of Edinburgh. I was a patient in the students' ward of the Edinburgh infirmary, and my case attracted some attention.

I had arrived in London suffering severely and was at first admitted to St. George's Hospital. On the 20th of May I entered the infirmary and it was not until July 1st, when my strength was much reduced that the operation was performed in Edinburgh. Professor Chiene operated in the presence of 17 surgeons, several of whom have since become famous. The surgeon whom I had selected to be his assistant being Dr. Joseph Bell,³⁴ the original of Sherlock Holmes. Professor Chiene was not more pleased than I was at having removed the spear point. A year later, he gave a dinner in honour of my recovery. When he expressed his intention of sending my parents a model of the spear head in gold. It was very pleasant for me to hear this, and I wrote to my parents in Australia, telling them of the gift that would soon reach them. But the gift was never sent. In 1895, I was again in Edinburgh, graduating from my doctorate and it was pleasant for me again to meet the professor to whom I owed so much. He then said to me: "Man, I have long intended to send your father a model of the spear head *in silver.*" I again wrote to my parents in Australia, telling them that they will shortly receive this valuable souvenir, but the model was never sent. Some years later when I met the cautious Professor a third time, I was disappointed that he did not offer to send me a model of the spear point in bronze. But this by the way.

---

32 A marginal note in the MSS says: "? longer—does not tally with the dates" Indeed not; from the date of the injury (3 October) until Prof. Chiene's successful operation (1 July), 271 days had elapsed.

33 John Chiene, 1843–1923, professor of surgery at Edinburgh University; president of the Royal College of Surgeons. The Chiene Medal is to this day presented to the top surgery graduate of Edinburgh University. Morrison was to study under him.

34 Morrison was correct in saying that Bell, 1837–1911, was credited with being the inspiration for Conan Doyle's celebrated detective. Bell was a pioneer of forensic science; he emphasised the importance of close observation in diagnostic work and he occasionally assisted police in their investigations.

I was in the Edinburgh Infirmary for 80 days, leaving on the 7th of August 1884. After my recovery, I went on with my medical course in Edinburgh. I previously had been in at the medical classes in Melbourne, and the time I spent there was allowed to count towards my graduation. I was able to begin work on the 6th of January, 1885 and providentially I passed on the 6th of July 1887, having in two years and six months passed the preliminary first, second and final examinations. There is no question but that I worked hard. I was anxious to finish my course as quickly as possible, and travel around the world. On the first of August, I graduated and a few days later, having fortified myself with a certificate and at the emigration depot in Edinburgh, testifying that I was a bona fide emigrant and with £15 in my pocket, I started for St. John's in Newfoundland, in the S.S. *Hibernia* of the Allan line.

I went as an intermediate passenger having paid £6 for my passage and being entitled to better treatment than a passenger in the steerage. Three other passengers shared my compartment. One I remember well, he was a pork sausage manufacturer of Glasgow, he used to tell me, one pound of pork will give the flavour of pork to 40 pounds of inferior meat and that which costs three pence per pound can be sold for six pence. For years he had made he assured me £700 profit a year. And he was now on his way to become a prosperous farmer out west.

From St. John's I went to Philadelphia, arriving there in time to be present at the celebrations on the 15th, 16th, and 17th September of the Centennial Anniversary of the adoption of the American Constitution. I saw General Phil Sheridan[35] riding at the head of the American troops and I was present on the day when addresses were delivered by President Cleveland and other celebrities and the Commemoration hymn by Marion Crawford[36] was sung on the great staging at the back of Constitution Hall.

---

35 Philip Henry Sheridan, 1831–1888, a protege of Ulysses S. Grant in the American Civil War, was instrumental in forcing the surrender of Robert E. Lee at Appomattox in 1865. He subsequently fought against the plains Indians and rose to become General in Chief of the US Army.

36 F. Marion Crawford, 1854–1909, was an American writer now largely forgotten. *A National Hymn* is dated 1 August 1887 and begins:
"Hail, Freedom! thy bright crest / And gleaming shield, / thrice blest ..."

11 | 'REMINISCENCES'

Aimlessly I wandered about Philadelphia for some days. Strolling one day along the river, I saw a steamer unloading bananas from Jamaica. At once it occurred to me that I ought to go to Jamaica. I went to the agent and asked him the price of passage. My imagination pictured Jamaica as a small island which could be crossed in a day's walk. The agent said $50. "Nonsense", I replied, "I can go to New York and go to an Atlas Steamer for $50." He said, "what are you willing to pay?" Assurance failed me. Instead of offering $10 which was more within my means and compounding for $20, I offered $20 and we compromised with $30, but I forgot to ask what part of Jamaica the steamer was going to, and was surprised when I found myself landed in St Ann's Bay on the north of the Island, when my destination was Kingston on the south.

By this time, I had little money left, and when I bought my passage to Ewarton my pocket was almost empty. In Kingston I took a room with a negro lady in 54 Duke Street, and then set about trying to obtain employment as a doctor. I applied for a post in the medical service of the island, but there was no immediate vacancy. When my resources were exhausted, I had no alternative but to go into the interior, and endeavour to obtain employment upon a sugar plantation. I took passage by train to Ewarton, arriving there in the evening, and walked on in the beauty of the night.

In the morning hearing that a doctor was in the neighbourhood, I walked over to him. Nothing could exceed the kindness that was shown to me by this generous man. His name was Dr. Frank Rand. When I told him of my circumstances, he said at once that there was no possibility of my obtaining the appointment I was looking for. He advised me to leave the Island and said he would lend me the money to enable me to make a short tour before doing so. With the money he lent me I started on foot and walked over to Falmouth, and from Falmouth around the coast to Montego Bay, and then crossed back over the island to Black River, and finally home to Porus, and from there came back by train to Kingston. Travelling as I did, a "walk-foot buccra"[37] I excited the derision of the niggers and still more of my white countrymen. A white man walking in Jamaica, they said, was an "insult to the Almighty."

---

37 An African-American word to describe a white person.

Morrison brooding at Ellenville, New York, 1887.
Mitchell Library, Sydney

In Kingston I learned that opportunities of employment were open to me on the mainland, either at the Panama Canal, or on the Costa Rica railway. Agents were engaging men in Jamaica, but not professional men of my class. In each case the answer to my request was the same. Gladly would gladly would employment have been given me had I only known Spanish. It may seem ridiculous, but I detected in this, it but I detected in this the hand of Providence directing me to go to Spain, and I remembered the intercourse I had had at the Cockatoo Wells in South Australia with a shanty keeper who had lived in Spain and his stories that country of ancient glory had fascinated my imagination. I determined to go to Spain. That intention beset me and was not to be shaken off. But Spain was far distant from Kingston, immensely far for a man whose pockets were empty. At this critical time opportune help was given me in Kingston I had become known to two men: one a namesake of my own, was the editor of the *Colonial Standard* and heard my story. He gave me a little money, another Captain W. Peploe Forwood,[38] the agent in Kingston of the Atlas Steamship Co., did better than give me money. He offered to give me free passage back to New York, shipping me as an Assistant Purser. For New York then I started, determined to make my way to Spain.

On the Atlas steamer "Alps", if work it could be called where work was none, I worked, sitting on a chair with my heels on the rail, keeping tally of the oranges and bananas brought on board the steamer at Morant Bay and Port Antonio, where we loaded our hatches before setting out for New York.

On my arrival in New York on the 4th of November, I was the possessor exactly of $7.13. The month was bitterly cold. I was clad as for the tropics, and the outlook was not good but I secured a room at 203 West 19th Street with a Mrs. Davis, paying $2 a week for the room in advance. It was way up the top of the building and was very cold. I warm

---

38 Captain Wellington Peploe Forwood, 1851–1916, was a prominent English shipping agent and civic leader based in Kingston, Jamaica. Morrison kept in touch with him. In 1896 he wrote to Morrison to thank him for a copy of *An Australian in China* he had sent him. He called him "one … honest man that I have met in my travels, referring, of course, to you and your sending the company ten shillings." Morrison repaid his debts. ML MSS 312/42.

the room by keeping the gas burning, but on the second day the scheme failed, the landlady telling me that when lodges paid only $2 a week in advance, they're expected to put out the light at night at 9 o'clock. Then I was colder than ever. I tried for various appointments in New York. Among others, I applied for the post of warder at $30 a month at the New York Hospital in 15th Street. With a motley crew I waited in the ante-room, and we passed in one by one, and were questioned by the secretary as to our qualifications. When it came my turn, I showed him my testimonials. He said, "How do I know that these have not been written by yourself?" I said, that had they been, they would have been more flattering. He said, "You would have to obtain the guarantee of some reputable citizen of New York that the testimonials were genuine, and while doing that I could obtain a hundred competent to fill the post. He spoke to me kindly but there was no hope of my employment.

Little by little I pawned by things. The first thing I parted with, and reluctantly, was my cardigan jacket, the only warm piece of clothing I possessed. I left this with Simpson's of 171 Bowery. What did I want for it, he asked? I suggested $5. He offered me $1, and I accepted it with much unwise alacrity, that he picked up the garment again, saying that he had not observed a certain disproportion between the length of the body and the length of the arm. Now that he noticed this he could only, he said, offer me 75 cents. It was ungenerous, but I had no alternative. For all I know the jacket is still in his possession. A small surgical instrument case kept me in food for some time. But I fared badly having, only one meal properly so called every second day, when I went to Beefsteak John's in the Bowery, and had some pork and potatoes for 10 cents.

Finally, a man I met named Junner M. Croll,[39] seeing from my credentials that I was a genuine case, and knowing that I wished to go back to Scotland, with great generosity obtained from your passage to Glasgow for $30. I undertook to pay this amount on my arrival in Glasgow, and he gave me an undertaking that if I did not pay him the passage he would do so.

---

39 Junner M. Croll, 1852–1916, was born in Edinburgh and emigrated to the US. He is buried in New York.

11 | 'REMINISCENCES'

Thus, after 24 days of poor feeding, I left New York on the 28th of November on my return to Scotland to look for employment in Spain. My steamer was the Anchor liner Ethiopia bound for Glasgow, and I shared a cabin with two men. One had been a valet to Sir Arthur Hayter,[40] and had a marvellous knowledge of the interrelations of the British aristocracy. He was a Walking Peerage. The familiarity which during our fortnight's crossing I then acquired with the names of our hereditary aristocracy, has ever since served me in good stead, especially among English people, who have sometimes mistaken my familiarity with the name for familiarity with the person. From my childhood I had reverent love for our hereditary aristocracy, the noble type sent to Australia, either as Colonial Governor or as remittance man having permanently impressed my admiration.

My other cabin mate was a recent but earnest convert to Mormonism who was in the oil trade in Liverpool. His domestic life was unhappy. His wife was a termagant. He confided to me in picturesque detail how he would like to "knock the (blank) thing's head off." He had been in this frame of mind when a Mormon apostle had approached him and urged him to change his faith. He had gone to Salt Lake City intending to marry again and start life anew, but to his discomfort he found he could only become sealed to a second wife provided he had obtained the consent of the first one. He was now ruefully returning to Liverpool on this forlorn quest. Some years after I was in Liverpool and saw my old merchant. He had never returned to Utah.

As soon as possible after my arrival in Glasgow I came through to Edinburgh where I was known, and set about obtaining employment in Spain. To everyone I told the same story that I wanted to go to Spain. I did not know what appointments were open. I knew no one in the Peninsula, but I felt confident that as it was my intention to go there a place would be found for me. As time went on and I was still in Edinburgh, my friends would joke with me upon my failure to go to

---

40 Arthur Divett Hayter, Baronet and 1st Baron Haversham, 1835–1917. Liberal politician in Gladstone's government, 1880–85, first as a Treasury minister, then the War Office.

Spain. One evening, I met Littlejohn,[41] the present Professor of Medical Jurisprudence in Edinburgh. He said to me:

"You want to go to Spain?"

I said I did.

He said, "There's a doctor from Spain at present in Edinburgh. I know nothing more. I don't even know his name."

Here was my chance. Without loss of time I made inquiries, and very soon I learned that there was a Dr. J. S. Mackay in Edinburgh who was the senior medical officer of the Rio Tinto Co. in Spain. I found his address and went to see him and told him that it was my wish to go to Spain. I gave him my credentials, and told him how I had passed the previous years of my life. He said he would do what he could to help me and, and advised me to apply to him formally for a post in Rio Tinto. Then, while I was waiting, I found to my disappointment that he had been suddenly called back to Spain. Since my money was exhausted, there was nothing else for me to do, but to go as *locum tenens* in the country and await developing. I got to post as *locum tenens* in Portree in Skye and remained three weeks and heard nothing more about Spain. Then I came back to Edinburgh. Captain David Gray[42] of the "Eclipse", the famous Arctic whaler, sailing from Peterhead, offered me the post of surgeon on board his ship going to the Arctic, but the idea of going to Spain obsessed me and I refused the offer. So I waited on, and yet no news came. Then I was tempted by the offer of a post as surgeon on a steamer trading to the West Coast of Africa. I was given until 10 o'clock on a certain Monday morning to accept the post or not, when providentially late on Saturday night a telegram was handed to me containing the words, "All right buy Spanish grammar Mackay" In a few days, I received a letter from Dr. Mackay confirming his telegram saying I had been appointed assistant surgeon in the Rio Tinto mines on six months probation, and I was to go to London and report myself

---

41 Sir Henry Littlejohn, 1826–1924, famous for his work in public health, and forensic medicine.

42 David Gray, 1829–1896, commanded the *Eclipse*, a steam powered whaler that was built for him. He was her captain from 1867–1890.

to Mr. Hugh Matheson,[43] the head of Matheson and Co., the London agents of the Rio Tinto Co.

In London, I saw Mr. Matheson. He was a pietistical Presbyterian elder, who was confident, he told me, that I would fulfil my duty as well, and at the same time, could help to bring the word of Grace to the heathen in Rio Tinto.

Sailing from Cardiff, in a cargo steamer bound for Huelva, the port of the Rio Tinto mines, I arrived there on the 8th of May 1888, and immediately proceeded to the mines to take up my duties. Huelva itself possesses little of interest, but on high land, on the other side of the harbour, is the famous monastery, La Rábida,[44] where Christopher Columbus received help when preparing for his voyage to the New World. Lineal descendants of his fellow voyagers still live in the neighbourhood. I think I can boast that lineal descendants of the discoverers of the New World have been under my benevolent care.

Three months after my arrival in the mines, Dr. Mackay resigned his post as senior medical officer, and I was appointed in his stead. There was a staff of eight Spanish doctors and three British doctors, and a medical attendance had to be given to 9500 workmen and their families. Nothing of interest marked my time in Rio Tinto. It was a godforsaken spot. Sulphur smoke pouring forth from the calcining of the copper ore devastated the country from miles around. I was thankful to be able to leave Rio Tinto. On August the 7th 1889 I sent my resignation. The immediate cause of my resignation was this. As head of the medical service I had discovered an extensive series of frauds involving several thousands of pounds per annum in the druggist department attached to the medical department. On my sending the Company a report upon the fraud, I received an admonishing letter in reply expressing the grave disapproval of the directors at the unbecoming language in which my report was couched. I resigned two hours after getting the letter.

---

43 Hugh Mackay Matheson, 1821–1898, was a Scottish industrialist, businessman, and minister who was a senior partner in Matheson & Co. and founder of the Rio Tinto corporation. He declined an invitation to join his uncle's firm, Jardine Matheson, because of its involvement in the China opium trade.

44 Founded in 1261 by the Franciscans. Columbus visited it in 1490 and discussed with the monks his plans for a voyage of discovery.

Portrait of Morrison taken in Huelva, Spain, 1888.
Mitchell Library, Sydney

11 | 'REMINISCENCES'

It appears that the frauds I discovered were insignificant compared with other frauds that soon came to light of which even some of the directors who had admonished me had not been guiltless.

My relations with the Spanish were friendly, and I had no unpleasantness. But their ignorance was astonishing. There was considerable feeling against the medical department, for the maintenance of which 1% of all men's wages were allotted, and the chief of the department had to go warily. For example, it was difficult to expel from hospital anyone who declared that he had been injured at his work. He might obviously be malingering, but he could not be discharged so long as he merely declared that he was ill. In these cases we had a consultation in the presence of the malingerer. Suppose a man pretended that his knee had been injured at his work. There might be no evidence of the injury, the man might be a bad character, and known to be shamming. The consultation was held by his bed-side. There was the patient, there were the Spanish nurses, there was the fat old English matron, there was Don Jesus Alonso, the senior of the Spanish doctors, Don Miguel Sanchez, the second myself. I had to speak first. I would say:

"No injury can I find in this knee. The trouble must be very deep seated. What do you advise and what do you advise? Don Jesus?"

Don Jesus: "There is no other remedy. We must explore the knee with a red hot cautery. "

"But," said Don Manuel, "the pain of doing that is something infernal."

"Yes," added Don Jesus, "and what is worse, the patient must suffer. You cannot in that operation, give the patient chloroform."

Then we would adjourn to the other room to finish the consultation. It invariably happened that a few minutes afterwards, the patient, fully dressed would come into my office, and say that he was leaving the hospital. I would advise him not to leave. He would persist in going, whereupon he will be given a pass which stated that he had left the hospital against the doctor's orders. This meant that he could not come back again under any conditions.

The miners were a rough class, the best workers coming from the province of Galicia. One day I had occasion to dismiss a workman named Antonio Tanco, who, having lost a leg by accident was being taught the trade a bookmaker in a boot-shop (*zapateria*) connected with the hospital. Early the next morning, a messenger came to my house asking me to come at once that a body was lying dead on the hill side by the path leading from the village to the hospital. With others I went over, and then we found the dead body of a young strolling player who was known to have been in the company of Tanco the previous night and had been the last seen alive when the two had left the end together. He had been stabbed in the back. He had fallen in his tracks, had risen to his feet, gone a few paces and again fallen: had again risen and again fallen a few steps further on and there had died. His struggles were marked by pools of blood.

Leaving the body we went over to the small one-room compartment in which Antonio lived, in a low terrace built by the Company for the workmen. The door was not locked. We entered and found Antonio, fast asleep in bed. There was no pretence—he was really asleep. We woke him and asked him why he had killed his friend. He seemed in no way abashed, but answered he killed him in self-defence. "And where is the *cuchillo*? (the knife) we asked. He said it was under the bed, and here we found it all bloodstained. For this murder. Antonio was sentenced to two years imprisonment.

One night I was returning from the town by the same steep path when I overtook a number of Spaniards who had been drinking, and were loitering along the way. One of them was carrying a goatskin of wine. As I passed among them, a young man pointed to the wineskin said to me, "Do you care to taste, Señor?" I said, "No, many thanks." I went on a step or two when the same man stepped after me repeated in a somewhat louder tone. "Do you care to taste, Señor?" I again said, "No many thanks," and I walked on through the men, when a few yards further on the same man a third time in peremptory terms said to me, "Do you care to taste, Señor?' As he said it I felt something prick into my leg. I turned quickly round, and found the man pointing at me with his rapier. My first impulse was to pull out my revolver, for we always carried a revolver, but I first said politely speaking, as if to the assembly:

"Caballeros, I'm the doctor of the hospital up there," pointing to our hospital. "I am on my way to attend to your sick compatriots. Do you wish me to see them when I am full of wine?"

11 | 'REMINISCENCES'

With one voice they cried, "The señor is right (*El señor tian razon*) and I walked on unmolested many of them saying to me, "Good night, go with God."

I left Rio Tinto on the 9th of November 1889. Returning by train to Huelva, whence after a day or two I made an excursion to the Tharsis mines where local tradition declares the Queen of Sheba obtained her riches. Then I went to Jerez and to Cadiz. In Cadiz I was present at the trials of a submarine invented by a young Spanish engineer named Isaac Peral.[45] All Spain went mad about this discovery. Pictures were seen in every shop in the peninsula, depicting the Peral restoring to Spain her ancient naval glory, every town in Spain and I believe every town in her possessions oversea gave the same Peral to one of its streets. In those days, I have heard spendings discussing the submarine and gravely declaring that among its miraculous merit, not the least, was the power at possessed of being able to travel more quickly under the water than on the surface. An immense crowd mounted the ramparts of Cadiz to witness the triumph. At the trials no proof was given that the vessel could move under water. The Spaniards were quickly disillusioned.

In Cadiz I lived in a hotel in the Plaza de la Constitución. At the head of the table sat a colonial set of Colonel Fernandez who was representing the Spanish government in connection with negotiations then proceeding for the purchase of American small arms. At the other end of the table set an American dentist whom I had met two years before in Philadelphia. I said to Colonel Fernandez, "It's a curious coincidence, but that American," pointing to the dentist, "and I stood together in Chestnut Street, Philadelphia, on September 17th 1887 and witnessed the march past of the American troops with general Sheridan at their head."

He replied in Spanish. "It is only the mountains that never meet. Where did you stand?" he added.

"Opposite to Drexel's Bank."

He said, "I'm married to a daughter of Drexel."[46]

---

45 Isaac Peral y Caballero, 1851–1895, a naval officer and designer of the Peral submarine, the first electric-powered submarine, whose maiden voyage was in 1888.

46 Colonel Fernandez had married well. The Drexels were a storied family of America capitalism in the so-called Gilded Age and prominent financiers. The bank Morrison

From Cadiz I crossed over to Tangier in Morocco. It was my wish to visit the interior, but I did not have that I did not know how this could be accomplished. One Saturday evening, I was calling upon a Greek chemist, Nicholas Dassoy.[47] When he said to me:

"Excuse me for being in a hurry, but I am leaving on Monday for Fez."

I said, that is a place I'd very much like to visit.

He said, "Then come with me."

"Done," I said, and so it was arranged.

It appeared that he had been called to attend the son of the Shereef of Wazan,[48] in the sacred city of Kazan. He spoke Arabic perfectly, and a score of other languages. He called himself, by the way, a British subject. I asked him how he could call himself a British subject, seeing that by his admission, his father was a Greek, his mother was an Italian, and he was born on a ship in New York harbour, and educated in Cadiz. He said the ship he was born on was flying the British flag—that made him a British subject.

I went with Dassoy to Wazan, and operated upon the Sharif. I lived in the Palace at Wazan, and had the run of the park and some Partridge shooting. From Wazan we went on to Fez to hand to the Sultan a wounded soldier, who had been shot in the leg on the occasion of the Sultan's visit to Tangier, some months before.

Shortly before my visit three English tourists, Lord Edward Cecil,[49] Captain Lindsay, and an English officer detached from his regiment in Gibraltar, had been in Wazan and had occupied the same rooms that

---

saw had already merged with J. P. Morgan's bank to become Drexel, Morgan & Co. It later became just J. P. Morgan & Co in which Drexel held a minority interest.

47 This may be Nicholas D. Dassoy, b. 1850, who, in 1871, was listed in the Gibraltar census as a "druggist."

48 The Sharif was one Sidi al-Hadj Abd al-Salam ben al-Arbi, d. 1891, leader of the Wazzanyyia Sufi order, and who, remarkably, married an Englishwoman, Emily Keene, styled *Shareefa*. She published a book in 1911 *My Life Story* which provides a rare glimpse of Moroccan life from a western female perspective. Situated in northern Morocco, Wazan is today known as Ouazzane.

49 Lord Edward Herbert Gascoyne-Cecil, 1867–1918, saw extensive service in the Near East and Africa. In the years up to World War 1 was a member of the Liberal government.

I was living in. Many years afterwards I was speaking of this visit at a dinner table in Peking, when our Military Attaché, Colonel G. Pereira[50] said quietly. "I was that officer."

In Fez, I met Kaid Harry MacLean,[51] the commander of the Shareefian Army, and the British Vice-Consul, Mr. Bewick, the brother of Mrs. Archibald Little[52] whom I was to know so well in China in after years. Returning to Tangier by Mequines, Larache[53] and Alcasar, I crossed over to Gibraltar and then for the next few months, I wandered through Spain, going from one end of the peninsula to the other, returning finally to Huelva and from there going back to England.

From England, I went to Paris to study at the Salpêtrière under Professor Charcot.[54] Unfortunately, the only day that I went to the Hospital, Charcot was not there. But I can truthfully assert that I did go to Paris to study at the Hospital Salpêtrière. In France I very quickly spent the money I had saved when in Rio Tinto, and when I finally returned to Australia, after an absence of five years and eight months I had in my possession only seven francs, and a very poor outfit, and owed £63 for my passage money.

I reached Australia on the 3rd of December 1890 and four months later, on the 21st of April 1891. I was appointed resident surgeon of the Ballarat District Hospital, an appointment I held for two years. This was

---

50 Brigadier General George Edward Pereira, 1865–1923, was the first European to walk from Peking to Lhasa. He died while en route from Yunnan along the Tibetan boarder.
51 (Kaïd) Sir Harry Aubrey de Vere Maclean, 1848–1920, Scottish soldier and Moroccan Army instructor. 'Kaïd' is Arabic for commander or leader.
52 Morrison is here being a little disingenuous. Cyril Pearl (p. 148) tells us that he always referred to her as "that awful woman" or "the detestable." Little prompted great soul-searching by Morrison about his relations with women when she observed to him in 1904 that he was "very shy with women." He brooded on this and was perhaps fortunate to meet shortly thereafter Miss May Ruth Perkins, a woman of appetites, with whom he had an affair, itself the subject of an erotic novel by Linda Jaivin, *A Most Immoral Woman*.
53 A city in northwestern Morocco. It is on the coast where the Loukkos River meets the Atlantic.
54 Jean-Martin Chalcot, 1825–1893, a celebrated French neurologist dubbed "the Napoleon of the neuroses," who in 1882, established a neurology clinic at Pitié-Salpêtrière Hospital in Paris, which was the first of its kind in Europe. Sigmund Freud studied with him shortly after the time Morrison went to Paris.

in some ways the most coveted hospital appointment in Australia, for the city is interesting, the climate glorious and the pay was generous. In giving me the appointment the committee paid attention to other factors than mere vulgar medical knowledge. On paying my visits before the appointment was made, I called first on the most aggressive member of the committee, Mr. George Smith,[55] a market gardener who had been in his time a handy man with his fists. When I spoke to him of my desire to be appointed, he said:–

"Wasn't you the young man walked across Australia." I said I was.

He said:– "We all admired that plucky feat. I don't think we will go far wrong if we appoint you."

And when I was appointed the press notices while generously referring to my going to Paris to study at the Salpêtrière, laid special stress upon the circumstances that I carried my swag across the continent of Australia.

For two years I remained in Ballarat then other arrangements were made. I decided to go to China, and having refused the post of surgeon on board one of the China's steamers, I took passage on the steamer "Tai Yuan" and came to Hongkong. Then I went over to the Philippines, hoping to get an appointment there because of my knowledge of Spanish and my possession of the Spanish authorization to practice, but I was unsuccessful. Returning to Hongkong, I went up the coast to Shanghai and then crossed over to Tiensin[56] and Peking.

After a few days in Peking, I returned to Shanghai and then crossed over to Japan. Most of my time in Japan was spent in the Seamen's Refuge in Kobe, the cheapest place that I have yet stayed in. The manager of this home was an ancient Englishman, who had, he declared fought, in the Battle of Chillianwallah.[57] His accounts of that battle in which he played

---

55 George Smith, 1828–1896, an Englishman who trained as a horticulturalist at Kew Royal Gardens. He was employed for four years at Windsor Castle and emigrated to Australia in 1854, lured by the promise of gold. In Ballarat he founded a horticultural business which prospered. Baron Von Mueller, who designed the Royal Botanic Gardens in Melbourne, proposed him for a fellowship of the Royal Horticultural Society of England.

56 Tianjin today.

57 One of the bloodiest battles of the British East India Company's conquest of India and the Punjab. Fought during 1842 in the Chillianwala region of Punjab (now Pakistan)

a conspicuous a part as Bill Adams[58] had done in the Battle of Waterloo, caused me infinite amusement, and I committed them to paper.

I was really hard up in Japan, in Kobe, when I sold my telescope for $12. I truthfully wrote to a friend in Australia telling him that I had come round from Yokohama on my first shirts studs, that I was at present living on my telescope, and that I hope to return to Shanghai on my surgical instrument case. And that happened. In Kobe I had conceived the idea of crossing China to Burma, and on my return to Shanghai, I telegraphed home for money, and with the assistance then send me I set out on my journey, an account of which I have published in *An Australian in China*.[59] On my arrival in Rangoon, at the end of the journey, I went round by British India steamer to Calcutta, and there I have narrated in my book, I nearly died from remittent fever.[60] When I was well enough to go on board a steamer I shipped as surgeon on board the steamship "Port Melbourne" bound for Auckland in New Zealand. Good luck now attended me. Five days out, an accident occurred. The rope of the ash bucket broke, and the filled bucket dropped down the sink. This was not an unusual occurrence, but what was unusual was the presence at that moment of Lascar fireman at the bottom of the sink. The ash bucket fell on his head and split his delicate skull from the frontal bone to the occiput. He was then brought on deck in a state of collapse: I cleaned the wound thoroughly, and by some miracle the man got well I was put ashore alive at Singapore. So pleased was the Captain with my skill that he would not forget the service I had rendered, and on arriving in Auckland he gave me free pass via Wellington to Sydney, whence I went on my home in Victoria.

This was in the end of November 1894. What was I now to do? Two alternatives were before me. I was offered £1,000 a year to stay in Victoria as a doctor, and found that I could go home to England as a

---

    in what is called the Second Anglo-Sikh War. Both sides claimed victory.
58 'Bill Adams' was a comic creation of George H. Snazelle, 1848–1912, who told a 'yarn' about Adams helping Wellington win the Battle of Waterloo. He toured Britain, the United States and Australia with his act.
59 Published in London in 1895.
60 Remittent fever is a fever that generates variable body temperatures throughout the day and is associated with typhoid and brucellosis.

surgeon, arriving in London with £30 and the manuscript account of my journey across China. There was never any doubt as to the decision. The craze of travel had bitten me. I had never seriously contemplated the discomforts of medical practice. I decided to go home.[61]

I shipped a surgeon on board the Lund liner "Warrego", Captain Ilbery, who afterwards went down in the ill-fated "Waratah".[62] No passengers were carried. I paid £10 for my passage to London, and did the medical work on board. As a rule surgeons who came home under these circumstances are callow youths fresh from the University, of whose inexperienced sailors are apt to take advantage. Two days out from Melbourne, the steward came to me and said:

"There's a man very sick and the fo'csle, sir. He would like to see you."

When I went to the fo'csle I found the most powerful man on the ship lying on his bunk groaning.

"I'm awful bad, doctor," he said. I examined him and was suspicious.

"Get up," I said, "and come aft" and I walked out. It was obvious that my examination had surprised his shipmates. Sheepishly the man came aft to the saloon, and there I mixed him in a thick tumbler of draught of quinine and castor oil and everything abominable I could find in the medicine chest, colouring the nauseous mixture with tincture of rhubarb, so as to make it look like ink. I handed it to my friend, and said:

"I think that will make you all right."

He touched his forehead, and said, "All right, sir. I'll take it forrard."

"No, you won't," I said, "you'll take it here. I want the glass. So I stood by, while he took the nauseous mixture, every drop. Then I told him to stay on deck, "keep your watch, don't turn in. The fresh air will do good." I saw no more of him for some days. Then one day he came to me looking really ill very sheepish and humble.

---

61 Morrison's friend Theodore Fink tried to get him a job on *The Argus* then the more prestigious newspaper than *The Age*, but its editor Edward Cunningham, said: "It's impossible. He can not write up to our standard." Not for the first time Melbourne's loss was London's gain. See Pearl op. cit. p. 72.

62 The SS *Waratah*, a passenger and cargo steamship of the Blue Anchor Line, went missing in July 1909 off the coast of Natal, Southern Africa, with the loss of 211 on board. Captain Joshua Edward Ilbery, 1840–1909, was in command.

Dr Morrison, Edinburgh, 1895.
Mitchell Library, Sydney

He said, "I'm not coddling yer this this time, sir."

I said, "I don't think you coddled me last time. How did you like that dose?"

"I think you know a thing or two, sir," he said.

"You fool, I said, "I have been in the fo'csle myself." I had no further trouble with the sailors during the voyage.

In London then I arrived with £30 and with a meagre outfit. I took a room in Burton Crescent at 6/6 (six shillings sixpence) a week and lived within my means. That was on the 15th of February 1895. On the voyage home, I had completed the account of my journey, and in London I tried to find a buyer. Eventually the manuscript, on the recommendation of Mr. Douglas Sladen,[63] was purchased by Mr. Horace Cox[64] of "The Field" for £75,[65] a sum with which I was well content. This was in April. While waiting for the book to be published I worked in the British Museum, writing a thesis for my doctorate on the subject of the "Hereditary Transmission of various Malformations and Abnormalities." These weeks were amongst the happiest of my life. My thesis was accepted, and on August 1st I graduated M.D. in Edinburgh.

During all this time, I had been endeavouring to obtain employment on some newspaper. There was trouble at the time in Venezuela, and in Cuba, and I thought that my knowledge of Spanish in my experience of travel might enable me to obtain an appointment, but every newspaper I applied to sent me the same stereotyped reply, that the staff was complete. Mr. Cooper[66] of the Scotsman advised me to try *The Times*, and Sir Henry Norman,[67] who was then doing brilliant work for the

---

63 Douglas Brooke Wheelton Sladen, 1856–1947, English author, poet, and first professor of history at the University of Sydney. Lived in Melbourne. Returned to England. Was a friend of Morrison and Sir John Monash. He wrote two volumes of memoirs.

64 Morrison had offered to manuscript to MacMillan and to Longman (he kept their rejection letters) before Horace Cox (died 1918). Cox was more noted as a publisher of specialist directories, among others, notably *Crockford's Clerical Directory* and *The Law Times*, and magazines such as *The Field*.

65 About £8,500 in today's money.

66 Charles Alfred Cooper, 1829–1916, journalist and writer, editor of *The Scotsman* from 1880 until 1906.

67 Sir Henry Norman, Bt, 1858–1939, British journalist and politician. When Morrison first met Norman he was Assistant Editor of the Daily Chronicle. He was a Liberal MP from 1900–1923. He was made a baronet in 1915.

Daily Chronicle, also counselled me to make application to The Times, but I never ventured to do so. In London Sir William Gowers,[68] the great authority on nervous diseases, had been struck by something I had said in my book regarding the blunted nerve sensibilities of the Chinese,[69] and he asked me to come and see him. At his house, I met Sir Henry Howorth,[70] the author of the standard history of the Mongols. To them I confided my desire to find employment on a newspaper. One day at the Athenaeum club I understand that Sir William Gowers spoke to Mr. Buckle[71] the editor of The Times, telling him of my wish and that he communicated the message to the manager, Mr. Mobley Bell.[72] The result was that on Tuesday, October the 22nd, to my profound astonishment, I received a letter signed C. F. Mobley Bill asking me to call on him "at about 3.30 pm Wednesday, Thursday or Friday". When I received the letter, I was worth considerably less than one sovereign. Every day, therefore, it was of importance, and I purposed calling on Wednesday, but confided my intention to Thomas Waters, retired British Consul General from the China service, whom I had got to know in London he said to me, "That would be bad policy. They will think you too eager. Better go on Thursday." So I went on Thursday, and Mr. Bell said to me:–

68 Sir William Richard Gowers, 1845–1915, was a pioneering British neurologist and hailed as one of the greatest clinical neurologist of all time. Morrison would maintain a correspondence with Gowers for many years.
69 See Morrison's, *An Australian in China*, London, 1893, pp. 97–8.
70 Sir Henry Hoyle Howorth, 1842–1923, Conservative politician, barrister, historian. He wrote a three-volume history of the Mongols and a separate biography of Genghis Khan and his ancestors, together with a three-volume history of the English church up to the eighth century.
71 George Earle Buckle, 1854–1935. Buckle was appointed editor of *The Times* at the age of 30 and remained editor for 28 years, until 1912. His career was marred by the publication of forged letters attributed to Charles Parnell, an Irish nationalist. In retirement Buckle completed the biographer of Disraeli started by Moneypenny (see note 73) and edited and published three volumes of Queen Victoria's letters.
72 Charles Frederick Moberly Bell, 1847–1911, was Managing Director of *The Times* from 1890 until his death in 1911. He was hired to improve *The Times'* business operations, having reported from Egypt, about which he published three books. Under his management *The Times* expanded its foreign coverage, launched its still published Literary and Educational Supplements, and entered into business with the *Encyclopaedia Britannica*.

"I don't know where I heard of you, but I read your book. Would you care to go to Peking as our correspondent?"

I said:– "I will have to think over the matter."

"If you went," he asked me, "what salary would you require?"

I told him that in my two previous appointments, I'd been paid the equivalent of — pounds a year. He replied, "You will have at least that." Then he said, "But why do you hesitate to go?"

I said, "Because for some time past I had been studying the subject of Siam and French Indo-China. Relations between England and France regarding Siam have been critical. My hope was that I might be sent there as a correspondent."

He said, "Compared with China, Siam is of minor importance to us. Will you come and dine with us quietly one evening?"

"I am in an embarrassment," I said, "because I have no dress clothes. I was hard up," I added hastily, "and I sold them."

This made him laugh. He said, "Never mind about your dress clothes, but come and dine with us". I agreed to it. And among other things, he said to me was:–

"Have you read the articles by our Special Correspondent who has lately been in China?" I had read them. They were the articles by Mr. Valentine Chirol,[73] which were afterwards republished in a book called *The Far Eastern Question*. He said:–

"If you come to dinner, you will meet the author of those letters." I said I wished him to understand at once that I could never hope to approach the standard of excellence, the power and the literary ability displayed in those letters.

I went to dinner and met them Mr. Chirol, Mr. W.F. Monypenny,[74] the biographer of Disraeli and later in the evening, Mr. Buckle, looked in

---

73 Sir Ignatius Valentine Chirol, 1852–1929, was a distinguished journalist, author, historian and diplomat who was head of he Foreign Department (Foreign Editor) of *The Times* from 1892 until 1912. He coined the term 'Middle East' for a series of articles he wrote for the paper and published as a book in 1903. An arch imperialist he was described by Sir Neill Malcolm, "as the friend of viceroys, the intimate of ambassadors, one might almost say the counsellor of ministers ... one of the noblest characters that ever adorned British journalism."

74 William Flavelle Monypenny, 1866–1912. Journalist, editor, author. He was Buckle's assistant from 1893 until 1898 when he became editor of *Johannesburg Star*. He

on his way to the office. This was the turning point of my career in a few days it was arranged that I should have my wish that I should leave for Siam and Indo-China on November the 21st on probation for six months to carefully study and report upon to *The Times* only the political, financial and commercial position and prospects of Siam. My mission was to be a confidential one. A sum of — pounds was to be entrusted to me. I was to travel as an Australian doctor interested in the commercial development of Siam and Australia, and I was to report especially upon the truth of the alleged action of the French government in registering the Cambodians as French subjects. At St. Erwin's Mansions, I saw Sir Donald Mackenzie Wallace,[75] who was then in charge of the Foreign Department of *The Times*, and he outlined what I was to do in Siam. He gave me letters to Sir Thomas Sanderson[76] of the Foreign Office and an official in the India office.

My movements were the object of considerable suspicion inevitable under the circumstances. At Pnom Penh[77] an interpreter was supplied to me by the French authorities, and he made careful note of all my actions. He was master of all the vices, he drank, smoked opium and lied unblushingly. I sent him back from Battambong.[78] From Pnom Penh I crossed by the Great Lake to the Cambodian provinces of Siam stopping first at Siem Reap to visit the glorious runs of Angkor Wat

---

participated in the Second Boer War after which he resumed editorship of the *Star*. He returned to England, made a director of *The Times*, and accepted an invitation to write Disraeli's biography. He lived to complete the first two volumes; a further four were written by Buckle.

75 Sir Donald Mackenzie Wallace, 1841–1919, was a writer, newspaper correspondent, and public servant with a formidable education gained at the universities of Edinburgh, Glasgow, École de Droit in Paris, Berlin and Heidelberg, the last from which he graduated with a doctorate in law. He moved between journalism and royal service (he was private secretary to the future George V, political officer to the future Tsar Nicholas II, and private secretary to Lords Dufferin and Lansdowne in India) and wrote about Empire. Chirol replaced him as head of the Foreign Department (Foreign Editor) of *The Times*.

76 Thomas Henry Sanderson, 1st Baron Sanderson, 1841–1923, diplomat and, when Morrison met him, Permanent Under Secretary of State fo Foreign Affairs, Britain's top civil servant for foreign affairs.

77 Phnom Penh is the standard spelling today.

78 Battambang is the standard spelling today.

and Angkor Thom[79], the most remarkable monuments of Eastern Asia, and afterwards at Battambong, and then continued my journey to the ruby and sapphire mines of Boh Pailin.[80] Elephants were provided for me here, and I rode on to Chantaboon, the port which had been in the occupation of the French pending the fulfilment of the terms of the Treaty of 1893. At the fort I was received in a friendly manner by Commandant Arlabosse,[81] an acquaintance which I was to renew some years later during the military occupation of China following the Boxer rebellion, when the Commandant was appointed the representative of his country on the Tientsin Provisional Government.

A small steamer, a rusty, stuffy little craft that client between Chantaboon and Bangkok, took me round to Bangkok. On the deck was the Siamese boy who spoke good English. To him I said incautiously, "To whom does this wretched toy belong?" To my surprise he answered, "To my father." "And who is your father," I asked. To my greater surprise he replied, "His Royal Highness Prince Chaosai."

On January 15 1896, a day or two before I arrived in Bangkok, the Anglo-French Treaty, guaranteeing the integrity of the central portion of Siam, and defining the British and French spheres of influence, has been signed by Lord Sailsbury and Baron de Courcel.[82] There was much satisfaction in diplomatic circles—through the French Colonial party was little pleased, speaking of the Agreement as the Néfaste[83] Convention—for the Agreement had removed the most serious crisis that had jeopardised relations between England and France for many years. The Convention guaranteed the integrity of the central portion

---

79 Angkor Wat was built in the early 12th century (1113–1150), an Hindu temple dedicated to Vishnu and later transformed into a Buddhist site. Angkor Thom, primarily Buddhist in design, was built in the late 12th century (1181–1220) and was the last great capital of the Khmer Empire.
80 A province in western Cambodia.
81 General Louis Eugène Auguste Arlabosse, 1856–1924. Born in Algeria to French parents, his father was in the military. Arlabosse saw service in Sudan, Indo-China, and World War 1.
82 Baron Alphonse Chodron de Courcel, 1835–1919, French diplomat and politician. Presided over the Olympic congress in Paris in 1894 where it was decided to reestablish the Olympic Games.
83 Néfaste means *harmful* in French.

of Siam, recognised all Siamese territory east of the guaranteed area as within the sphere of influence of Great Britain. Practically, therefore, the Agreement stayed French Aggression and guaranteed the integrity of the whole of Siam, for it was obvious that it France moved into her sphere of influence England would make a corresponding move and the territory which France would occupy would be that defined on the maps as Regions Marécageuses,[84] while that over which Great Britain would become sovereign would contain the rich teak forests of the Salween Valley, the vast tin deposits of the Siamese Malay states and the Isthmus of Kra. The cutting of which, deemed practicable by many, would shorten the voyage from Europe to Bangkok. Or Saigon by four days. The agreement was therefore, one wholly agreeable to Siam, and was so recognised by the king and by his responsible ministers in Bangkok, I stayed for two weeks in the British negation with the British *chargé d'affaires* Mr. de Bunsen,[85] a statesman-diplomatist, who has left grateful memories in Siam of his tactfulness, his wisdom and his ready sympathy and who has since deservedly risen to one of the highest posts in the service of his sovereign. Accompanied by Mr. Warrington Smyth,[86] of the Department of Mines, the author of a standard book on Siam, I went along the railway, then only partially constructed from Bangkok to Korat. The contractor himself came with us. For several years the railway had been under construction that had made but little progress. Incessant friction with the authorities had delayed the work. Tenders had been called for its construction. The successful tenderer was an English contractor, the unsuccessful competitor was the German representative of Krupp. With that curious absence of trust characteristic of the Oriental the Siamese, after the contract had been signed, appointed the German unsuccessful tenderer to supervise the

---

84 French for 'swampy regions'.
85 Sir Maurice William Ernest de Bunsen, Bt, 1852–1932, a British diplomat of German extraction (his grandfather was the Prussian ambassador to London) was Consul General in Bangkok 1894–1897. He went on to be Ambassador in Lisbon, Spain and Austria. He was influential in British policy towards the Ottoman Empire and South America.
86 Herbert Warrington Smyth, 1867–1943, went to Siam in 1891 and was secretary of the government Department of Mines from 1891–1895 and Director General from 1895–1897.

construction work of the English contractor. Endless wrangling was the inevitable result, and the work suffered accordingly.

The latter half of the journey to Korat had to be made on horseback. From Korat, leaving Smyth, I struck north-west across Siam to Chiengmai,[87] travelling sometimes in bullock cart, sometimes on horseback, frequently on foot and occasionally on elephants. Every kindness was shown to me by the people, the letters given me by Prince Damrong[88] and other Siamese authorities ensuring me every consideration and assistance.

At Utardit I struck the Menam Valley travelling thence northwards to Muang Nan, doubled back over the hills to Muang Pré, again north to Muang Ngao, and then by zigzag route through Nakawn Lampang to Chiengmai, a picturesque city, the second in importance in Siam, situated in the midst of a plain of extraordinary richness. From Chiengmai I rode for two days to Chieng Rai, and two days later, having left behind my Siamese escort, who were forbidden to enter the 25 kilometre zone, I reached Chieng Sen on the banks of the Mekong.

Stationed here I found the French *Agent Commercial*, M. Ngin, a brave Cambodian, decorated with the Legion of Honour, who for 10 years 1885 to 1895 had been the trusted companion of M. Alphonse Pavie,[89] the famous traveller and in his time the greatest living authority on Siam, Laos, and Indochina. With him was an Irishman, a noncommissioned officer in the foreign Legion. Elephants were provided for me in Chieng Sen and I crossed the frontier into Burma, my intention being to push my way north to Yunnan City. Here all transport failed me: I was unable to obtain horses, and though I paid

---

87 Now usually spelt Chiang Mai. The largest city in northern Thailand and second largest, after Bangkok, in the country.
88 Prince Tisavarakumarn, the Prince Damrong Rajanubhab, 1862–1943, was instrumental in creating the Thai educational system as well as the country's modern provincial administration. He was the half-brother of King Chulalongkorn.
89 In a rare error Morrison has mis-named Pavie, 1847–1925; his forename is Auguste Jean-Marie. Explorer and civil servant, Pavie is credited with establishing French control of Laos where he became French minister plenipotentiary in 1894. He conducted extensive surveys of Indo-China which were published in seven volumes from 1879–1895.

11 | 'REMINISCENCES'

freely for everything I had considerable difficulty in engaging coolies to carry my scanty kit.

Keng Tung[90] town, the point for which I was now making, is the chief town in the most important of the southern Shan states: it is the farthest Eastern garrison town of the British empire in India. It lies in a valley which seemed to me the fairest spot I had seen in Asia with its sequestered villages in picturesque woods on the edge of the hills with the town itself with its matte grass thatched houses, its red tiled temples and gilded pagodas, with its busy commingling of the most picturesque races of Eastern Asia.

The town is six marches from the Siamese frontier. I marched this distance on foot mostly barefoot, for I'd hurt my ankle, and I could not wear a boot. I arrived in Kong Tung town somewhat lame.

At this time, the town was garrisoned by a Gurkha regiment, under the command of Lieutenant Colonel Presgrave. The British commissioner was Mr. G. C. B. Sterling a trained official of exceptional experience. Associated with the Frontier Boundary Commissioner under the leadership of Mr. now Sir J. G. Scott[91] he had been left in charge of Mong Hsing, the small state east of the Mekong, pending the settlement by diplomatic agency of future ownership of this malaria stricken district. When it was decided to hand back the state to France. It was Mr. Sterling, upon whom fell the unpleasant duty of conducting the formalities required for its transfer. I retain a vivid recollection of his kindness to me, especially during the attack of fever, by which I was frustrated. Up to this point, I had two servants, a Lukchin or Chinese Siamese half-caste name Ah Heng, a man of exceptional courage, resource and linguistic ability who spoke good English, Siamese, Lu Shan, and Swatow Chinese, and a gentlemanly Siamese named Mom Luang Sook, from the survey department in Bangkok. Unable to sustain the fatigues of the journey Mom Luang Sook was compelled to leave me in Keng Tung. Sometime later he died on his way back to Chieng Mai.

---

90 Kengtung is now a town in Shan State. It was formally the seat of government when it was a minor principality.

91 Sir James George Scott, 1851–1935, Scottish journalist, and colonial administrator in Burma where he became Deputy Commissioner. He is credited with bringing the Shan States under British control.

My intention now was to cross the Chinese frontier and march up through the Chinese Shan states (Sip Sawng Panna) and Yunnan Province to Yunnan City. But I had much difficulty about my passport. Our agreement with China stipulated that a British subject wishing to cross the frontier from Burma should be provided with a passport written in Chinese. There was no one in Keng Tung who could write Chinese. The Acting Chief Secretary of the Government of Burma, Mr. Thirkell White,[92] when asked to help me, wired back "Is not journey risky at this unhealthy season?" It was, however, impossible for me to wait until the season became healthier. I wired back to him, telling him that I was travelling for *The Times*, and appealing to him to expedite my journey, and I was permitted to proceed on the understanding that if any objection was shown to my crossing the frontier I would return. Mr. Sterling gave me a document written in English, Shawn and Lü calling upon the Chinese authorities at the frontier to allow me to proceed to Yunnan City, but as I have said, there was no one in Keng Tung town who could translate it into Chinese. This missive I put into the largest envelope that I could find and I then decorated the outside with a large seal stamped from the top of a Van Houten's cocoa tin. An official character which it otherwise lacked was given to the document.

Thus fortified, on June the 12th I set out for the frontier. It was the middle of the rainy season. Every day it rained and travelling in the jungle had many discomforts. Keng Tung, the Shan State, the most easterly of the British Shan states, marches with Keng Hung, the most distant of the Shan states of the Chinese Empire. From the town of Keng Tung to the Chinese frontier is a distance of 54 miles, and the town of Keng Hung in the state of the same name on the Mekong River, is 81 miles further. When I reached the frontier the chief of the district called upon me, and squatted down with me on the floor of the Wat. With reverence I showed him the document, and asked him to help me to reach the town of Keng Hung where there resides a small there resided, a small, a very small, Chinese frontier official. He had

---

92 Sir Herbert Thirkell White, 1855–1931, rose to become Lieutenant-Governor of Burma (1905–10). He is best known for *A Civil Servant in Burma* (1913) which was based on his 32 years in Burma.

previously met Colonel Woodthorpe[93] and some other members of the British Boundary Commission, and was very friendly and did all he could to help me.

My party was a humble one. It consisted of Ah Heng, two ponies and seven coolies. I was quite unarmed. In Bangkok, Prince Damrong discussing my projected journey, reminded me that I had crossed China unarmed. "There is even less need for you to carry arms in Siam than in China," he said. In my haste I said I had intended also traveling in Siam unarmed, the fact being that at the time I had given the subject no thought. Afterwards I regretted my careless compliance. There was no need for arms in Siam or Burma, but once I had crossed the border into the Shan states of China, I would have been more secure, my journey would have been more interesting, and I should have been saved much anxiety had I been armed.

Travelling was not unpleasant although it was the rainy season; the men were working in the paddy fields and there was often delay in getting labor. Leeches and mosquitoes were the chief annoyance, the former, especially. By pressing coolies from village to village I reached Keng Hung town without difficulty. The country is rich, fertile and well peopled. Cultivation is highly developed. The people are thriving, prosperous and contented. Every village has its Temple and Guesthouse. Houses are built on piles high off the ground. Frequently my fellow travellers were Chinese Traders from Southern Yunnan—Mohammedans all who had knowledge of foreigners and were always cheery and hospitable.

Keng Hung itself is a straggling village scattered around the steep western slopes of a jungle crowned promontory that projects into the Mekong. High up on the hill slope is the Palace of the Sawbwa commanding a splendid view of the great river as it comes into view from the mountains to the north, sweeps away to the East past the promontory, and then rolls on in majestic volume southwards to the sea. Keng Hung is a place of considerable importance. It is the chief town of the Sip Sawng Panna, the twelve Shan states tributary to China,

---

93 Robert Gosset Woodthorpe, 1844–1898, Major-General, explorer, maker of maps for the Indian Survey Department.

lying between China and Burma and Tongking it is the residence of the Chinese frontier official: it is the spot where the future railway to Ssumao will cross the river Mekong.

On the second day after my arrival, I visited the Sawbwa.[94] He was a young man of 32 of prepossessing appearance, but much addicted to opium. His town was steeped in opium. I met no man, not even a priest, who did not smoke opium. I was received politely in a large hall, and given a foreign easy chair, the Sawbwa seating himself nearby at a table on which his opium lamp was still lit. Spectators sat on their haunches in rows filling the hall, the more important head man being grouped near the chief. Outside the rain was descending in cataracts. A Shan clerk who by the payment of a special fee had been induced to come with me from Keng Tung acted as interpreter, but he spoke in tones so respectfully humble and so low as to be quite inaudible. I interrupted him and called upon my Luk-chin. Ah Heng spoke in a loud and confident tone as became the interpreter of the one whom he persistently referred to as the 'Chau Luang'. "No damn fear," he explained to me afterwards, "but I make these buffaloes (thus referring to the Sawbwa and his court) know that my master is the number one big man." Chao Luang is, I believe, the title due to the Chief Commissioner of Burma.

The Sawbwa began to speak, and at once, as I had expected, suggested difficulties. Was I aware that this was the worst route to Yunnan? I said I could not believe so, seeing that it was the route selected by all the Chinese caravans in their annual journeys from Yunnan to Keng Tung. Did I know that I had chosen the worst period of the year to come here? "Is it true?" I replied, raising my voice above the deluge "that a few drops of rain have fallen, but then how cool it is. To one coming from a cold country the summer heat is intolerable." "True," he said, "true." I asked permission to go through to Yunnan city. He said that this was a question which would have to be settled by the Chinese Commissioner whom I should see tomorrow. Then conversation ensued. Which people now possessed Bangkok—the English or the French?" "Neither," I said, "the Siamese, whose independence, by the friendly concurrence of

---

94 Sawbwa is the Burmese title given to the hereditary rulers of the Shan states. The British recognised them and they were given a degree of autonomy in their fiefdoms.

11 | 'REMINISCENCES'

England and France has been forever guaranteed." "But I know that the Minghoon Prince is now in Cambodia and that the French are to give him Burma, for he is the son of King Theebaw[95]." I asked the chief where he had heard this nonsense. He said, from the Myosa of Monghsing, who was now in the Sip Sawng Panna. The French had promised to restore him to authority in Monghsing, at the same time they would restore the throne of Burma, the Minghoon Prince now a refugee in Indo-China.

I came away well pleased. The next day I saw the Chinese 'Commissioner', a humble official of slender authority. He was really the Chinese clerk of the of the Sawbwa. He wished me to remain in Keng Hung until he heard from his superior officer in Ssumao. I was insistent, however, and he gave way. He was suffering from an irritative skin affection of his neck, for which I gave him an elixir in the form of a cake of much advertised soap. He was grateful and gave me the necessary letter authorising me to proceed. It was not my fault that his letter somewhat imaginatively described its bearer as the "Chao Sala. a prince Doctor specially sent by the Queen of England at the urgent entreaty of the Viceroy of Yunnan to save the sick and dying."

Trouble began after I left Keng Hung. I was now to traverse the Sip Sawng Panna, that congeries of 12 small Shan states lying on each side of the Mekong as far as the border of Yunnan, each self-governed under its own chief and head man all owing allegiance more or less shadowy to Keng Hung, which state itself is a tributary of China. The ferry over the Mekong is three miles above the town, the stream is more than a quarter of a mile wide, with a deep and powerful current. We crossed safely. On the other side of the bamboo grove near the river bank is the village of Bam Ta Kaw. We camped in in its splendid wat.[96] "The Prince Doctor may travel all through the Sip Sawng Panna, and not find another temple like this," said the Chief Priest. It was built by Chinese traders to protect them from the dangers of the crossing. From the river we were deceitfully led into the hill country, away from the main

---

95 Thibaw Min, 1859–1916, the last king of the Konbaung dynasty of Burma. His reign ended when his army was defeated by the British in the Third Anglo-Burmese War in November 1885.

96 A Buddhist monastery.

track, and dumped into a hill village in which it was difficult to obtain assistance in continuing our journey. For days I was wondering about these hills among the aborigines, zigzagging from village to village until finally I reached Ssumao.[97] We used to sleep in the head man's house and were kindly treated. Dark skinned aborigines of primitive customs, the Khalawa as they are known are without priests or temple, have their own language, their own dress, their own ornaments, worship, worship nats, unable to read or write. Exceptionally hard working, inoffensive and industrious, they are treated like dogs by the Lüs, or Shan and periodically oppressed by the Sawbwa. Goitre is very common among them. They are allied to the Lolos and those many indigenous tribes along the border of Yunnan—a multitude of races, who will one day be merged into the Chinese. Men and women climb the hillsides like goats. They do not smoke opium, but are fond of home distilled samshu,[98] smoke home grown tobacco and drink tea. The tea plant grows on all the hillsides. Stop their weapons are the invariable dah, protecting them alike from visible and invisible, the crossbow and poisoned arrow. Throughout the country splendid maize was grown, the plants waving high above my head as I rode my pony back. Chinese mud villages were passed. The houses are like the poorest Irish cabins and quite as dirty. All the talk was of man eating Tiger. It was said to have killed 13 men and many buffaloes and bullocks. My man declared that they could hear it mewing in the jungle. We saw its fresh footprints. I measured them but never saw the tiger. If a native killed a tiger, he was compelled to give the skin and bones to the Sawbwa of Keng Hung who paid him a reward of seven rupees, and thus had all the best of the bargain for the skin was worth 25 rupees and the bones even more. Ground into powder they are sold as a sovereign remedy for failing courage, in accordance with the primeval idea that the body imbibes the qualities of the thing eaten.

As I proceeded, the appearance of the villages improved. The people slept under mosquito curtains: they wore home made cottons, some had coloured turbans brought from upper Burma. On the 7th July we emerged from the valley that led to the southern gates of Ssumao, the

---

97 Simao, today a district of Pu'er.
98 A strong alcoholic beverage made from rice.

gateway of South Western China; the Golden Esmok of earlier writers. Our reception was alarming. People poured into the street to see us pass, jeering at us as foreign devils. But for the speedy intervention of the officials, it might have gone hard with me and my solitary companion. No sooner, however, had the magistrates heard of our rival that he came over personally to see us, to welcome us and assure us of his friendship and protection. Quarters were found for us in the comfortable inn, and after two or three days the excitement of the people subsided, and we were allowed to wander about unmolested. Ssuamo had recently been opened as a Treaty Port, and the French Consul, M. Pierre Bons D'Anty,[99] was then within a few days of the city, some of his stores being already unpacked in the very next inn to the one we occupied.

One could wish to live in no pleasanter spot and Ssumao. The plain is a lake of paddy, gleaming green and gold, skirted by thickly wooded hills recessed with valleys of paddy. Across the plain a paved road winds temples gleam white from the groves of pines and bamboo. Every yard of arable land is under cultivation. What a contrast from the Sip Sawng Panna to China, from the straggling Lü bush village and mountain bridle path to the well-built compact Chinese town, walled and approached on all sides by paved causeways. Order is preserved by the mere semblance of authority by a few antiquated guns and a few opium eating soldiers of the type described by Baber[100] as armed to the teeth with an opium pipe and an umbrella.

For some days I stayed in Ssumao, and then on July 14, set out for Yunnan city, distant 19 stages of 363 miles in all. There was the recurring difficulty about my passport. Two days further north is the prefectural town of Pu Erh Fu,[101] famous throughout China for its tea. This town passed there would be no further difficulty. The Ssumao magistrate gave me a letter to the prefect, and provided me with an escort of two

---

99 Pierre-Remi Bons d'Anty, 1859–1916, French diplomat who served throughout China and north Vietnam from 1885 until his death in 1916.
100 Edward Colborne Baber, 1843–1890, English diplomat and traveller. While working in the British legation at Peking he made three journeys into the interior of China: to the Burmese border (1876), Sichuan, and last (1878), north from Chongqing. He saw service also in Korea and Burma.
101 Famous for its red tea, Pu'er is located in the south west of Yunnan.

soldiers on whose dress were affixed the broad cotton discs marked with the character for valour. The traveller did not fail to note that the discs are stitched to the back of the uniform, in which position they are more likely to be seen by the enemy. Two coolies and one pack pony carried my meagre outfit. I secured the services of a Chinese interpreter who could speak Lü.

As I was leaving Ssumao, a fellow lodger at the inn, a Chinese merchant, asked earnestly if he might have the privilege of accompanying me as far as his home in Yuan Xiang. I gladly accorded him permission. An amiable and transparently good man, the merchant had made an unfortunate speculation in opium and was returning empty. He had lost his whole parcel. Unwilling to vaunt his wares he had declared on his arrival at the gate when interrogated by the likin officials that his stock, two horse loads, consisted exclusively of personal goods upon which no duties were leviable. Had he any opium? he was asked. He was surprised at the question, No, he had none. Was he a man to traffic in this nefarious drug which was sapping the life blood out of his nation? Had he any opium? he was asked again. No, he had none. Might Heaven have no need for him if what he said was not the truth. But they searched his saddlebags and found false linings and much opium. His stock was forfeited, but this did not represent all his loss. To buy perilous immunity from a bambooing,[102] he had to spend much silver; yet he was quite cheerful regarding his loss as one of those incidents invariably in the career of a conscientious trader seeking to resist the outrageous sanctions of the likin officials. I found him pleasant. I found him a pleasant companion.

At Ssumao the friendly official had given me a pass to Pu Erh Fu fu, but could not guarantee me being permitted to pass it, for the Prefect was his superior officer. And thus it happened. I reached the city in the afternoon. In the evening the district magistrate came to see me. He said to me:

"Where is your passport from Peking?"

I said, "I have no passport from Peking. I came from Burma, provided with letters of application from the British Commissioner."

---

102 A caning using bamboo sticks.

11 | 'REMINISCENCES'

He said: "You have no passport from Peking, then you will go back tomorrow."

I protested against this arbitrary treatment. He had no right to send me back, seeing that I had complied with all the requirement, all the seeing that I had complied with all the requisite formalities, with the exception of my passport. He, however, repeated that as I had no passport from Peking, I would have to go back tomorrow. But he added: "You have been put to great expense in coming thus far, the sum of 20 tales will be given to you to defray your expenses." I laughed scornfully at his offer and ostentatiously sat down and began writing a number of figures on a sheet of paper. The room was crowded, and everyone was keenly interested to see what I was doing. The magistrate could not hide his curiosity. "What was the teacher doing?" he asked. I replied that I was making note of all the expenses I had been put to in coming thus far, and the loss I had sustained, and the estimate cost of the affront now being inflicted upon a high British Official who had given letters of application.

"What does it amount to?" he asked.

I said, my heart was in sorrow. I would not speak now, but I would tell him in the morning. He was very civil in his demeanour and left me, promising to come again in the morning and undertaking that when I returned, I would be provided with a safe escort back to Ssumao.

In the morning the magistrate and the same crowd came back to see me. I was handed a packet of 20 tales of silver. With my stick I disdainfully pushed it off the table as if it were dirt. Then I handed the official two large envelopes, one addressed to the Viceroy of Yunnan and the other addressed to the Tsungli Yamen at Peking[103], both written overnight, and in which I had made a detailed statement of my case claimed 10,000 tails, compensation for the loss I had sustained. In handing them to the magistrates I told him to whom they were addressed, and told him they contained a demand for compensation which would no doubt have to be paid to me by the local authorities. He asked what was the amount I had claimed? I said, airily:

---

103 The short form for the 'Office for the General Management of Affairs Concerning the Various Countries', the Qing term for their agency dealing with foreigners.

"Knowing how poor is China, I have only asked for ten thousand taels."

The amount seemed to astonish him, the crowd took it up and "ten thousand taels" you can hear pass from man to man out into the street. A demand of this kind appeals strongly to the mandarins concerned, for they know that although the applicant may never receive the money, they may nevertheless have to pay it. An escort was provided for me, and I rode back the two days journey to Ssumao. The people along the road were friendly, and I had no unpleasantness whatsoever. At Ssumao immediately on my return, I was visited by the magistrate and by the local military official. They were distressed at what had happened. I declared that the very next day I would return to Burma and report my case to the British frontier Commissioner. They begged me to postpone my departure for only three days. Stop, there was a mistake, they assured me, which could easily be rectified. I yielded to their entreaties and consented to remain. On the third morning a messenger came from Pu Erh Fu saying that a mistake had occurred, and begging the stranger to return and continue his journey to the capital. The authorities kindly offered to defray all my expenses. They had treated me well, however, and I would not, of course, accept any such payment. On my return to Pu Erh Fu I consented to take back the two letters I had written and then continue on my way to Yunnan city.

North of Pu Erh Fu, the road bifurcates, one branch going to the capital, the other to Talifu. It was a mountainous road flagged all the way. The Papien was crossed, a deep and powerful stream that mingles its waters some 300 miles to the east with the Red River of Tongking. For a few miles. The road follows the winding course of this river as it flows between mountains of inaccessible steepness and then crosses the river by a splendid suspension bridge, an engineering work that would attract attention in any country. It is one span, 320 feet long, from buttress to buttress, 13 feet six inches wide, formed of parallel chains of linked rods of iron. Iron mines that have been worked for centuries are a few marches distant.

Five days out from Pu Erh Fu I met a long procession of pack animals carrying the French tricolour, and later on the same day, I met the French Consul, M. Bons D'Anty proceeding to Ssumao to take up his official residence. M. Bons D'Anty had spent his official career in China.

11 | 'REMINISCENCES'

La rue du Marché, Mongtze, Yunnan, c. 1895.
Mitchell Library, Sydney

Few French officials have acquired so great a knowledge of China, or have studied more clearly the conditions as they are, even at this time he had traveled far afield, he has since acquired an unusual knowledge of China and its borders so far distant as the frontiers of Yunnan and of Kwangsi and the marches of Ssuch'uan (Sichuan) and Tibet.

Eleven days later I reached Yunnan city. Ill luck befell me, and I was very ill, but I was among friends, staying with Mr. Christian Jensen, the director of the Chinese telegraphs in the province of Yunnan, and I was nursed back to health. When after a long stay I recovered sufficiently, I went south east to the treaty port of Mêng tzu[104], and after a few days spent my spent with my friend Mr. Campbell McAllum[105] of the Maritime Customs, started westwards on October 1st along the base of the Yunnan plateau to return to Ssumao. It was my intention to march southwards to Siam, visiting on my way the small state of Mong Hsing in the Sip Sawng Panna.

---

104 Mengzi today.
105 Campbell (Christain) Alexander McAllum, 1867–1918.

My stay in Mêng tzu, the most distant from Peking of the Maritime Customs stations then opened in China, was exceptionally interesting. Mr. W. F. Spinney,[106] a graduate of Harvard and a noted snipe shot, was in charge. Working under him were the well-known botanist Dr. Augustine Henry,[107] the author of the *Economic Botany of China* who had found in the flora of the Yunnan plateau almost a virgin field for his researchers, and Mr. Campbell McAllum, a remarkable man of striking presence and imposing personality. Among the able men of that cosmopolitan service, few men have ever had more interesting experiences than McAllum. The services he rendered in South Formosa at the time of the rebellion following upon the termination of the war between China and Japan, although known to many, have never received any adequate recognition.

It will be remembered that war between China and Japan terminated on April 17, 1895 by the signature at Shimonoseki of the Treaty of Peace, one of the conditions of which was the session to Japan of the island of Formosa. Lord Li Ching-fang,[108] afterwards minister to London, one of the signatories to the Treaty was deputed by his government formally to give effect to the transfer of this unwelcome task he carried out on June 2nd fulfilling the requisite formalities not on land but on a Japanese Man of War, lying off Kelung the most northerly harbour of the Island. Five days later, the Japanese occupied Taipeh, the Capital of which Kelung is the harbour.

Li Ching-fang had been afraid to land in the Island. Chinese authority no longer ran there, for in the interval between the signing of the Treaty and the formal transfer of the island, the literati and people of Formosa, that is to say, the officials of Formosa prompted thereto with characteristic duplicity by Chinese high authorities on

---

106 William Franklin Spinney, 1828–1917, also worked for the Imperial Customs Service in Anping (Taiwan) where he was acting Commissioner in 1884. In 1904 he was awarded the Order of the Double Dragon, but the Qing authorities.
107 Augustine Henry, 1857–1930, plantsman and sinologist. He sent more than 15,000 specimens and seeds to Kew Gardens in London.
108 Li Jinfang, 1854–1934, statesman. Li was the nephew and adopted son of Li Hongzhang, China's pre-eminent statesman of that age. Li signed the Treaty of Shimonoseki in the elder Li's stead. He held senior diplomatic posts in London and Tokyo. He received a British knighthood. He ended his public service as head of the Chinese postal service.

11 | 'REMINISCENCES'

the mainland, foremost of whom was the Viceroy Chang Chih-tung,[109] and determined to resist subjection of Japan, had declared foremost an independent Island Republic. Tang Ching-sung,[110] a Kwangsi man, the Island Treasurer, was nominated first President with General Tcheng Ki-tong,[111] the notorious ex-military attaché of the Chinese Legation in Paris as his Minister of Foreign Affairs. The Island was divided into three military districts, the most important division that of the South, with Anping as its headquarters being entrusted to Liu Yung-fu,[112] the former leader of the Black Flags in the struggle with the French on the borders of Tongking, who now at the head of 10,000 Invincibles had sworn to resist to the death the Japanese occupation.

In the north, the Republic endured just 13 days from the 23rd of May to the 5th of June, when President Chang and his valorous general fled to the mainland But in the South, Liu Yung-fu proved himself of sterner metal. Declaring himself President "elected by the people", he prepared to resist the Japanese advance. The Commissioner of Customs at Anping having left the port on June 29, McAllum, who was then on the outdoor staff, took charge of the customs property, assisted Liu in the maintenance of order and at his request assisted him in obtaining money for the paying of his troops, issued bank notes and postage stamps, which are now philatelic curiosities and advised him in all things relating to foreigners. But no serious resistance was ever contemplated. Unchecked the Japanese moved southwards, reaching the

---

109 Zhang Zhidong, 1837–1909, a prominent Qing official known for his efforts to modernise China yet retain traditional Confucian values, best encapsulated by the phrase "Chinese learning as the essence, Western learning for practical use." He held the most senior positions in provincial government from Shanxi to Guangdong and Hunan and Herbei. He was involved with defence modernisation, and, in Hubei and Hunan, industrialisation in founding cotton mills, tanneries, and iron works. With Yuan Shikai he led the abolition of the Imperial examination system and the promotion of western learning in 1904.
110 Tang Jinsong, 1843–1903, Chinese general who commanded the Yunnan Army in the Sino-French War, 1884–1885. Appointed governor of Taiwan in 1894.
111 Chen Jitong, 1851–1907, diplomat, general, shipbuilder, scholar. He was one of the first Chinese to travel to Europe (1876).
112 Liu Yongfu, 1837–1917, was a bandit and warlord who commanded the Black Flag Army against the French when the latter took over Tongking (north Vietnam) in the 1880s. In 1895 her led the resistance to the Japanese takeover of Formosa (Taiwan).

neighbourhood of Anping in the middle of October. The place became too hot for the President. He prepared to forsake his trusty braves. On the 18th, disguised as a coolie, he went on board the British ship *Thales*, and escaped to Amoy. On his way the ship was boarded by Japanese officers, but on its arrival in Amoy, the British Consul, Mr. Christopher Gardner[113] who had no love for the Japanese, having once himself been pitched into a ditch by some Japanese soldiers in Seoul, permitted Liu Yung-fu to land. His leaderless braves left behind in Anping where they were in imminent danger of Japanese reprisals were taken in charge by McAllum, who, assisted by two other Englishmen, hotly induced them to lay down their arms, guaranteeing them security from molestation to the number of nearly 8000 the arms were stored in the Customs House. The Japanese entered into possession of Anping on October 21st and faithfully respected the engagement and peace thus terminated what at one time was a very serious situation indeed. For some unexplained reason, no reward was ever given to either belligerent to the Englishmen for their service, but Sir Robert Hart who was fond of citing this case in illustration of the self reliance and promptitude in action, so often displayed in critical times by members of his service, testifies to his appreciation and gave McAllum a substantial promotion.

From Talantcing, one of the most picturesque towns on the road to Ssumao and the centre of the gold mining district of future possibilities, I turned southward over the hills, following mountain paths not previously visited by European, until I reached the neighbourhood of Ssumao. The faithful Ah Heng was still with me and we were both mounted. Two coolies and one pack pony carried our modest outfit. An escort of two opium-smoking braves accompanied me. For a short distance we followed the main road and then turned abruptly to the south among the hills inhabited by Lolo aborigines, in shady woods with many butterflies, by running streams meeting long files of native people gentle in speech and manner, the men in Chinese garb, the women wearing their own characteristic dress of many colours with earrings of silver and neck strings of beads. As we advanced the country

---

113 Christopher Thomas Gardner, 1842–1914, British diplomat who was an authority on East Asian coins, especially Korean and Chinese. His collection is in the British Museum.

became more difficult and broken and my coolies traveled badly. When I remonstrated with them they would ask me reproachfully, "Are we horses that we that eat grass?

We started from Talantcing on the 14th October. Next day, one of my soldiers left me and the day after Ah Heng and I got separated from the other three men. Rain came on. The country became a tangle of jungle, ravines and water courses and we never saw our coolies again. Fortunately, distrusting the men, I had transferred to the pack pony all the indispensable article articles for our journey. Held up by flooded rivers and much delayed but treated with invariable friendly friendliness by the hill men, we finally reached Ssumao on October 31st. There were no bridges but happily my ponies feared no flooded river. Their courage was remarkable. Called by their masters from the other bank they would hear the cry would prick up their ears, then take to the water like ducks. With Blondin-like[114] skill they would walk along a narrow plank, flung for them across a foaming rivulet.

In Ssumao I stayed at the same in as on my first visit. It was now trading season and the rooms were filled with hardy Mohammedan Chinese preparing for their annual journey to Chiengmai in Siam, many of whom had come from Ta-ch'ian-lu in Western Sichuan on the border of the Tibetan marches. Assistance was given me by M. Bons D'Anty, the French consul, so that I could continue my pilgrimage. Leaving on November 4th I was again to pass south through the Sip Sawng Panna, the special object of my journey being a visit to Mong Hsing, that small state the possession of which had strained the relations of England and France, which had been for sometime in British occupation but which by the far reaching convention of January 15, 1896 had been handed over to France. My route thus kept me from for the most part to the east of the Mekong and I did not cross the river until I reached the ferry at Chien Lap.

On the 16th day out from Ssumao, having the previous day crossed the border of Mong Hsing State, I reached the town of Mong Hsing and found this paltry village of 160 native wooden houses was the chief town

---

114 A reference to the famous tightrope walker Charles Blondin (born Jean François Gravelet), 1824–1897. He crossed the 1,100 ft Niagara Gorge on a tightrope.

of a jungle-covered malarious district, scantily peopled by an enfeebled race steeped in opium.

To think that possession of this "clump of hatched villages in the fever jungles"[115] once nearly involved England in France in war! Truly the quarrels of nations have often strange origins. It is, however, a magnificent game country: a virgin field for the sportsman. Its disadvantage, and it was a formidable disadvantage, was the curse of leeches. People did not fear the tiger and the leopard, but they were afraid of the leeches. Leeches were literally on every blade of grass. In charge of the State at the time of my visit, his jurisdiction extending to the banks of the Mekong, was the resident commissioner M. Henri Sévénier, a courageous Frenchman of much promise, assisted by one foreign secretary, and a native interpreter and guarded by an escort of 24 Luang Prabang soldiers. Nothing could exceed the courtesy with which I was received by M. Sévénier. Himself in some straits from the non-arrival of his stores from Luang Prabang he generously offered to assist me from his slender stock, but I was only five marches from the Burma frontier and help was no longer necessary. Pushing on through the jungle, I crossed the Mekong at Chieng Lap and found myself once more in British territory. On my way, I had abundant evidence of the good name left behind by my countryman during the occupation of Mong Hsing. We have had more experience than the French dealing with such peoples. Our methods at the time—I speak of 1896—were more considerate than the French methods and were better adapted to the native character. To give only two examples—we paid for work, the French levied a tax in the form of an unwelcome corvée. We found that the rupee was the coin whose size exactly met the needs of the people. The French introduced their trade dollar, the Piastre de commerce, and by means of arbitrary exchange hoped to drive out the rupee. But the coin was too large for the native taste, and the effect of an attempt to enforce an unwelcome currency was not to drive out the rupee but to drive out the people who moved in considerable numbers across the Mekong to British territory. On my journey I found fields neglected, and

---

115 Morrison's footnote reads: "Lord Dufferin, speech to British Chamber of Commerce, Paris, March 1894." Dufferin was British Ambassador in Paris when he gave this speech.

11 | 'REMINISCENCES'

the harvest in many places rotting the men having been commanded for telegraph construction.

On the evening of November 23rd, I came to the village of Mong Long and went as usual to the Sala or rest house. But it was already occupied and the small temple was also unavailable. So with Ah Heng I went across to see the head man. He was in his courtyard, hewing wood. Ah Heng asked him to find accommodation for me. He said let him go to the Sala, and he went on with his work. But there is no room in the Sala, Ah Heng said. Still continuing his work the head man said, "Let him go to the temple." Then my servant became angered. Speaking with energy he said,

"Is this the way you treat the English gentleman who has done you the honour to call upon you."

The man stopped work. "English," he said.

"Yes, can't you see he is English," said Ah Heng.

The head man laid down his axe, came over to me, and without another word led me up the bamboo steps to his own home and seated me in the place of honour in the best room in it. He could not do enough for us both. He had thought he said I was a French traveler and speaking bit he added: "My village is empty. Paddy is ready for harvesting, but is rotting in the fields or feeding swarms of birds, because there are no men to gather it. Every man, and some of the women, are at the corvée on the French telegraph lines."

From Chang lap I traveled southwards to the border, crossed into Siam, and rode by my former route to Chieng Mai. Here I sold my horses and engaged to native boat floating down the Menam arm to Raheng and Bangkok.

In Bangkok messages from *The Times* were delivered to me asking me to proceed at once to Peking. They were delivered to me personally by Mr. V Chirol, who prior to taking up the position so long held by Sir Donald Mackenzie Wallace as director of the Foreign Department of *The Times* had run around the world to reorganize the service, to appoint new correspondents and to freshen up our knowledge, already unrivalled, of our Eastern affairs and foreign affairs generally. For the next 15 years, Mr. Chirol was to be my chief. I am afraid I was not the most satisfactory of his correspondents but I yielded to none in admiration of his amazing memory, his and encyclopaedic attainments, the noble English by which he adorned everything he wrote, the genius for friendship and broad sympathy which bound to him in every quarter of the world hosts of friends of every class in life. He had come to Bangkok partly to meet me. I felt that my work for *The Times* had been of little advantage to the paper, but Mr. Chirol encouraged me and promised me his help and faithfully fulfilled his promise. In a written dispatch sent to me after his return to Printing House Square I was given broadly the features of what was expected of me. "For our purpose," wrote Mr Chirol, "the incident and adventures of travel must always be merely subsidiary to the general information and enlightenment we require for the furtherance of British interests and of an imperial policy. In one word what you seem to me to lack in some measure is a sense of perspective. You must try and focus your lens to our eyes, remembering always that we are a very long way off and only want to look through the big end of the telescope. Picturesque details should be garniture, not the foundation of your work ... All I can say with regard both to notes and separate articles is: condense as much as possible, giving us a maximum of information and instruction in the minimum of space."[116]

One of the first man I met in Bangkok on my return from the interior was the Japanese Colonel Fukushima,[117] an officer who had already distinguished himself and who was destined to make a conspicuous part and the great movement which was to advance his country to its place among the world's great powers. An alert, active man of determined face breaking easily into laughter, small of stature, but of unusual physical strength, he impressed me by the keen intelligence of his questions. Of his career I knew but little. That he was one to achieve greatness I felt confident and recorded my impressions at the time. In 1874 when quite young, before he became an officer, he had been attached to the Japanese expedition sent to punish the offending savages of Formosa as

---

116 For the full text of this letter see Lo Hui-Min, *The Correspondence of G. E. Morrison 1895–1912*, Cambridge, Cambridge University Press, 1976, p. 38, n. 1.
117 Fukushima Yasumasa, 1852–1919, soldier, statesman, linguist, poet. He represented Emperor Meiji at the coronation of Edward VII in 1902 and was part of the team negotiating the Anglo-Japanese Alliance. He became a General in the Imperial Japanese Army and saw service in the Sino-Japanese War of 1894–95. See p. 37.

11 | 'REMINISCENCES'

English interpreter to Major General Saigo[118] and had travelled widely through the Chinese districts of the Southern part of the island. From 1887 to 1892 he was military attaché to his legation in Berlin and on the completion of his service he rode overland through Europe and Asia from Berlin to Vladivostok and when he landed in Japan in June 1893 was received with as much honour "as though he were Moltke[119] returning from the Franco-German campaign." His subsequent career is recorded in every history of the Far East.

After a fortnight delay in Bangkok, during which time I was again ill with fever brought on by a fall into the river at midnight when, returning from dinner at the American Legation, I took steamer for Hongkong still accompanied by the faithful and fearless Luk-chin who had cheerfully shared the probations of my journey.

From Hongkong, I proceeded up the coast of China calling at the treaty ports and after passing a few days of my colleagues in Shanghai went on to Peking, where I are where I arrived on March 15th 1897. My new life was now to begin.

That first summer in Peking, I recall with shuddering. Everything was in darkness. The work was unfamiliar. Ignorance of the springs of Chinese action was universal and I was the most ignorant of all. But from the beginning I received help and encouragement from Sir Claude MacDonald,[120] just as in Bangkok, ready assistance had been given me by Mr. De Bunsen. Sir Claude had only recently been appointed British

---

118 Saigo Judo, 1843–1902, member of the reformist Satsuma clan that led the Meiji Restoration of 1868. Saigo commanded Japanese forces in the Taiwan Expedition of 1874.
119 A reference to Helmuth von Moltke the Elder, 1800–1891, chief of the Prussian and then German General Staff.
120 Colonel Sir Claude Maxwell MacDonald, 1852–1915, British soldier and diplomat, who held important diplomatic positions in China and Japan. Until the mid-1880s MacDonald was on army service in Africa where he ended up Commissioner and Consul-General in Brass in the West African Oil Rivers Protectorate (present day Nigeria). He left the army in 1896 and, having caught the eye of Lord Salisbury, was that year appointed HM Minister in China with representation in Korea as well. He negotiated the 99-year lease on the New Territories adjacent to Hong Kong which expired in 1997 and resulted in the reversion to Chinese sovereignty of Hong Kong in its entirety. He distinguished himself as leader of the foreign community on Peking during the Boxer uprising of 1900. That year he swapped jobs with Sir Ernest Satow in

minister in succession to Sir John Walsham,[121] the *chargé d'affaires* in the interval being Mr. W. N. Beauclerk,[122] who was married to a daughter of Sir Robert Hart.[123] Sir Claude was one of the favourites of fortune from the Commissionership of the Oil Rivers Protectorate without any previous diplomatic training he had been unexpectedly transferred to one of the most important and difficult posts in the service. Envy denounced his appointment. He was attacked as imperfectly educated, he was weak, flippant and garrulous, he was described as the type of military officer rolled out a mile at a time and then lopped off in six-foot lengths. His only claim to the post was the fact that some years before he had been a gunnery instructor in Hongkong for a period of one year! Such were the criticisms levelled against a British officer of singular charm of manner, who had not sought the post thrust upon him by Lord Salisbury,[124] and who quickly inspired to the to an unusual degree the confidence of his famous chief. Never did a minister receive more frequent congratulations. We ought to be proud, said Lord

---

Tokyo, becoming ambassador there when the status of the legation was raised to that of an embassy.

121 Sir John Walsham, Baronet, 1830–1905, was a diplomat.
122 William Nelthorpe Beauclerk, 1849–1908, diplomat.
123 Sir Robert Hart, Bt, 1835–1911, British official serving the Qing dynasty as Inspector-General of China's Maritime Customs Service from 1863–1908 which Hart staffed with a cadre of brilliant foreign linguists, mostly British but also Americans and Western Europeans. Himself a formidable linguist, with equally formidable powers of organisation, he transformed Chinese Customs into the single most important source of revenue for the Chinese Government and expanded its operations to include managing lighthouses, China's first postal service, and source of diplomatic advice. To the extent that the Chinese trusted any foreigner they trusted Hart—his Chinese nickname was "our Hart". He was given Chinese honours of the highest rank including the Red Button, a Peacock's Feather and the Order of the Double Dragon, among others. He was created a baronet in 1893. He married Hester Breedon in 1866 and had three children with her; they separated in 1882 when Hart went to live with his Chinese mistress, Ayou, with whom he also had three children.
124 Robert Arthur Talbot Gascoyne-Cecil, 3rd Marquess of Salisbury, 1830–1903. Lord Salisbury was three time British prime minister, foreign secretary known for his policy of "splendid isolation" from entanglements abroad, especially in Europe. His last period as PM was 1895–1902. A man of formidable intellect but of melancholy disposition, a Victorian titan indeed.

Salisbury in his speech at the Albert Hall, to live in an age which has produced great generals like Lord Kitchener and Sir William Lockhart, and great statesmen and diplomatists, like Lord Cromer and Sir Claude MacDonald. Even then there were not wanting those who declared that Sir Claude on reading the singular compliment had remarked with a sigh "Why drag in Cromer?"

The technical work of the Legation is in the hands of linguists, or dragomans, Chinese secretaries as they are called officially, who are selected from the Consular service for practical knowledge of Chinese. On my arrival, the Chinese Secretary was Mr. Henry Cockburn,[125] a man of acute mind and ready wit, who played a conspicuous part in the troubled times preceding the Boxer outbreak. With him was associated Mr. C. W. Campbell,[126] who had an unusual knowledge of the interior of China and had written the best report on Korea ever published. Our military attaché and the first to hold the post was Colonel G. F. Browne, DSO. Of the Foreign Ministers in Peking the most formidable was August Gérard,[127] the French minister, who had signed on June the 20th 1895 the convention which his name has since been associated. Profiting as he described it, by the privileged position gained by France in China as a consequence of joining Russia and Germany in forcing from Japan the retrocession of the Liaotung Peninsula and Port Arthur, he had induced China to permit the extension of the Annamite border as far as the river Mekong. In acceding to this suggestion for what is known as a rectification of the frontier, China conceded to France, two states Muang U and Muang U-tai belonging to territory which she had previously undertaken not to cede to any other nation without previously coming

---

125 Henry Cockburn, 1859–1927, was born in Calcutta (his father a judge in India), and he served in China for 25 years until 1905 when he was sent as Consul to Seoul, Korea at the beginning of the Japanese occupation. His son, Claud, was a famous leftwing journalist and editor of *The Week* in the 1930s. Claud's sons, Alexander, Andrew and Patrick, have all distinguished themselves in journalism.

126 Charles William Campbell, 1861–1927, an experienced Consul-scholar who also wrote *Travels in Mongolia, 1902: A Journey,* London HM Stationary Office, 1904.

127 Auguste Gérard, 1852–1922, French diplomat who served as ambassador at Peking 1893–1897 and Tokyo 1907–1913. He wrote memoirs of his embassies to both countries.

to an agreement with Her Britannic Majesty.[128] Sir Nicholas O'Connor, the British minister, had discovered the intrigue, and unavailing he had endeavoured to prevent signature. Actually, he was seated in one room in the Tsungli Yamên, waiting to see the Chinese ministers while the convention was being signed by Prince Ching in another room. This action of France caused considerable resentment. It was China as usual who had to suffer and shortly before my arrival in Peking on February the 4th 1897, she had made reparation and had consented to a further rectification of the Burma frontier, to the advantage of Great Britain.

M. Gérard was unmarried. He had spent several years in Germany and he was reputed, I know not with what truth, to be the author of a book that had more than passing success entitled *Society in Berlin*.[129]

Almost equally energetic and the trusted colleague of M. Gérard was M. A Pavlov,[130] the Russian *Chargé d'Affaires*, an ex-naval officer who had taken charge of the Legation on the departure for St. Petersburg of the Minister, M. Cassini[131] with *his* famous Convention in his pocket. So was Baron von Heyking[132] who played later so conspicuous apart in

---

128 Britain would use this failure of China to consult as a pretext for extending its territory—the so-called New Territories—around Hong Kong. See p. 494 of this narrative.

129 Comte Paul Vasili (Auguste Gérard). *La Société de Berlin, Augmenté de lettres inédites*, Paris, Nouvelle revue, 1884. A bitchy and acid account of the power elite in Berlin in the late 1870s. Gérard, as Morrison suggests, might be the author.

130 Alexandr Ivanovich Pavlov, 1860–1923, Russian diplomat and spy stationed in Peking in the mid-1890s until transfer to Seoul in 1904–05. He returned to Shanghai where his attempt to set a branch of the Russian Secret Service in Shanghai was exposed in 1907–08. He died in obscurity in France.

131 Arturo Paul Nicholas Cassini, Marquis de Capuzzuchi de Bologna, Count de Cassini, 1836–1919, was a diplomat with the Russian government for 55 years, and who, in 1891, was appointed to the post of envoy extraordinary and minister plenipotentiary to the Chinese Imperial Court at Peking. He refused to present his credentials to anyone but the Emperor, something the Chinese finally complied with. Russia was building the Trans-Siberian Railway and wanted a warm water port in the east. After the Sino-Japanese War Cassini was instrumental in depriving Japan of its territorial gains and winning for Russia significant presence on the Liaotung peninsular, especially Port Arthur and Talien (Dalien) Bay.

132 Edmund Freiherr von Heyking, 1850–1915, German diplomat. Ambassador at Peking 1896–1899.

the extension of German influence in the Far East, a Livonian educated at Dorpath, Baron von Heyking had been in the Russian government service, had edited a paper in Riga, had become suspect and had withdrawn to Germany and become naturalised finding favour with Bismarck. He had entered the German government diplomatic service, was consul general in Calcutta and afterwards in Cairo. He was in Cairo during the Fashoda[133] incident, but was antagonistic to Lord Cromer and was recalled when his position became untenable. From Cairo he was promoted to Peking.

Japanese interests were in the care of Fumio Yano[134] whose first secretary, Gonsuke Hayashi[135] had been *Chargé d'Afaires* after the departure of Baron Tadasu Hayashi,[136] of whom by the way, he was in no way related. Both subsequently rose to the highest posts in the service Gonsuke to be Baron Hayashi Ambassador in Rome, Tadasu to be Count Hayashi Ambassador in London and Foreign Minister.

The American and the American minister and Dean of the diplomatic body was the honourable Charles Denby,[137] a man of striking presence, as handsome as a Greek god to use the phrase by which he was justly described by Sir Robert Hart.

---

133 The name given to an international incident involving France and Britain in the scramble for territory in East Africa. Fashoda (today Kodok) is in South Sudan and was reinforced by Egypt to counter the east African slave trade. It was also the place where Franco/British imperial ambitions collided. France was defeated.
134 Yano Fumio, 1850–1931, Meiji era intellectual, spent the last 39 years of his life as writer and journalist.
135 Hayashi Gonsuke, 1860–1939, Japanese diplomat from a distinguished samurai family in Aizu (now Fukushima Prefecture). His diplomatic career was a succession of increasingly important appointments in China and Korea with a stint, in 1920–25 as Ambassador in London towards the end of his career.
136 Count Hayashi Tadasu, 1850–1913, politician and diplomat. Born Sato Singoro, he took name by which his is known to history following adoption. He was an early Japanese visitor to Britain after the Meiji Restoration, especially keen to learn about modern engineering methods. Prior to his appointment to Peking in 1895 he was Vice-Minister for Foreign Affairs. He was the first Ambassador to Britain in 1905 when diplomatic relations were upgraded.
137 Colonel Charles Denby, 1830–1904, fought for the Union in the Civil War and resigned his commission to pursue the law. He was an active Democrat and was appointed Minister in Peking in 1895–98 during Grover Cleveland's first term.

English was the main language of diplomatic intercourse and almost without exception, all the foreign ministers spoke English well. There had however, been an occasion recently when English had been nearly displaced by French, equal voting had required the casting vote of the dean. There was a moment of there was a moment of suspense for Mr. Denby prided himself upon his knowledge of Parisian. Once speaking in French in public, he had complimented Baroness von Heyking, who spoke English like an English woman, upon her wisdom, aspirating that she was *la plus sage femme* of Peking, but when the vote was taken he could not pass by his own language, so English held its ground for some time longer.

Among Chinese officials at the time, the most powerful was Prince Ching, president of the Tsungli Yamen the most cumbrous body that ever mismanaged the affairs of a nation, but the best known was another Minister of the Tsungli Yamen, the ex-Viceroy Li Hung-chang,[138] who

---

138 Li Hongzhang, 1823–1901, was an official who tried to modernise China. He was for a time de facto in charge of China's foreign relations and he administered a large area of China centred on Tianjin. A brilliant scholar-official, Li was a statesman, diplomat, politician and military leader. In his day, he was compared to Bismarck, the dominant continental European politician of the final quarter of the 19th century. However, unlike Bismarck, who built a nation, it was Li's lot to preside over the breakup of the Chinese Empire. He was unable to prevent the collapse of the Qing dynasty's 'tribute' system, which kept Vietnam, Korea, Okinawa, among others, quiescent and in the Chinese orbit. He forged an alliance with the Russian Empire that took vast tracks of Chinese territory.

From 1870–1895, Li was Viceroy at Tianjin and from that position was China's principal interlocutor with foreigners, especially in times of crisis. On his watch Korea's bonds to China were severed and he settled the Franco-Chinese war in 1885 by ceding Vietnam to France. He represented China after its defeat in the Sino-Japanese War of 1894–95, signing the Treaty of Shimonoseki which ceded Taiwan and Okinawa to Japan as well as the Liaoning peninsula, which Japan was later forced to retrocede to Russia.

In business, he started the China Merchants Steamship Company in 1872 (a company later resurrected by Deng Xiaoping after China's re-embrace of modernisation in the 1980s), coal mines in Kaiping, producing 250,000 tonnes a year, and he favoured railways which brought him into opposition with the Empress Dowager. He told Ito Hirobumi, the Japanese statesman, in 1895 that, "Affairs in my country have been so confined by tradition that I could not accomplish what I desired ... I am ashamed of having excessive wishes and lacking the power to fulfil them." For a fuller account of Li's life and career see 'Li Hung-chang', by William J. Hall in A. W. Hummel, *Eminent*

had recently returned from his mission to Russia indoctrinated with belief in Russian friendship. Li Hung-Chang lived in Hsien Liang Ssu, the Temple of Worthies. His private secretary was W. N. Pethick,[139] an American scholar who served the viceroy with single minded devotion for more than 20 years.

Early among my experiences in Peking, was the revelation of the untrustworthiness of the Chinese telegraph office. Shortly after my arrival I received from the telegraph clerk, whom I knew slightly a brief note enclosing a code message. The note said, "The under mentioned tele sent by Dr. Dudgeon. Can you make out the above news?" I never attempted to. Dr. Dudgeon, formerly of the London mission, was at the time Reuter's Correspondent. He was also the representative of a Syndicate seeking gold mining concessions in Mongolia. A learned scholar he had introduced the art of photography to China and the Chinese terms for photographic phenomena were of his devising. He had written books of permanent value upon the opium question and upon Russian ecclesiastical mission to Peking. For Trübner's Oriental Series he had translated into English four learned works of Bretschneider.[140] No man in Peking was better known. Distressed by the prevalence of the vice, he had introduced morphia pills to check the opium habit, and this had led to the of severance of his connection with the London Mission, of which he had been one of the most conspicuous workers. But his interest in mission work never ceased: nor the mission alleged did his interest in morphia pills. Another field of activity claimed his attention. He undertook to provide the Chinese with a loan of £16,000,000 on behalf of the British Syndicate and on May 1897, signed a preliminary contract to this end, going immediately afterwards to the telegraph office to cable the news to Reuter for the

---

Chinese of the Ch'ing Period. U. S. Government Printing Office, Washington DC, 1943, vol. 1, pp. 464–471. Li's life cries out for a modern biographer.

139 William Pethick was one of Morrison's most important sources. Pethick went to China after the American Civil War with a letter of recommendation from Abraham Lincoln. Pethick was for 30 years in the employ of Li Hongzhang. Pethick distinguished himself during the 1900 Boxer Uprising, leading a group of 10 US soldiers to save Chinese Christians. He died in 1901, the same year as Li.

140 Emil Bretschneider, 1833–1901, a Baltic German, sinologist. He wrote about early contact between China and the west, and botany.

information of the world. Dr. Dudgeon, undertook to pay 100,000 taels forfeit if he failed to give effect to the contract. Unfortunately, however, he was never able to sign the final contract, nor was he ever able to pay the forfeit.

Li Hung-chang entrusted to his friend, Mr. Louis Spitzel[141] the task of recovering the 100,000 taels promising him a commission of 30%. But Mr. Spitzer was unsuccessful. His dunning of Dr. Dudgeon caused some pain to that worthy scholar during the last few years of his stay in Peking.

Then and for some years afterwards, Mr. Louis Spitzel was a power in China. A British stalwart as his named denotes, born in Trieste of Israelite parents Mr. Spitzel had come to China animated, he himself assured me, by a patriotic desire to further British interests. He had expected a more cordial reception than was accorded to him at the British Legation, whose methods he thought contrasted unfavourably with the wholehearted support given to his American brother Adolf at the American Legation, and his German brother Fritz at the German Legation. A dealer in jewels and in discarded arms, Mr. Spitzel, early won the confidence of Li Hung-chang by his expert knowledge. Li Hung-chang was parsimonious to an exceptional degree and was always disgusted—it was Pethick who told me—when foreign decorations were given to the Empress, for she would take out the jewels and set them in bangles and then send the decorations to Li Hung-chang to have new jewels substituted. This continued until Louis showed the advantage in such cases of the use of paste and his friendship was grounded upon a rock. Before coming to China, Mr. Spitzel had been had been a jeweller in Victoria and in Queensland, and had considerable experience of bankruptcy court and both colonies. For a long time, his success was most marked. Probably the most inferior consignment of arms, whichever the Chinese had ever purchased was planted upon them by Mr. Spitzel, who overrode all objections by communicating

---

141 Spitzel is a shadowy figure of uncertain ancestry. Australian newspaper reports have him born in Cracow, Poland, and trading there as a diamond cutter. In 1878 he was working in Melbourne in the jewellery trade. He left Australia in 1887 for China where Morrison becomes aware of him. He lost his fortune in England in a series of trades involving British, French and German stocks, was destitute. He evidently remade his fortunes, and died in 1906 with an estate reportedly valued at £2 million.

in confidence to the wise men of the Board of War that the markets he was selling them that the muskets he was selling them were the identical arms, so help him, with which England had won the Battle of Waterloo. Mr. Spitzel was a man of considerable courage. In the case of Bainbridge versus Spitzel, when the return of money was claimed which it was alleged had been obtained by false pretences, Mr. Justice Farwell paid tribute to his courage. Never have I met, he said, a more audacious witness. Mr. Spitzel amassed a fortune during the Russo-Japanese war. His death was a serious loss to British prestige in China.

When I first came to Peking, Mr. Spitzel was in the partnership with another gentleman and American named W. F. Sylvestre, whose earlier name had been Fred Sutterle, a name to which he has since reverted. Later Mr. Sylvester became correspondent of the *Daily Mail*, and his picturesque and veracious description of the massacres of the Legations in Peking, was one of the greatest scoops ever made by that enterprising paper.

Very early in my work, I learned the futility, contrary to general belief of purchasing secret news. One day a Japanese colleague asked me if I would join with him in buying certain information regarding Russian action in Korea. I was glad to do so. But a few days later, my colleague came to me and frankly told me the information he had bought was useless—it was wholly fictitious—and he would not let me share the expense he had been needlessly put to. During the many years I have been in China, I have never, with one exception when publication was a question of urgency, to be mentioned later, paid money for news. I have never employed a secret service. To give an illustration of the danger of following a different course. At the time of the Japanese negotiations in Peking in December 1905 following upon the Portsmouth peace treaty, correspondence which Japanese newspapers were naturally anxious to obtain early knowledge of the terms of China's adhesion, a friend of mine, a Japanese colleague of high character, was offered one day for $400 what purported to be the complete text of the agreement. It was so cleanly worded that it bore apparent evidence of authenticity. My friend paid the $400 and cabled the text to Tokyo, published without misgivings in Japan, it was telegraphed to Europe to *The Times* and reproduced in many other papers. Yet the text was wholly fictitious. (Vide the Appendix).[142]

On my arrival in Peking, and for long afterwards, Russian influence was paramount in North China. Russia, combined with France and Germany, had taken the lead in compelling Japan to relinquish the chief fruits of her victorious war against China[143] and still further playing upon China's fears had been amply rewarded for doing so. The authenticity of the Cassini convention, the secret treaty signed with Li Hung-chang in Peking, and carried back by Count Cassini to Russia, though questioned at the time was afterwards abundantly manifest. A version of the convention somewhat garbled, but correct in its main provisions, had come into the possession of *The Times* correspondent in Shanghai, and had been telegraphed to London but the story he revealed, was not believed at headquarters, and instead of being thanked for his zeal, he was dismayed to find his famous message damned by the apologetic preface "Among the English in China," said *The Times*, "the belief in a secret treaty between China and Russia, facilitating the advance of the latter to the Gulf of Pechili,[144] seems to be proof against all official and semi-official denials. As an illustration of the current rumours we are giving the following telegram which we received last night from Shanghai from which it is evident that the inventors of current reports have more imagination than knowledge." He was still further dismayed to learn that his services had been dispensed with.

On the occasion of the Imperial coronation in Moscow (May 26 1896) Li Hung-chang was charged with a special embassy to convey gifts to the Tsar. A year later return gifts were sent by the Tsar to the Emperor in Peking. The special Ambassador entrusted with their delivery,

---

142 No longer in Morrison's papers.
143 This is the Sino-Japanese War that was concluded with the Treaty of Shimonoseki in 1896 which, inter alia, ceded large tracts of land situated on in Liaoning peninsular, including Port Arthur (Lushun), to Japan. Russia, Germany and France forced Japan to relinquish control of the peninsula to Russia. One of the best accounts of the war is S. C. M. Paine's *The Sino-Japanese War of 1894–1895 Perceptions, Power, and Primacy*. New York: Cambridge University Press, 2003.
144 Now known as the Bohai Sea.

being Prince Hesper Ockhtomsky,[145] the editor of the St. Petersburg "Vledomosti" an authority on Tibetan Lamaism. The companion Tsar while still Czarovitch on his journey through Asia, an account of which he had written into monumental volumes and the President of the Council of the Russo-Chinese bank. Prince Ockhtomsky landed in Tentsin on May 17th, and on the 21st he arrived in Peking by the first train that ever carried passengers to the walls of the city. His mission and especially his coming by train profoundly stirred the Chinese imagination. All of us foreigners rode out to witness the arrival. An immense concourse of people swarmed in serried masses across the dusty plain beyond the South Gate to the rail head at Ma Chia Pu. Charles Denby Jr,[146] who in the absence of his father was in charge of the American Legation rode with me to the platform. "What is it," asked Mr. Denby of the Chinese as we threaded our way through the crowd. The answer came back in every case the same. "It is the brother of the Tsar who brings tribute to the Emperor."

At his first audience with the Emperor the ceremony to be observed was the same as that provided for the reception of other foreign envoys. Chinese present, however, declared that never before had a foreigner been received with such extraordinary honour. At the second audience when Prince Ockhtomsky presented to the emperor the presents sent to the Empress Dowager by the Tsaritsa, the Son of Heaven rose to receive them from the Envoy's hands. No similar mark of Imperial condescension had been recorded in China since her gates were first forced open to foreign intercourse. Pethick, who heard of the audience from Li Hung-chang wrote to me in the morning: "At the audience today the Emperor stood up to receive the gifts handed to him by the Russian Ambassador. This is the first instance on record of a Chinese emperor rising to the occasion." Among the gifts was one deserving special mention for his undergone strange vicissitudes. It was the allegorical representation in silver, of the "Emancipation of Bulgaria by the intervention of Russia." Originally designed as a gift for Prince Alexander of Battenburg, the prince of Bulgaria from his uncle the

---

145 Prince Esper Esperovich Ukhtomsky, 1861–1921, orientalist and confidant to Tsar Nicholas II. Morrison uses an older version of his name.
146 Charles Denby Jr, 1861–1938, Chinese scholar, first secretary at Peking for US Legation.

Tsar Alexander II, it was still in the artist's studio when the Tsar was assassinated and by the time it was completed Prince Alexander had fallen from grace and lost the Imperial favour. The group remained in the possession of the imperial family. Fourteen years later Japan was compelled to relinquish possession of Dalny[147] and Port Arthur. When return gifts were being gathered for presentation to the Chinese emperor, what more natural than to send to His Majesty the silver model originally intended for the Prince of Bulgaria. Few alterations were needed to convert the statuette from the Emancipation of Bulgaria by the Intervention of Russia, to the Emancipation of Manchuria by the Intervention of Russia. In its new guise, the group was carried by Prince Ockhtomsky to Peking. Later in 1900 when Peking was in the possession of foreign troops the silver group with its strange allegory resting on a black wood table in one of the Emperor's Dowager's apartments, was an object of much curiosity to those foreigners who had access to the inner recesses of the palace.

Tangible results followed the mission of Prince Ockhtomsky not the least important being the sanctioning by Russia Imperial ordinance of the articles of Association of the projected Russian railway across Manchuria, for the construction of which a concession giving effect to the terms of the Cassini Convention had been granted to Russia in the previous year. The attention of the world was directed to this railway by which the pacific conquest of Manchuria was to be achieved. To inspect the course of the railway and report upon its possibilities was now imperative. Accordingly, in the last week of July 1897, having completed my arrangements, I set out for Siberia on this mission, accompanied by the same Siamese half-caste who had travelled with me to Yunnan and followed my fortunes to begin, a born traveller, Ah Heng had looked forward with keen interest to the journey through Siberia and across Manchuria from Mongolia to Vladivostok. During his stay in Peking, he had added to his other languages, a working knowledge of Chinese. From Peking I went by Shanghai to Nagasaki, where I took passage to Vladivostok in the Russian volunteer steamer Kostroma. Then I went by train to Imaum on the Ussuri river, where I embarked on a river

---

147 The Russified name of Dalian on the Liaoning peninsula.

11 | 'REMINISCENCES'

steamer and floated downstream to Habarovsk. Letters of introduction had been given me by M. Pavlov and these ensured me a correct if not a cordial reception. General Duhovskoi,[148] the Governor General of Eastern Siberia, was ill and I did not see him. But I met the Chief of Staff, General Grodekoff,[149] the famous Chief of Staff of General Skobeleff,[150] who had a company that famous military adventurer in Central Asia, and had been present at the massacre of Keok Teppe, and had been the historian of his achievements.

In a crowded steamer, Ah Heng and I travelled up the Amur. At Blagovestchensk, the prosperous river port of the Zeya gold fields, I frequently met Colonel Grombtchevsky,[151] the stormy petrel of Russian advance in Central Asia, the engineer explorer and companion of Prjevalski.[152] At the time of my journey Stretensk on the Shilka was the limit of steam navigation, the starting point of the overland mail to the Siberian rail head at Virknei-udinsk.[153] By the Amur I had gone north and west and south around three sides of Manchuria. I now left the river and doubled back by land across Manchuria to my original starting point.

Leaving Stretensk in a Tarantass[154] kindly lent to me by a Russian merchant, who had frequently visited Peking, I drove my post stages eastwards through Russian territory as far as Nerckinski Savod, where Major General von Sünnerberg a charming old soldier, helped me to hire a fresh tarantass, in which I drove through steppes swarming with

---

148 Sergei Mihailovich Dukhovskoi, 1838–1901, Russian military officer.
149 Died 1914.
150 Mikhail Dmitriyevich Skobelev, 1843–1882, Russian general who conquered Central Asia. The massacre to which Morrison refers was in 1881 at Geoktepe fort in Turkestan where Skobelev put down Tekke Turkman resistance to Russian control. Some 8,000 Turkmen soldiers and civilians were killed in addition to 6,500 who died inside the fortress. Skobelev was relieved of command and transferred to Minsk.
151 Bronislav Ludwigovich Grombchevsky, 1855–1926, Polish officer in the Imperial Russian Army and noted explorer/spy in central Asia.
152 Nikolay Mikhaylovich Przhevalsky, 1839–1888, Russian geographer and explorer of Central Asia.
153 Today known as Ulan-Ude, the capital of Buryat-Mongol Autonomous region of the Russian Federation.
154 A four-wheeled Russian travelling-carriage without springs, on a long flexible wooden chassis.

partridges and wildfowl southwards down the Russian treeless border of Mongolia, crossed into Chinese territory and continued with Mongol escort to Hailar, then an unimportant village, now an important town on the Russian railway. My Russian driver had frequently made the journey, spoke Mongol well, and was at home among the Mongols. From Hailar my course was directed east again, across the width of Manchuria. In high wheeled Mongo carts, springing in light, I drove across the steppes and through the forest of the Khingan Mountains to Tsitsihar, the capital town of the province of Hei-lung-chiang.[155] Russian engineers with Russian guards were everywhere in evidence. There was still uncertainty as to the railway route. Engineers was searching for the easiest alignment. Leaving Tsitsihar where our light Mongol carts were exchanged for heavy springless Peking carts drawn by three animals, the route I followed was not the one ultimately adopted for the railway. Through haunts of wild geese and along the banks of the Nonni. I came to Fetune, crossed to Kirin, the capital of Kirin province, one of the most picturesque and interesting of Manchurian cities, and then journeyed on through that glorious country of forests teeming with pheasants, which lives between Omoso and Ninguta. At Ninguta I met our Military Attaché, Col. G. F. Browne DSO,[156] who had also travelled in Manchuria, and had just finished a journey of immense hardship over the mountains from Sansing. A few stages further I crossed the frontier at San Chia K'ou and took train at Nikholski to Vladivostok, where I cable to *The Times*, a message about my journey.

Every Russian engineer of authority met on the journey had spoken of Port Arthur as the hoped for terminus of their railway. With this knowledge in my possession, I telegraphed to *The Times* that a preliminary survey from the projected trans Manchurian railway was about to be made to Port Arthur. Fearing, however, that the words Port Arthur would not be permitted to pass over the wire, I wrote instead, its Chinese name, Lu Hsuan Kao. But the name was unfamiliar. It was printed as Lu Ksuan kan and was unintelligible. No attention, therefore

---

155 Today Heilungjiang.
156 Major General George Fitzherbert Browne, 1851–1935, was Britain's military attaché in Peking 1896–1903, although not present during the Boxer rebellion.

was given to the announcement, and in view of what happened shortly afterwards, this was very unfortunate.

Vladivostok I reached on the 22nd of November and a few days later, I left by steamer for Chefoo.[157] "What is the news?" was the first question I put to our Consul at the treaty port. "Germany has seized Kiaochao Bay," he replied. Hastily he told me the story. On the 14th November following the murder on November 1st of fathers Nies and Henle[158] at Kuyeh-hsien in Shantung province, Germany had entered into possession of one of the finest harbours in Eastern China, and a new chapter in Far Eastern history had opened. A few days later, I was in Peking.

Of the German occupation of Kiaochao and the causes which led up to it much has been written. Baron von Heyking conducted the negotiations with uncommon dexterity. Prior to the occupation, his chief anxiety was the need of ascertaining whether China was under any antecedent obligation to Russia with regard to this harbour. But his doubt was set at rest at an interview with Li Hung-chang at the Tsungli Yamên in September 1897, when he satisfied himself that he could demand the cession or "lease" of care of Kiaochao, without involving Germany—whatever might be the case with Chin—in difficulties with the Northern Colossus.[159]

In 1896 Baron von Heyking had decided upon securing Kiaochao Bay for Germany, but by the terms of the Cassini convention Russia had some prior claim to lease the harbour for a term of years and to erect their coaling sheds, docks and barracks and otherwise to use it as a convenient calling place for her Far Eastern squadron. Was such a claim well founded or not? Fear of raising suspicion compelled him in

---

157 Know now as Yantai, it is situated on the south eastern coast of the Bohai Strait and was a Treaty Port. Today it is an important fishing port.
158 Franz Xaver Nies, 1859–1897, a German catholic missionary and Richard Henle, 1863–1897, both with the Society of the Divine, were killed in the Juye Incident early in the morning of 2 November (All Souls' Day) having celebrated mass for All Saints' Day that evening. Both priests were German and the Germany government used their murder as a pretext for territorial expansion in Shandong and the takeover of its strategic ports. This move by Germany began a grab by other powers for territory in China.
159 i.e., Imperial Russia.

the meantime to keep silence. He waited till September 1897, when in the Tsungli Yamên one day he said to Li Hung-chang: "It is the wish of my government that our ships during the coming winter may visit the northern ports of Port Arthur, Wei Hai Wei and Kiaochao. In regard to the two former I apprehend there is no difficulty, but in the case of Kiaochao, I understand that Russia has some prior claim, so we should ask Russia if there be any objection." Li Hung-chang jumped at once. "What has Russia got to do with it?" he asked petulantly. "I understand that some arrangement exists between Russia and China," said Baron von Heyking blandly. "None exists. The matter does not concern Russia. It has to do with China only."

Baron von Heyking had learned all he wanted. On the 5th October, he went south in the Prince Heinrich and called at Kiaochao on the way. Pretence was made that the machinery had broken down. Divers were sent overboard and a hasty inspection of the harbour made. He went on to Hankow, and there he heard of the murder of the Shantung missionaries. The Chinese had played into his hands. He returned to Shanghai, where Admiral von Diederichs[160] alone was admitted into his confidence. Two German ships under the Admiral proceeded to Kiaochao Bay, the third being left in dock in Shanghai. Baron von Heyking came straight to Peking, and the admiral occupied Kiaochao on November 14th. The Baron told me that the only man to suspect German action in Kiaochao was Henry O'Shea, a clever Irish journalist in Shanghai.

M. Pavlov was furious: the Russian Foreign Office were furious, but could do nothing, trammelled as they were, by the assurance given by the Tsar, to the German Emperor. On the occasion of their famous meeting at Darmstadt, (October 10th, 1896) that in the matter of Kiaochao Russia was quite *disinteréssé*. No reprisals, therefore, against Germany where possible, but history repeated itself and China was punished—the weak China which had shown itself defenceless to German aggression.

---

160 Ernst Otto von Diederichs, 1843–1918, was a German admiral of the Prussian Navy who served both the Kingdom of Prussia and the German Empire. He was the first governor of the German Jiaozhou Bay concession in China.

11 | 'REMINISCENCES'

When the German marines landed it Kiaochao. The Chinese garrison were quite ignorant of their intention. Soldiers turning their old fashion jackets inside out so as to conceal their military character, ran down to the landing to assist the boat ashore and earn a few cents by carrying the luggage of the German crew. Could any illustration given be more significant of the absence of Chinese national spirit? The Chinese were no more awake to the consciousness of nationality than they were in 1860 when Cantonese coolies assisted the British and French landing parties in the operations at Taku,[161] or then they were in 1884 when diplomatic relations continued amicably with the French delegation and Peking while the French fleet under Admiral Courbet[162] were bombarding the forts at Foochow.[163]

Back in his Legation in Peking Baron von Heyking began the negotiations "intended to strengthen the bonds of friendship uniting the two countries" which ended on March 6 1898 in the Kiaochao Convention and the formal "lease" to Germany for 99 years of the finest harbour on the coast of China, and the guaranteeing to Germany of all manner of preferential advantages, railway rights, mining rights, preferential employment rights both men and capital throughout the provinces of Shantung, a province as large as England and Wales.

Throughout these disastrous negotiations China was represented by two men whose names are famous in the history of the empire, Li Hung-chang, whose inability to recognise modern conditions and whose policy of playing of one power against the other invariably involved his country in costly difficulties with both powers, and Weng Tung-ho,[164]

---

161 This refers to the August 1860 battle of Pei Tang where an Anglo-French force took the Taku forts. This action was a prelude to their march on Peking which was captured in October that year.

162 Anatole-Amédée-Prosper Courbet, 1827–1885.

163 The Battle of Fuzhou, August 1884, occurred during the Sino–French War 1883–85, a war fought by France in pursuit of its demand to colonise Vietnam (and much else in Indochina), until then a tributary state of China's. Courbet was ordered to destroy the naval yards at Fuzhou (constructed with French capital!) in retaliation for a perceived Chinese sleight during talks to resolve the war. In action Courbet only inflicted damage on the yards but destroyed nine of the 11 ships that constituted China's Fujian fleet.

164 Weng Tung-ho (Tonghe), 1830–1904, Confucian scholar who, in 1856, was named top scholar in Imperial examinations and admitted to the prestigious Hanlin Academy.

the Grand Councillor, the greatest scholar of his time, who had been the Emperor's tutor.

To increase still further the prestige of Germany and the Far East, to soften the blow struck at Kiaochao, and in the hope of giving China face, Prince Henry of Prussia, was sent on a visit of courtesy to the Emperor.

On the 16th December 1897, the German emperor was present at the farewell banquet in Kiel Castle, given in honour of "My dear Henry", his brother, when he threatened helpless China in flamboyant terms that provoked laughter throughout Europe. "Should anyone essay to detract from our just rights or to injure us, then up and at him with your mailed fist, and if it be God's will, weave your youthful brow a wreath of laurel, which no one in all the German Empire will grudge you."

The ship in which Prince Henry sailed was the Deutschland, an obsolete ship of war, whose journey was frequently delayed by the breakdown of its engines. In sarcastic terms it was described by a paper reputed to be the most scholarly of English newspapers as "witless William's old iron." Yet it arrived safely. Within three years, the Boxer outbreak had burst upon an astonished world. Fleets of many powers hastened to the Far East. No more striking illustration of the enormous advance made by the German navies since the voyage of the Deutschland could be could be given than the fact that among that assemblage of warships the German men of war were second only to the British in power, speed and equipment.

With the seizure of the Kiaochao Bay a new era began in the Far East. Peaking became the centre of international activity. The energies of Russia, England and France were aroused. No sooner had the Kiaochao landing been effected and the "friendly overtures" began for the cession of the harbour that it was announced that the Russian fleet would pass the winter in Port Arthur.

On December the 22nd 1897 the Tsungli Yamên informed Sir Claude MacDonald that permission had been given to the Russian fleet, which was already in the harbour, to winter at Port Arthur. On December 28th two British Men of War, the Immortalité and the Iphegenia, as they

---

In addition to his role as tutor to the Emperor (both Tongzhi and Guangxu) he was President of the Board of Revenue, Director of the Censorate and President of the Board of Punishments. He was a member of the Grand Council.

had every right to do, anchored in the harbour. On the same day Lord Salisbury telegraphed to Sir Claude MacDonald informing him that the government (urged thereto by the China Association)[165] had under consideration a project to lend China money and thereby enable her to recover immediate possession of Wei Hai Wei, which by the terms of the Shimonoseki Treaty was to remain in Japanese possession until the final payment of the War Indemnity, the amount at the time still outstanding, being £16,450,490. Lord Salisbury asked Sir Claude for suggestions as to the conditions to be attached to the loan, which was to be £12 million, as everyone knows, so Claude suggested as one of the conditions the opening of Talienwan a port close to Port Arthur as a treaty port.

On January 10th, the Immortalité was withdrawn from Port Arthur and on the 27th the Iphegenia was also withdrawn in deference to the protests of Russia, or rather in acceptance of the assurances of count Mouravieff,[166] upon which Lord Salisbury stated British policy was based. Meantime, our loan proposals were under consideration. On January 8th Lord Sailsbury telegraphed the terms upon which England was prepared to advance China £12 million. One of the conditions was the opening of Talienwen as a Treaty Port. So exceptionally favourable were the terms that they naturally excited suspicion even among the Chinese whose goodwill they were designed to win over. To no other country in the world would we have lent money on such generous terms. After they had become well known and had been the subject of diplomatic protest I cabled them to *The Times*. The Foreign Office saw fit to blame me at the time and I have often been since censored for what was termed my "premature disclosure" of the conditions, but the criticism was undeserved.

At that time our conception of diplomatic reticence among the Chinese was immature. We had failed to profit or the lessons of experience. On January 8th Lord Salisbury cabled Sir Claude

---

165 The China Association was an important business lobby on behalf of the China trade. Its chairman was Sir William Des Voeux, former governor of Hong Kong, whose name lives on as an important thoroughfare in Central, Hong Kong island.

166 Count Mikhail Nikolayevich Muravyov, 1845–1900, Russian statesman and architect of its Far East policy.

MacDonald the offer to lend money to the Chinese on terms implying a confidence in China's credit equal to that in British Consols.[167] On the 9th Sir Claude communicated the terms to Li Hung-chang and the next day the British ships anchored in Port Arthur. What other interpretation could the Russian government give to this action than that it was minatory to enforce compliance with the terms of the loan and to gain some advantage and Port Arthur in return for advancing China money on such a split on such suspiciously favourable terms.

Li Hung-Chang, having received the dispatch on the 9th at once sent for M. Pokotiloff,[168] the manager of the Russo-Chinese Bank (afterwards minister to Peking) and submitted the project to his judgement. The same afternoon I found Mr. Pethick when I called on him at the Hsien Liang Ssu, busy with Archer's tables, working out this sum: "What is the rate of interest on a loan that by a service of 4% per annum can be extinguished in 50 years?" No secrecy was maintained. The office speedily became common knowledge. Not an official in Peking interested in the question need have been ignorant the terms of the proposal. On January 12th M. Hanotaux[169] discussion the question with Edmond Monson[170] in Paris disclosed knowledge of the conditions. On January 15th Sir Claude MacDonald was officially informed at the Tsungli Yamên that M. Pavlov, under instructions from his government, had protested in the strongest manner against the conditions of the loan, especially that which provided for the opening of Talienwan[171] as a treaty poured. His protest implied that he had known the terms some days earlier, for he had in the meantime communicated with his government. On the 15th the local weekly paper published in Tiensin commented in an editorial on the terms of the loan: "there seems every reason for believing" it said "that the negotiations between the British and Chinese Governments have reached that final point

---

167 The name given to the Consolidation of British government debt that occurred in the 1750s. By Morrison's time Consols were issued at 2.75%.
168 Dmitry Pokotiloff served as Russian ambassador at Peking from 1905–08.
169 Albert Auguste Gabriel Hanotaux, 1853–1944, French statesman who and historian who was France's minister of Foreign Affairs from 1894 to 1895 and 1896 to 1898.
170 Sir Edmund John Monson, 1834–1909, a British diplomat who was minister or ambassador to several countries, including Paris, 1895–1905.
171 Dalian, a major port on the Liaoning peninsula.

where a satisfactory issue becomes practically and assured fact ... We have every confidence that the terms will be such as to satisfy even the dismal pessimist, as such a low rate of interest clearly points to some offset of a very advantageous nature to British interests."

The terms having thus become public property I cabled them to London on January 16th and they were published in *The Times* on January the 17th. The same day Sir Claude, under instructions, and in pursuance of our policy of accepting Russia's assurances, withdrew our amount for the opening of Talienwan, and on February 3rd China, in deference to Russian opposition, formally refused the British offer.

The Foreign Office so fit to excuse its blundering by declaring that my premature disclosure had lost Britain alone. My telegram did nothing of the kind. It was not a disclosure, it was not premature and Britain did not lose the loan. Where the government had failed the Hongkong Shanghai Bank succeeded, and through its agent in Peking signed on February 19th a preliminary contract undertaking to lend China the sum of £16 million on terms much more favourable to British capital than those proposed by the British government.

In this transaction the British bank was acting in conjunction with the Deutsche-Asiatishe Bank, and the final contract completed on March 1st was signed by the representatives of both banks. This was the first of the Anglo-German loans which were to be so prominent a feature in Chinese finance for the next few years. In the previous year, the two banks had agreed to participate in Chinese government business on equal terms, pooling their respective advantages—British financial experience in China to be associated with the favourable position temporarily secured by Germany by her alliance with Russia and France in depriving Japan of the fruits of her victorious war and compelling the retrocession of Port Arthur and the Liaotung Peninsula.

No overt opposition was offered to the loan while negotiations were in progress but the Russian legation was bent upon its undoing and secretly was preparing for the coup which was to shake the bosses of Europe and profoundly modify the course of history. On the day of the ratification of the loan the blow was delivered.

At this time the Russian delegation, as I have already said, was in charge of M. Pavlov, an ex-naval officer who owned his rapid promotion to the protection of Count Cassini, but the power behind delegation was M. Dimitri Pokotiloff the manager of the Russo-Chinese Bank.

In this generation there has been no abler man in Peking than Pokotiloff. A tall, handsome man, swarthy of complexion, a born linguist who spoke Chinese with unusual fluency, he had gained an insight into Chinese methods and modes of thought rarely acquired by a foreigner. Under his masterful influence, Li Hung-chang became a "fervent apostle of Russian ascendancy." Posing always as a friend of China, straining his energies to prevent the threatened aggression of the Russian Legation he would counsel Li Hung-chang to accept the terms suggested by Russia urging that they were the mildest terms possible and that but for his opposition Russia would have demanded and might still demand if her proposals were rejected, terms that might be disastrous to China.

His influence was at its height, when, to the profound dismay of Li Hung-chang, M. Pavlov presented China with a peremptory demand for the cession of Port Arthur and Talienwan and the right to construct a railway from the Trans-Manchurian railway and on the same condition southward through Mukden to these ice free ports. China was given a time limit of five days for compliance, the Agreement had to be signed within one month of the event of non-compliance Russia threatened to tear up the Cassini convention.

On the evening of Saturday, March 5th, I received a note from Mr. Pethick, asking me if it would be convenient for me to come and see him. He was living in the temple which Li Hung-chang always occupied during his stay in Peking. I went over it once. I found him walking up and down his room in a state of suppressed agitation. He asked me if I were prepared to do a service to China, in whose employ he was. Was I prepared to publish, without disclosing the source from which I had obtained the information, a statement which he could show me? Any indecision on my part would imperil his future. He then showed me the telegram which Li Hung-chang had instructed him to send to Prince Ockhtomsky at St Petersburg. It was written in English in Slaters code arranged between Li Hung-chang and Prince Ockhtomsky during the latter's mission to Peking. It contained a brief summary of the Russian demands and a threat to annul the Cassini Convention and it begged the Prince to see the Tsar and induce him to withdraw the demand.

Next day I cabled the substance of the telegram to The Times and it was published on the morning of the 7th.

In my cable, which, by a curious coincidence, was put on the wires immediately after a telegram from Baron von Heyking to his government announcing that he had just signed the Kiaochao Convention, I purposefully omitted a reference to the Cassini convention, knowing that the existence of the Convention had been denied, and fearing therefore, that its citation would weaken the force of my message. In its stead I inserted the threat that Russia in the event of non-acceptance would move troops into Manchuria, for I had met them during my journey, and had spoken of them in the detailed report of my journey across Manchuria which, by good fortune, was published in The Times on the very same day as the announcement of the Russian demands. An immense sensation was caused by the telegram. It almost created a financial panic. The agent of the Hongkong Bank wrote to me on the 9th saying that he had high authority for declaring that I was mistaken and begging me in the interests of Anglo-German loan to modify my message. Sir Robert Hart still more strongly assured me that I had been misled. Sir Chanting Liang, confidential secretary of the Tsungli Yamên had convinced him that no threat had been made only a friendly proposal. So Robert Hart begged of me, if I wish to avoid wrecking my reputation at the outset, to withdraw my message. When I left him I walked up and down outside his garden wall for a few minutes, thinking the matter over, and then I walked over to over to the telegraph office and wired to *The Times*: "The Chinese Government, while admitting that it has received Russian demands, denies that they were pressing or in their nature of an ultimatum. Despite this denial, I reasserted the correctness of my message on Sunday." The message was published in *The Times* of March 10th.

It may be as well to state that before sending the information to *The Times,* since the question was one of national importance, I informed Sir Claude MacDonald of my intentions. But it was impossible to tell Sir Claude in what way the information had reached me. Sir Claude was cautious and very properly cautious and did not give full credence to the story, and when asked by the Foreign Office for information could only venture to say that there had been negotiations but there was "no indication of anything in the shape of an ultimatum nor so far as he was aware, he had any time limit been given for a reply, as represented in the Press."

The Foreign Office at the time resented the publication of my telegram: they were concerned with the immediate effect it might have on Anglo-German loan negotiations rather than upon the future of Manchuria. As a result of Sir Claude's official message I was charged with having accepted without discrimination the information of a "Mandarin probably prompted by the Russian Legation for the purpose of hampering British negotiations by the premature publication of incomplete information."

On March 22th, the Anglo-German loan was offered for public subscription, but the issue was a failure, the subscription amounted to only 25% of the portion of the loan offered in London.

China agreed, as it was inevitable she must agree, to all the Russian conditions, a statement of which fact I telegraphed on the 24th. My message being published on the 25th the same evening, the 25th, Mr. Curzon,[172] speaking in the House of Commons said, "We have no confirmation of the rumours referred to." *The Times* characterise the situation as a "time of exasperating doubt and perplexity." But Lord Salisbury was in no doubt as to the acceptance, for after reading the message and *The Times* he wired Sir Claude MacDonald, instructing him to demand the reversionary lease of Wei Hai Wei, which had been offered to us on the 25th of February but the offer Lord Salisbury then thought premature, on the same terms as the lease or Port Arthur to Russia in order to restore the balance of power in the Gulf of Pechili so materially affected by the surrender of Port Arthur. On the 27th March the Port Arthur Convention was signed at Peking, the signatories being M. Pavlov, Li Hung-chang and Chang Yin-huan[173] the leading Cantonese in China a member of the Tsungli Yamên who had formerly

---

172 George Nathaniel Curzon, 1859–1925, 1st Marquess Curzon of Kedleston, Conservative grandee, foreign secretary to Sailsbury, Viceroy of India. His quip about journalists intelligently anticipating facts was applied to Morrison.

173 Zhang Yinhuan, 1837–1900, joined the civil service in 1864 and rose steadily through provincial appointments. He gained the support of powerful Manchu princes in the Board of Revenue. He lost out in the palace coup of 1898 which ended, temporarily, China's reform movement and he was exiled to Urumchi in Sinkiang. In 1900, with the Boxer Rebellion in full sway, he was sentenced to death and executed.

been minister to the United States and had represented China at the Queen's Jubilee. And on the 29th Mr. Curzon, in a reply to a question of Mr. Dillon (not to correct in its substance) asking for an explanation of the of the facts that *The Times* had on several occasions published facts of the utmost public importance several days before the Foreign Office had obtained information in respect to them, defined the difference in functions of a diplomatist and a correspondent in the following terms, one phrases of which have often been quoted:

"I think the explanation asked for is not far to see. It is the business of Her Majesty's representatives abroad to report to us facts of which they have official cognizance, and to obtain confirmation of them before they telegraph. I hesitate to say what the functions of a modern journalist are, but I imagined they do not exclude the *intelligent anticipation of facts even before they occur*,[174] and in that somewhat unequal competition I think the House will see that the journalist, whose main duty is speed, is likely sometimes to get the advantage over the diplomatist whose main duty is accuracy."

Demands for the redress of the balance of power and invariable compliance with those demands followed now with bewildering rapidity. A week after the signature of the Kiaochao Convention, before the expiry of the Russian ultimatum, M. Dubail,[175] the French Chargé d'Affaires demanded the lease on the port of Kwangchowwan as this by which Kiaochao Bay had been granted to Germany. On the 2nd April, China complied with the British demand for the set for the cession of Wei Hai Wei and three days later gave her consent to the demands of M. Dubail. A few days later still, on April 27th, China gave Japan a compensatory undertaking regarding Kuhkien Province[176] where Japan has special interests by reason of its geographical relation to Formosa.

While nearly every Englishman rejoiced at the transfer to our flag of the harbour of Wei Hai Wai, and recognise that its possession to some degree counterpoised the Russian occupation of Port Arthur,

---

174 Morrison's emphasis.
175 Georges Dubail, 1845–1932, first went to China in 1876, and was ambassador from 1902–05.
176 I think Morrison here means Fukien, the coastal province opposite Taiwan (Formosa since cession to China in 1896).

serious blunders sensibly reduced the advantages of its acquisition. When our demand for its lease was granted, Mr. Balfour was in charge of the Foreign Office, in the absence of Lord Salisbury through illness. And no sooner was it granted than Mr. Balfour ill-advised gratuitously conveyed to Germany on April 7th the unfortunate undertaking, not to injure or contest the rights and interests of Germany in the province of Shantung, and not to construct any railroad communication from Wei Hai Wei and the district least therewith with the interior of the province of Shantung. And this was not our only blunder. Instead of demanding the cession by lease of Wei Hai Wei for so long time as Port Arthur was in the occupation of "another power", as diplomatic usage dictated parliamentary strategy required that British electors should be impressed with the resolution of our government to abandon the policy of climbing down and their determination to oppose Russia at all reasonable hazards. Therefore, our Convention specified that we would occupy Hai Wei Hai "for so long a period as Port Arthur shall remain in the occupation of Russia."

A few years later, after the Russo-Japanese war, and the Portsmouth peace treaty, when China gave her adhesion to the transfer to Japan, of all Russian rights in South Manchuria, we failed at the same time to arrange with China, as we easily could have done, an amendment to our Convention requiring the alteration of only one word, the substitution of the word Japan for the word Russia. In the latter case, however, this oversight is explicable by the confusion due to the elections and the change of government in England.

Excitement due to the crisis in China brought many correspondents in haste to Peking. Among them the latest unobtrusive was Herr Eugen Wolff, the correspondent of the *Berliner Tageblatt*, an able writer whose work was, however, often disfigured by rather acrid personalities. Herr Wolff had represented his paper in German East Africa and had caused considerable disquiet in Germany by his allegations of unrest in the colony due to the maladministration of the German authorities. These charges form the subject of questions in Parliament.

11 | 'REMINISCENCES'

Inquiries were addressed to the governor, Baron von Soden,[177] as to the truth of the story is transmitted by the Correspondent. His laconic reply when read in the Reichstag, was received with much laughter. It said: "All is quiet in German East Africa except Eugen Wolff." Unconsciously the Baron was anticipating the phrase published many years after in the private correspondence of the Marquess of Dalhousie, who, writing on 30th June 1850, makes similar reference to his arch opponent, Sir Charles Napier, the Commander-in-Chief. "Everything in India continues quiet except the Commander-in-Chief."

Peking at this time was the storm centre of the world. According to Reuter sent here its most distinguished war correspondent, Mr. H. A Gwynne,[178] who has since risen to the highest ranks in the profession of journalism. He remained here throughout 1898, leaving for South Africa in the spring of 1899 in time to organise Reuter's service before the War. His admirable dispatches from Peking, sane, lucid and well balanced, contributed more than anything else written at the time to the to an intelligent understanding of the situation.

Spring and early summer of 1898 were chiefly occupied by the War of the Concessions and the dispute with Russia. The somewhat inglorious part we played in these events—is it not recorded in the Blue Book[179] No. 1, 1898, the most severely criticised of modern Blue Books, the Blue Funk Book as it was dubbed by the cynics!

It was said at the time that to Lord Salisbury the name of China was anathema. His policy in China was a succession of failures yet he

---

177 Alfred Graf von Soden, 1886–1943, later served as Flügeladjutant (Aide-de-Camp) to the Kaiser from 1904. Later as a Generalleutnant in WW1 he was German Military Commander of Brussels. Der Held von Pekin (the Hero of Peking) died at Lübek in April 1943 and was buried with full military honours.
178 Howell Arthur Keir Gwynne, 1865–1950, was a British author and editor of the *London Morning Post* from 1911 to 1937. Gwynne's reputation was dealt a fatal blow by his embrace, in 1920, of the spurious Protocols of the Elders of Zion which he used in an anti-Semitic diatribe about world communism. He was godfather to Ian Morrison.
179 Blue Book is the name given to the publication of diplomatic correspondence and reports by the British Foreign Office. The practice dates back to the early 17th century but reached its height during the 19th century when the British Empire expanded. They represented the 'official view' of events and policies and were issued for parliamentary briefing and public information. Many other countries issued 'colour' books as well.

understood the Chinese better than many of his advisers. His sarcastic references to the Chinese, to their capacity for being squeezed, to the difficulty of reforming those who did not wish to be reformed, contained, often deep truths. His most severe critic was Sir Lepel Griffin,[180] who wrote a series of papers on the "Art of Climbing Down" taking as his text the saying of Bismarck that Salisbury was the lathe of wood painted to look like iron. To meet these charges Lord Salisbury was driven to boast of successes that exist only on paper. On May 4th, speaking at the Primrose League[181] about Living and Dying nations, he referred to his Far Eastern policy and to the concession recently granted for the opening of the inland waterways of China. "We have gained" he boastfully declared "results from China, which we have longed for years. We have induced her to open all the waterways of the Empire to English boats and to English trade." Lord Salisbury omitted to mention an essential condition on the concession, namely that Sir Robert Hart was entrusted with the framing of the regulations. The distinguished I. G. did frame them and when his work was finished he had whittled away the major advantages of the concession. In the words of Sir William Harcourt, Lord Salisbury's squibb fizzled out.

When the political atmosphere in Peking became clearer, Prince Henry of Prussia paid his promised to visit. He was received with the honour due to the brother of the German Emperor, but it cannot be said that the Chinese welcomed his coming. Following so soon after the German occupation of Kiaochao Bay, the Chinese were unable to understand what was the object of his visit. One high official remarked on the day of his departure: "Uninvited he came, unmourned he left." Yet there was no question as to the success of his visit. The Prince made himself universally popular. He was a fine manly fellow, the best type of naval officer. His visit broke down much of the exclusiveness of the barbaric Court, and did much to reconcile conflicting interests in Peking.

180 Sir Lepel Henry Griffin, 1838–1908, diplomat, administrator in India for the Raj. He was a writer, and proponent of Anglo-American political union.
181 A political association for promoting Conservative policies in Britain. Its motto *Imperium et libertas* was not ironic.

11 | 'REMINISCENCES'

There was delay in the coming of the prince to Peking he was expected in April but when he didn't arrive until May 13. Seasons change quickly and peaking. intense cold is rapidly followed by almost tropical heat. Days and weeks passed and the prince did not come with increasing anxiety. The ladies among whom was the brilliant authors of "Letters which never reached him", observed that their dress is were becoming unsuitable for the season. As often happens, Baron von Heyking, invoked the aid of the Press, and asked the correspondent of Reuter and *The Times* correspondent, whether they would see their way to telegraph to their principals stating that the Chinese were much "disappointed" at the non-arrival of Prince Henry. Conscientiously Reuter accepted this view, and on April the 28th wired "Much disappointment is expressed in Chinese circles owing to the postponement of the date of Prince Henry of Prussia's visit to Peking." I equally conscientiously said that if I telegraphed at all, I would have to say that the Chinese would still be more delighted if the Prince didn't come at all. Subsequently I asked Pethick whether the word "disappointed" or "delighted" conveyed the correct impression of the Chinese attitude towards the delayed arrival. He said "elated" would have been the correct word for my suggested message.

The Prince was received in audience by the Empress Dowager. His interpreter was Baron von der Goltz, the Chinese Secretary of the German Legation, who later became minister to Siam. The Prince was struck by the feeble appearance of the Emperor, which contrasted with the singularly well preserved features of the Old Buddha. Gifts some great value had been sent to the Chinese Court. Among them was the Black Eagle set in brilliants[182]—in the whirligig of time it passed into the possession of an enterprising Shanghai stockbroker—and a pair of magnificent vases made in the mirror in the Imperial porcelain works in bought Berlin. They were exquisitely coloured with a forest scene with dead leaves floating in the wind. The Tsungli Yamên were asked to take delivery of these gifts. A common street Cooley, with a carrying pole and two baskets, was sent to receive them as he was leaving the legation with his precious burden. The wretched string with which the basket was

---

182 Diamonds cut so as to capture light.

tied broke. One vase fell and was smashed to fragments, the minister, the master of ceremonies, when he learned of the disaster, came to the legation and suggested to Baron von Heyking, that he should purchase at Carl Imbeck's store a vase to take its place. He seemed to imagine that the Imperial vase was one which could be bought for a few dollars.

Prince Henry left Peking on the 25th of May having been present the evening before at the Queen's Birthday Ball at the British Legation four days before on May the 21st, There had been signed at the Tsungli Yamên the Shansi Concession of the Peking Syndicate, whose representatives was the Cavaliere Angelo Luzzatti,[183] another of those stalwart champions of British interests, whose services have contributed so masterfully to the maintenance of British prestige in far eastern Asia. I had known of the Cavaliere in Siam, where he was concessionaire of the ruby and sapphire mines at Boh Bailin, and of the Bang Ta Pan gold mines in the Siamese Malayan States, and it was instructive and characteristic that in both ventures the enterprise lasted just as long as, and no longer than the capital.

Signor Luzzatti had been in Peking for some months when first concession was obtained from the Chinese. He was insistent upon receiving from the Italian Chargé d'Affaires, the Marquis Salvago Raggi,[184] who was said to groan when he saw his countrymen approach and mutter fervently, "Why did not Pharaoh overtake the flying Israelites?"

But the concession contained no right to build railways to carry the material mined away from the province. Signor Luzzatti then received instructions to remain in Peking and to obtain a more definite concession, and he did so, adapting himself to Chinese ways and gaining much personal popularity with those officials with whom he was associated. His chief Chinese assistant was a man of many parts name,

---

183 Angelo Luzzatti, b. 1858. No relation to Luigi Luzzatti, Italian statesman. He was successful in acquiring mining licences in Siam which gave him an entree to business circles in London.

184 Giuseppe Salvago Raggi, 1866–1946, a diplomat, ambassador to China 1899–1901. He was subsequently ambassador to France and then held a series of administrative roles in Italy's North African colonies.

11 | 'REMINISCENCES'

Ma Kien-chong.[185] Educated in Rome as a Jesuit priest, Ma Kien-chong on his return to China abandoned the Church and became one of the confidential secretaries of Li Hung-chang. When that curious incident occurred "unique in the annals of diplomacy" in connection with the erasure of certain characters in the text of the Fournier convention of Tientsin of May 17th 1884[186] regarding the handing over of various fortresses on the Annam frontier to the French, which incident led to the reopening of hostilities, the capture of the Min Forts and the Blockade of Formosa, the declaration issued to the world by Li Hung-chang, testifying that with their own eyes they had seen Captain Fournier with his own hand make the erasures which he strenuously denied having made, was signed by Low Feng-loh, who was afterwards minister to London and Ma Kien-chong. In 1885 he was sent to Korea as delegate of Li Hung-chang, and there he settled a vexed question by the effective if primitive method of kidnapping the father of the Emperor, the Tai Wen Kun, and carrying him off to China, where he was interned for three years in Paitingfu. Ma Kien-chong later spent some years in Europe, and on his return he again entered the service of Li Hung-chang and was with him in Peking as one of his confidential secretaries, when he came to the assistance of Signor Luzzatti.

Events were now to take place of historic importance in China. During the month of August the Emperor came under the influence of the Cantonese reformer Kang Yu-wei[187] and issued a series of reform decrees which amazed the Empire.

No one doubts the sincerity the young Emperor: no one denies the wise tendency of the reforms that he was attempting to institute.

---

185 Ma Jianzhong, 1845–1900, studied to be a priest in Shanghai and Paris, where he abandoned his seminary studies, instead enrolling in the Sorbonne from which he graduated in 1879 becoming the first Chinese to graduate from a European university. He became and interpreter for Li Hongzhang. He authored the first systematic grammar of classical Chinese (1898) revolutionising Chinese linguistics.

186 It was concluded on May 11. Ernest François Fournier, 1842–1934, was naval officer and diplomat.

187 Kang Youwei, 1858–1927. F. W. Mote provides a sympathetic and scholarly appraisal Kang's thought in his *China and the Vocation of History in the Twentieth Century: A Personal Memoir*, East Asian Library Journal in Association with Princeton University Press, New Jersey, 2010, pp. 68–79.

But the pace was too fast. He had failed to calculate the forces against him. Princes and officials, mandarins and literati were trembling. The Empress Dowager trembled for herself. Urged by the reactionaries she suddenly resumed the office from which she had retired ten years before and seized the throne. On the 15th September all Peking heard with amazement that Weng Tung-ho, the Imperial tutor, believed to be the most influential commoner in the empire, was abruptly dismissed from office. He had introduced Kang Yu-wei and his brother to the Emperor, and this was the fount of his offending. On the night of the 20th Kang Yu-wei escaped from Peking but his brother and five other young reformers, one of whom Tan Ssu-t'ung a Hunanese was the son of the governor of Hubei, were arrested and summarily executed. Next day the Peking Gazette published the first of a series of decrees annulling, one by one, the reform decrees issued by the Emperor under the influence of Kang Yu-wei. The life of no one was safe. There was universal excitement among the Chinese in great anxiety amongst the foreigners. On the morning of the 22nd we were shocked to hear of the arrest of Chang Yin-huan, the best known Cantonese in China, as a sympathiser with Kang Yu-wei, his fellow provincial and a member of the Tsungli Yamên who had represented China at the Queen's Jubilee in 1897 and had been decorated with the GCM G.[188] As soon as I heard of the arrest, I wrote to Sir Chen Tong Liang, his confidential secretary, also a Cantonese who had accompanied him on his mission and had been given the KCMG asking him if the news of the arrest were true. This was his reply:–

Private.   *Thursday (22/9/1898)*

Dear Mr. Morrison,

I'm happy to write to you, Chang Tar-jen (Chang Yin-huan) has not been deprived of his office, nor has anything happened concerning his property. It was this: yesterday morning secret Imperial Edict ordered Kang Yu-wei and brother to be arrested. The Manchu

---

188 Grand Cross of St Michael and St George—an important British knighthood which carries with it the right to the prefix Sir. It is the top honour traditionally given to senior British Foreign Office officials at or near retirement.

general proceeded quite early to ransack Kang's house outside the city, but not finding him there, the police suspected that Kang might have been spending the night with Mr. Chang, hence several guards remained outside Chang Tar-jen's house, waiting for Hang to come out. (This was done without Imperial instruction or order from the general.) Therefore rumours were circulated that Chang Ta-jen was also concerned in the matter. Chang Ta-jen was in the Yamen as usual yesterday and received Mr. Conger. Of course this new change of things is most unfortunate, and it might lead to many high officials retirement.

The Regency has already been proclaimed in last evening's Gazette, and we all watch the movements of the new power thus formed with greatest anxiety.

*Yours truly,
Liang Chang.*

Kang Yu-wei left Peking day before yesterday. His brother was immediately arrested.

Looking back to this time of upheaval, and comparing things with what they were during the recent revolution in China, it is interesting to recall how closely associated were the Japanese with the reform movement of those days. Mr. Narahara, the son in law of the Marquis Saigo who led the Japanese expedition to Formosa in 1874, a Japanese who had written a standard work upon the commerce of China, and who had a greater knowledge of Chinese officials than any other foreigner of the time, was in Peking prior to the *coup d'état* include close intercourse with the reformers. He was the forerunner of the Marquis Ito, who was actually in Peking during the *coup d'état* having arrived in the Capital on September the 11th, been received in Audience on the 17th, entertained at dinner by Li Hung-chang on the 24th, and on the 28th was present at an "At home" given in the Japanese Legation by the Chargé d'Affaires Mr. Gunsuke Hayashi[189], and left Peking on his return to Japan on October 2nd.

---

189 Hyashi Gunsuke, 1861–1939, distinguished Japanese diplomat, intimate with Japan's relations with China and Korea, served as ambassador to Britain 1920–25, represented Japan at the League of Nations.

The Times suggested that the visit of the Marquis Ito to Peking "set fire to the straw", this impression having been fostered by the fact that every one of the six men arrested had been on terms of interstate intimacy with the Japanese. At the time it was generally believed, but the statement was subsequently denied by Mr. Hayashi that Kang Yu-wei spent his last night in Peking in the company of the Marquis Ito. Certainly they were on very intimate terms.

I saw Marquis Ito before he left Peking. He despaired of reform in China. In Peking he could find no statesman willing to take responsibility, no statesman standing conspicuously above his fellows. No reform in the court was possible, he said to me, so long is Peking remained the capital. And no reform of the finances in his opinion was practicable until the problem of Manchu pensions had been grappled with, and the vast expenditure involved in the upkeep of useless hordes of Manchu retainers abolished. The Manchu pension list he estimated he said at £3 million per annum.

While Japan supported Kang Yu-wei and his reforms, Russia on the contrary favoured the policy of reaction. One of the tenants of Kang Yu-wei's faith was an alliance with Japan, the adoption of Japanese reforms on the model of Japan, the training of Chinese officers in Japan, the reorganisation of the Chinese fleet under Japanese officers. One of the first books that he called to be translated was *The History of the Reformation in Japan*. He had urged the Emperor to shake off the bondage of his court and proceed on a tour of inspection to Tientsin. This was to be the first stage of a longer journey to the Emperor of Japan himself, but all these schemes were frustrated.

While Russia was hostile, and Japan sympathetic, England remained indifferent. Mr. Timothy Richard,[190] the most ardent of his foreign supporters, was upbraided at the British legation for his association with Kang Yu-wei. Yet Kang Yu-wei owed his life to England. He escaped from Tientsin on board a British steamer, the "Chung king". Rewards were offered for his capture dead or alive. At Chefoo the steamer called on its way to Shanghai. Kang Yu-wei went ashore and wandered and

---

190 Timothy Richard, 1845–1910, Welsh Baptist minister who joined the Baptist Missionary Society in 1869. Politically involved after the Boxer uprising and became influential in establishing two universities in China, one in Taiyuan, the other in Shanxi.

11 | 'REMINISCENCES'

noticed among the crowd. The Taotai received an urgent message ordering him to arrest Kang Yu-wei. Prudently he kept the telegram in his pocket without decoding it. Detectives in numbers were waiting for him at Shanghai. Proclamations issued by the Shanghai Taotai offered a price for his head where he to land in Shanghai his life would be forfeit. Hastily the British authorities arranged that his steamer was to be met at the entrance to the river leading up to Shanghai and the reformer was to be taken off and transferred to the British Mail steamer *Ballaarat* bound for Hongkong. To prevent possible interference with the British ship from Chinese gunboats HMS *Bonaventura* was detailed to convoy the *Ballaarat* to Hongkong. Mr. J. O. P. Bland, the Secretary of the municipal council and *Times* Correspondent in Shanghai, was asked to meet the Chung king and warn Kang Yu-wei of his peril. His mission (on September 24th) was was successful. The brilliant study of Kang Yu-wei and the Reform Party written for *The Times* by Mr. Bland and published in its issue of November 26th contained only a modest reference to his rescue of the 'Modern Sage' whose labours changed the course of Chinese history. Two passages in this article show singular clearness division. Speaking of Kang Yu-wei Bland says: "As matters stand, the 'Modern Sage' is in exile and those whose followers who have escaped the wrath of the Empress Dowager are scattered far and wide; but the good seed of progress has been sown in many of the eighteen provinces and unless Kang Yu-wei should fall victim to the hand of the assassin the day must come when he shall again become a power in the land." And again. "The day may come when England shall rejoice that she protected the reform-leader, half-heartedly though it was done."

Kang Yu-wei passed into exile. His name became a household word far beyond the borders of China. From a safe retreat he denounced the Empress Dowager and all her minions, denounced her comprehensively in her private life and her public career, impeached her for her immorality, for her illicit relations with the spurious Eunuch,[191] for her savage despotism. Of her minions no one more passionately than Yuan Shih-kai charging him with perfidy to the young emperor whose person

---

191 This appears to be a reference to Li Lien-ying, Chief Eunuch, noted for his cupidity and intimate relationship with Tsu Hsi.

he was in duty and honour bound to support. His views prevailed for many years. But his judgement of Yuan Shih-kai has been reversed by history. Years later Yuan Shih-kai gave me in writing his own story of his action during this formidable crisis.

At the time of the *coup d'état* Yuan Shih-kai was the most powerful military commander in the province of Chili.[192] On the restoration of peace after the disastrous war with Japan he had been entrusted with the command of a new army of 5000 men who were to be trained experimentally by Western methods and station at Hsiao Chan, a camp one day's march SW of Tientsin. This was the real beginning of China's modern army. His camp was a model of efficiency and attracted worldwide attention. He showed what Chinese troops could become with proper training. Instead of the ill fed, ill clad, disorderly braves of the old type, Yuan formed and efficient, well-trained force recruited from a good class of men from the rural districts of North China, and guaranteed by the local authorities. Soldiering became an honourable calling. He established military schools, from which military instructors were drafted into other provinces. The discipline of his force was admirable. He rolled his men with a rod of iron.

In 1897, Yuan was appointed provincial Judge of Chili, but he retained his military post, and continued his work of army reorganisation. In the autumn of 1898, the Reform Party led by Kang Yu-wei, considered that the late Empress Dowager and the viceroy of Chili, Jung Lu[193] blocked

---

192 Chili (Zhili) was and administrative area surrounding Peking. Yuan was later to become Viceroy of Chili, a post that oversaw civil and military affairs in Hebei and Tianjin.

193 Jung-lu (Ronglu), 1836–1903, Manchu, member of the Plain White Banner. Official in the Ching government starting in the Board of Works. During the British and French invasion of Peking in 1860 he was in charge of the police in the suburbs of Peking. He was soon noticed by the Empress Dowager. He 'retired' in 1879, under a cloud, but retained his rank as commander of the Peking Gendarmerie. He was recalled in 1887, made a chamberlain of the Imperial Bodyguard, followed by Tartar General of the Manchu garrison at Sian in 1891 until 1895. He returned to Peking in 1895 to head the police and serve in the Tsungli Yamen. At the end of the Sino-Japanese War in 1895 he became president of the Board of War and in 1896 Associate Grand Secretary. He led the reorganisation of the army and was responsible for Yuan's appointment to Chili. He was opposed to reform and was anti-foreign; in 1895 'memorialised' (petitioned) the Emperor advising against the establishment of railroads, mines, telegraph lines,

11 | 'REMINISCENCES'

the way to their reforms, conspired for their removal. Jung Lu was to be put to death in his Yamen in Tientsin, the Empress Dowager was to be interned as a state prisoner. Yuan Shih-kai, whose progressive views were well known, was to execute these plans. He was to go to Tientsin, put Jung Lu, his 'Blood Brother' and benefactor, to death, and was then to return immediately to Peking with his foreign drill troops and their seas and imprison the Empress Dowager.

On the night of September 18th 1898, the reformer T'an Ssu-t'ung,[194] one of the K'ang You-wei party, and the Secretary of the Grand Council, called on Yuan Shih-kai. After ordering all the servants out of their presence, and after a few words of introduction, he denounced Jung Lu in scathing terms, and laid his plans before the general, saying that scheme had the Emperor's consent and approval. At the conclusion of his speech, he produced a rough draft of the proposed plot, written in ordinary black ink and invited you and cooperation. Yuan Shih-Kai replied that there was no imperial order for him to undertake the task. T'an Ssu-t'ung said that on the 20th a secret order from the emperor would surely be given. On Yuan's further objecting that such a plan could not be executed suddenly, but needed mature deliberation and Vermilion Decree T'an said, "I have the Imperial Order with me" and forthwith handed a document to Yuan. Instead of the Imperial Order written in vermillion it was a document in black ink, neatly written, couched, however, in the Emperor's phraseology. It stated that His Majesty was bent on reform but since conservative opposition was met everywhere, Yang Jui, Liu Kwant-ti, Lin Hsu, and T'an Ssu-t'ung (four the most active members of the Reform Party) were to devise some "sound plan of action." Yuan Shih-kai once more objected that the document was not an Imperial Order, since it was not written in

---

paper currency, factories, a modern army and navy, Westernized schools, and even the post office. The only foreign thing he did not condemn was firearms which could be used to oppose foreign aggression. He kept his head down during the Boxer uprising and in spite of his tacit support he managed to profit from it. He was appointed Grand Secretary in succession to Li Hung-chang who had recently died. Jung-lu died soon afterwards.

194 Tan Sitong, 1865–1898, philosopher, poet and reformer key to the 100 Days programme associated with Kang and the Guangxu emperor. He was arrested and beheaded in September 1898 on the orders of the Empress Dowager.

Vermillion ink, nor did it mention the execution of Jung Lu and the confining of the Empress Dowager in the Summer Palace. T'an said that the vermillion order was in Lin Hsu's hands, and that what was produced was only a copy and added that in truth and Imperial Order had been issued three days before. He assured Yuan that the phrase "sound plan of action" referred to the disposal of Jung Lu and the imprisonment of the Empress Dowager.

As Yuan insisted on a vermilion order from the Emperor and T'an could not show one, nothing definite could be arranged. On taking leave T'an said: "We depend on you." Yuan decided at his audience on the 20th to which he had already received the summons, he would sound the Emperor on the subject by referring to the reform movement. Accordingly, when he was present at an audience, he spoke of the new reforms and their difficulties, and the Emperor was much affected by Yuan's words, but made no reference to the "sound plan of action."

While the reformers were busy with their plans, the Conservatives were not inactive. Secret emissaries went often to Tientsin and deliberated with Jung Lu, who was well informed what was going on by private communications with the reactionaries.

When Yuan retired from the audience he started from the railway station, where he waited for a friend with whom he proceeded to Tientsin. On his arrival in Tientsin that evening, he called on Jung Lu, who was who said to him: "You have come from my head. You had better confess all because a man (Yang Ch'ung-i), whose son married the daughter of Lord Li Ching-fong, who was here just before you came, has told me everything." Yuan answered: "What you have heard is but a plot of a few political schemers. His Majesty the Emperor said nothing to me about such a plan, and he is innocent of such intrigue." When they got as far as that part of the conversation, the late Admiral Yeh Chih-ch'ao was announced, and later on another official arrived. They stayed till 11pm, and Yuan seeing no chance of renewing the conversation returned to his quarters. Next morning, September the 21st Jung Lu called on Yuan and said: "Lately friends from Peking have repeatedly informed me of the reformers' minutest movements. Their daring is astounding. We must rescue the Emperor from their clutches." Jung Lu returned to his Yamen and sent for Yuan in the evening. Yang Ch'ung-i was present, and produced an edict sent by wire, informing Jung Lu that the reformers' plot had been exposed in Peking. On dismissing Yuan from his presence, Jung Lu pointed to the teacup and said: "You can drink there is no poison in your tea." Four days afterwards, on September the 25th, Jung Lu was called to Peking and given the rank and power of generalissimo.

Such is the story translated from Yuan Shih-kai's own words.

Kang Yu-wei escaped from Peking. Not so fortunate was Chang Yin-huan. Arrested, falsely charged, banished for life to the New Dominion in far western China, he was taken under escort from the temple of Tien Ling-ssu where he had been confined since his arrest, a number of us including Hugh Grosvenor, of the British delegation, who afterwards died in tragic circumstances in Vienna, offered to rescue him and bring him for protection into the British legation. We claim the right to rescue one who had been decorated by the Queen. Sir Chentung Liang, to whom we disclosed our plan, approached Chang Yin-huan afterwards informed us that it was not his masters desire to interfere with the course of Imperial justice. Two years later, under circumstances of great barbarity, Chang Yin-huan was put to death in Tihuafu, the capital of the new dominion, his place of exile.

The very day that Chang Yin-huan set forth on his sad pilgrimage from which he was never to return, Reuter's agency in London distributed a communication from Loh Fang Liu, the Chinese minister in London, Laughing Loh as he was popularly called, which gave with oriental exactitude the official version of the coup d'état, but made no reference to the exile of Chang in one he had received he said, "a telegram from Peking stating that the greatest harmony prevailed between the Emperor and the Empress Dowager. The latter, seeing the danger to the Emperor which would inevitably arise if the great and sweeping reforms which His Majesty was being advised to sanction were carried out, has again left her retirement in order to give His Majesty the benefit of her councils and the management of affairs and in the manner of introducing the reforms which circumstances have shown to be necessary. Of the injudicious counsellors who have been urged on the Emperor the adoption of the ill-advised and inopportune measures of reform, six have been put to death, while two others named Kang Yu-wei and Liang Chi-chao have not yet been arrested, one having escaped on board a British and the other onboard a Japanese ship."

So unsettled work conditions in Peking that foreign guards were brought to guard the legations they arrived on October 7th by special train provided by the Tsungli Yamên, all foreigners in Peking going out to welcome them. China saw no loss of face in thus providing facilities for bringing foreign troops to Peking. On the contrary Hu You-fen, the Governor of the city, and official much esteemed by foreigners, was deputed to head the procession. Not since the city's surrendered to the Anglo-French force in October 1860 had Peking been entered by foreign troops marching in military order.

With the departure of Kang Yu-wei and the annulment of the reform decrees and the array and the reconstitution of the Regency, the young emperor practically became a prisoner. He was interned on an island in the Palace. It was even reported that he had been put to death. So widespread was this belief that the Diplomatic Body suggested that the Emperor should be visited by a foreign physician "to knock the bottom out of all these Shanghai rumours" as Sir Claude MacDonald phrased it.

I was much disappointed that in the choice of doctors I was passed over, for I was the doctor who ought to have been selected. I was the senior doctor in Peking. Admittedly, I had higher qualifications than the French doctor and since the object of the visit was the establishment of the fact and its announcement to the world that the Emperor was not dead, it was in every way fitting that I should have been asked to see him. But despite the support of my friend, Gwynne, Sir Claude MacDonald would not accept this view. He considered I was out of court because I was *Times* correspondent and gave his approval to the appointment of the French legation doctor on the ground that he was the only medical man attached to a foreign legation at that moment in Peking. Accordingly, on the 18th of October, the memorable inspection was made by Dr. Dethève,[195] accompanied by M. Vissière,[196] the distinguished Sinologue. Dr. Dethève published an account of his visit and of his diagnosis but no adequate examination was permitted.

---

195 Claude Dethève, 1867–1936.
196 Arnold Vissière, 1858–1930, distinguished Sinologist.

11 | 'REMINISCENCES'

In the midst of the interest aroused by all these occurrences Lord Charles Beresford[197] arrived in Peking as the delegate of the associated Chambers of Commerce of London. The Admiral was placed on record the impressions of his journey. The title given to his book *The Break-up of China* exactly defines the impression left upon the mind of an able and energetic man of action, by the inefficiency, the lack of responsibility, the obsolete misdirected methods of the government of China to cope with the new situation. No other visitor to China ever received a more hearty welcome. No other visitor ever devoted to his task greater energy and enthusiasm. He arrived in Peking on October the 15th, staying at the British Legation and was given the assistance of Mr. H. E. Fulford,[198] the Chinese Secretary, a dragoman[199] of unusual readiness and flexibility, one of the ableist interpreters in the Chinese consular service. Mr. Fulford's capacity was put to a severe test. New Chinese phrases had to be coined on the spot. 'Open Door', 'Spheres of Influence', 'Spheres of Interest' and other such phrases were freely used. The climax of the difficulty of translation came at the meeting between Lord Charles and Jung Lu on October 23rd. Lord Charles had called on Prince Ching, the President of the Tsungli Yamên, had been courteously received and had many compliments, but when it came to business—the unfolding of a scheme for the reorganisation by British officers of the Chinese army—the admiral was advised to see Jung Lu, the most powerful official in Peking. To Jung Lu accordingly he went, was again courteously received, was again the recipient of many compliments, but when the business upon which he came was announced, he was politely requested to call upon Prince Ching, the official most conversant with affairs. But his patience was exhausted. "Ask him," said the visitor, with

---

197 Charles William de la Poer Beresford, 1st Baron Beresford, 1846–1919, was a British admiral and member of parliament.
198 Henry English Fulford, 1859–1929, British diplomat. Educated at Melbourne Grammar School (his English father, an Anglican priest, worked in Melbourne) Fulford joined the British Consular Service in 1880. He accompanied Francis Younghusband on the latter's tour of Manchuria. He was successively Consul General in Yingkou, Shenyang, Hankou, and finally Tianjin. He returned to Australia in 1917 and was found dead by his daughter in a bedroom of his Melbourne residence, apparently by his own hand.
199 A dragoman is an interpreter and a guide and was originally applied to practitioners in countries where Turkish, Arabic or Persian is spoken.

a brisk indignation, "if he thinks that a British Admiral has come all this way to cruise around after their old fossils."

Success did not attend Lord Charles's visit to Peking. Reaction had set in. Anti-foreign feeling was being aroused. All foreigners were looked upon with suspicion. The outlook in China was now blacker. Every reactionary force was at work. Tung Fu-hsiang,[200] the fanatical Mohammedan leader from Kansu, was brought to Peking and his undisciplined rabble was stationed on the railway at Lu kuo chi, near the famous bridge known as Marco Polo's bridge, on the first section of the line then under construction to the Yangtse. On October the 23rd, a grave assault was committed by soldiers upon Mr. C. W. Campbell of the Chinese Secretariat and Mr. A. G. Cox, the Australian Engineer of the railway. They narrowly escaped their lives. Prompt action was called for and a peremptory demand, supported necessary by armed force, was urgently needed. But Sir Claude, hampered no doubt by the weakness of the Foreign Office, feared to act independently and summoned a meeting of the diplomatic body to devise concerted action, as if any concerted action were conceivable, with ministers most of his time and energy, were devoted to intriguing and plotting one against the other. Indignant at what seemed to me, our unnecessary vacillation and weakness. I cable to *The Times*:

> It is an unfortunate indication of the altered position of British influence in Peking, that in that in a strong case affecting Englishmen only, and requiring firmness only to compel the Chinese to make whatever reparation is demanded we should hesitate to act independently but should invite the code the

---

200 Dong Fuxiang, 1839–1908, Chinese general from the western province of Gansu who commanded an effective force of Muslim Hui soldiers. He participated in the Dugan Revolt, 1862–1877, on the side of Yaqub Beg but defected to the Qing forces in exchange for official position. In 1890 he was stationed at Aksu, Kashgaria in the far west of China but was brought east by the Sino-Japanese War of 1894. He returned to the west in 1895 to put down another Dungan revolt. In 1898 he and his force of 10,000 were in Peking for preparation for war against foreigners. He supported the Boxers in 1900 and lost all official positions after the rebellion was put down. He returned to Gansu with a personal force of 5,000, and died there.

conjoint assistance of the Belgian, Dutch, Spanish and other Ministers.

Sir Claude did demand severe punishment of the offenders and the removal of the force to another province, but his demand was not pressed home, his dispatch was ignored and the assailants were never punished. They were probably rewarded.

In the light of later knowledge it can be argued that had the troops with Tung Fu-hsiang been removed from Peking and sent back to their own province much of the problem trouble that subsequently came to China—the Boxer upheaval and the siege of the Peking legations in which Tung Fu-hsiang played so conspicuous apart—might have been averted.

Reaction was in the air. The only feature redeeming the gloom was the presence in the province of the highly drilled force of Yuan Shih-kai. What part they were to play in the future?

Early in January 1898 there came into my possession a confidential report upon the construction of this force, which numbered 7000 men and was stationed at Hsiao Chan, a camp 24 miles from Tientsin. A copy, which I gave to Sir Claude, was sent by him to the war office, on January the 16th. It reached me through a distinguished Japanese officer, Colonel Kamio,[201] who was then military attaché in Peking, and subsequently after the war with Russia became Major General commanding the Japanese forces in North China. This report detailed the formation of the force, its organisation, equipment and pay and was drawn up by Captain J. W. N. Munthe,[202] a Norwegian officer, who had been seconded from the maritime Customs Service to join the Chinese army after the war with Japan. Attached to Yuan Shih-kai as cavalry instructor at Hsiao Chan, Captain Munthe then and afterwards

---

201 Kamio Mitsuomi, 1856–1927, was a Japanese general in the Imperial Japanese Army who commanded the allied landing forces during the Siege of Tsingtao in World War 1.
202 Johann Wilheim Normann Munthe, 1864–1935, was a Norwegian soldier who joined the Chinese Maritime Customs Service in 1886. He mastered Chinese, joined the Chinese army and fought in the First Sino-Japanese War (1894–95) where he came to the notice of Yuan Shikai. Promoted lieutenant general and the only foreigner to be an advisor to the Ministry of War. He died in Peking.

faithfully followed the fortunes of China's great man, serving him with devotion and beyond all praise. Justly rewarded, he has risen through the grades of the service to the rank of Lieutenant General. His report was written then with firsthand knowledge. Appended to it were brief appreciations of the different leaders. That of Yuan Shih-kai speaking of his ambition, his power and resourcefulness, showed unusual insight and prescience. Writing in 1897 of him who 15 years later, was to become China's first president, Captain Munthe has said, "He will undoubtedly set his mark on Chinese history, but whether he will die with his head on his shoulders or not, remains to be seen."

Yuan Shih-Kai was already a personage in the province. He was soon to become one of the most powerful persons in the empire, to rise to great authority and influence to fall more suddenly, to be driven into retirement, to emerge and save the country and become the first president of the Recognised Republic of China. All of us in Peking were watching the career of this forceful man. In later years it has been pleasant to recall how early some of us foretold the greatness which was to come to him. To no one did this conviction come more forcibly than to Mr. Gwynne, the correspondent of Reuter. Telegraphing to his agency on October the 27th 1898, he said, "The only force now capable of overawing the turbulent soldiery is the division of foreign-drilled troops under Yuan Shih-kai stationed in the neighbourhood of Tientsin. The police however, stand in dread of this commander, who would even seem to be regarded at the moment as practically holding the destinies of China in his hands."

Lord Charles Beresford visited this fourth force and was much impressed. He spoke to Yuan Shih-kai with a strait-forward directness which shook the equanimity of that imperturbable oriental. In picturesque language, he suggested that Yuan Shih-kai might tie the Old Buddha (the Empress Dowager) in a blanket and hold her suspended above a wall. A mandate decreeing her own retirement would be handed to her. "Sign that," she would be told. If she refused, she would suddenly she would be such she would suddenly be she would be suddenly lowered into darkness. She would soon be brought to reason. So pleased was he with his suggestion that Lord Charles cabled to Lord Salisbury asking permission to be allowed to accompany the force should Yuan Shih-kai elect to march on Peking and seize the government. He had inspected the camp of Yuan Shih-kai near Tientsin and found their 7000 well drilled capable men. Probably without firing a shot these troops could seize Peking and Yuan Shih-kai could then conduct the government under the orders of Sir Claude MacDonald in the interests of all. Lord Salisbury sent in a sarcastic reply. "The idea would have been attractive at the beginning of the century. But any attempt to take over the government of China in defiance of the vast mass of the Chinese and all the European powers would be too exhausting a task for England." To the dispatch, which was sent in on November 8th and reached Lord Charles at Newchwang, Sir Claude MacDonald had airily added the endorsement "Better stick to trade and commerce."

Lord Charles stayed in Newchwang for several days and I also. Everybody called upon him and among others the Russian Engineer Titoff, an eccentric, hairy Muscovite, who had assisted me in my journey across Manchuria and had since been stationed at Newchwang in connection with the branch railway connecting the port with the South Manchurian railway that under construction. He called upon Lord Charles and denounced me in heated terms as a Russophobe whose malevolent articles in *The Times* had gravely misrepresented Russia's mission and the Far East. In the midst of his tirade, I walked in. Titoff saw me and crying, "My dear friend" ran towards me with arms outstretched and embraced me warmly. He had met his long-lost brother and he could not have displayed more warm-hearted joy. Lord Charles stood by and roared with laughter and when the hairy one left us told me that Titoff had for the last half hour been urging him to use his influence to have me recalled. Subsequently Titoff drove me to the railway station and wept—actually wept—as he testified to his joy at meeting me once more.

From from Newchwang, Lord Charles Beresford proceeded to Shanghai, and I returned to Peking in time to see Li Hung-chang before starting on his mission to Shantung. Li Hung-chang had been removed from the Tsungli Yamên on September 7th on some slender grounds and the British legation had prided itself in the belief that his removal was a success for British diplomacy. It was never made clear, however, in what way could the infliction of an affront upon the most prominent statesman in China react to the advantage of British influence. As a matter of fact our policy was for years a policy of antagonism to

Li Hung-chang, with the inevitable result of driving him into the arms of Russia. Removed from the Tsungli Yamên, Li Hung-chang still retained his post his Grand Secretary and on November 13th 1898 he was given the much coveted and lucrative post of Commissioner to the Yellow River and was instructed to proceed to Shantung and cooperate with the Governor in concerting measures to prevent inundations. Missions of this kind have existed from time immemorial. Fifty years ago the methods of enrichment attaching to such an office were indicated in a classic passage by George Wingrove Cooke:[203] "The life and state papers of a Chinese statesman abound in the finest sentiments and the foulest deeds. He cuts off 10,000 heads and cites a passage from Mencius about the sanctity of human life. He pockets the money given him to repair an embankment and thus inundates the province: and he deplores the land lost to the cultivator of the soil."

The Yellow River is China's Sorrow now, as it has been China's sorrow for centuries. The bursting of its banks is the most appalling danger with which China is ever confronted. Any year this may happen, every year the calamity becomes nearer. Sediment is brought down in vast quantities, so that its water is constantly rising, and the Chinese know no other means to restrain the river within its banks than by raising the banks above the level of the water. For many miles, the great river flows through country, which is on a lower level than its own bed. No planting is being done along the banks: on the contrary, all timber, shrubs grass are ruthlessly stripped from the soft soil, and every day the great catastrophe is drawing nearer when the river will pour across the thickly populated country to the sea, causing death and destruction incalculable. Such a catastrophe nearly occurred during a cloud burst in June 1906 near the city of Khaifeng, which lies 26 feet below the level of the river flowing past a few miles to the north. Should such a breach occur, provinces will be flooded, millions will perish. "Earth will feel the wound."[204]

---

203 George Wingrove Cooke, 1814–1865, British lawyer and historian. He covered the Second Opium War for *The Times* as special correspondent in 1857 which resulted in the book *China* in 1858.
204 This is a line from Milton's *Paradise Lost*, when Eve eats the forbidden fruit, book 9, line 783.

11 | 'REMINISCENCES'

No systematic attempt has ever been made to deal with this problem. Methods hitherto used have been primitive as the methods for fighting the flames in a Chinese city. High officials were every year appointed to investigate. Large sums were allocated for expenses and were duly pocketed. In 1898 Li Hung-chang was entrusted with this lucrative mission. He was accomplished by a remarkable Chinaman the 'General' Tcheng Ki-tong,[205] who had been military attaché in Paris and had their lent his name as author to various books, *Les Chinois chez eux* and others written by M. Doudon de Foucarde, which had a considerable vogue in their day.[206] On his return to China, he had been appointed Secretary for Foreign Affairs to the President of the Republic of Formosa,[207] a post which he retained for 13 days before skipping to the mainland. The general had a French wife and spoke French with fluency. To the mission, upon his offering to pay his own expenses, was also attached the Belgian engineer Armand Rouffart. On his return to Peking Li Hung-chang was astonished to find that he was called upon to pay a large sum for the expenses of the Foreigner, but he paid and said nothing and only later discovered that Tcheng Ki-tong had unknown to Rouffart presented a claim on his behalf and pocketed the proceeds.

The year closed with attention chiefly directed to Manchuria where Russia was working with feverish haste to consolidate her power. Railway construction was being pressed forward with unexampled rapidity. Not less than 140,000 of the finest labourers in the world were working overtime along the course of the railway. Russia's sphere of influence was well defined and England had admitted that the special interests of Russia extended at least as far south as the Great Wall. England herself had defined, although less explicitly, her sphere of influence in the

---

205 Tcheng Ki-tong, 1851–1907, was a notable Chinese diplomat, writer and scholar. He graduated from the Fijian Naval Academy and went to France where he studied at Sciences Po and represented China diplomatically.
206 Morrison is referring to Tcheng-Ki-Tong's, *Les Chinois Peinte Par Eux-Mêmes*, Paris, Calmann Lévy, 1884. This is a collection of essays depicting Chinese life and customs.
207 One of the shortest-lived republics in history, the Republic of Formosa (Taiwan) came into existence under Qing tutelage on 23 May 1895 and was extinguished in 21 October the same year when Japan took control of the island under the terms of the Treaty of Shimonoseki. Taiwan was known for long periods during the 20th century as Formosa, Portuguese for 'beautiful'.

Yangtze Valley, and everything was ready for the agreement which the two powers signed in at St. Petersburg on April 28th 1899. It seemed to many of us that the enforcement of the policy of the 'Open Door' would constantly become one of increasing difficulty and that events were tending to a clearer definition of Spheres of Influence and of the admission within those spheres of rights of interposition if not of exclusion.

In China herself, reaction supported by Russia, had become everywhere manifest. Everywhere the tendency was shown to displace officials who had manifested any sympathy with reform and progress. In the Tsungli Yamên the notorious Prince Ching[208] was President and with him were associated five of the most incompetent old fossils that were ever entrusted with the Foreign Affairs of any country. Their chief recommendation in the sight of the Empress Dowager was their complete ignorance of Foreign Affairs. While above all, was the Old Buddha, the Empress Dowager, plotting schemes for the extermination of the foreigner, who would who was soon to lead her country to the verge of destruction.

At the close of the year, having visited the treaty ports, and forts on the Yangtze and other defences on the coast of South China I was in Hongkong and saw the old year out on the British flagship.

Then I took passage to Bangkok. It was a great delight to me to return to Siam. I have I have a feeling of sincere affection for the beautiful country and its attractive people. My first work for *The Times* was done in Siam. From one end of the country to the other I have travelled when

---

208 I-k'uang, 1836–1916, descended from the emperor Kao-tsung, his family fell from prominence but was raised up again by his efforts. He was famously corrupt, preferring to negotiate the size of emolument himself rather than through the usual way, an intermediary. He inherited family estates in 1850 and in 1884 he was made Prince of the Second Degree to which was attached his historic family's designation Ch'ing. That year he was made chief member of the Office of Foreign Affairs, the Tsungli Yamên. In 1885 he was appointed on of the controllers of the Board of Admiralty. In 1894 the Empress Dowager raised his to the Prince of First order. He fled Peking with the court in 1900, returning in 1901 to participate with Li Hung-chang in the peace settlement. In 1903 he became chief Grand Councillor, the most powerful official in the empire. From May-November 1911 he was Prime Minister. He resigned and was made Privy Councillor. P'u-i abdicated in December 1911 and Ch'ing resigned and moved to Tientsin where he subsequently died.

11 | 'REMINISCENCES'

fresh and strong and vigorous, open to every impression, finding a new joy every day, attracted by the kindly sympathetic people, and charmed by the picturesque beauty of their surroundings. So vivid to this day, are the recollections of my journey, that travelling as I have so often done for long periods alone, I have passed frequently, the best part of a weary day in recalling in imagination stage by stage my journey through the Kingdom, from the splendour of the ruins of Angkor Wat, and Angkor Thom[209] through Battambong[210] and Chantaboon[211] to Bangkok and on through the interior to far distant Chiengmai and the mighty Mekong. Of all the countries I have visited since leaving in Australia Siam is the one which I would most gladly revisit. My heart thrills when I think of Siam, its beautiful temples, its silent waterways, its gliding beats, its splendid forests and grain clad valleys, and I shall always rejoice that as correspondent of the great London paper I was able to help a little towards a better understanding of the people in their struggle to raise themselves in the scale of civilization and preserve the integrity of their enchanting country.

I had first seen Siam when after fierce international rivalry breathing time had been given to the country. The king, crushed and humiliated by the French occupation—an occupation that might have been permanent but for fear of England—remained for some time in retirement. But he had pulled himself together and with the loyal assistance of his brothers had set himself the task of reorganising the administration of his country. Every step he then made was a step forward. Wise in his generation, he engaged the services of selected foreign experts and station them in various departments of state. Not only did he invite their advice but, wise above the oriental, he listened to their advice and acted upon it. Far above the average in administrative capacity, able and sympathetic, energetic and receptive, he had been specially fortunate in his brothers who seconded his efforts with a single heart of devotion

---

209 See note 75.
210 Now Battambang in present-day Cambodia. From 1795–1907 it was annexed by Siam (Thailand) and designated Inner Cambodia. Originally founded by the Khmer Empire in the 11th century.
211 Now the Chanthaboon Waterfront Community of Chanthaburi Province, eastern Thailand.

that set an example to every official in the kingdom. That capriciousness of appointment so conspicuous in China was absent. There was none of that precariousness of office tenure which had been such a blemish in China. The king and his brothers were cast in a different mould from the Regent and his brothers and China. They had been nurtured gently and had been trained in western knowledge. They had been free from the degrading influence of Eunuchs. The king himself spoke admirable English with a musical rotund voice, while his two distinguished brothers Prince Damrong[212] the Minister of the Interior and Prince Devawongse,[213] the Minister of Foreign Affairs, had brought gifts to their high office which would have made them conspicuous in any country in the world. By their help I had travelled through Siam alone and unarmed welcomed everywhere with the most charming kindness. Small wonder then that I rejoiced to have an opportunity of returning to their country to record the changes that had taken place during my two years' absence.

My visit was well timed. That, I believe, has been admitted. Misleading reports especially disseminated by the local correspondent of a Parisian daily his mischievous activity brought its own retribution had created in Europe a feeling of impatience which it was essential to counteract. Where there's smoke there must be fire the critics said and these reports in the French papers must have their origins in fact however much distorted their presentation may be. I believe there had been informal consideration of the possibility of exchanging our interests in Siam for advantages territorial or other on the west coast of Africa. France was to be allowed to work her way in Siam in return for granting England compensatory treatment in Africa. That, broadly, was the suggestion. The world had been kept in ignorance of the true state of affairs in Siam. Correspondents had passed it by. Diplomatic reports and failed to impress the people. No one had brought home to the people of England the great changes that had been quietly and

---

212 Prince Tisavarakumara, the Prince Damrong Rajanubhab, 1862–1943, was the founder of the modern Thai educational system as well as the modern provincial administration.
213 Devan Udayawongse, the Prince Devawongse Varoprakar, 1858–1923, was a Siamese prince and diplomat.

unostentatiously effected in Siam by the king and his brothers, aided by a number of foreign advisors, chief among whom were the British officials led by the Burmese government, who had learned their business in "that great school of statesmanship" the Indian service. With exceptional qualifications, accustomed to the same climatic conditions, to deal with the same problems and trained to work in cooperation with cognate oriental peoples, their success was most remarkable. It was only necessary to state facts and support them by evidence for opinion to change and this would be done by The Times with the help of their correspondent.

I left Hongkong on January the 17th by direct steamer for Bangkok my fellow passenger being Phya Dejo, Major General A. D. C. to the King and his brother-in-law Luang Anuchit. Phya Dejo had been educated in England and had recently accompanied his sovereign in his journey to Europe. He was the grandson of the Krolshome, the Regent who placed King Mongkut on throne. Luang Anuchit had been with Mr. Slade in the Foreign Department in North Siam when that service was reorganised. Both officials gave me a reassuring account of the progress that had been made in Siam during the last two years. Progress, they said, could be seen in every department of state. There had been financial and currency reform, reform of all the revenue producing departments in the customs and forestry and land tax. The cadastral survey had been extended preparing the way for land reform. Improved methods of irrigation had been introduced. Prince Damrong the Minister of the Interior had introduced the Burma village system and reorganised the provincial administration. Siamese authority had been consolidated in the Lao states previously autonomous. Administration of law and justice had been reorganised. Gaols had been purged. "Buddha had come again," said the common people. The police system had been reorganised. Communications was still backward, especially railway communications but post and telegraph had been improved as had education and sanitation. Both spoke modestly of what had been accomplished. Yet the picture they gave was not over-coloured and my own inquiries confirmed what they said.

I arrived in Bangkok on the 23rd and was cordially received this to George Greville,[214] the British minister had spent two years in Peking (1880–1881) and seemed pleased to meet one coming fresh from that centre of international intrigue. The foreign advisors, at the head of whom were the learned jurist, Rolin-Jacquemyns,[215] who had introduced far reaching reforms in the administration of justice, and thus prepared the way by which Siam was to recover her extra territorial rights, and the Accountant-General from Burma, Mr. Rivet Carnas, a member of the distinguished Indian family and other foreign experts were glad that a correspondent could testify to the work they had so quickly accomplished. Prince Damrong gave me every help: the King himself received me with much heartiness. "Welcome to my Kingdom," he said, "there is no one more welcome than you are." It was manifest that Siam's relations with foreign countries had been had much improved. Even with France her communications are now more friendly than there had been at any time since 1893. With England they were unusually cordial and it was not difficult to believe that British prestige and gained by the incident of Fashoda.[216]

As a result of my inquiry, I cable to *The Times* on January the 30th a succinct résumé and followed up my message with a comprehensive survey of what might have what had been achieved during the two years that had passed since I left the country. It was pleasant to sit down and record some of the improvements effected during those astonishing two years. It was gratifying to recall how closely identified were Englishmen with the movement which was so rapidly transforming Siam.

No work that I have done since I joined the service of *The Times* gives me greater pleasure to look back on than the writing of this report. The great journal accepted the conclusions of its correspondent and in two striking leaders altered the opinion of England with regard to Siam,

---

214 Sir George Greville, 1851–1937, diplomat.
215 Gustave Henri Ange Hippolyte Rolin-Jacquemyns, 1835–1902, was a Belgian lawyer, diplomat and Minister of the Interior (1878–1884). From 1892–1901 he lived in Bangkok and assisted the Siamese government to modernise and codify the country's legal system. He also advised on foreign affairs.
216 Fashoda (Kodok today) is a south Sudanese city that was the scene of Anglo-French rivalry in 1898 for control of east Africa. Kitchener led an Anglo-Egyptian army. France withdrew without serious conflict.

drawing attention to the remarkable telegram from their correspondent describing the "progress achieved within the last two or three years by an Asiatic monarchy, not only sunk in torpor, and to all appearances effete" *The Times* reminded us that only three years ago, the "decadence of Siam seemed to have reached a pitch which constituted a serious danger to her European neighbours. To the eye of competent observers the collapse of the kingdom appeared to be at hand the signs which usually portend the downfall of decrepit monarchies were present." Giving praise where praise was due *The Times* concluded its editorial: "It is to the sagacity, the energy and the devotion of the sovereign that Siam owes, in the first instance, the solid progress she has already attained, and the brilliant change in her prospects for the future."

When my work was completed in Bangkok, I returned by a coasting steamer to Hongkong and hurried north to Peking, arriving there on the 25th of February just in time to be an eyewitness of the first appearance of Italy on the scene in China.

Rumours regarding Italian action in China were first broached in Tibuna of January the 22th Important demands, commensurate with the dignity of Italy's place among the nations, were to be submitted to China. The British government had undertaken to assist Italy diplomatically but not to take any steps which would require armed support and I have received instructions as to the course I was to follow in the laconic message "Morrison Peking remember Marconi friendship Times."

This new departure required careful piloting. The situation was one which called for high exhibition of tact and urbanity a calm judgement and aplomb and the mission was entrusted to Signor de Martino, the minister to Peking, a diplomatist who had represented his government in Brazil and in Japan and who was the brother of the senator who afterwards became governor of Italian Somaliland. Temperamentally no man was ever more unfitted to succeed in a task of this kind. Signor de Martino was a highly strung, excitable man, superstitious to a degree, who was guided in all his actions by omens and portents. On one occasion he was proceeding to an important engagement in Rio de Janeiro, to sign in fact a convention at the Foreign Office, when a squint-eyed woman crossed his path. He hurriedly returned. No inducement could make him sign an agreement on a day of such ominous portent. In

Japan M. de Martino had formed that attachment to a Japanese lady who accompanied him to China. While he was conducting his negotiations in Peking she remained in Tientsin. Her husband, unknown to M. de Martino, was in the employ also of the diplomatist and he, I suspect, gave friendly assistance to the Japanese correspondents who throughout the ensuing negotiations were more than usually well informed.

Sir Claude MacDonald was still the British minister, the first secretary being Mr. H. G. O. Bax-Ironside,[217] a gentleman of imposing guide who had gained very experienced in Constantinople, Cairo, Washington and Persia, and who enjoyed in the service and unusual reputation for skill as a card player. M. Pichon,[218] who subsequently became Minister of Foreign Affairs was the French minister, while German interests was still in the safekeeping of Baron von Heyking.

The Italian demands which England agreed to support comprised the lease of San Moon Bay on the coast of Chekiang,[219] the right to construct a railway from the bay to Poyang Lake and preferential railway and mining rights along the course of the railway. Of these demands Signor de Martino first spoke to the Tsungli Yamên on the 28th of February embodying them afterwards in a dispatch which he submitted on March 2nd. In somewhat flamboyant style he reminded the Chinese government that Italy was one of the great powers that had her place in the European Concert justified her in requiring that a position similar to that granted to other great powers should be conceded to her in China. The dispatch laid emphasis on the 'Sphere of Influence' that was to be given to Italy and her and here the difficulty of rendering such phrases in Chinese was manifest, for the nearest characters possible were equivalent to those of 'Protectorate'. Moreover none of the ministers of the Yamên could recognise in their Chinese characters the name of the bay which he had led demanded. In my own account of the dispatch I referred ironically to the Chinese translation of the word 'European Concert', saying that it was understood that the character is

---

217 Sir Henry George Outram Bax-Ironside, 1859–1929, British diplomat.
218 Stephen Jean-Marie Pichon, 1857–1933, journalist, diplomat, politician. Minister at Peking 1897–1900 including the Boxer uprising. He was close to Georges Clemenceau and was his foreign minster at the end of WW1 and at the Paris Peace Conference.
219 Zhejiang today.

11 | 'REMINISCENCES'

used with those commonly used for theatrical performance. My words were taken seriously in Italy and to my regret did some passing injury at headquarters to the Chinese secretary of the Italian delegation, Baron Guido Vitale,[220] one of the most accomplished scholars and linguists who have ever been in Peking.

Astonishment filled the Chinese when they received the Italian demands. Wholly ignorant of the place of Italy among the great powers, they had some vague impression that it was a minor state whose troops had been defeated by some black barbarians in Africa. They discussed the dispatch with ponderous gravity and then accepted the suggestion of one of their wiseacres that the most friendly act they could do to save face of the Minister who had presented such an unprecedented petition was to send it back to him. And this they accordingly did next day. No affront was intended. I am confident that they believed they were doing a friendly act: they were certainly wholly unaware of the gravity of their offence. But the excitable Minister was furious and frantic at what had been done, and in the muddle that he created he involved the British Legation. When on March 2nd Signor de Martino handed in his dispatch he informed the British legation that he had done so. Sir Claude had gone to Tientsin on March 1st and De Martino went down on 3rd to see his Japanese friend. It happened that Baron von Heyking was also in Tientsin. Sir Claude telegraphed instructions to Peking to send in his dispatch supporting the demands of his colleague and this was handed to the Tsungli Yamên and on 4th, the Italian's dispatch having been returned to the Italian delegation on the 3rd. Thus the British Minister sent in his dispatch supporting the demands after these demands had been rejected in the most discourteous manner known in diplomatic intercourse. Signor de Martino[221] knew that his dispatch had been returned but kept Sir Claude in ignorance. For the evening of the 3rd he called it the German consulate in Tientsin where Baron von Heyking was staying, to tell him that he had just received a telegram from Baron Vitale saying that the dispatch had been returned. "Will you

---

220 Noted for his collection and Chinese edition of Chinese Merry Tales which were rendered into English in 1909.
221 Renato De Martino, 1858–1903, Italian diplomat. He left China after the debacle described here for Brazil and then Japan.

not tell Sir Claude?" asked Baron von Heyking. "No", said the Italian. "But," said the Baron, "Sir Claude has not yet sent in the note supporting your demands." M. de Martino said he would not inform Sir Claude and naturally, Baron von Heyking preserved his discretion and said nothing. Our note caused the Chinese even more astonishment than the Italian. What policy is it they asked, which offers to protect China from the aggression of Russia and now aids Italy and her aggression upon China. Courteous reply was sent to the British Note expressing the impossibility of accepting the demands of Italy. Later the Chinese indicated their willingness to take back the dispatch, but this concession was regarded as inadequate unless in doing so they would state their readiness to enter into negotiations. Signor De Martino continued in a state of wild excitement. His judgement outran his wits. On the evening of the 10th he presented an ultimatum demanding the acceptance of Italian demands and calling for a satisfactory reply within four days and on the 11th he ran off again to Tientsin and his lady love. Next day on the 12th I met Baron Vitale. He said, "Between yesterday and today much has happened." This put us all on the *qui vive*.[222] Signor De Martino returned in the evening and was off again to Tientsin in the morning. He would transact no business on the 13th. He would not even speak of the day as the 13th: in conversation with his with Sir Claude he called it "the day of the fox." He was back in Peking on the 14th and I went to see him. He would not receive me. I went home and wrote him a short note and called later. He was lying down, groaning, on the sofa when I came in but rose to meet me. "But why did you send me that ultimatum," he said. "Ultimatums seen the order of the day," I replied, "but it was not meant for an ultimatum. I have instructions to give you support and I naturally want to know how things are going." "But you need not have written me in those peremptory tones," he said as if inviting sympathy, "you know I'm always glad to see you." And then he proceeded to read me a statement he had prepared for the press. Everything was going well: the Chinese had consented to take back their dispatch: he had sent no ultimatum he had only affixed a time limit of four days because it was customary in China etc, etc. As he spoke I got more and more indignant,

---

222 French for 'on the lookout'.

11 | 'REMINISCENCES'

seeing that he was misleading me, besides a hint had reached me from a Japanese friend who was an intimate terms with the envoy's *mousmè*.[223] Somewhat angrily I stamped my foot and said, "I will tell you what they say outside M. de Martino." He pricked up his ears. "They say that your action has been repudiated by your government that you've been recalled." He was seated when I said this, but he jumped to his feet and said passionately, "Ah, which of my dear colleagues told you that. Was it my friend MacDonald?" So I left him and was able to cable to London that he had been recalled and that the British minister would take charge of Italian interests. Thus the episode ended. M. de Martino had misunderstood his instructions. He had sent in his ultimatum and had delayed for 24 hours to inform his government that he'd done so. In the meantime, the Italian Foreign Minister Admiral Canevaro in good faith denied to the British ambassador the existence of the Italian ultimatum and thus unwittingly deceived the British government whose diplomatic support had been given conditionally on the engagement that Italy would resort to no measure of violence to obtain the concessions she was seeking. In the circumstances Italy had no alternative but to discern the actions of the eccentric gentleman to whom had been confided this important mission. Signor de Martino returned to Italy and was succeeded in Peking by the Marquis di Salvago Raggi.[224]

While the Italian question was reaching its last phase in Peking negotiations of another kind, affecting the status of all Italian and other Catholic missionaries,[225] were being conducted between the Chinese government and the Catholic bishop of Peking, Monseigneur Alphonse Favier.[226] M. Pichon was the French minister in official charge of the

---

223 Mistress.
224 Marchese Giuseppe Salvago Raggi, 1866–1946, was Italy's ambassador at Peking 1899–1901; he was then involved in Italy's colonial administration in Somaliland and Eritrea 1906–1915, and thence to Paris as Ambassador 1916–1918.
225 The relations between the Chinese government and the Vatican are long and complicated. For a thoughtful discussion of the Yongzhen's emperor's ban on Catholic proselytisation, see Eugenio Menegon, *Yongzheng's Conundrum: An Emperor Confronts Christianity and the Heterodox*, <https://chinaheritage.net/journal/the-christian-conundrum-of-yongzheng/>.
226 Known as Monsignor and later Bishop Favier, 1837–1905. His account of the Chinese capital (*Péking histoire et description*, Peking, Imprimerie des Lazaristes au Pe-Tang,

protectorate of all Catholic missions in China, except the German. With his knowledge, but without it, it is thought, his wholehearted approval, and certainly without his direct intervention, discussions were in progress, which were to end in a success for the able prelate, such as rejoice the hearts of all Catholic missionaries. Monsignor Favier suggested to the Chinese that it would be material that it would materially contribute to the better understanding between Christians and non-Christians if China were to grant official rank to the Catholic hierarchy. With admirable skill he induced the Tsungli Yamên to give ear to this proposal. They appointed one of their own number, a Chinese Bannerman named Yü Keng,[227] who had been received into an American Protestant congregation, as their representative to confer with the bishop and the result of their deliberations, was incorporated in a memorial which the Tsungli Yamên submitted to throne and which received the sanction of an imperial edict on March the 15th 1899. The Chinese did not realise what they were doing. By the terms of the edict it was proclaimed that a Catholic bishop was entitled to the rank and dignity of a Chinese viceroy with the right to direct input intercourse and on a footing of complete equality; that similarly a pro-Vicaire[228] was to be treated with the honour due to the Provincial Treasurer, and that even ordinary missionary priests were to rank with Chinese Prefects. The Chinese did not realise that in signing this agreement they were granting to the Catholic missionaries throughout vast areas of China, Manchuria and Mongolia, higher rank than that held by their own officials.

There were at the time eight Chinese viceroys, the ninth being created some years later and three governors (Shantung, Shansi and Honan) have equal rank to a viceroy—in all 11 Viceroys and Governors and there were 46 Catholic bishops and six Protestant bishops who could claim the same favoured treatment as their Catholic brethren. And there were 1100 Catholic priests who could claim equality with

---

1897, 2 volumes) is highly regarded. He was too successful for the Catholic Church's own good, as Morrison details here. Morrison successfully intervened in 1909 to have the Catholic church's privileges reversed.
227 He died in 1905 in Shanghai.
228 A Provincial, generally a bishop or archbishop.

the Chinese Prefects, a number far in excess of local authorities of similar rank, so that in vast areas, the highest official in the district was the Catholic ministry. Missionary, the rescript when it became known was not favourably received by the Protestant bishops and it met with hostile criticism from many prominent Catholics.

At a conference held in Shanghai on October the 21st, 1899 at which were present the Protestant bishops of China, English and American and the bishops of Hongkong and Korea the question was discussed whether they should have they should acquire for themselves and their missionaries the same privileges that had been conceded to the Roman Catholic hierarchy by the Edict of March 15th 1899. The bishops unanimously decided that it was inadvisable to take such a step. They had no wish to "complicate their spiritual responsibilities by the assumption of political rights and duties, such as have been conceded" in the Edict referred to. The resolution of the conference was communicated on October 31st 1899 by the British *Chargé d'Affaires* to Lord Salisbury, and was by him submitted to the Archbishop of Canterbury, who approved of the decision taken by the bishops, considering "that both as a matter of principle and a policy, it was undesirable that Protestant missionaries in China should claim the privileges" conceded by the Edict. The British government concurred in this view and the British *Chargé d'Affaires* in Peking was instructed by dispatch to take no further action in the matter.

Catholic Writers did not hesitate to condemn the folly of this Edict. Throughout the memorial, the words "France" and "French" do not occur. France with some exceptions, was the protector of the Catholic religion in China and Bishop Favier conducted the negotiations not as a French but as a Catholic bishop. One of the leading authorities in France, M. Henri Cordier, speaking with exceptional authority, said in his work *Histoire des Relations de la Chine aves les Puissances Occidentales*[229] [that] *"Jamais la France n'eut du laisser commettre cette faute."*[230] He saw in the decree no insignificant factor in the cause which were to lead to the Boxer Rebellion and he declared *"Ce décret interpratif et impolitique doit être rapporté la plus tôt possible."*[231]

---

229 History of China's relations with the Western Powers. Published in Paris in 1901.
230 "France should never have allowed this mistake to be committed."
231 "This explanatory and impolitic decree must be revoked as soon as possible."

At the time we wondered why M. Pichon gave his sanction to an Agreement which was to increase the responsibilities of his legation at the same time belittled the authority of his own officials in relation to the Catholic missionaries. For example—and specific instances should be given—the French Consul General having failed to settle a case with the Taotai, the Chinese official whose rank corresponded with his own, calls to his aid his subject the French Bishop or his protégé the Belgian or Dutch or Italian Bishop who arranges the dispute directly with the Viceroy with whom he is permitted by the decree to treat on equality.

When M. Pichon was in Peking it was no secret that, personally, he considered the Protectorate disadvantageous to France, leading as he often did to embroilment with the Chinese authorities, in cases in which French interests were not directly affected.

France at one time exercised an undisputed protectorate of all Catholics in China. Every Catholic missionary, irrespective of nationality, obtained his passport through the French Legation, or through the French Consul. China still recognises the validity of such passports although they are often necessarily misrepresentations of fact. An Englishman a Dutchman, or Belgian or Spaniard or Portuguese being a Catholic missionary can claim a passport from the French authorities. This passport speaks of the bearer as "our countrymen", that is, declares him to be a Frenchman and affirms that the bearer "enjoys a good reputation in our country," that is in France, though he may never have been to France. There are many Ministers Plenipotentiary to Peking who are unable to issue passports to their own Catholic missionaries.

Germany renounced the French protectorate in 1882, informing the French government that in future the Fatherland would protect its own Missionaries, but the separation did not become finally effective until the 22nd of July 1891 when the German Minister in Peking presented the Catholic German Bishop of Shantung to the Tsungli Yamên.

Italy next attempted to break away when during the War with France in 1884–1885, Signor de Luca, the Italian minister, then resident in Shanghai in response to an appeal from the Italian mission in Hankow, whose interest France seemed unable to safeguard, proceeded to Hankow and assumed the protectorate over his countrymen on the Yangtze. At the Italian mission he received the visit of the Viceroy

11 | 'REMINISCENCES'

under the Italian flag, but his act was regarded as unofficial and at the end of the war the mission resumed its former dependency upon the French Legation. An attempt by China at the end of 1885 to enter into direct relations with the Vatican was foiled by the French government. That year, prompted there by the same restless Lazarist Père Favier who afterwards became Bishop and by the remarkable German G. Detring,[232] who was for many years his most trusted counsellor, Li Hung-chang entrusted an extraordinary mission to Rome to an Englishman named John George Dunn who was to convey to the Pope an invitation to appoint a Legate to China. 'Mysterious Dunn', as he was nicknamed, was a culture gentleman who represented in China the telegraph interests of Sir John Pender.[233] He conducted his mission with ability was well received, and was so far successful that the Vatican even nominated Monseigneur Agliardi,[234] afterwards Cardinal Archbishop of Albano, as the first Legate to Peking, but then France intervened and insisted upon the scheme being abandoned, threatening if it were not to denounce the concordat.

Thus at the time of the issue of the Imperial Rescript France still exercise the protected over all Catholics in China, except the Germans, and the immense indemnities exacted from time to time throughout the interior for the destruction of Catholic lives and Catholic property were always arranged through the French legation.

China had not realised what she had done. But she was persuaded that she had done well and she accordingly rewarded Yü Keng,[235] the Chinese Bannerman who had drafted the memorial on behalf of the Tsungli Yamên with the Legation at Paris, a post he filled with success, being aided by his Eurasian wife, and by his accomplished daughters,

---

232 Gustav Detring, 1842–1913, was a German-born British official of the Imperial Customs Service.
233 Sir John Pender, 1816 – 1896, was a Scottish industrialist who formed the group to lay an under sea cable between Ireland and Newfoundland. He was a Liberal member of Parliament, and, in addition to the almost 140,000 km of undersea cable he controlled, had interests in railways in the United States.
234 Antonio Agliardi, 1832–1915, was an Italian archbishop, cardinal and papal diplomat.
235 Yu Keng, 1836–1905, was a Chinese diplomat with postings in Tokyo and Paris. His daughters were influential figures in the Empress Dowager's court on account of their foreign language proficiency.

who subsequently became Ladies in Waiting to the Empress Dowager. The younger daughter, under the name of the Princess Der Ling[236] has recorded in an interesting book her experiences in the service of that remarkable woman.

Sir Claude MacDonald left Peking on March 23rd on leave of absence. He had been in charge during troublous times when the problems presented would have taxed the ability of the most highly trained diplomatist. He was a special favourite of Lord Salisbury, who gave him signal marks of approval. Perhaps his most notable service was the extension he obtained of Kowloon territory on the mainland opposite Hongkong, where a small area was conveyed to England as compensation for certain lapses from good faith on the frontier of Tongking and Burma. Negotiations for the extension had been prolonged interminably. Probable explanation of the delay could be found in the fact that at the opening session Sir Claude produced and subsequently used a map of the territory larger than was the map of the whole of China with which the Chinese delegates were provided. Misapprehension as to the size and importance of the territory whose cession was asked for was engendered in the Chinese mind. Had Sir Claude taken with him and ordinary map of China and marked it on a microscopic point, representing the area sought for and ostentatiously always regarded this through a magnifying glass it is thought that he could have obtained the concession in as many days as it required months. The Convention was signed on June 9, 1898, but formal transfer of the territory ceded took place only after Sir Claude MacDonald's departure from Peking.[237] There was some local opposition to the British

---

236 Lizzie Yu Der Ling, 1881–1944, also known as Elizabeth Antoinette White after her marriage to Thaddeus C. White. The book Morrison refers to is *Two Years in the Forbidden City*, New York, Moffat, Yard and Company, 1911. It is the first of eight books she wrote about old China in additions to numerous magazine articles.
237 This is the Treaty governing the New Territories of Hong Kong—separate from the Kowloon peninsula and Victoria Island which Britain held in perpetuity—were ceded to Britain for 99 years and reverted to Chinese sovereignty with much pageantry on the rainy and windswept night of 30 June 1997, in the presence of the Prince of Wales, now, King Charles III, Jiang Zemin, General Secretary of the Chinese Communist Party, and Chris Patten, the last British governor of the colony.

occupation. A Blue Book has been devoted to the operations of the occupation The accounts of the "very heavy hostile artillery fire" and the "courage and military bearing under heavy fire displayed" while clearing the territory of some misguided villagers armed with matchlocks and spears are described in as grave language as were later dispatches from the front in the South African war. Happily, no one was injured except one Commissariat mule.

The British Legations Guards left Peking the day before Sir Claude. There was no need to detain them any longer. They had served their purpose. But observers noticed that the German Legation Guard still remained in Peking. They had not yet served *their* purpose. There was a railway contract to be signed and the astute Baron von Heyking, who was in charge of the negotiations, had let the Chinese understand that the troops would not be withdrawn until after signature. A powerful incentive this to Chinese! The contract provided for the construction by German and English finance of the important trunk line traversing China from Tientsin to Pukow a port opposite Nanking on the Yangtse, a railway which has since been constructed and has been of the highest importance to the development of the country. Two-thirds of the railway was to be German, one third British and the effect was to define more clearly than ever German special interests in Shandong Province.

Under pressure the contract was duly signed on May 18th, and Baron von Heyking, whose successor was to be Baron von Ketteler, German Minister to Mexico, left Peking on June 1st accompanied by his Legation Guard, whose departure completed the withdrawal of the Legation Guards who had been stationed in Peking since the previous October.

Baron von Heyking had added greatly to German prestige in China. Of all the ministers who have been in China in my time he is the one who seems to me to have accomplished the most. His seizure of Kiaochao was masterly: he upset the plans of Russia. For his country, he obtained a priceless harbour, preferential rights of every kind throughout a province as large as Norway and Sweden and equal participation for the German bank in all Chinese government business with the powerful British bank, the Hongkong and Shanghai Bank. No other Minister ever left Peking, who could with justice claim to have obtained for his country, greater advantages than he had done. Yet he left Peking more or less in disfavour.

For some time before the departure of the German Minister the attention of the Correspondents in Peking was directed towards the rapprochement of China and Japan, and we were all keenly interested seeking to unravel the significance of the secret Mission of Narahara and the mysterious movements of Japanese and Chinese special service envoys.

On a previous occasion, at the time of the *coup d'état*, I have referred to the mission of Narahara, the stormy petrel of Japan, the confidential messenger of the Marquis Ito. Narahara was a remarkable man of fine soldier intimate with the foremost Chinese officials. He had been educated in Edinburgh, had an exceptional knowledge of China and had written in Japanese a standard work on the trade and commerce of the Chinese Empire. The son-in-law of the Major General (afterwards Marquis) Saigo who led the expedition to Formosa in 1874, he was held in much respect by official Japan and being a man of discretion and resource he was frequently employed on special missions to China. After the *coup d'état* of September 1898, he returned to Japan with the Marquis Ito. Some months later in April 1899 he came back to Peking bringing with him a letter from the Marquis Ito to Li Hung-chang. This letter, the contents of which became known in due course, was of higher significance. It urged a better understanding between the Yellow Races,[238] it lamented the decay of China and warned China to reform ere it was too late. Speaking to me on April 30th, and discussing the Mission of Narahara, the German Minister described Marquis Ito as the "Arch Conspirator who was striving for the post of Counsellor-General in China" and this fairly represented the uniformed opinion of the diplomatic body in Peking. But the Marquis Ito had a higher mission to perform in life than that of an *employé*, however exalted, of the Chinese government. The mission of Narahara created a profound impression. A return mission was sent to Tokio, but as so often has happened in the history of China the men entrusted with the delicate task of proposing not only a better understanding but, in the hopes of China and alliances offensive and defensive between China and Japan, were selected by Court favour who were to profit by the immense sum

---

238 The Chinese refer to themselves as the sons of Huangdi—the Yellow Emperor.

allotted for the expenses of their embassy: they were in no sense men of educational standing or ability. To this delicate mission to a proud and sensitive people China appointed Ching Kuan a Manchu and Member of the Imperial Clan and Liu Hsüeh-hsün[239] a wealthy Cantonese who had been lessee of the Wei Hsing Lottery in Canton and had gained the favour of the throne by raising a large provincial contribution to the expense of the war with Japan. Ching Kuan once before had obtained some feeble notoriety. At the time of the *coup d'état* he had been especially deputed to effect the capture of Kang Yu-wei dead or alive. From the outset the mission was doomed to fail, and although they were granted audience by the Emperor of Japan the Japanese resented the folly of entrusting a mission to two men, one of whom had made his fortune in gambling and the other had been the paid agent seeking the head of a reformer much esteemed by Japan.

The two commissioners left Peking on June 8th and Shanghai July 8th carrying valuable presents and Imperial credentials provided by Prince Ching and approved by the Empress Dowager. The Russian delegation was most suspicious. To Sir Ernest Satow,[240] the British minister in Japan, Viscount Aoki, the Minister for Foreign Affairs, admitted that negotiations for a better understanding were in progress, but nothing more was contemplated than giving assistance to China to reorganise her fleet, her army and her defences. Japan, he said, naturally designed to maintain the status quo and Korea. Excitement among the Russians increased. On the 22nd of July, the Russian Minister M. de Giers, pressed the Tsungli Yamên for information regarding the object of the mission, but they denied all knowledge of any mission of Alliance. Captain Brinkley, writing to *The Times* on September 6th said "it would be an egregious error to suppose that any alliance of the nature suggested by recent rumours is possible between China and Japan.

---

239 Liu Hsueh-hsun achieved the rank of Expectant Prefect (an official awaiting appointment) in the early 1900s. Aside from the mission to Japan in 1898 little is known of him.

240 Sir Ernest Mason Satow, 1843–1929, diplomat and scholar, notably of Japan its history and culture. He and Sir Claude MacDonald swapped jobs, Satow was in Tokyo, in 1901. He authored *Satow's Guide to Diplomatic Practice*, currently in its 7th edition and still in print, the standard work.

To afford every reasonable aid towards the development of her neighbour's capacities in of self defence is certainly in Japan's mind, but to conclude any agreement which would pledge her to share the vicissitudes of China's future is a project she does not entertain for a moment."

But although the mission was a failure many observers believe that the dream of Ito will come true and that an alliance of the Yellow Races is within possible distance or accomplishment. Speaking to me on July 25th, when the mission to Japan was still the chief subject of diplomatic talk in Peking, Pethick, who as confidential secretary to Li Hung-chang, had intimate knowledge of the communications that had passed between Ito and the Chinese Statesman, said to me, "Ito is the Prime Mover for the Alliance of the Yellow Races and in this connection is supporting the Chinese claims for Chinese to be given the same rights of residents in the interior of Japan that have been granted to other nations since the revision of the old treaties and the abandonment of extraterritoriality."

A few days later, on July 28th, Major Aoki, at that time, and for many years afterwards, military attaché in Peking and one of the most distinguished and most trusted of Japanese intelligence officers, said to me, "That was a great *canard* that got into circulation—an alliance between China and Japan! What has China to offer for such an alliance? Better understanding Yes that is necessary for it is necessary that China should attempt the reorganisation of her forces. Alliance, however, is impossible. The recent manoeuvres at Shan Hai kwan showed that the rank and file were excellent but the officers were thoroughly incompetent. In one year or even less than one year Japan could make them an effective force."

We spoke of Russia's fear for the mission and of the legacy of distrust that Russia had bequeath to China by her action at Port Arthur when the major said—and this was the view already forming in the minds of many of us "Japan can drive back Russia. It is not Japan that is afraid of Russia. It is Russia that is afraid of Japan. That port (Masampho)[241] she is scheming to obtain on the coast of Korea, nearly opposite to Japan,

---

241 Masan, today.

is of the greatest strategical importance. Japan will never allow Russia to obtain a base in Masampho. Japan can drive Russia back into Asia." And then he spoke of the possibility, in the event of Russia being engaged in war, of a simultaneous rising in Poland and Finland.

I record this expression of view which I wrote in my diary immediately after the interview, because the time had come when the predominant question of the Far East was the growing antagonism between Russia and Japan. Relations were becoming strained. Japan was making preparations for the inevitable struggle and Korea was the storm centre. To Korea then I now turned my steps.

On August the eighth I left Peking and four days later landed at Chemulopho ...[242]

[*This is where Morrison's account of his life ends.*]

---

242 This is the old name for Inchon, the port for Seoul.

Bibliography

Correspondence Respecting the Insurrectionary Movement in China. London: Her Majesty's Stationary Office, July 1900.

Anon. "American Who Advised Li-Hung-Chang Is Dead." *New York Times*, 21 December 1901.

Bickers, Robert. *Out of China: How the Chinese Ended the Era of Western Domination.* London: Allen Lane, 2017.

Biehl, Dominique. "The Boxer War and International Memory." In *Sites of International Memory*. Edited by Glenda Sluga, Kate Darian-Smith and Madeleine Herren: University of Pennsylvania Press, 2023.

Bland, J. O. P. *Li Hung-Chang,* London: Constable, 1917.

Bland, J. O. P. and E. Backhouse. *China under the Empress Dowager, Being the History of the Life and Times of Tzü Hsi.* Philadelphia: J. B. Lippincott Company, 1910.

Clark C. M. H. *Select Documents in Australian History 1851–1900.* Sydney: Angus and Robertson, 1955.

Dikötter, Frank. *The Tragedy of Liberation: A History of the Chinese Revolution 1945–1957.* London: Bloomsbury, 2013.

Fairbank, John King. *The Great Chinese Revolution 1800–1985.* London: Chatto & Windus, 1987.

Fairbank, J. K., and S. Y. Têng. "On the Ch'ing Tributary System." *Harvard Journal of Asiatic Studies* Vol. 6, No. 2 (1941): 135–246.

Fleming, Peter. *The Siege at Peking.* London: Rupert Hart-Davis, 1950.

Garnaut, Anthony. "From Yunnan to Xinjiang: Governor Yang Zengxin and His Gungan Generals." *Études Orientales* 25, No. 1er semestre (2008): 93–125.

Hippisley, A. E. "Obituary Dr G. E. Morrison." *The Geographical Journal* 56, No. 2 (1920): 149–50.

Hu, Hsien Chin. "The Chinese Concepts of 'Face.'" *American Anthropologist* New Series Vol. 46, No. 1 Part 1, pp. 45–64 (1944).

Hummel, Arthur W. *Eminent Chinese of the Ch'ing Period.* Washington DC: US Government Printing Office, 1943.

Jaivin, Linda. *A Most Immoral Woman.* London: Fourth Estate, 2009.

Kaufman, Alison A. "The "Century of Humiliation" and China's National Narratives." Testimony before the U.S.-China Economic and Security Review Commission. Washington: US Government, 2011.

Kennan, George F. *American Diplomacy 1900–1950*. Chicago: University of Chicago Press, 1951.

Kennedy, Paul. *The Rise of Anglo-German Antagonism 1860–1914*. London: George Allen & Unwin, 1980.

Kotkin, Stephen. *Stalin: Paradoxes of Power, 1878–1928*. London: Penguin Books, 2014.

Lo, Hui-Min. *The Correspondence of G. E. Morrison*, Vol. 1 1895–1912. Cambridge: Cambridge University Press, 1976.

———. *The Correspondence of G. E. Morrison*, Vol. 2 1912–1920. Cambridge: Cambridge University Press, 1978.

Mackinder, H. J. "The Geographical Pivot of History." *The Geographical Journal* 23, No. 4 (1904): 298–321.

Marr, Andrew. *My Trade: A Short History of British Journalism*. London: Pan Books, 2005.

Matsuzato, Kimitka. *Russia and Its Northeast Asian Neighbours: Chin, Japan, and Korea, 1858–1945*. Lanham: Lexington Books, 2017.

Morrison, George Ernest. *An Australian in China, Being the Narrative of a Quiet Journey Across China to Burma*. London: Horace Cox, 1895.

Mote, F. W. *Imperial China 900–1800*. Cambridge, Massachusetts Harvard University Press, 1999.

Paine, S. C. M. *Imperial Rivals China, Russia and Their Disputed Frontier*. London and New York: Routledge, 1996 (2015).

———. *The Sino-Japanese War of 1894–1895 Perceptions, Power, and Primacy*. New York: Cambridge University Press, 2003.

Pearl, Cyril. *Morrison of Peking*. Sydney: Angus and Robertson, 1967.

Pelliot, Paul. "Les Publications Du Tōyō Bunko." *T'oung Pao* 26, No. 4/5 (1929): 357–66.

Peyrefitte, Alain. *The Collision of Two Civilisation: The British Expedition to China 1792–4*. Translated by Jon Rothschild. London: Harvill, 1993.

Share, Michael B. "The Great Game Revisited: Three Empires Collide in Chinese Turkestan (Xinjiang)." *Europe-Asia Studies* 67, No. 7 (September) (2015): pp. 1102–29.

Shen, Jiawei. *Old China through G. E. Morrison's Eyes* (Revised Edition). Hong Kong: Hong Kong University Press, 2007.

Simpson, John. *We Choose to Speak of War and Strife: The World of the Foreign Correspondent*. London: Bloomsbury, 2016.

Spence, Jonathan D. *The Search for Modern China*. New York: W. W. Norton & Company, 1990.

———. *Chinese Roundabout: Essays in History and Culture.* New York: W. W. Norton and Company, 1992.

Teng, Ssu-yü, and John K. Fairbank. *China's Response to the West: A Documentary Survey 1839–1923.* Cambridge, Massachusetts: Harvard University Press, 1979.

Thompson, Peter, and Robert Macklin. *The Man Who Died Twice: The Life and Adventures of Morrison of Peking.* Crows Nest: Allen & Unwin, 2004.

Trevor-Roper, Hugh. *Hermit of Peking: The Hidden Life of Sir Edmund Backhouse.* New York: Alfred A. Knopf, 1977.

Peking: Report of Captain John T Myers, 26 September, 1900, Naval History and Heritage Command, <https://www.history.navy.mil/research/library/online-reading-room/title-list-alphabetically/b/boxer-rebellion-usnavy-1900-1901/selected-documents-boxer-rebellion/siege-peking-may-august-1900/peking-report-of-captain-john-t-myers.html>.

Index

Agliardi, Antonio 493
Ah Heng 22, 46, 53, 221, 415, 428, 429, 431, 444, 445
Arlabosse, Louis Eugène Auguste 412, 412 (n. 81)

Baber, Edward Colborne 421, 421 (n. 100)
Backhouse, Sir Edmund 46, 46 (n. 90)
Baden-Powell, Warrington 380
Balfour, Arthur 458
Bax-Ironisde, Sir Henry 486
Bean, C. E. W. 43 (n. 85)
Beauclerk, William Nelthorpe 434
Bell, Charles Frederick Moberly 17, 17 (n. 32), 18, 19, 22, 39, 49, 409
Bell, Dr Joseph 389, 389 (n. 34)
Bell, Mark Sever 272, 272 (n. 368)
Beresford, Lord Charles 473, 474, 476, 477
Bland, J. O. P. 40, 81, 467
Blondin, Charles 429, 429 (n 114)
Bonavalot, Pierre Gabriel Èdouard 281, 281 (n. 279)
Bons d'Anty, Pierre Remi 421, 421 (n. 99), 424
Bowen, Lady Diamantina 364, 364 (n. 25)
Browne, George Fitzherbert 446, 446 (n. 156)
Brownrigg, Lady Beatrice 340
Buckle, Greorge Earle 16, 16 (n. 30), 327, 409
Bunsen, Maurice Ernest William de 49, 49 (n. 94), 50, 413, 433
Burke, John O'hara 4, 353, 354, 359, 387

Campbell, Charles William 255, 255 (n. 346)
Carles, William Richard 181, 181 (n. 251)
Cassini, Count Arturo Paul Nicholas 55, 55 (n. 104), 436, 442, 444, 454
Chamot, Auguste 112, 126, 143, 154, 160
Chang Yin-huan 89, 263, 263 (n. 353), 456, 464, 471
Chang Chih-Tung 91, 91 (n. 179), 140, 427
Chao Shu-chiao 104–105, 105 (n. 211), 116, 124, 127
Chao Ping-chun 332
Ch'en Chin-tao 320, 320 (n. 229)
Chen Pao-chen 90
Chien Lung (Emperor) 26, 33, 35, 280, 344
Chiene, Professor John 7, 389, 389 (n. 33)
Ching (Prince) I-k'uang 108, 108 (n. 215), 131–132, 168, 170, 179, 238, 438, 473, 480
Charcot, Dr Jean-Martin 8, 403, 403 (n. 54)
Chester, Henry Majoribanks 386, 386 (n. 30)
Chirol, Sir Ignatius Valentine 22, 22 (n. 40), 23, 23 (n. 44), 42, 47, 53, 56, 410, 431, 432
Choulet, Marie-Félix 255, 255 (n. 345)
Cockburn, Henry 146, 434, 434 (n. 125)
Conger, Edward Hurd 117, 117 (n. 225), 132, 154, 170, 171, 181,
Cook, George Wingrove 478, 478 (n. 203)
Cooper, Alfred Charles 404, (n. 66)
Cordier, Henri 97, 491
Courcel, Baron Alphonse Chodron de 412, 412 (n. 82)
Cox, Horace 15, 408, 408 (n. 64)
Crawford, F. Marion 390, 390 (n. 36)
Croll, Jenner 394, 394 (n. 39)
Cunningham, Edward 14
Curzon, George Nathaniel 18, 18 (n. 34), 19, 49, 456, 457

Damrong Rajanubhab (Prince) 22, 424, 417, 482, 482 (n. 212) 483, 484
Dassoy, Nicholas 402, 402 (n. 47)
Darcy, Eugène (Captain) 164, 164 (n. 249), 166, 182
Delane, John Thaddeus 223, 223 (n. 307)
Deken, Constant Pierre-Joseph de 281, 281 (n. 378)
Denby, Charles 437, 437 (n. 137), 438
Denby, Charles Jr 443, 443 (n. 146)
Dethève, Dr Claude 472
Detring, Gustave 493
Diederichs, Ernst Otto von 448, 448 (n. 160)
Dijk, Louis van 251, 251 (n. 342), 253
Donald, William Henry 335, 335 (n. 444)
Dorjief, Agvan 307, 307 (n. 408)
Dubail, Georges 457, 457 (n. 175)
Duhovskoi, Sergei Mihailovich 445, 445 (n. 148)

Fairbairn, Sir George 365, 365 (n. 33)
Favier-Duperron, Pierre-Marie-Alphonse (Bishop) 97, 97 (n. 192), 105, 124, 152, 153, 489, 490, 491, 493
Feng Kuo-chang 315, 315 (n. 419), 319, 346
Fez, Sharif of 8
Fink, Theodore 14
Fitzgerald, Sir Thomas 7, 388, 388 (n. 31)
Forwood, Wellington Peploe 393, 393 (n. 38)
Freud, Sigmund 8
Fukushima Yasumasa 37, 174, 175, 185, 185 (n. 253), 432
Fulford, Henry English 473, 473 (n. 198)

Game well, Francis Dunlap 121, 121 (n. 228)
Gardner, Christopher Thomas 428, 428 (n. 113)
Gaselee, Sir Alfred 185
Gascoyne-Cecil, Lord Edward Herbert 402, 402 (n. 49)
Gaylord, Frank 386
Gérard, Auguste 255, 255 (n. 347), 436
Goes, Benoit de 268, 269,
Goldie, Andrew 383, 384 (n. 26)
Goodnow, Francis 337, 337 (n. 451), 338 (portrait),
Gowers, Sir William Richard 15, 409, 409 (n. 68)
Gray, David 396, 396 (n. 42)

Greville, George 484
Grey, Dr Douglas 330
Griffin, Sir Lepel Henry 460, 460 (n. 181)
Grombchevsky, Bronislav Lundwigovich 62, 62 (n. 119), 73, 306, 445
Gwynne, Howell 348, 459, 459 (n. 178), 472, 476

Ha Han-chang 318, 318 (n. 426)
Hart, Sir Robert 40, 40 (n. 79), 41, 100, 143, 156, 177, 183, 434, 437, 455
Hammer, Joseph 267, 267 (n. 360)
Hanataux, Albert Auguste Gabriel 452, 452 (n. 169)
Hayashi Gosuke 437, 437 (n. 135), 465, 466
Hayashi Tadsu 437, 437 (n. 136)
Henry, Augustine 426, 426 (n. 107)
Heyking, Edmund Freiherr von 436, 436 (n. 132), 437, 447, 448, 449, 455, 462, 488, 495
Higgins, Justice Henry 346, 346 (n. 464)
Hillier, Edward G. 93, 93 (n. 180)
Hippisley, Alfred E. 41, 47
Howorth, Sir Henry Hoyle 16, 409, 409 (n. 70)
Hsu Hsi-chang 346, 347
Hsu Tung 110, 110 (n. 217)
Hsuan Chuang 282, 282 (n. 381)
Hughes, William Morris 345, 345 (n. 461)
Hung Hsiu-ch'uan 29
Hunter, George W. 265, 265 (n. 355)

Ijichi Kōsuke 206, 206 (n. 283)
Ito Hirobumi 90, 90 (n. 178), 91, 92, 165, 466, 497
Iwasaki, Baron 343

Jadot, Jean 191, 193, 193 (n. 259), 194, 196, 199, 200
James, Huberty 144
Jardine Matheson 190
Jiaqing 26–28
Jordan, Sir John 331
Jung-lu 94, 94 (n. 183), 118, 133, 144, 155, 167, 184, 198, 218, 468, 470, 473

Kamio Mitsuomi 475 (n. 201)
K'ang Hsi 26
Kang-i 94, 94 (n. 184)

INDEX

Kang Yu-wei 80, 80 (n. 159), 81, 84, 85, 89, 90, 463, 464, 466, 467, 472
Kennedy, Alexander 361 (n. 19)
Ketteler, Clemens August Freiherr von 124, 133, 134, 135, 137, 174, 495
Kondratenko, Roman Isidorovich 207, 207 (n. 289)
Kundera, Milan v
Kwang Hsu 42, 79, 80, 86, 176, 215

Labarousse, Cpt Alexis Jacques Henri 140, 140 (n. 237), 164, 182
Lan, Duke, *see* Prince Tuan
Lawes, William George 384, 384 (n. 24), 385
Liang Pi 318, 318 (n. 427)
Liang Chang 464, 465
Liang Shih-yi 335–337, 335 (n. 445)
Li, Hung-chang 13, 13 (n. 23), 14, 32, 39, 41, 56, 80, 84, 89, 100, 109, 143, 189, 190, 376, 438, 439, 440, 442, 447, 448, 449, 452, 454, 463, 465, 477, 478, 479, 493, 496
Li Ching-fang 426, 426 (n. 108)
Li Peng-Heng 105, 105 (n. 212), 110
Li Lianying 216, 216 (n. 297)
Li Yuan-hung 341, 341 (n. 456)
Liljeblad, Frederik Hillel 384, 384 (n. 25)
Lin, Qing 27–28
Liu Hsueh-hsun 497
Liu Yung-fu 427, 427 (n. 112)
Little, Alicia Ellen Neve 223, 223 (n. 321)
Littlejohn, Sir Henry 396, 396 (n. 41)
Livingstone, Dr David 3
Luzzatti, Angelo 462 (n. 183), 463

Ma Kien-chong 463, 463 (n. 185)
Macartney, Lord George 35, 344
Macartney, Sir George 292, 298
MacDonald, Sir Claude 93, 95, 96, 100, 113, 113 (n. 222), 115, 119, 146, 148, 161, 172, 173, 176, 179, 180, 183, 184, 186, 433, 434, 435, 450, 451, 452, 453, 455, 456, 472, 474, 475, 475, 477, 486, 487, 488, 494
Mackay, J. S. 396, 397
Mackeller, Dorothea 355
Maclean, Harry Aubrey de Vere 403, 403 (n. 51)
Makarov, Stefan Osipovich 208, 208 (n. 290)
Mao Zedong 34 (n. 66)
di Martino, Renato 485, 486, 487, 488, 489
Mass Hioki 333, 333 (n. 443)

Matheson, Hugh Mackay 397, 397 (n. 43)
McAllum, Campbell (Christain) Alexander 425, 425 (n. 105), 426, 427
Maurice, Auguste-Jean-Gabriel 241, 241 (n. 333)
Merzbacher, Gottfried 287, 287 (n. 383)
Moneypenny, William Flavelle 16 (n. 30), 410
Monson, Sir John 452, 452 (n. 170)
Munthe, Johann 475, 474 (202), 476
Muravyov-Amursky, Nikolai Nikolayevich 61, 61 (n. 115), 451
Myers, John Twiggs (Captain) 32, 139, 156, 159, 160, 503

Nie Shicheng 37, 118, 118 (n. 226), 123, 124
Nogi Maresuke 206, 206 (n. 283)
Nolan, Sydney 353
Norman, Sir Henry 404, (n. 67)
Northcliffe, Lord (A. C. W. Harmsworth) 223

Ockhtomsky, Prince Hesper 443, 443 (n. 145), 444, 454
Oliphant, Nigel 140, 159, 159 (n. 246), 162, 165
d'Orleans, Prince Henri 218

Patten, Chris 84 (n. 169)
Paterson, A. B. 'Banjo' 43, 50
Pavie, August Jean-Marie 414, 414 (n. 89)
Pavlov, Alexandr Ivanovich 436, 436 (n. 130), 445, 448, 453, 456
Pelliot, Paul Eugène 270, 270 (n. 364)
Peng, Ying-chia 243, 243 (n. 338), 252
Peral y Caballero, Issac 401, 401 (n. 45)
Pereira, George Edward 403, 403 (n. 50)
Perkins, Patrick 383, 383 (n. 22)
Pethick, William 32, 32 (n. 61), 41, 121, 143, 154, 439, 452, 454
Petrovsky, Nikolay Fyodorovich 293, 293 (n. 393), 301, 302
Pichon, Stephen Jean-Marie 486, 486 (n. 218), 492
Plender, Sir John 493, 493 (n. 233)
Pokotilov, Dmitri Dimitrievich 143, 452, 452 (n. 168), 454
Priestly, Susan 2
Przhevalsky, Nilolay Mkhaylovich 445, 445 (n. 151)

Richard, Timothy 466
Richie, Matteo 269
Richthofen, Ferdinand Freiherr von 268, 268 (n. 268)
Robertson, Sir John 383, 383 (n. 23)
Robin, Jennie Wark (Morrison's wife) 328, 329 (portrait), 375
Rockhill, William Woodville 222, 222 (n. 304), 333
Rolin-Jacquemyns, Gustave Henri 484, 484 (n. 215)
Rosthorm, Arthur von 143, 163,
Russell, William 17

Safder Ali Khan 288, 288 (n. 387)
Saigo Judo 433, 433 (n. 118), 465
Salisbury, Lord Robert Arthur Talbot Gascoyne-Cecil 44, 113, 113 (n. 223), 434, 451, 458, 459, 476, 477, 491,
Sanderso n. Thomas Henry 411
Salvage Raggi, Marquis Guiseppe 184, 462, 462 (n. 184), 489
Satow, Sir Ernest Mason 205, 205 (n. 282), 330, 497
Sayle, Murray 46
Scadding, Albert (Private) 146
Schaal von Bell, Adam 126, 126 (n. 126)
Scott, Sir James George 415, 415 (n. 91)
Semedo, Alvaro 239, 239 (n. 332), 241
Sévénier, Henri 430
Sheng (Sheng Xuanhuai) 198, 198 (n. 267)
Shereef of Wazan, 404, 402 (n. 48)
Sheridan, Philip Henry 390, 390 (n. 35)
Shiba Goro (Colonel) 128, 128 (n. 233), 157, 158,
Simpson, Bertram Lennox 332, 332 (n. 439)
Skobeleff, Mikhail Dmitriyevich 445, 445 (n. 150)
Sladen, Douglas Brooke Wheelton 404, (n. 63)
Smith, George 8, 404, 404 (n. 55)
Smith, John 365
Smyth, Herbert Warrington 413, 413 (n. 86)
Soden, Alfred Graf von 133, 149, 149 (n. 243), 154, 167, 459
Spinney, William Franklin 426, 426 (n. 106)
Spitzel, Louis 440, 441
Splingaerd, Paul 251, 251 (n. 343), 267, 268
Squires, Herbert Goldsmith 143, 143 (n. 240), 186

Stanley, Henry Moreland 3, 44, 380
Stein, Sir mark Aurel 270, 270 (n. 263)
Stössel, Anatoly Mikhaylovich 208, 208 (n. 291), 210, 211, 212
Strouts, Bernard Morton (Captain) 150, 169, 186,
Sugiyama Akira 96, 123,
Sun Yat Sen 51, 312, 313 (portrait), 332
Sung Chiao-jen 332
Sung Ching 198, 198 (n. 267)
Su (Prince) Shan Ch'i 127, 127 (n. 232), 144
Syme, David 4, 355, 282, 382 (n. 21), 387
Syme, George Alexander 381, 381 (n. 16)

Tang Ching-sung 427, 427 (n. 110)
T'an Ssu-t'ung 469, 469 (n. 194)
Tcheng Ki-tong 427, 427 (n. 111), 479
Thibaw Min 419, 419 (n. 95)
Thomann Edler von Montalmar, Edward Anton 145, 146, 164
Ting Pao-chuan (Ding Baoquan) 242, 242 (n. 335)
Tocqueville, Alexis de 311
Tsai Tao 318, 318 (n. 424)
Ts'ao K'un 315, 315 (n. 421)
Tsen (Cen Chunxuan) 198, 198 (n. 268)
Tseng Guo-fan 29, 29 (n. 57), 31
Tso Tsung-tang 33, 33 (n. 65), 222, 236, 247, 254, 257, 273
Tsu Hsi (Empress Dowager) 79, 79 (n. 157), 81, 82, 83, 84, 85, 94, 100, 101, 119, 174, 184, 189, 190, 191, 194, 195, 196, 197, 198, 199, 200, 201, 213, 214, 238, 264, 311, 467, 471, 476, 480
Tuan Ch'i-jui 315, (n. 422), 341, 343, 346
Tuan (Prince) 104, 104 (n. 210), 109, 127, 131–132, 222, 262, 264
Tuan Feng 238, 238 (n. 330)
Tung Fuh-siang 110, 110 (n. 120), 120, 123, 167, 253, 474, 475

Verbiest, Ferdinand 126, 126 (n. 126), 268
Vitale, Guido 487, 488
Vroublevsky, Nikolai Victorovich 140, 159, 160
Vrevesky, Baron lexander 307, 307 (n. 409)

Waldersee, Alfred Ludwig Heinrich Karl Graf von 255, 255 (n. 344)

INDEX

Wallace, Sir Donald Mackenzie 411, 411 (n. 75), 431
Walshman, Sir John 434
Wang Shih-chen 315, (n. 420)
Wang Shu-nan 262, 262 (n. 351)
Weale, Putnam (*see* Bertram Simpson)
White, Patrick 353
White, Sir Herbert Thirkell 416, 416 (n. 92)
Williams, Samuel Wells 369, 369 (n. 369)
Wills, William John 4, 353, 354, 359, 387
Wilson, President Woodrow 331
Wilson, Samuel 364, 364 (n. 27)
Woodthorpe, Robert Gosset 417, 417 (n. 93)
Wu Tiao-ching 93, 93 (n. 181)

Xi Jingping 84 (n. 169)

Yamagata Aritomo 205, 205 (n. 280)
Yano Fumio 437, 437 (n. 134)
Yaqum Beg 3 3, 33 (n. 64), 297, 297 (n. 397)
Ye Mingcheng 36
Yin Chang 320, 320 (n. 428)
Yong Cheng 26, 280
Yu Keng 493
Yu Der Ling (Lizzie) 494, 494 (n. 236)
Yuan, Shih-kai 26, 26 (n. 45), 50, 51, 103, 197, 198, 200, 310 (portrait), 312, 314, 315, 317, 331, 337, 339, 340, 346, 375, 468, 469, 470, 471, 475, 476
Yung Lu, *see* Jung Lu

www.ingramcontent.com/pod-product-compliance
Lightning Source LLC
Chambersburg PA
CBHW071256070526
44583CB00017B/2502